TKO STUDIOS

SALVATORE SIMEONE - CEO & PUBLISHER

TZE CHUN - PRESIDENT & PUBLISHER

JATIN THAKKER - CHIEF OPERATIONS OFFICER

SEBASTIAN GIRNER - EDITOR-IN-CHIEF

THE PULL #1-6.

Copyright © 2020

TKO Studios, LLC. All rights reserved.

Published by TKO Studios, LLC.

Office of Publication: 450 7th Ave., Suite 2107. New York, NY 10123.

All names, characters, and events in this publication

are entirely fictional. Any resemblance to actual persons

(living or dead), events, or places, without satiric intent,

is unintended and purely coincidental. Printed in the USA.

ISBN: 978-1-952203-10-7

TKOPRESENTS.COM

TKO PRESENTS A WORLD BY:

STEVE ORLANDO
WRITER

RICARDO LÓPEZ ORTIZ
ART

TRIONA FARRELL
COLOR ART

THOMAS MAUER
LETTERER

SEBASTIAN GIRNER
EDITOR

MARIAM FAYEZ
EDITORIAL ASSISTANT

RICARDO LÓPEZ ORTIZ & TRIONA FARRELL
COVER ART

JARED K FLETCHER
TITLE & COVER DESIGN

JEFF POWELL
BOOK DESIGN

the puLL

CHAPTER 1

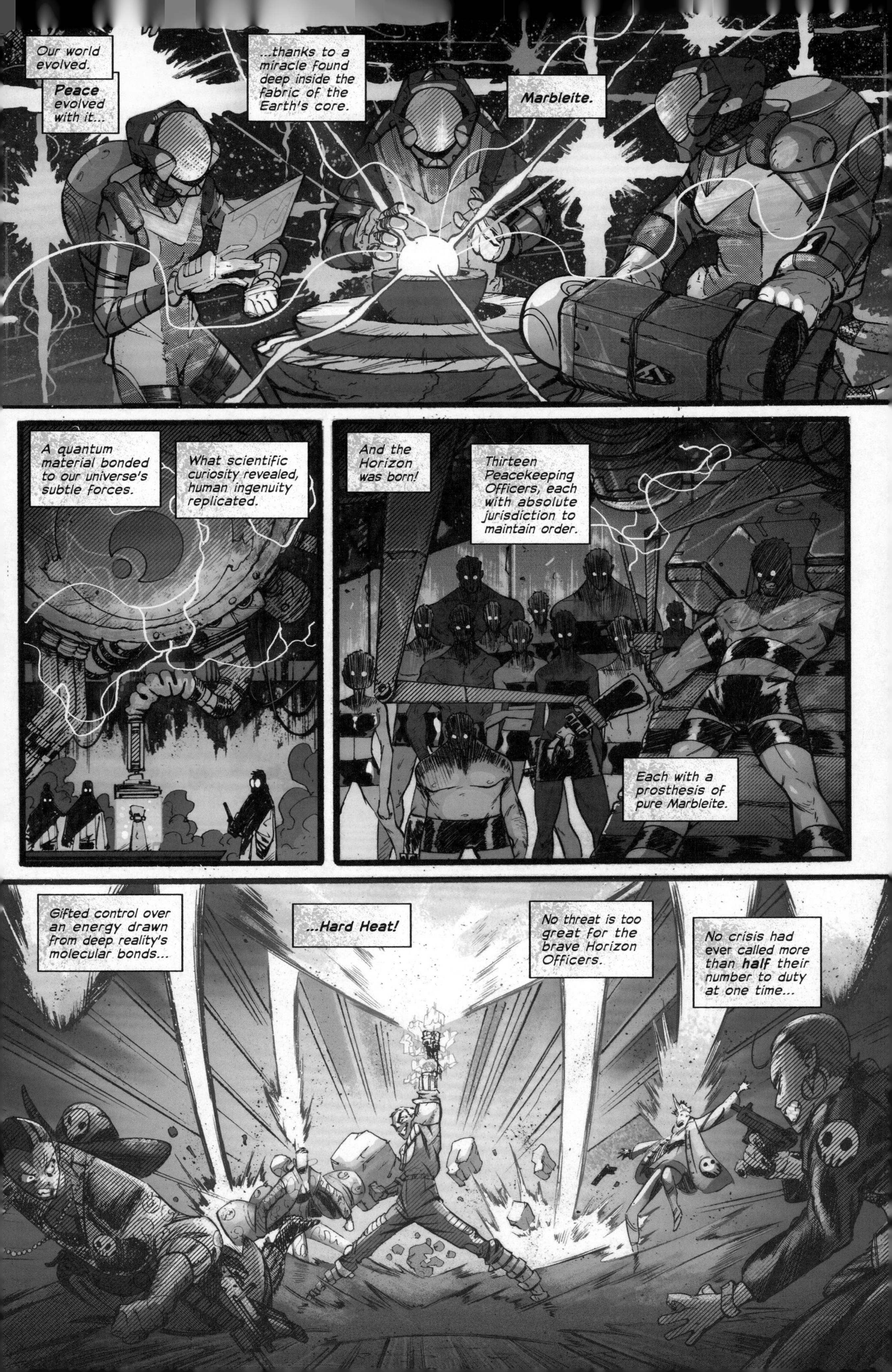
Our world evolved.
Peace evolved with it...
...thanks to a miracle found deep inside the fabric of the Earth's core.
Marbleite.
A quantum material bonded to our universe's subtle forces.
What scientific curiosity revealed, human ingenuity replicated.
And the Horizon was born!
Thirteen Peacekeeping Officers, each with absolute jurisdiction to maintain order.
Each with a prosthesis of pure Marbleite.
Gifted control over an energy drawn from deep reality's molecular bonds...
...Hard Heat!
No threat is too great for the brave Horizon Officers.
No crisis had ever called more than half their number to duty at one time...

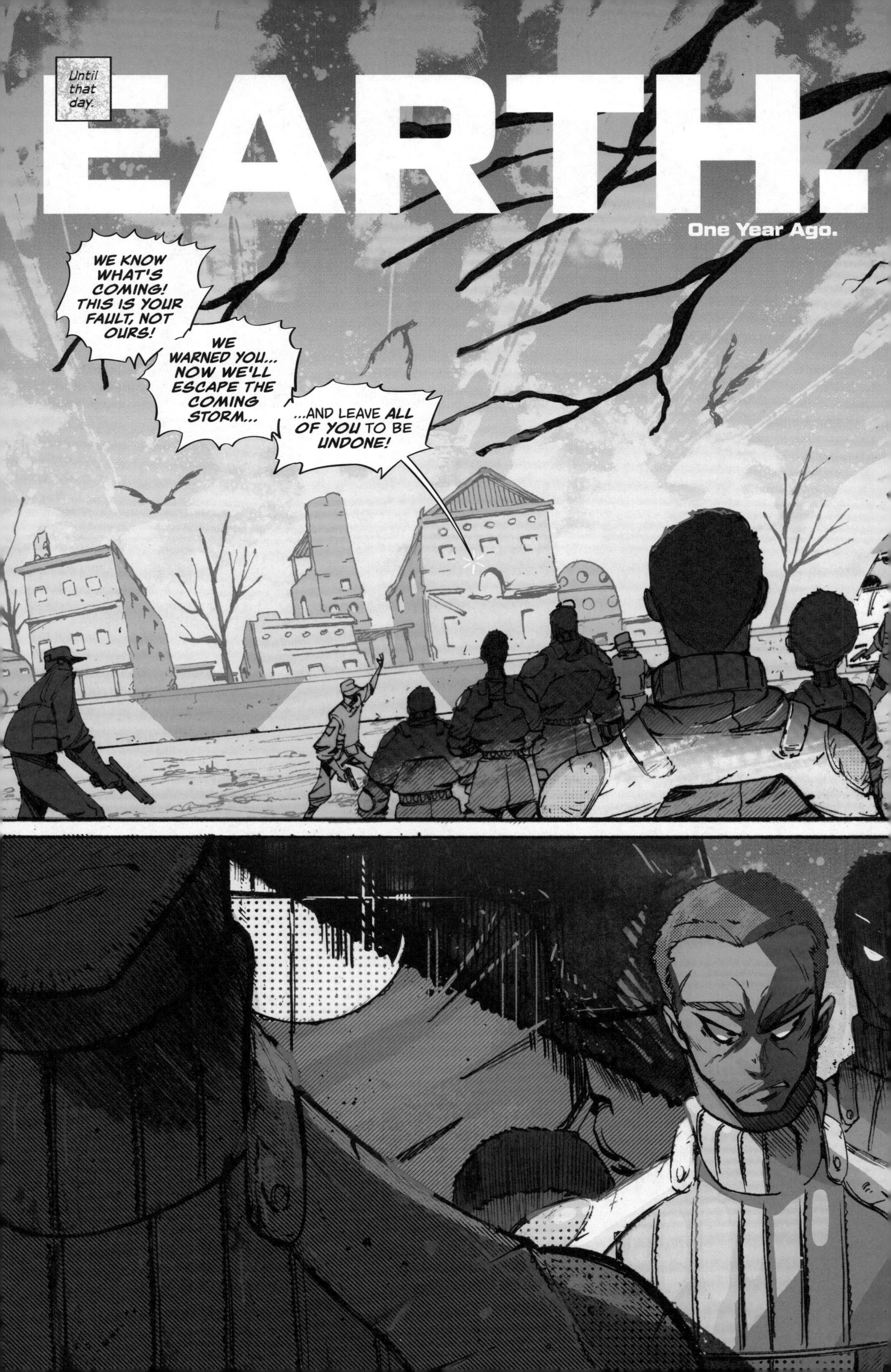
Until that day.
EARTH.
One Year Ago.
WE KNOW WHAT'S COMING! THIS IS YOUR FAULT, NOT OURS!
WE WARNED YOU... NOW WE'LL ESCAPE THE COMING STORM...
...AND LEAVE ALL OF YOU TO BE UNDONE!

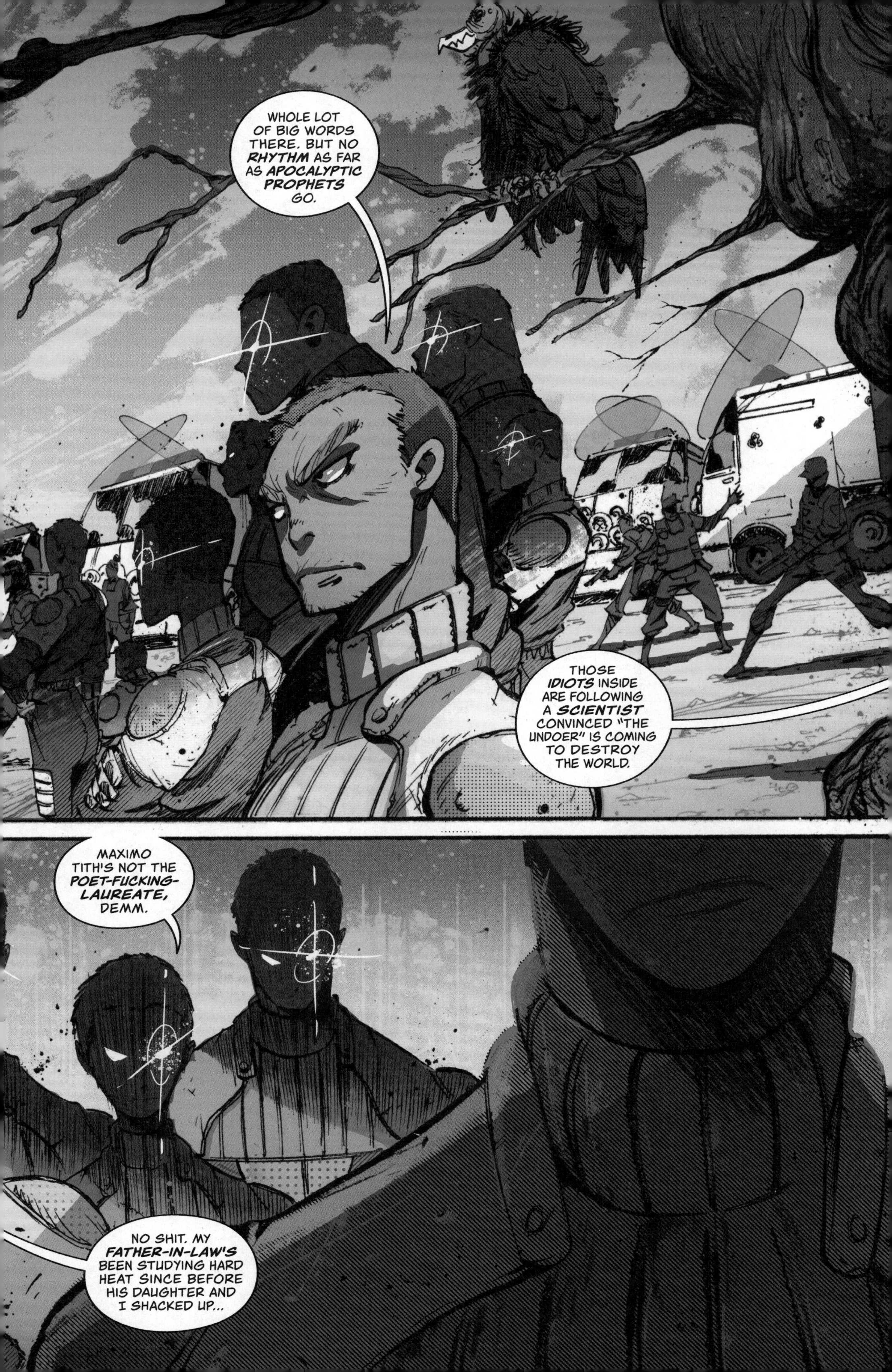
WHOLE LOT OF BIG WORDS THERE. BUT NO RHYTHM AS FAR AS APOCALYPTIC PROPHETS GO.
THOSE IDIOTS INSIDE ARE FOLLOWING A SCIENTIST CONVINCED "THE UNDOER" IS COMING TO DESTROY THE WORLD.
MAXIMO TITH'S NOT THE POET-FUCKING-LAUREATE, DEMM.
NO SHIT. MY FATHER-IN-LAW'S BEEN STUDYING HARD HEAT SINCE BEFORE HIS DAUGHTER AND I SHACKED UP...

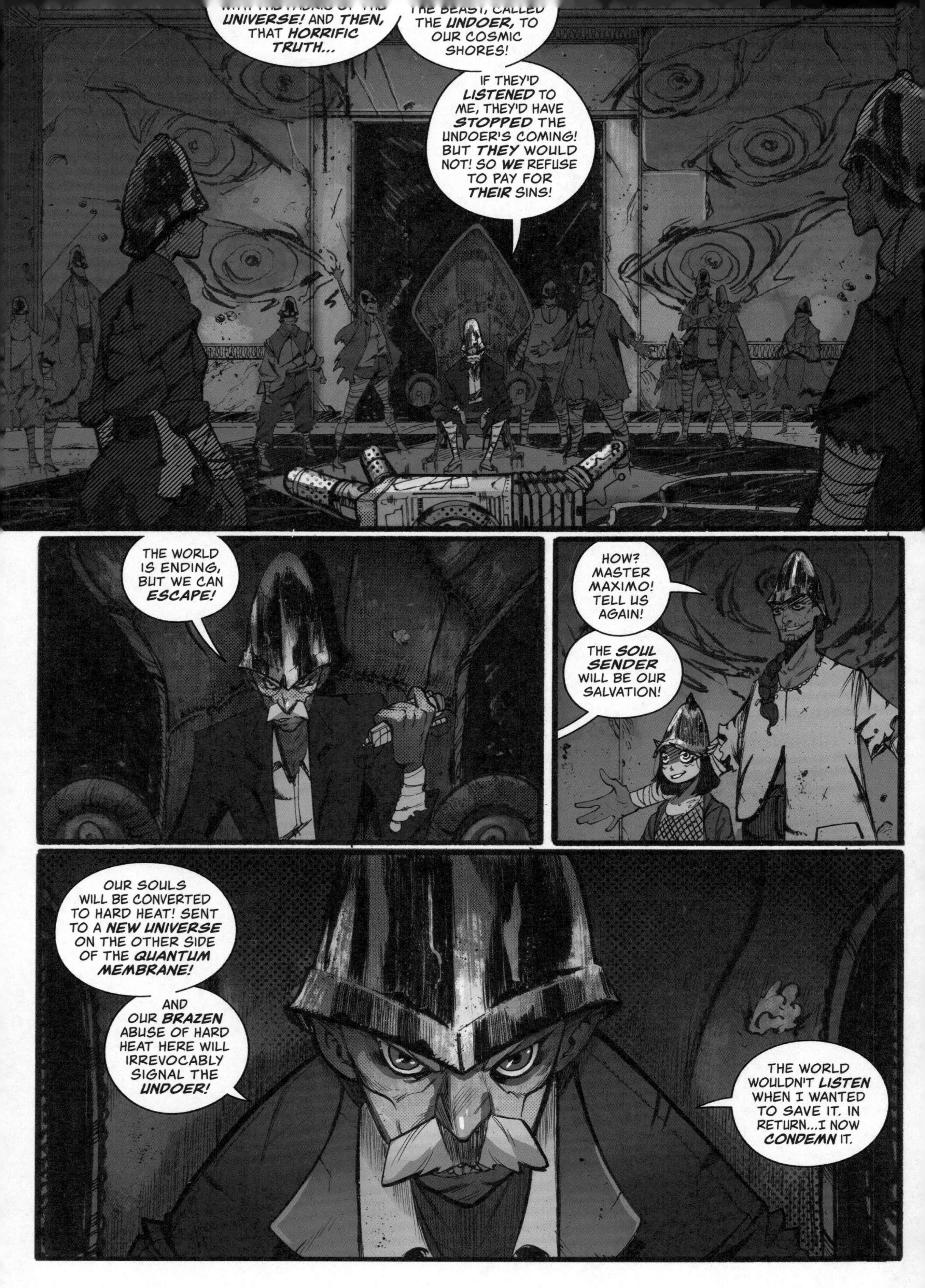
UNIVERSE! AND THEN, THAT HORRIFIC TRUTH...
THE UNDOER, TO OUR COSMIC SHORES!
IF THEY'D LISTENED TO ME, THEY'D HAVE STOPPED THE UNDOER'S COMING! BUT THEY WOULD NOT! SO WE REFUSE TO PAY FOR THEIR SINS!
THE WORLD IS ENDING, BUT WE CAN ESCAPE!
HOW? MASTER MAXIMO! TELL US AGAIN!
THE SOUL SENDER WILL BE OUR SALVATION!
OUR SOULS WILL BE CONVERTED TO HARD HEAT! SENT TO A NEW UNIVERSE ON THE OTHER SIDE OF THE QUANTUM MEMBRANE!
AND OUR BRAZEN ABUSE OF HARD HEAT HERE WILL IRREVOCABLY SIGNAL THE UNDOER!
THE WORLD WOULDN'T LISTEN WHEN I WANTED TO SAVE IT. IN RETURN...I NOW CONDEMN IT.

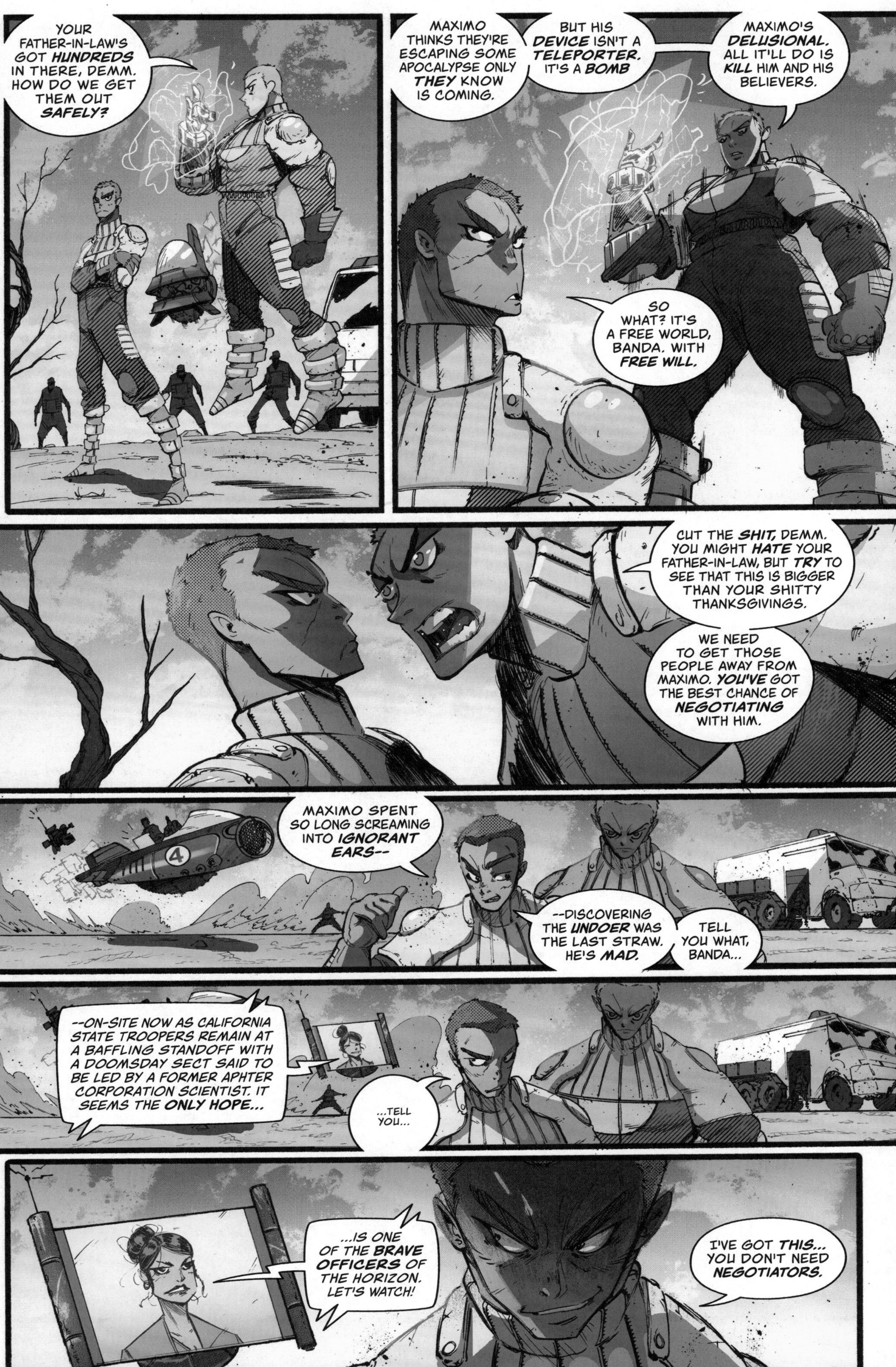
YOUR FATHER-IN-LAW'S GOT HUNDREDS IN THERE, DEMM. HOW DO WE GET THEM OUT SAFELY?
MAXIMO THINKS THEY'RE ESCAPING SOME APOCALYPSE ONLY THEY KNOW IS COMING.
BUT HIS DEVICE ISN'T A TELEPORTER. IT'S A BOMB
MAXIMO'S DELUSIONAL. ALL IT'LL DO IS KILL HIM AND HIS BELIEVERS.
SO WHAT? IT'S A FREE WORLD, BANDA. WITH FREE WILL.
CUT THE SHIT, DEMM. YOU MIGHT HATE YOUR FATHER-IN-LAW, BUT TRY TO SEE THAT THIS IS BIGGER THAN YOUR SHITTY THANKSGIVINGS.
WE NEED TO GET THOSE PEOPLE AWAY FROM MAXIMO. YOU'VE GOT THE BEST CHANCE OF NEGOTIATING WITH HIM.
MAXIMO SPENT SO LONG SCREAMING INTO IGNORANT EARS--
4
--DISCOVERING THE UNDOER WAS THE LAST STRAW. HE'S MAD.
TELL YOU WHAT, BANDA...
--ON-SITE NOW AS CALIFORNIA STATE TROOPERS REMAIN AT A BAFFLING STANDOFF WITH A DOOMSDAY SECT SAID TO BE LED BY A FORMER APHTER CORPORATION SCIENTIST. IT SEEMS THE ONLY HOPE...
...TELL YOU...
...IS ONE OF THE BRAVE OFFICERS OF THE HORIZON. LET'S WATCH!
I'VE GOT THIS... YOU DON'T NEED NEGOTIATORS.

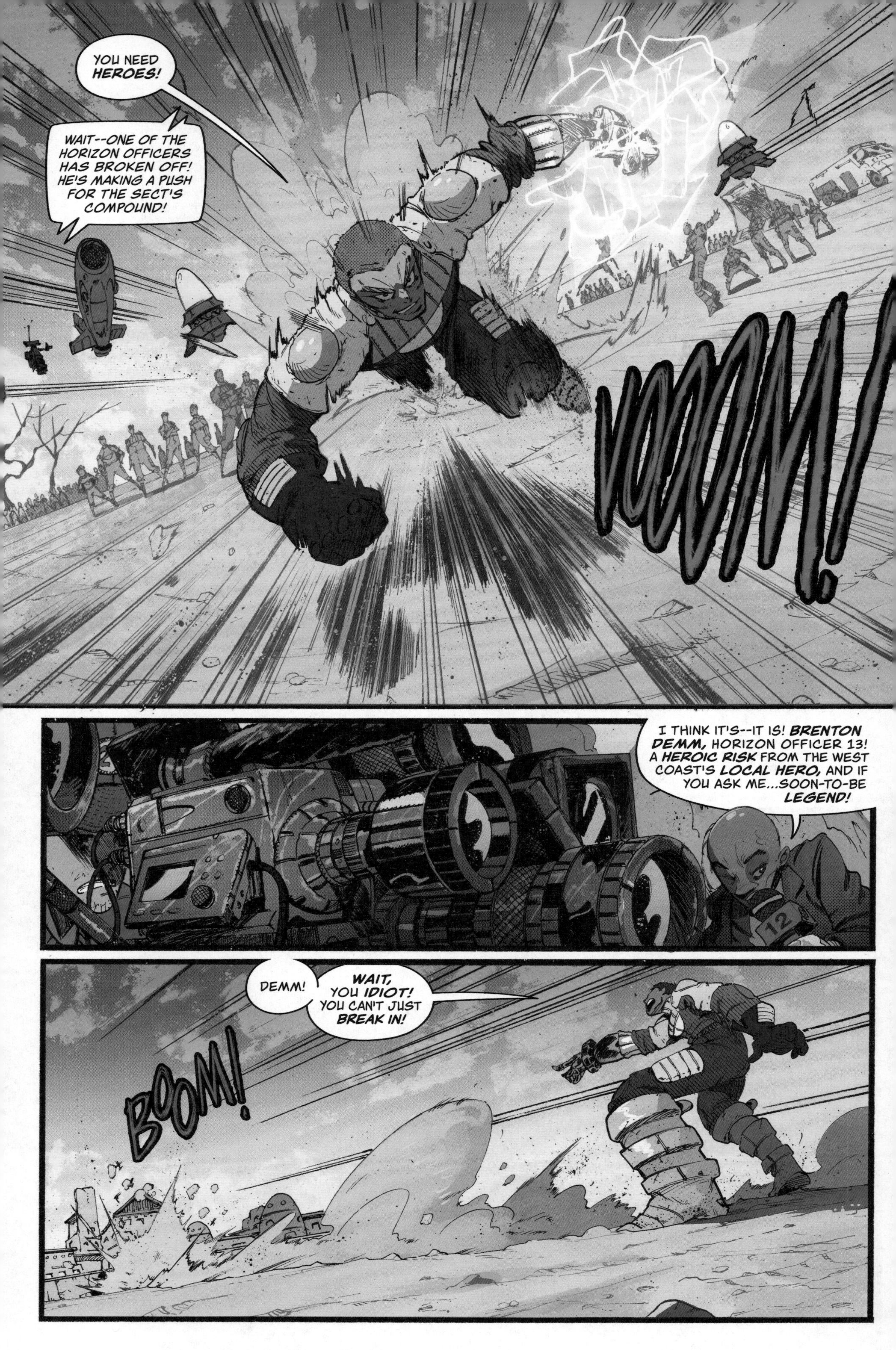
YOU NEED **HEROES!**
WAIT--ONE OF THE HORIZON OFFICERS HAS BROKEN OFF! HE'S MAKING A PUSH FOR THE SECT'S COMPOUND!
VOOOM!
I THINK IT'S--IT IS! ***BRENTON DEMM,*** HORIZON OFFICER 13! A ***HEROIC RISK*** FROM THE WEST COAST'S ***LOCAL HERO,*** AND IF YOU ASK ME...SOON-TO-BE ***LEGEND!***
12
DEMM!
WAIT, YOU ***IDIOT!*** YOU CAN'T JUST ***BREAK IN!***
BOOM!

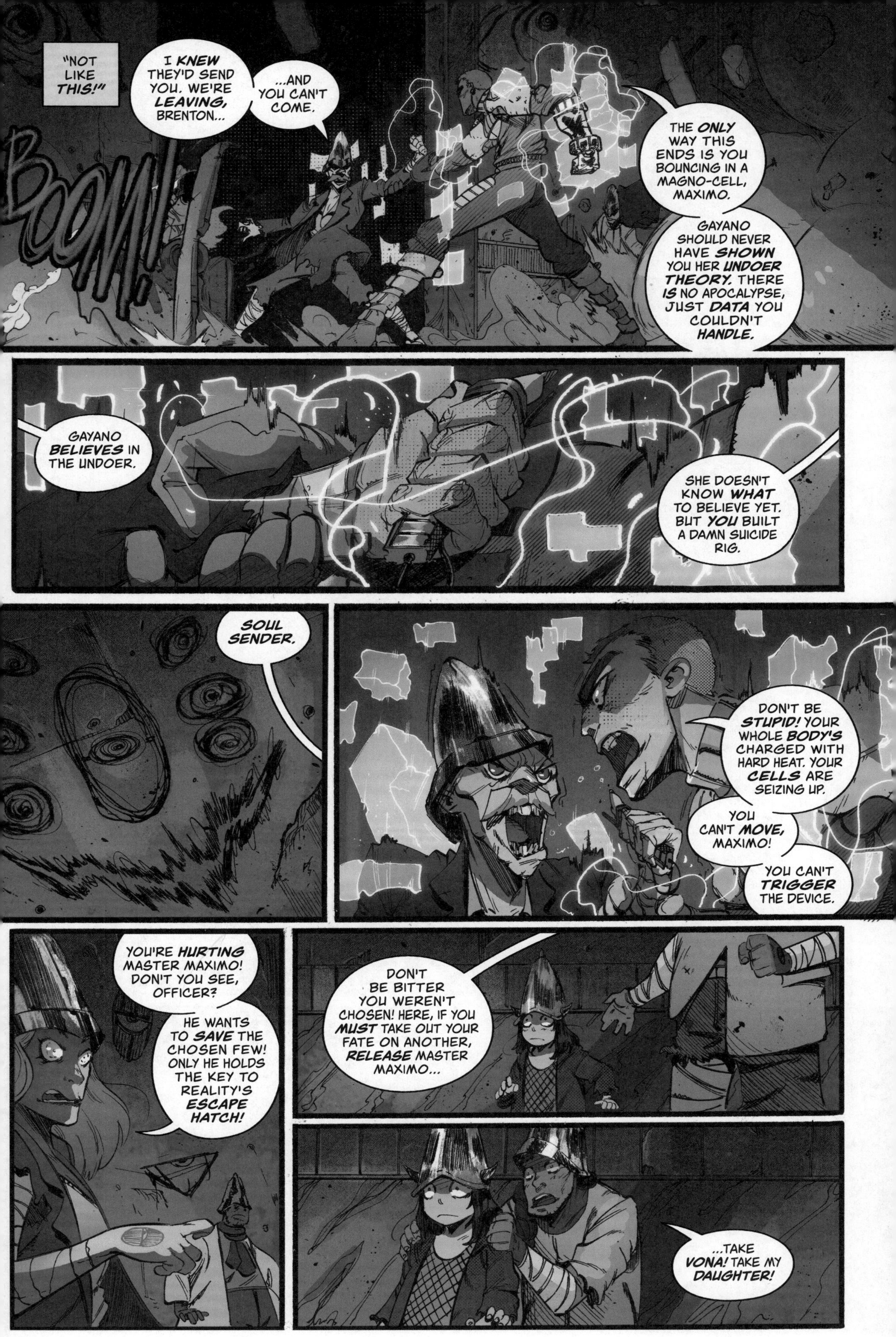

"NOT LIKE THIS!"
BOOM!
I KNEW THEY'D SEND YOU. WE'RE LEAVING, BRENTON...
...AND YOU CAN'T COME.
THE ONLY WAY THIS ENDS IS YOU BOUNCING IN A MAGNO-CELL, MAXIMO.
GAYANO SHOULD NEVER HAVE SHOWN YOU HER UNDOER THEORY. THERE IS NO APOCALYPSE, JUST DATA YOU COULDN'T HANDLE.
GAYANO BELIEVES IN THE UNDOER.
SHE DOESN'T KNOW WHAT TO BELIEVE YET. BUT YOU BUILT A DAMN SUICIDE RIG.
SOUL SENDER.
DON'T BE STUPID! YOUR WHOLE BODY'S CHARGED WITH HARD HEAT. YOUR CELLS ARE SEIZING UP.
YOU CAN'T MOVE, MAXIMO!
YOU CAN'T TRIGGER THE DEVICE.
YOU'RE HURTING MASTER MAXIMO! DON'T YOU SEE, OFFICER?
HE WANTS TO SAVE THE CHOSEN FEW! ONLY HE HOLDS THE KEY TO REALITY'S ESCAPE HATCH!
DON'T BE BITTER YOU WEREN'T CHOSEN! HERE, IF YOU MUST TAKE OUT YOUR FATE ON ANOTHER, RELEASE MASTER MAXIMO...
...TAKE VONA! TAKE MY DAUGHTER!

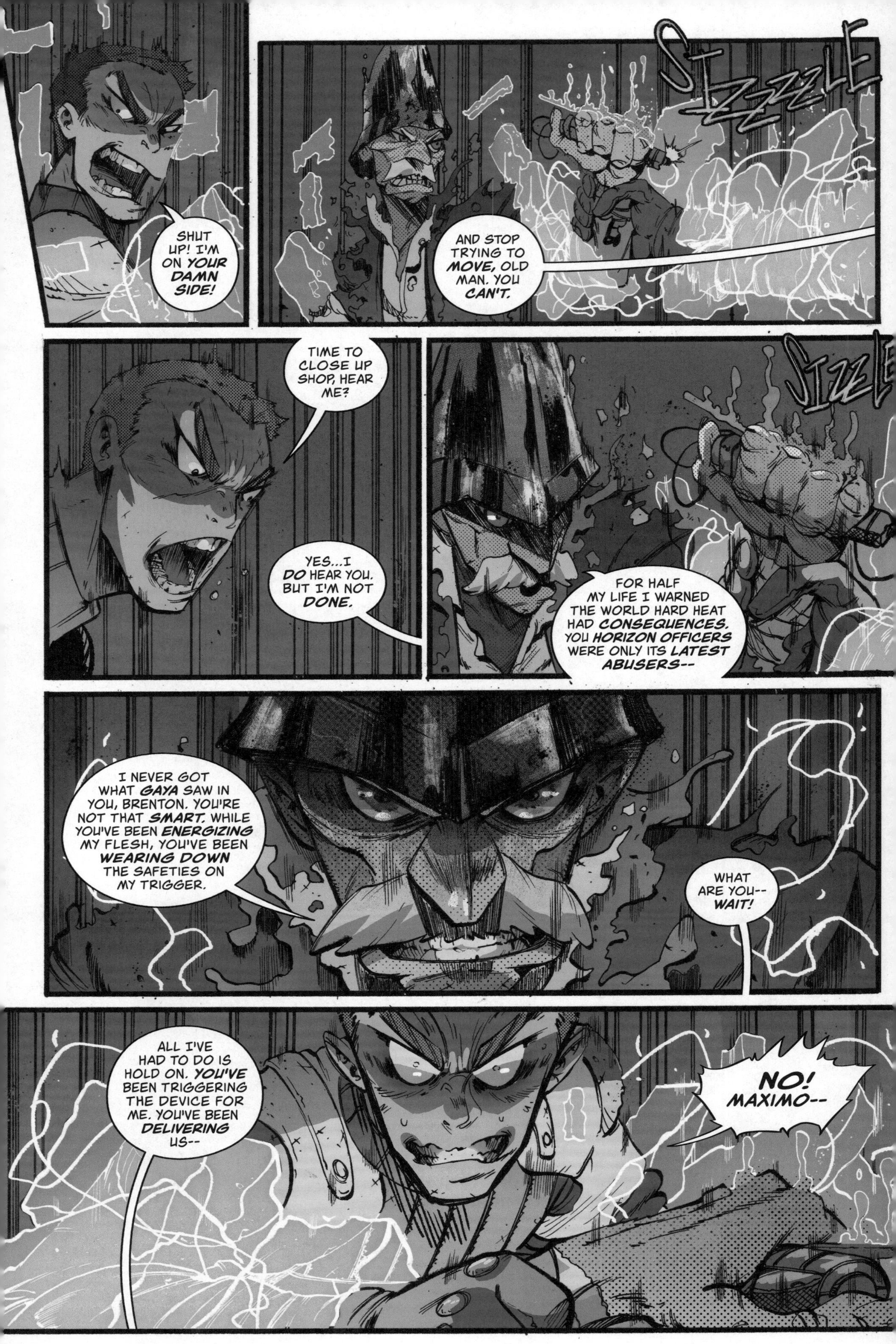
SHUT UP! I'M ON YOUR DAMN SIDE!
SIZZZZLE
AND STOP TRYING TO MOVE, OLD MAN. YOU CAN'T.
TIME TO CLOSE UP SHOP, HEAR ME?
YES...I DO HEAR YOU. BUT I'M NOT DONE.
SIZZLE
FOR HALF MY LIFE I WARNED THE WORLD HARD HEAT HAD CONSEQUENCES. YOU HORIZON OFFICERS WERE ONLY ITS LATEST ABUSERS--
I NEVER GOT WHAT GAYA SAW IN YOU, BRENTON. YOU'RE NOT THAT SMART. WHILE YOU'VE BEEN ENERGIZING MY FLESH, YOU'VE BEEN WEARING DOWN THE SAFETIES ON MY TRIGGER.
WHAT ARE YOU-- WAIT!
ALL I'VE HAD TO DO IS HOLD ON. YOU'VE BEEN TRIGGERING THE DEVICE FOR ME. YOU'VE BEEN DELIVERING US--
NO! MAXIMO--

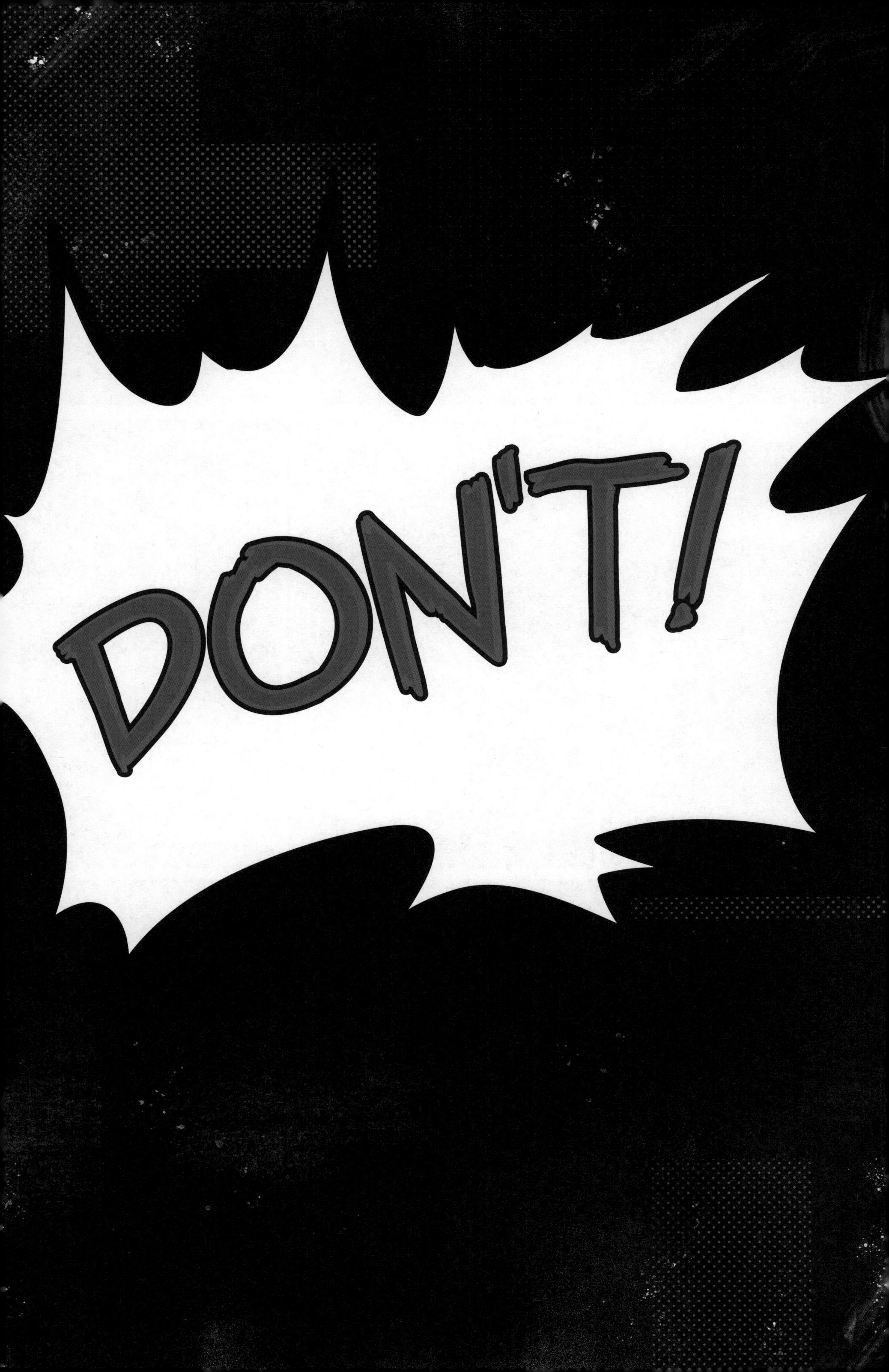
DON'T!

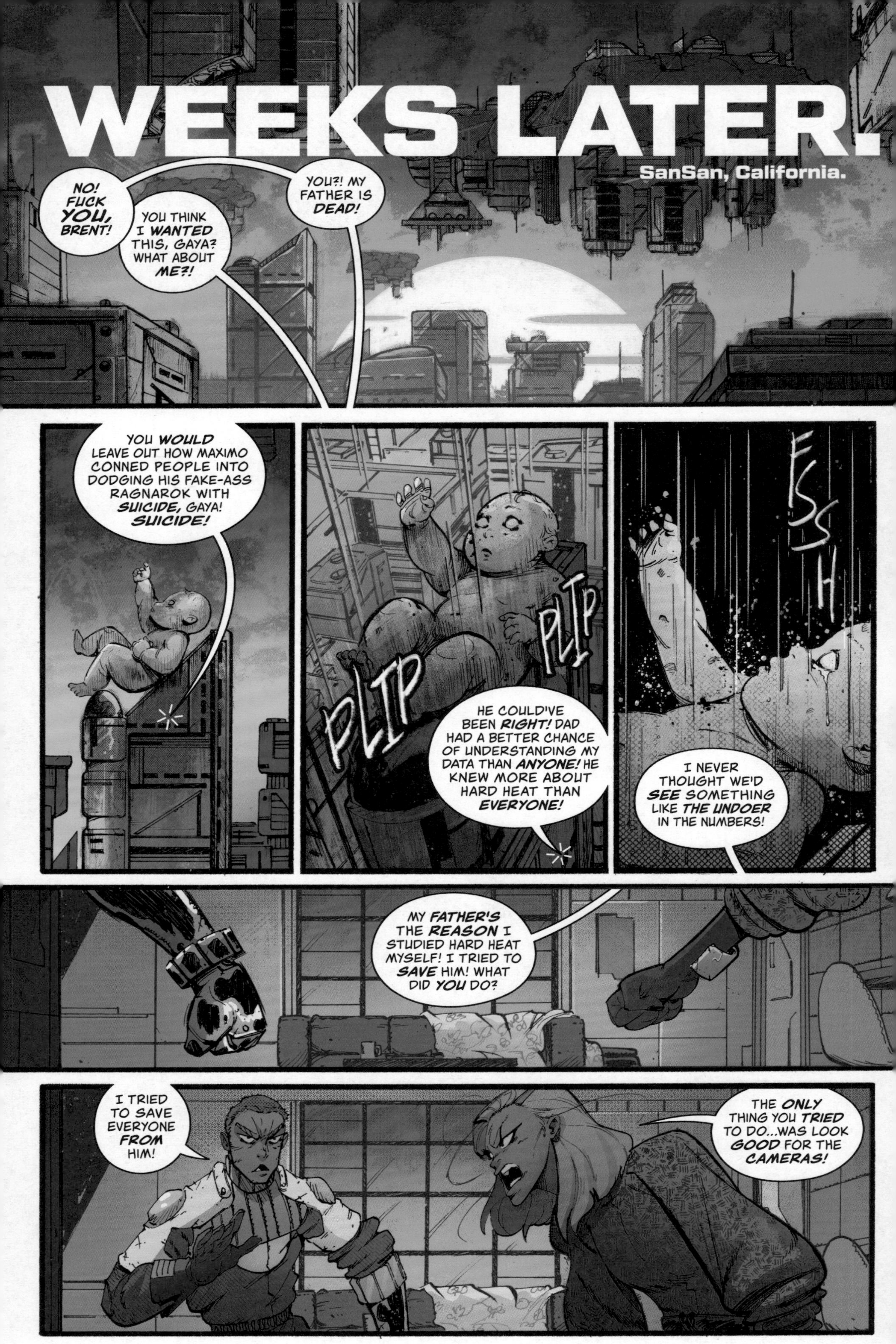
WEEKS LATER.
SanSan, California.
NO! FUCK YOU, BRENT!
YOU THINK I WANTED THIS, GAYA? WHAT ABOUT ME?!
YOU?! MY FATHER IS DEAD!
YOU WOULD LEAVE OUT HOW MAXIMO CONNED PEOPLE INTO DODGING HIS FAKE-ASS RAGNAROK WITH SUICIDE, GAYA! SUICIDE!
PLIP
PLIP
HE COULD'VE BEEN RIGHT! DAD HAD A BETTER CHANCE OF UNDERSTANDING MY DATA THAN ANYONE! HE KNEW MORE ABOUT HARD HEAT THAN EVERYONE!
FSSH
I NEVER THOUGHT WE'D SEE SOMETHING LIKE THE UNDOER IN THE NUMBERS!
MY FATHER'S THE REASON I STUDIED HARD HEAT MYSELF! I TRIED TO SAVE HIM! WHAT DID YOU DO?
I TRIED TO SAVE EVERYONE FROM HIM!
THE ONLY THING YOU TRIED TO DO...WAS LOOK GOOD FOR THE CAMERAS!

FUCK. YOU.

PEOPLE *DIED* BECAUSE YOU DON'T EVEN KNOW WHAT THAT THING ON YOUR ARM *DOES* BESIDES POINT-AND-SHOOT.

YOU COULDN'T FIGURE OUT YOUR DATA ON YOUR OWN! *YOU'RE* THE ONE THAT ASKED FOR MAXIMO'S HELP!

YOU TWO ALWAYS *DID* HOLD YOUR COLLEGE BULLSHIT OVER MY HEAD.

SCIENCE WAS *YOUR* THING. KICKING ASS AND PAYING THE RENT WAS *MINE*.

WE HAVE *ALWAYS* SPLIT OUR EXPENSES DOWN THE MIDDLE. AND YOU *KNOW* IT. YOU'RE LIVING IN A *FANTASY WORLD!*

DON'T YOU *GET* IT, BRENT? IF MY FATHER WAS RIGHT, IT'S THE *END* OF THE WORLD... AND THE CLOCK'S *TICKING.*

WHATEVER, GAYA. YOU CAN'T REALLY THINK--

SOON, WE'LL *KNOW.* YOUR *FUCK UP* HAS EVERY SCIENTIST IN THE *WORLD* STUDYING MY DATA NOW.

I TOLD MYSELF, YOU KNOW? SAID YOU WEREN'T SHOWING THE *REAL YOU.* SAID *THAT GOOD GUY* WAS SOMEONE ONLY *I KNEW,* MY SECRET *DISCOVERY.*

BUT I'VE BEEN *STUPID.*

I DON'T WANT TO SPEND WHATEVER'S *LEFT* GETTING IN THE WAY. THE *THREE* OF YOU DESERVE EACH OTHER.

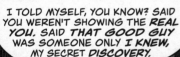

WIRSH

"YOU...YOUR *EGO,* AND NOW..."

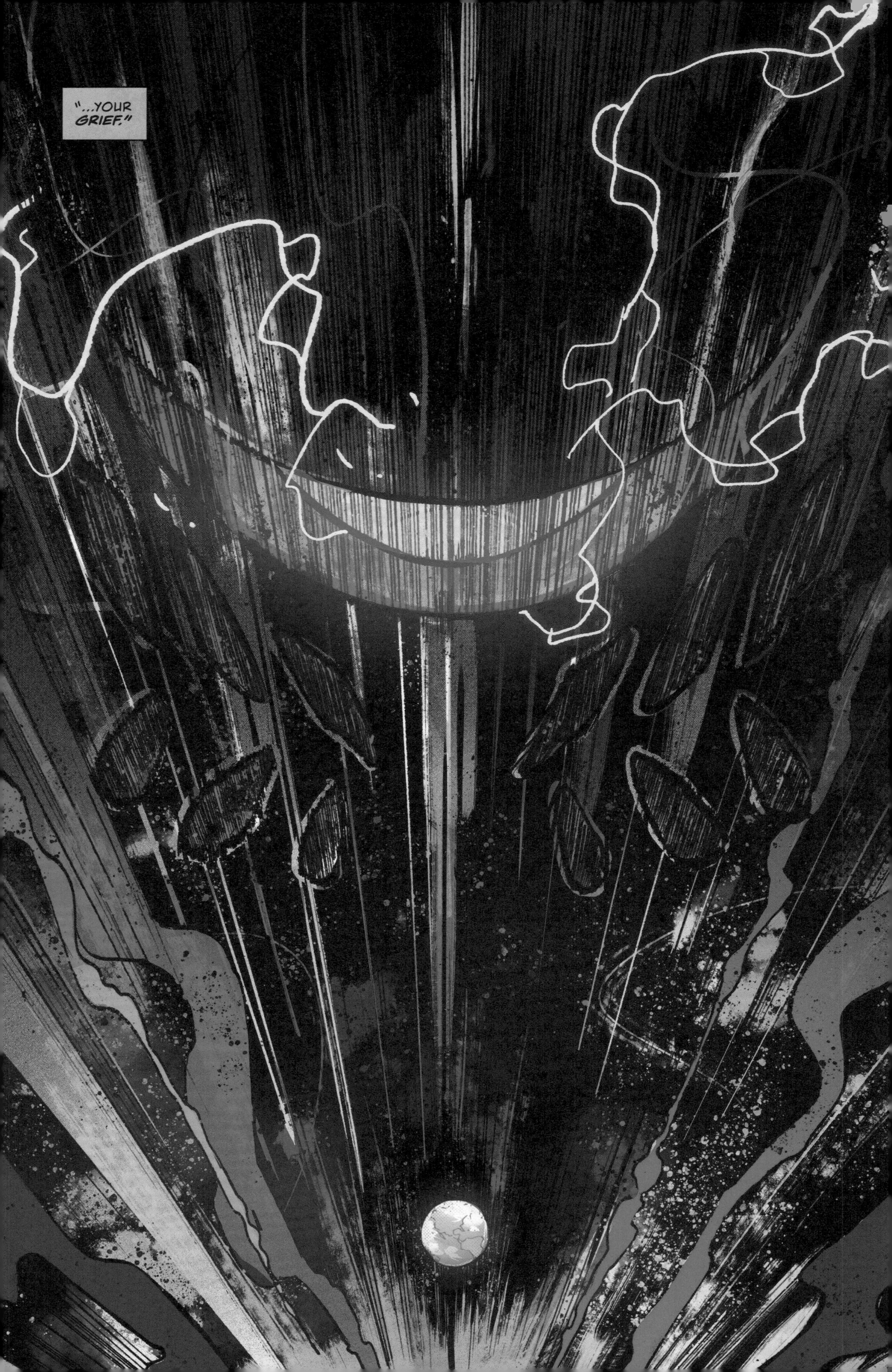
"...YOUR GRIEF."

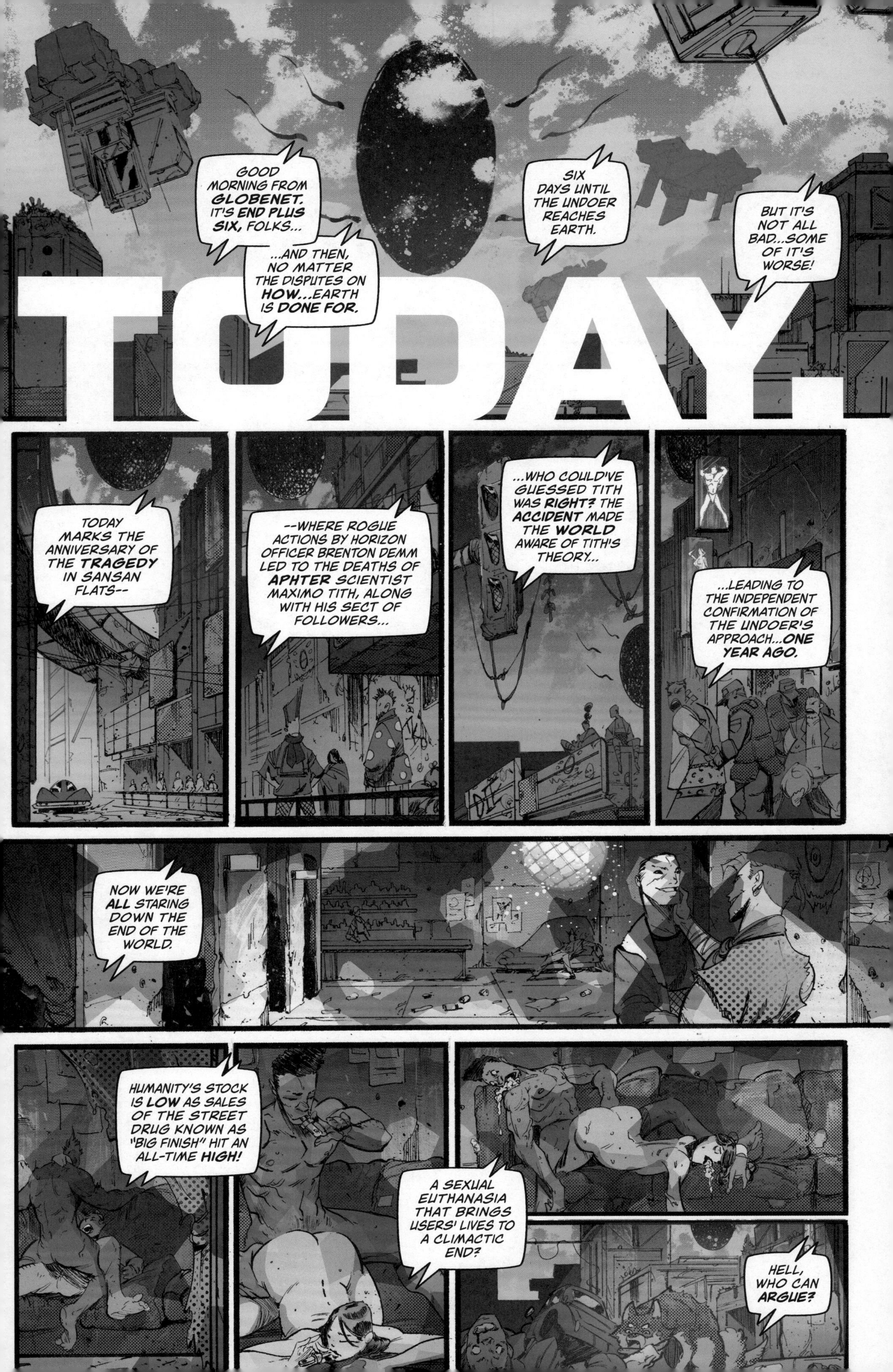
GOOD MORNING FROM GLOBENET. IT'S END PLUS SIX, FOLKS...
...AND THEN, NO MATTER THE DISPUTES ON HOW...EARTH IS DONE FOR.
SIX DAYS UNTIL THE UNDOER REACHES EARTH.
BUT IT'S NOT ALL BAD...SOME OF IT'S WORSE!
TODAY.
TODAY MARKS THE ANNIVERSARY OF THE TRAGEDY IN SANSAN FLATS--
--WHERE ROGUE ACTIONS BY HORIZON OFFICER BRENTON DEMM LED TO THE DEATHS OF APHTER SCIENTIST MAXIMO TITH, ALONG WITH HIS SECT OF FOLLOWERS...
...WHO COULD'VE GUESSED TITH WAS RIGHT? THE ACCIDENT MADE THE WORLD AWARE OF TITH'S THEORY...
...LEADING TO THE INDEPENDENT CONFIRMATION OF THE UNDOER'S APPROACH...ONE YEAR AGO.
NOW WE'RE ALL STARING DOWN THE END OF THE WORLD.
HUMANITY'S STOCK IS LOW AS SALES OF THE STREET DRUG KNOWN AS "BIG FINISH" HIT AN ALL-TIME HIGH!
A SEXUAL EUTHANASIA THAT BRINGS USERS' LIVES TO A CLIMACTIC END?
HELL, WHO CAN ARGUE?

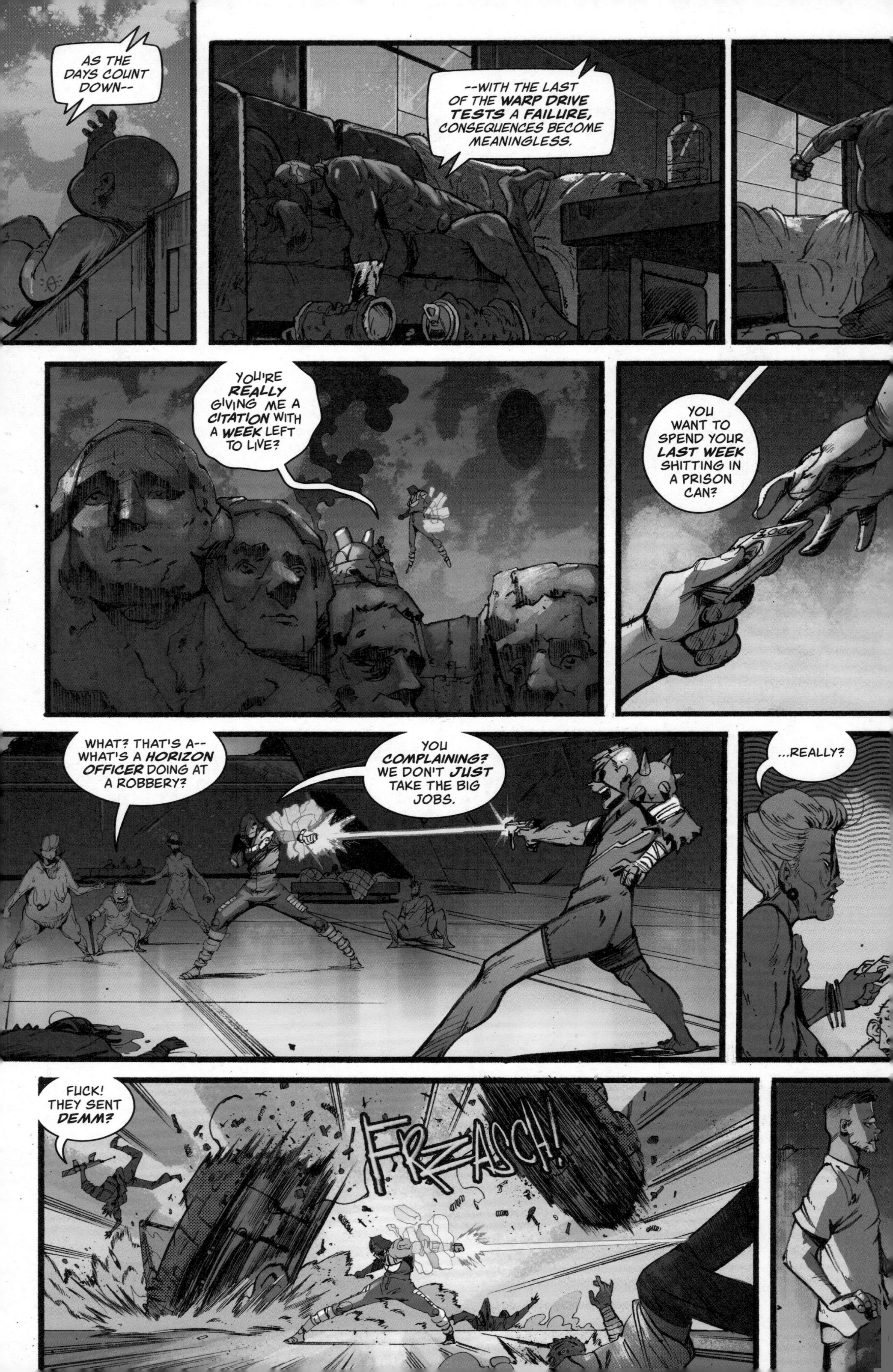
AS THE DAYS COUNT DOWN--
--WITH THE LAST OF THE **WARP DRIVE TESTS** A **FAILURE**, CONSEQUENCES BECOME MEANINGLESS.
YOU'RE **REALLY** GIVING ME A **CITATION** WITH A **WEEK** LEFT TO LIVE?
YOU WANT TO SPEND YOUR **LAST WEEK** SHITTING IN A PRISON CAN?
WHAT? THAT'S A-- WHAT'S A **HORIZON OFFICER** DOING AT A ROBBERY?
YOU **COMPLAINING**? WE DON'T **JUST** TAKE THE BIG JOBS.
...REALLY?
FUCK! THEY SENT **DEMM**?
FRZASCH!

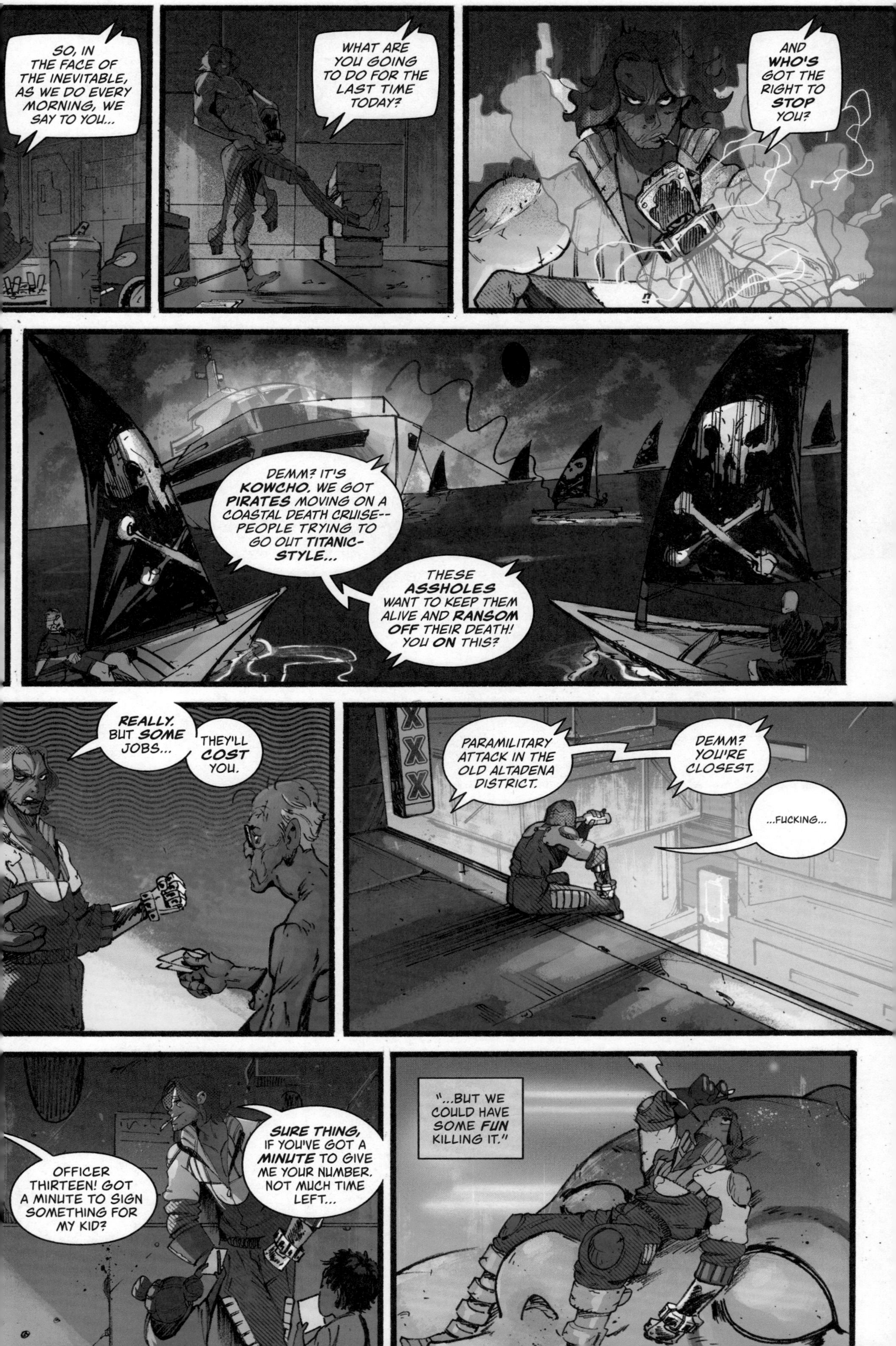
SO, IN THE FACE OF THE INEVITABLE, AS WE DO EVERY MORNING, WE SAY TO YOU...
WHAT ARE YOU GOING TO DO FOR THE LAST TIME TODAY?
AND **WHO'S** GOT THE RIGHT TO **STOP** YOU?
DEMM? IT'S **KOWCHO**. WE GOT **PIRATES** MOVING ON A COASTAL DEATH CRUISE-- PEOPLE TRYING TO GO OUT **TITANIC-STYLE...**
THESE **ASSHOLES** WANT TO KEEP THEM ALIVE AND **RANSOM OFF** THEIR DEATH! YOU **ON** THIS?
REALLY. BUT **SOME** JOBS...
THEY'LL **COST** YOU.
PARAMILITARY ATTACK IN THE OLD ALTADENA DISTRICT.
DEMM? YOU'RE **CLOSEST.**
...FUCKING...
OFFICER THIRTEEN! GOT A MINUTE TO SIGN SOMETHING FOR MY KID?
SURE THING, IF YOU'VE GOT A **MINUTE** TO GIVE ME YOUR NUMBER. NOT MUCH TIME LEFT...
"...BUT WE COULD HAVE SOME **FUN** KILLING IT."

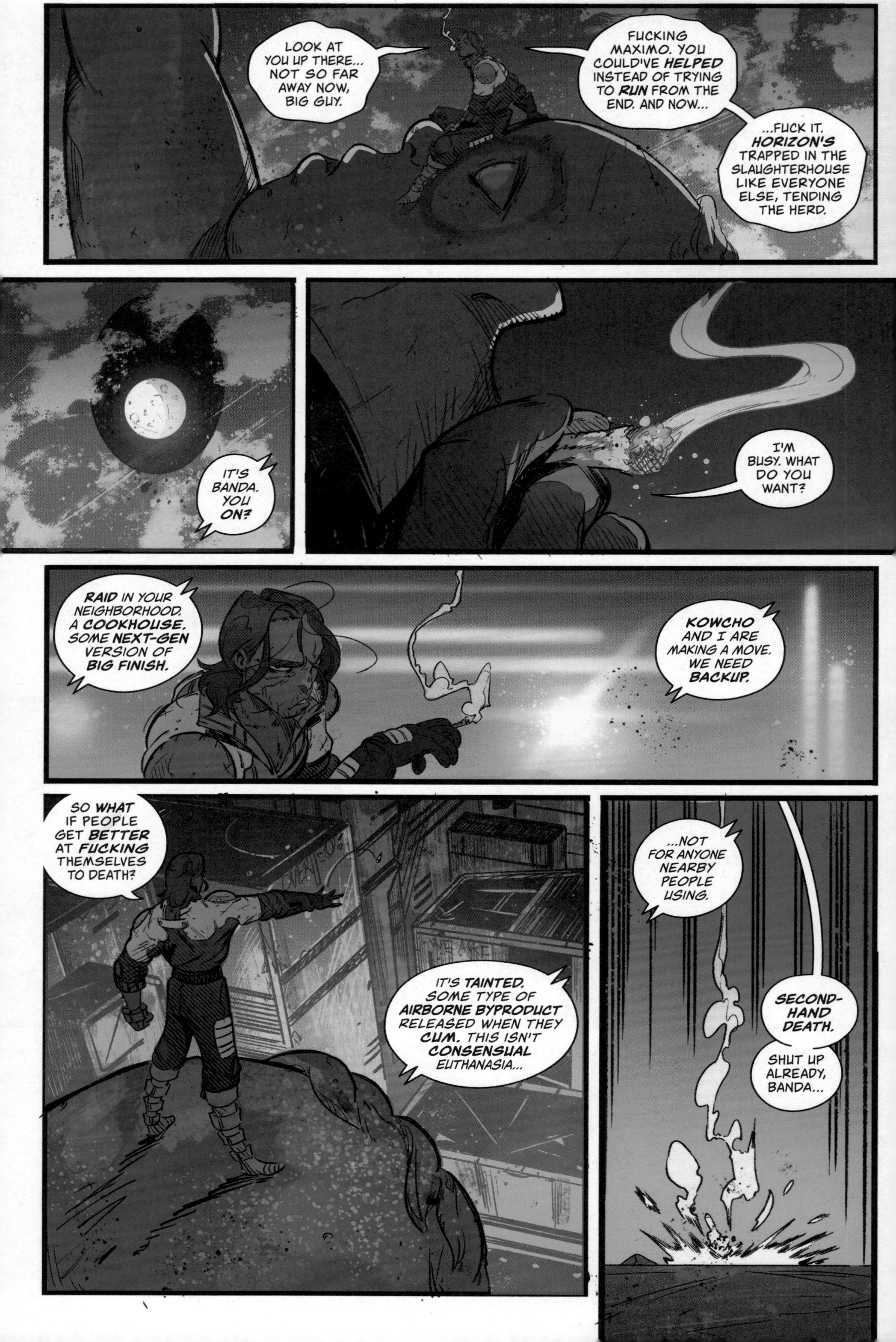
LOOK AT YOU UP THERE... NOT SO FAR AWAY NOW, BIG GUY.
FUCKING MAXIMO. YOU COULD'VE HELPED INSTEAD OF TRYING TO RUN FROM THE END. AND NOW...
...FUCK IT. HORIZON'S TRAPPED IN THE SLAUGHTERHOUSE LIKE EVERYONE ELSE, TENDING THE HERD.
IT'S BANDA. YOU ON?
I'M BUSY. WHAT DO YOU WANT?
RAID IN YOUR NEIGHBORHOOD. A COOKHOUSE. SOME NEXT-GEN VERSION OF BIG FINISH.
KOWCHO AND I ARE MAKING A MOVE. WE NEED BACKUP.
SO WHAT IF PEOPLE GET BETTER AT FUCKING THEMSELVES TO DEATH?
IT'S TAINTED. SOME TYPE OF AIRBORNE BYPRODUCT RELEASED WHEN THEY CUM. THIS ISN'T CONSENSUAL EUTHANASIA...
...NOT FOR ANYONE NEARBY PEOPLE USING.
SECOND-HAND DEATH.
SHUT UP ALREADY, BANDA...

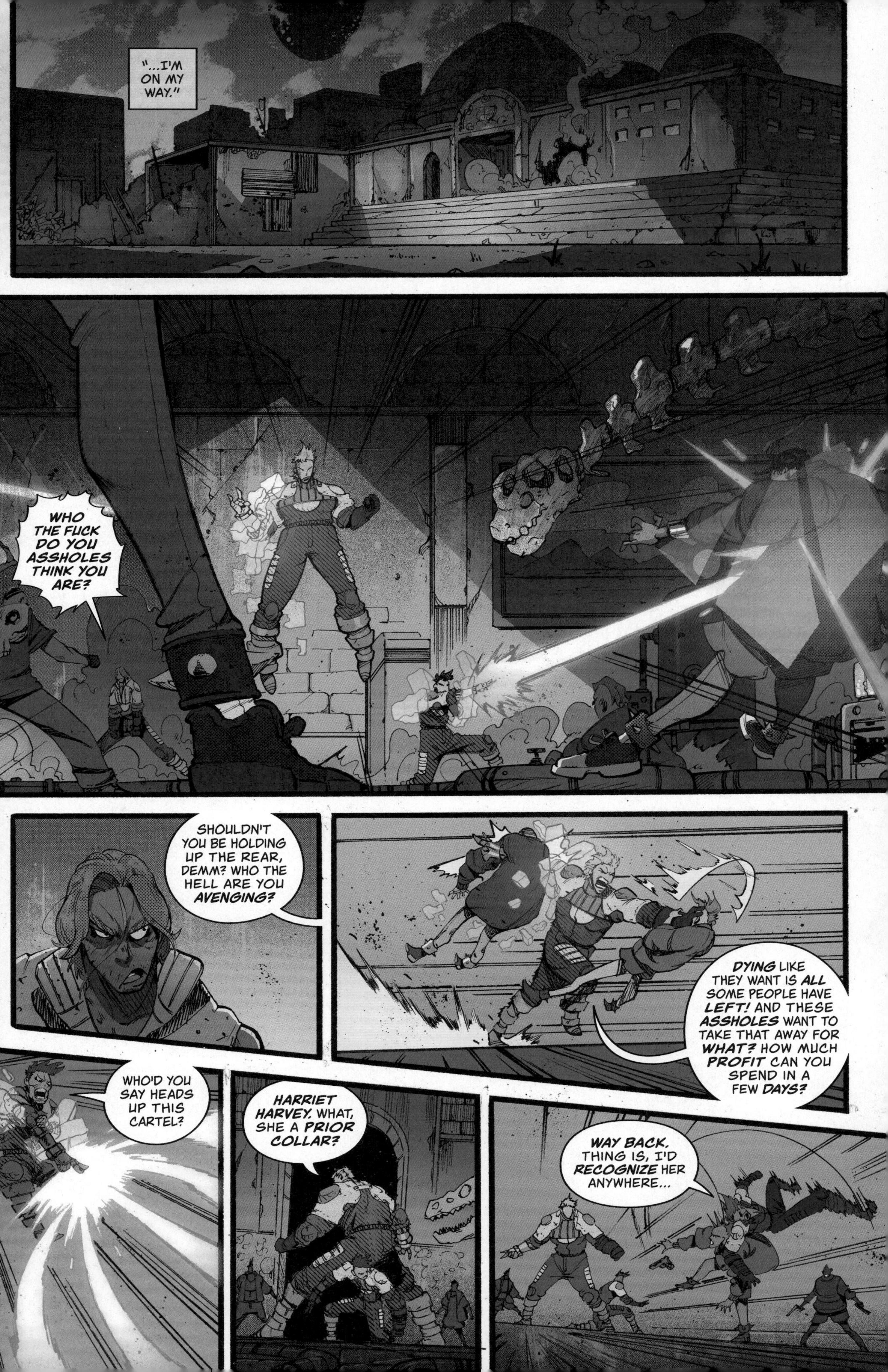
"...I'M ON MY WAY."
WHO THE FUCK DO YOU ASSHOLES THINK YOU ARE?
SHOULDN'T YOU BE HOLDING UP THE REAR, DEMM? WHO THE HELL ARE YOU AVENGING?
DYING LIKE THEY WANT IS ALL SOME PEOPLE HAVE LEFT! AND THESE ASSHOLES WANT TO TAKE THAT AWAY FOR WHAT? HOW MUCH PROFIT CAN YOU SPEND IN A FEW DAYS?
WHO'D YOU SAY HEADS UP THIS CARTEL?
HARRIET HARVEY. WHAT, SHE A PRIOR COLLAR?
WAY BACK. THING IS, I'D RECOGNIZE HER ANYWHERE...

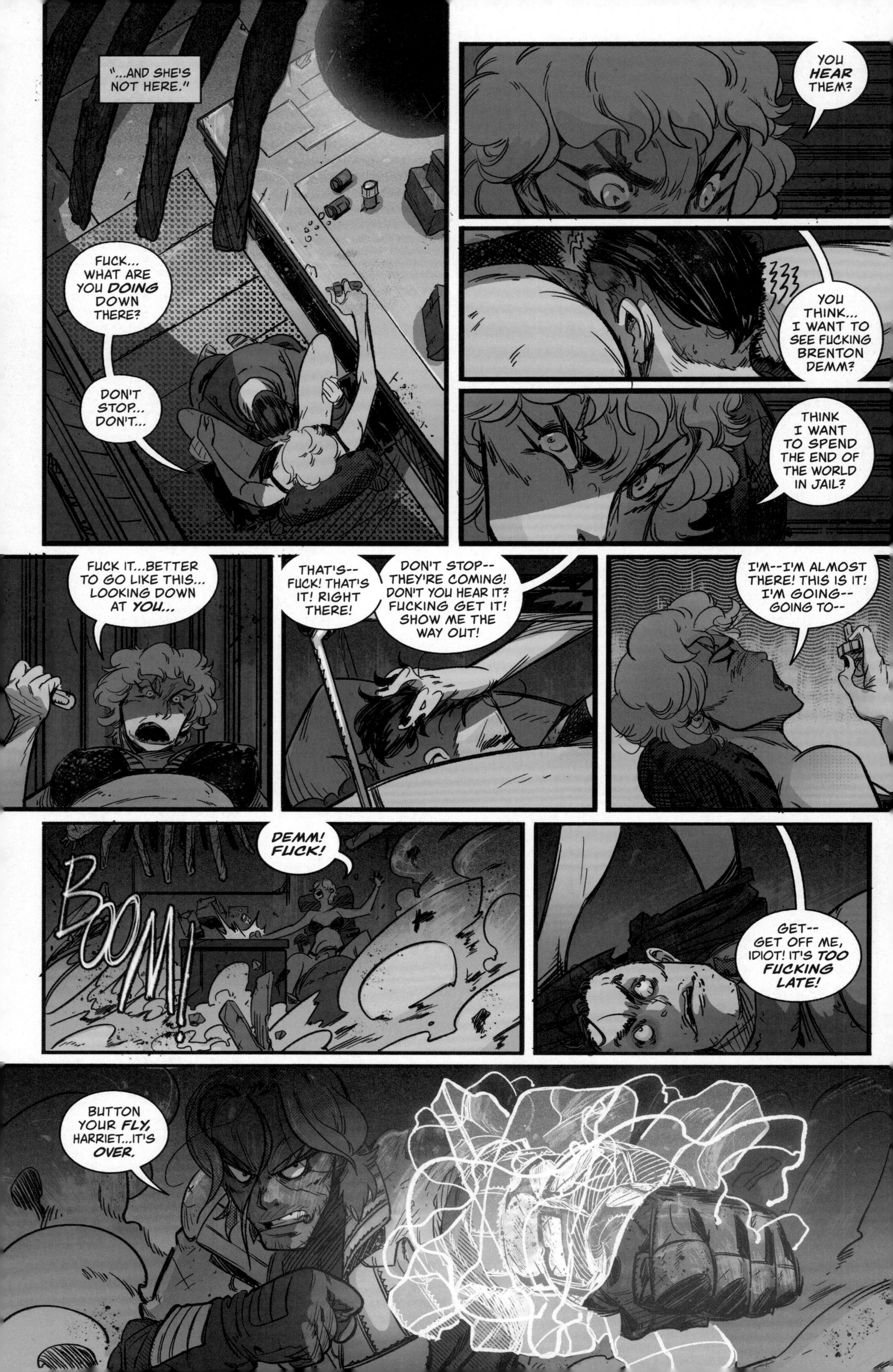
"...AND SHE'S NOT HERE."
FUCK... WHAT ARE YOU **DOING** DOWN THERE?
DON'T STOP... DON'T...
YOU **HEAR** THEM?
YOU THINK... I WANT TO SEE FUCKING BRENTON DEMM?
THINK I WANT TO SPEND THE END OF THE WORLD IN JAIL?
FUCK IT...BETTER TO GO LIKE THIS... LOOKING DOWN AT **YOU...**
THAT'S-- FUCK! THAT'S IT! RIGHT THERE!
DON'T STOP-- THEY'RE COMING! DON'T YOU HEAR IT? FUCKING GET IT! SHOW ME THE WAY OUT!
I'M--I'M ALMOST THERE! THIS IS IT! I'M GOING-- GOING TO--
BOOM!
DEMM! FUCK!
GET-- GET OFF ME, IDIOT! IT'S **TOO FUCKING LATE!**
BUTTON YOUR **FLY,** HARRIET...IT'S **OVER.**

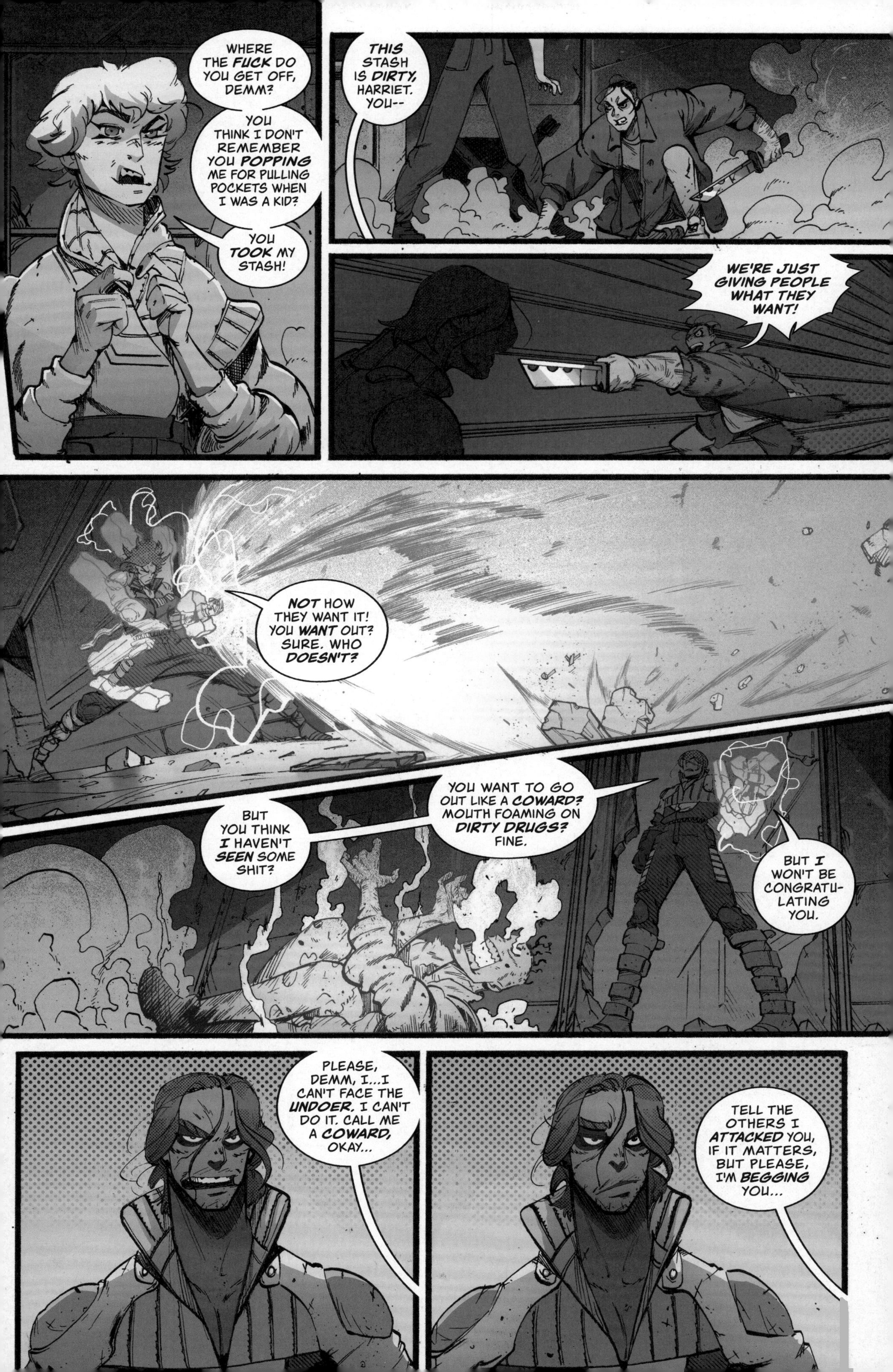
WHERE THE FUCK DO YOU GET OFF, DEMM?
YOU THINK I DON'T REMEMBER YOU POPPING ME FOR PULLING POCKETS WHEN I WAS A KID?
YOU TOOK MY STASH!
THIS STASH IS DIRTY, HARRIET. YOU--
WE'RE JUST GIVING PEOPLE WHAT THEY WANT!
NOT HOW THEY WANT IT! YOU WANT OUT? SURE. WHO DOESN'T?
BUT YOU THINK I HAVEN'T SEEN SOME SHIT?
YOU WANT TO GO OUT LIKE A COWARD? MOUTH FOAMING ON DIRTY DRUGS? FINE.
BUT I WON'T BE CONGRATU-LATING YOU.
PLEASE, DEMM, I...I CAN'T FACE THE UNDOER. I CAN'T DO IT. CALL ME A COWARD, OKAY...
TELL THE OTHERS I ATTACKED YOU, IF IT MATTERS, BUT PLEASE, I'M BEGGING YOU...

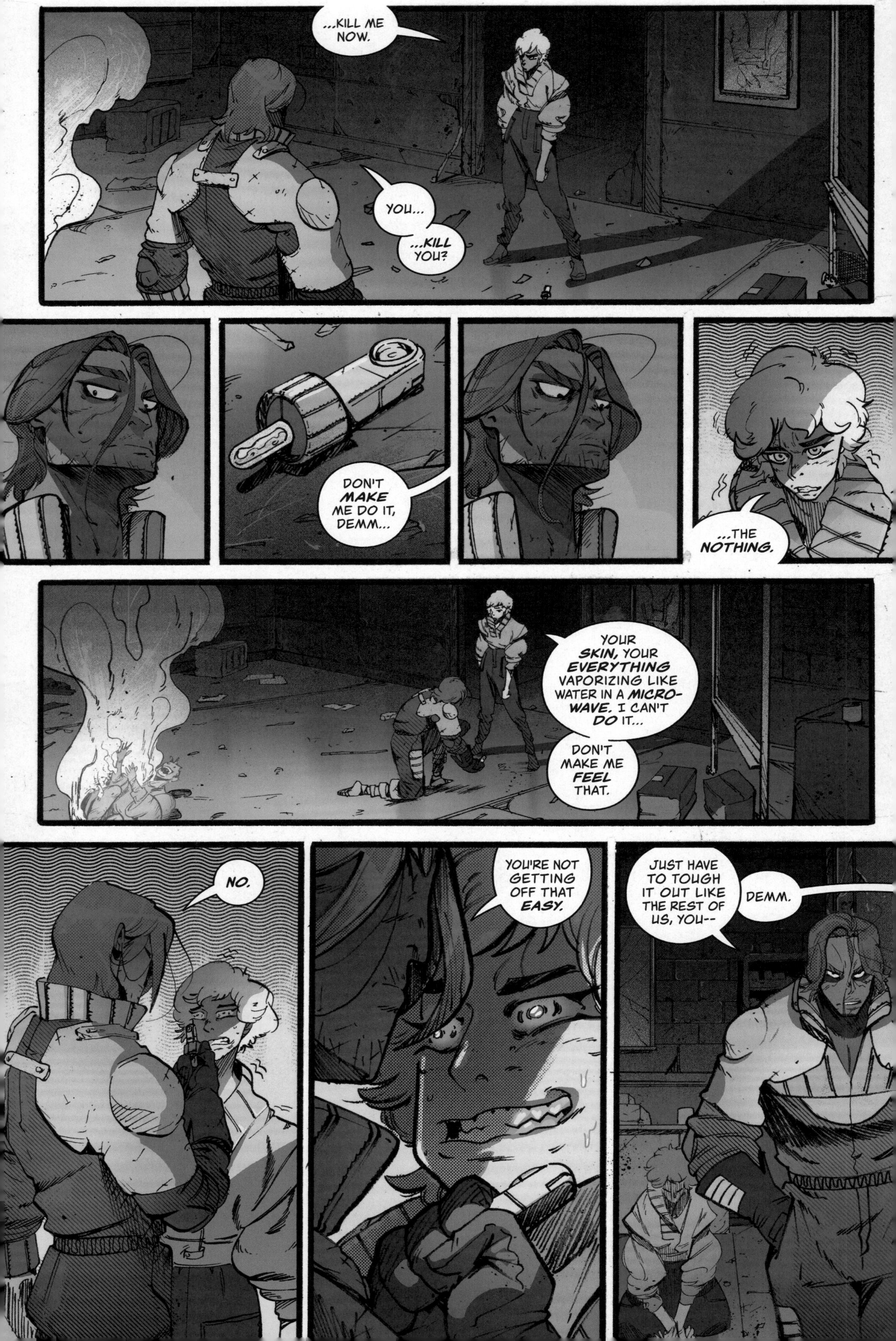
...KILL ME NOW.
YOU...
...KILL YOU?
DON'T MAKE ME DO IT, DEMM...
...THE NOTHING.
YOUR SKIN, YOUR EVERYTHING VAPORIZING LIKE WATER IN A MICRO-WAVE. I CAN'T DO IT...
DON'T MAKE ME FEEL THAT.
NO.
YOU'RE NOT GETTING OFF THAT EASY.
JUST HAVE TO TOUGH IT OUT LIKE THE REST OF US, YOU--
DEMM.

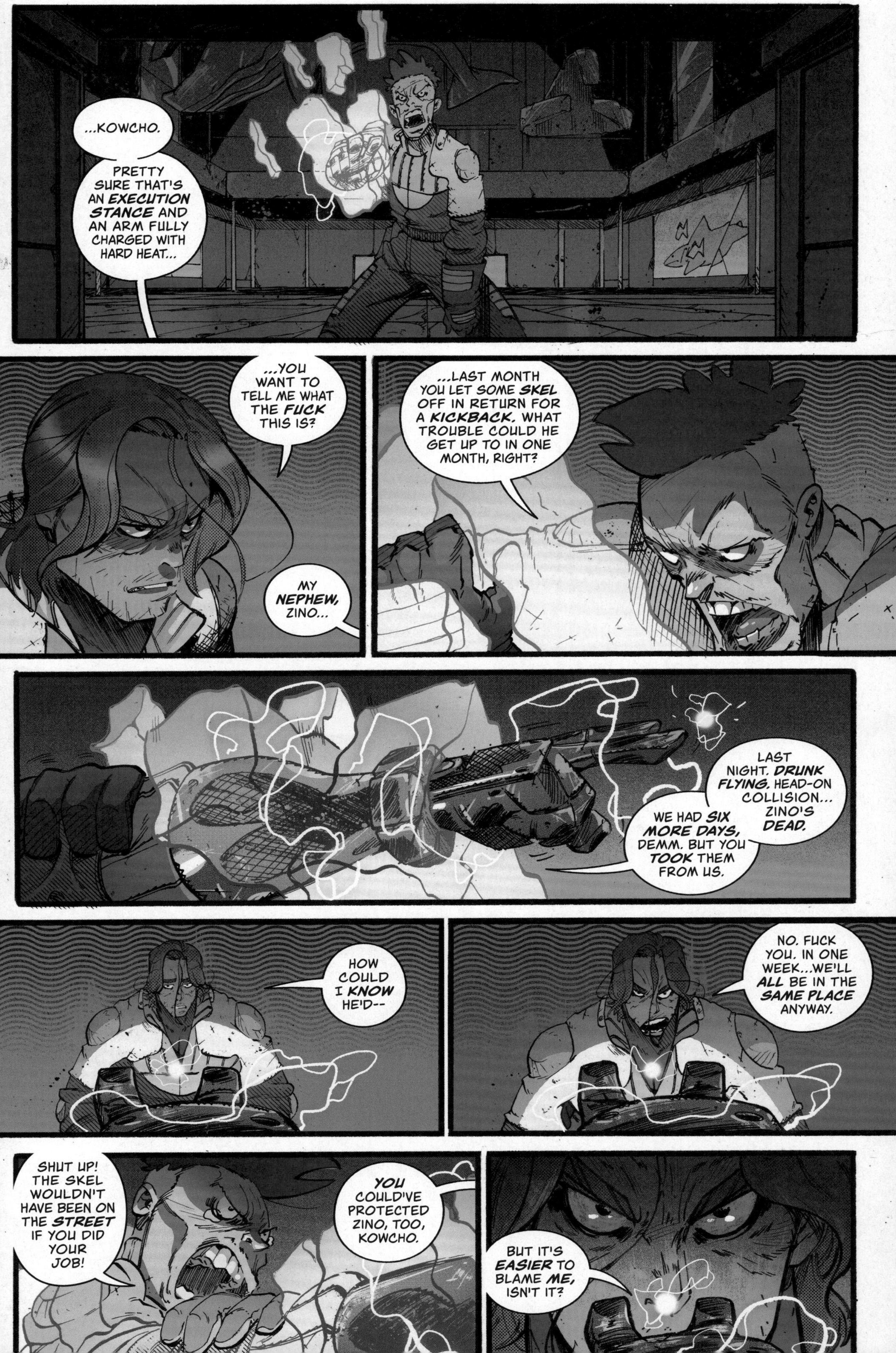
...KOWCHO.
PRETTY SURE THAT'S AN EXECUTION STANCE AND AN ARM FULLY CHARGED WITH HARD HEAT...
...YOU WANT TO TELL ME WHAT THE FUCK THIS IS?
MY NEPHEW, ZINO...
...LAST MONTH YOU LET SOME SKEL OFF IN RETURN FOR A KICKBACK. WHAT TROUBLE COULD HE GET UP TO IN ONE MONTH, RIGHT?
LAST NIGHT. DRUNK FLYING. HEAD-ON COLLISION... ZINO'S DEAD.
WE HAD SIX MORE DAYS, DEMM. BUT YOU TOOK THEM FROM US.
HOW COULD I KNOW HE'D--
NO. FUCK YOU. IN ONE WEEK...WE'LL ALL BE IN THE SAME PLACE ANYWAY.
SHUT UP! THE SKEL WOULDN'T HAVE BEEN ON THE STREET IF YOU DID YOUR JOB!
YOU COULD'VE PROTECTED ZINO, TOO, KOWCHO.
BUT IT'S EASIER TO BLAME ME, ISN'T IT?

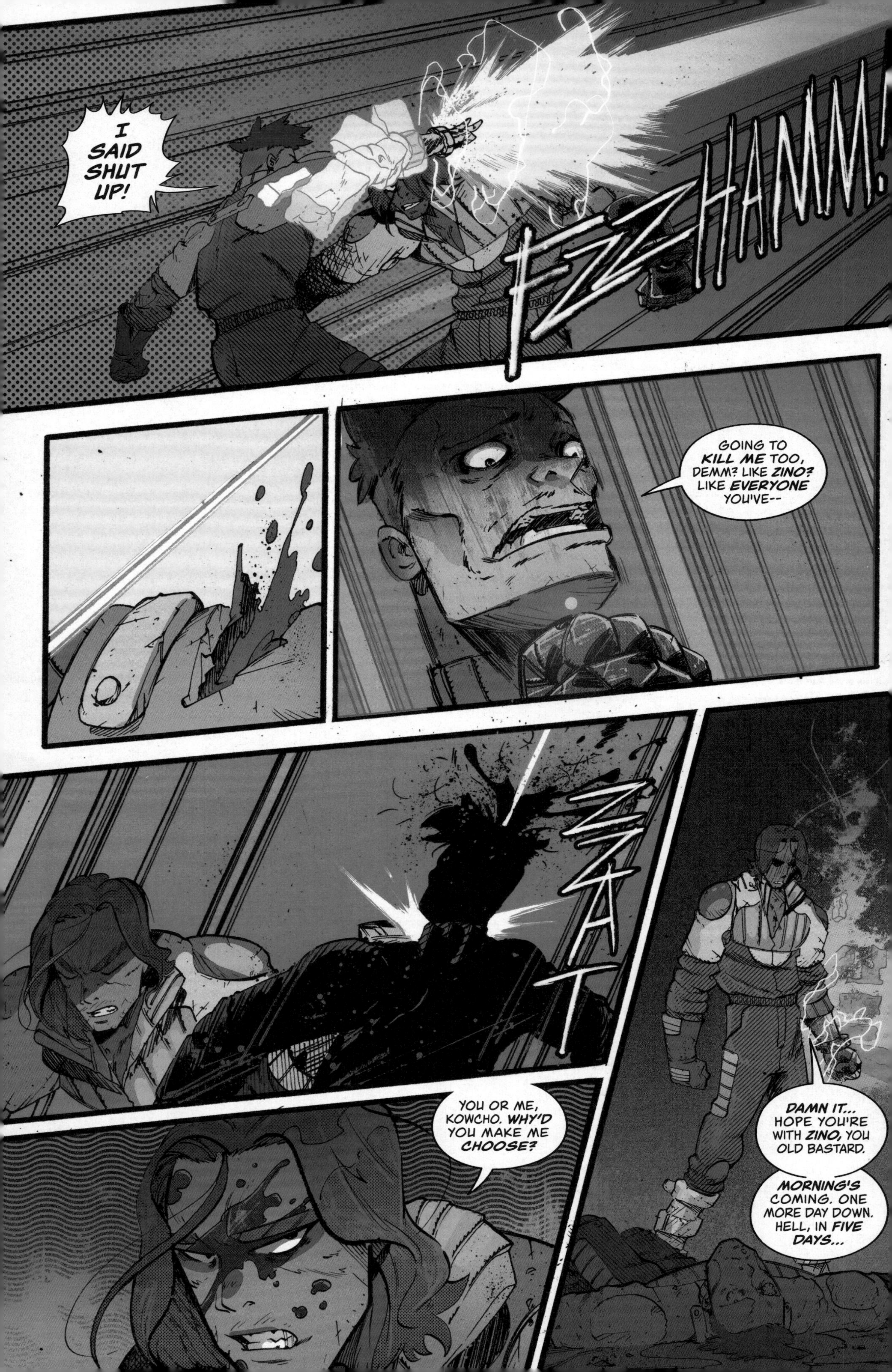
I SAID SHUT UP!
FZZHAMM!
GOING TO KILL ME TOO, DEMM? LIKE ZINO? LIKE EVERYONE YOU'VE--
THWAT
YOU OR ME, KOWCHO. WHY'D YOU MAKE ME CHOOSE?
DAMN IT... HOPE YOU'RE WITH ZINO, YOU OLD BASTARD.
MORNING'S COMING. ONE MORE DAY DOWN. HELL, IN FIVE DAYS...

"...MAYBE I'LL SEE YOU BOTH."

ANOTHER DAY *DOWN*, FOLKS...THE FINAL MOMENTS OF END PLUS SIX.

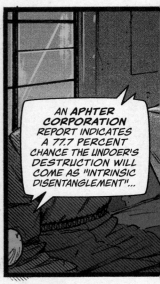

AN *APHTER CORPORATION* REPORT INDICATES A 77.7 PERCENT CHANCE THE UNDOER'S DESTRUCTION WILL COME AS "INTRINSIC DISENTANGLEMENT"...

...AS ALL MATTER ON EARTH DISASSEMBLES IN A FLASH. IT'S *SAID TO BE A PAINLESS END--*

RADIO OFF.

PAINLESS MY ASS.

GOOD SPIN. YOU KNOW...

MAYBE THEY'RE RIGHT. MAYBE THIS *IS* THE WAY.

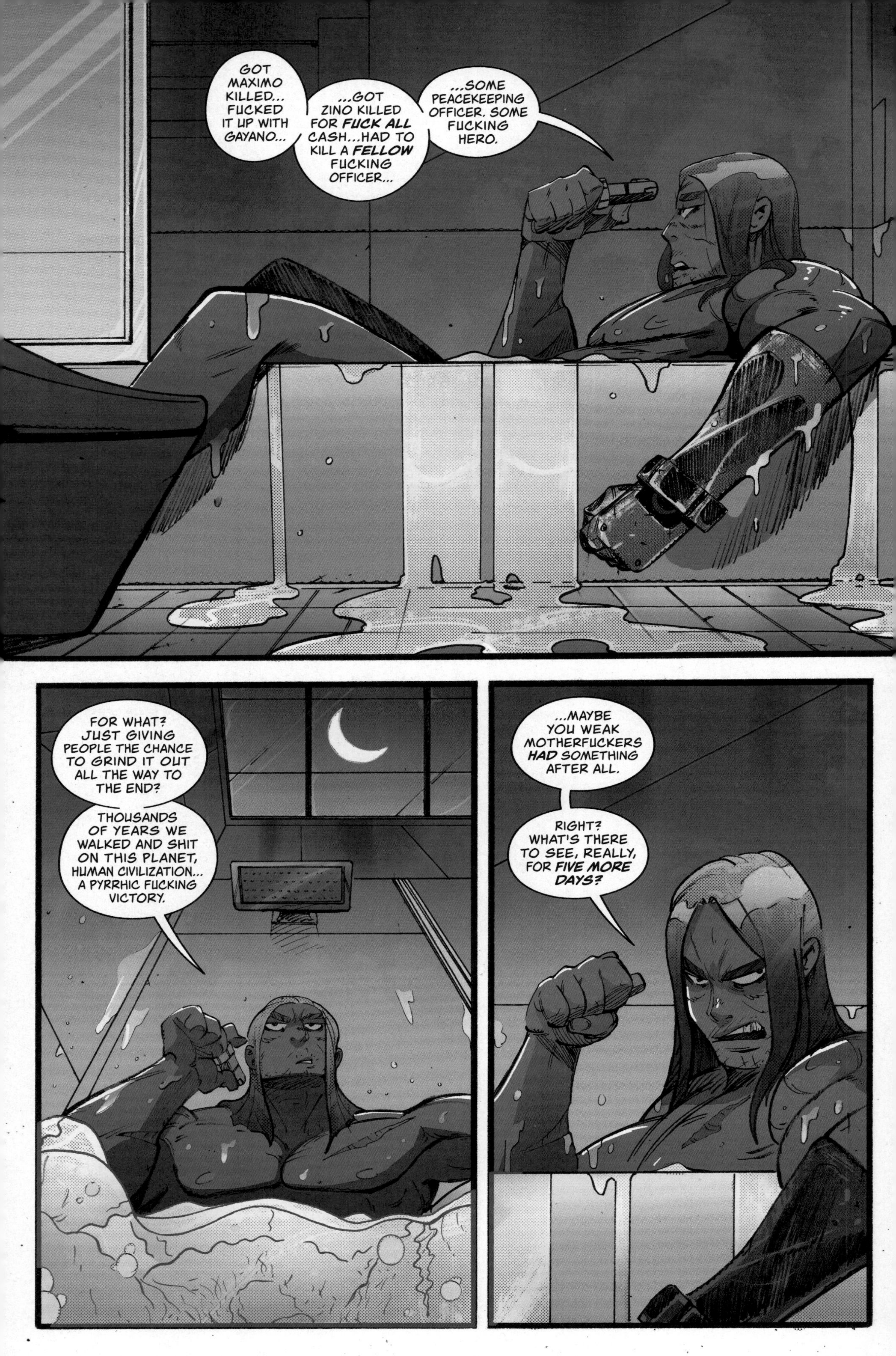
GOT MAXIMO KILLED... FUCKED IT UP WITH GAYANO...
...GOT ZINO KILLED FOR **FUCK ALL** CASH...HAD TO KILL A **FELLOW** FUCKING OFFICER...
...SOME PEACEKEEPING OFFICER. SOME FUCKING HERO.
FOR WHAT? JUST GIVING PEOPLE THE CHANCE TO GRIND IT OUT ALL THE WAY TO THE END?
THOUSANDS OF YEARS WE WALKED AND SHIT ON THIS PLANET, HUMAN CIVILIZATION... A PYRRHIC FUCKING VICTORY.
...MAYBE YOU WEAK MOTHERFUCKERS **HAD** SOMETHING AFTER ALL.
RIGHT? WHAT'S THERE TO SEE, REALLY, FOR **FIVE MORE DAYS?**

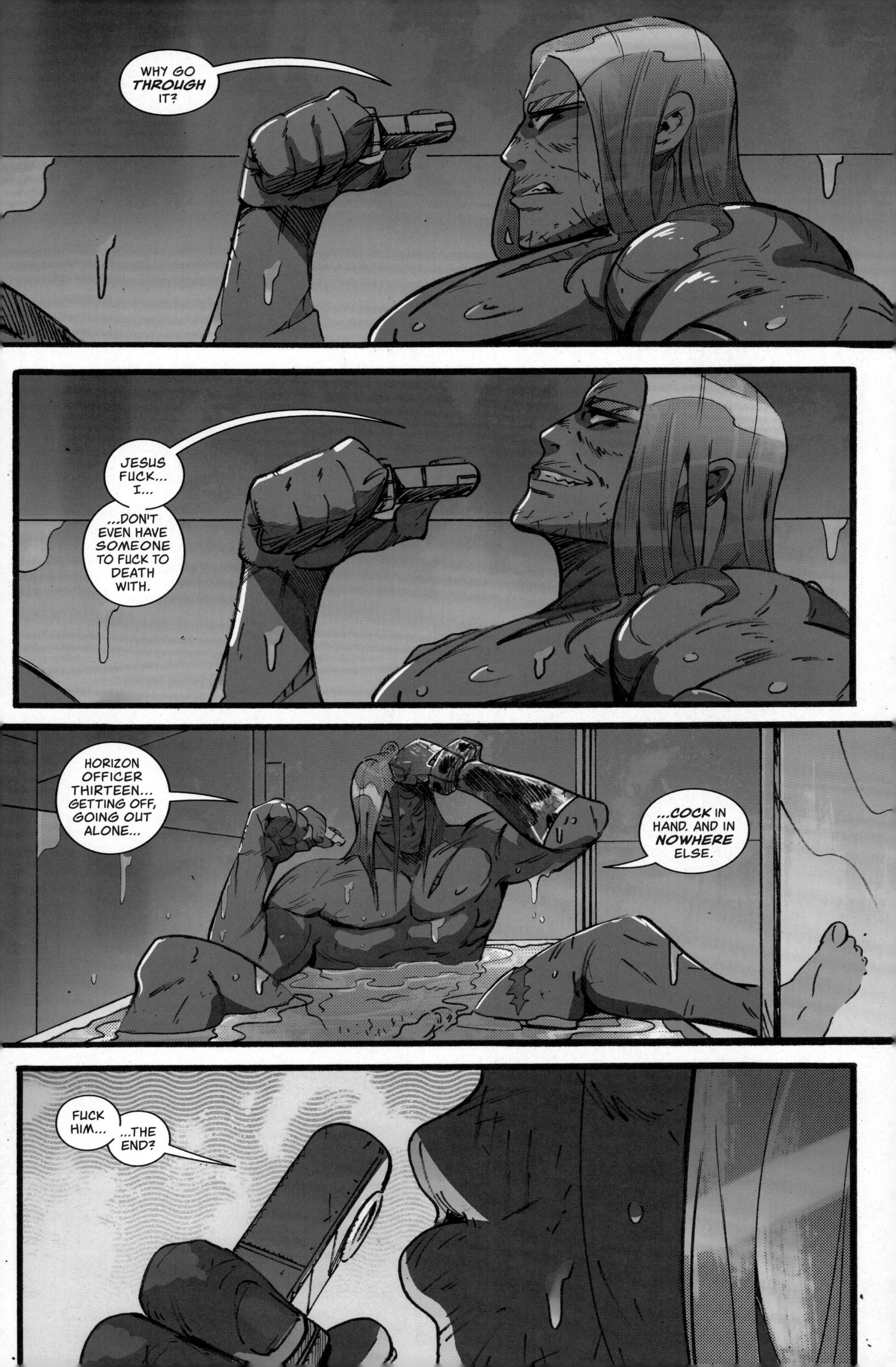
WHY GO *THROUGH* IT?
JESUS FUCK... I...
...DON'T EVEN HAVE SOMEONE TO FUCK TO DEATH WITH.
HORIZON OFFICER THIRTEEN... GETTING OFF, GOING OUT ALONE...
...*COCK* IN HAND. AND IN *NOWHERE* ELSE.
FUCK HIM...
...THE END?

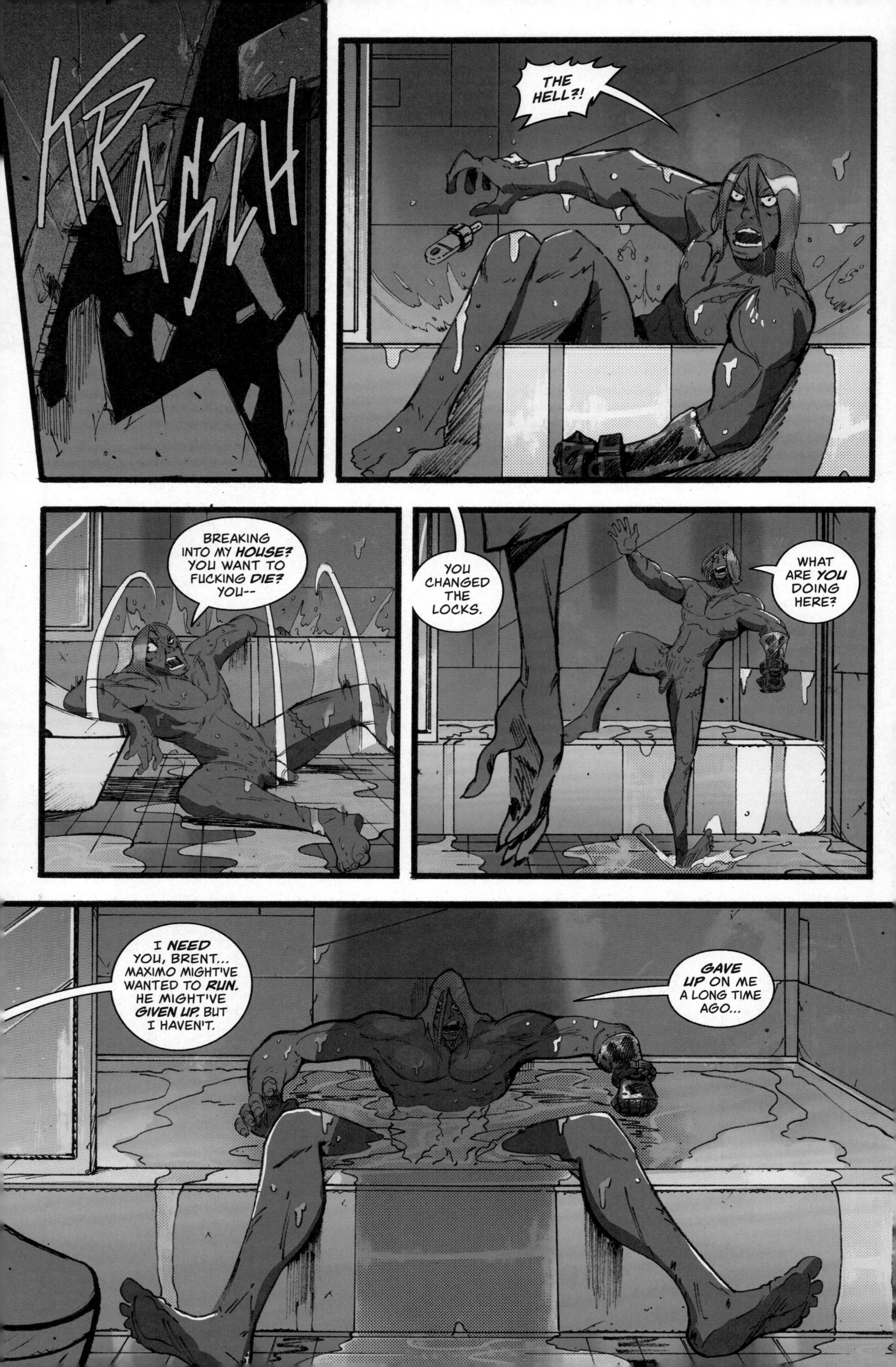
KRASZH
THE HELL?!
BREAKING INTO MY HOUSE? YOU WANT TO FUCKING DIE? YOU--
YOU CHANGED THE LOCKS.
WHAT ARE YOU DOING HERE?
I NEED YOU, BRENT... MAXIMO MIGHT'VE WANTED TO RUN. HE MIGHT'VE GIVEN UP. BUT I HAVEN'T.
GAVE UP ON ME A LONG TIME AGO...

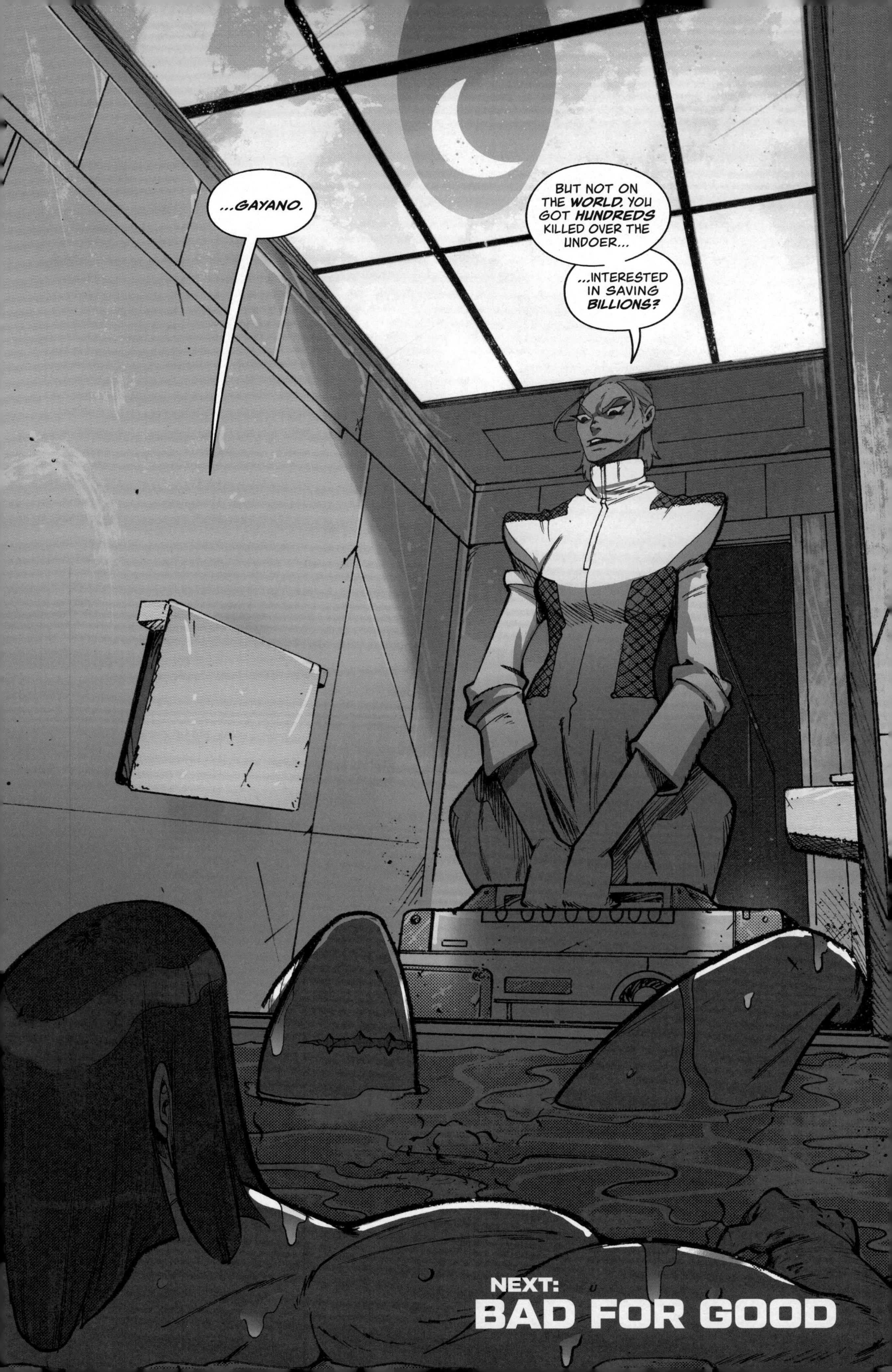
...GAYANO.
BUT NOT ON THE WORLD. YOU GOT HUNDREDS KILLED OVER THE UNDOER...
...INTERESTED IN SAVING BILLIONS?
NEXT:
BAD FOR GOOD

CHAPTER 2

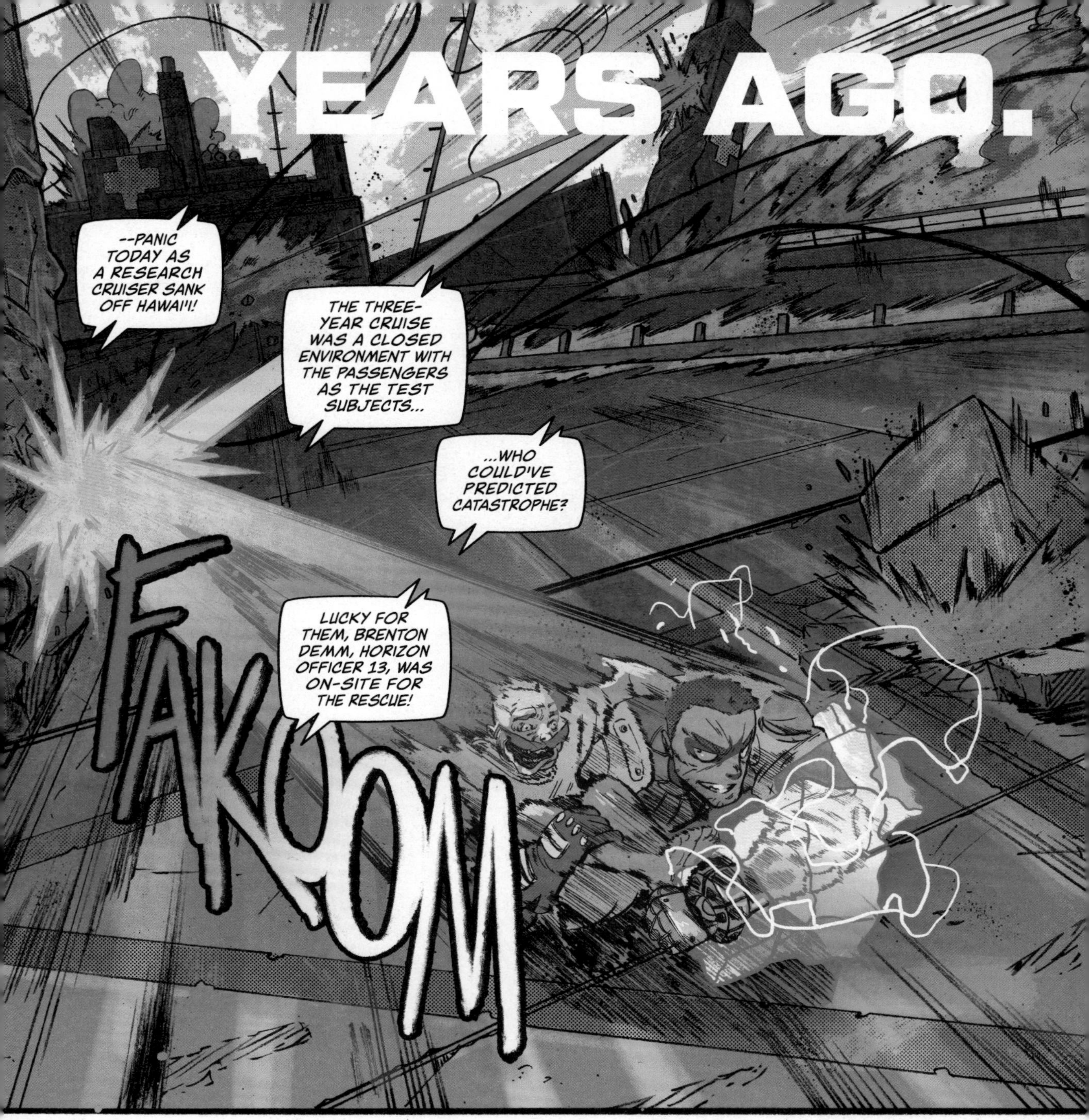
YEARS AGO.
--PANIC TODAY AS A RESEARCH CRUISER SANK OFF HAWAI'I!
THE THREE-YEAR CRUISE WAS A CLOSED ENVIRONMENT WITH THE PASSENGERS AS THE TEST SUBJECTS...
...WHO COULD'VE PREDICTED CATASTROPHE?
FAKOOM
LUCKY FOR THEM, BRENTON DEMM, HORIZON OFFICER 13, WAS ON-SITE FOR THE RESCUE!
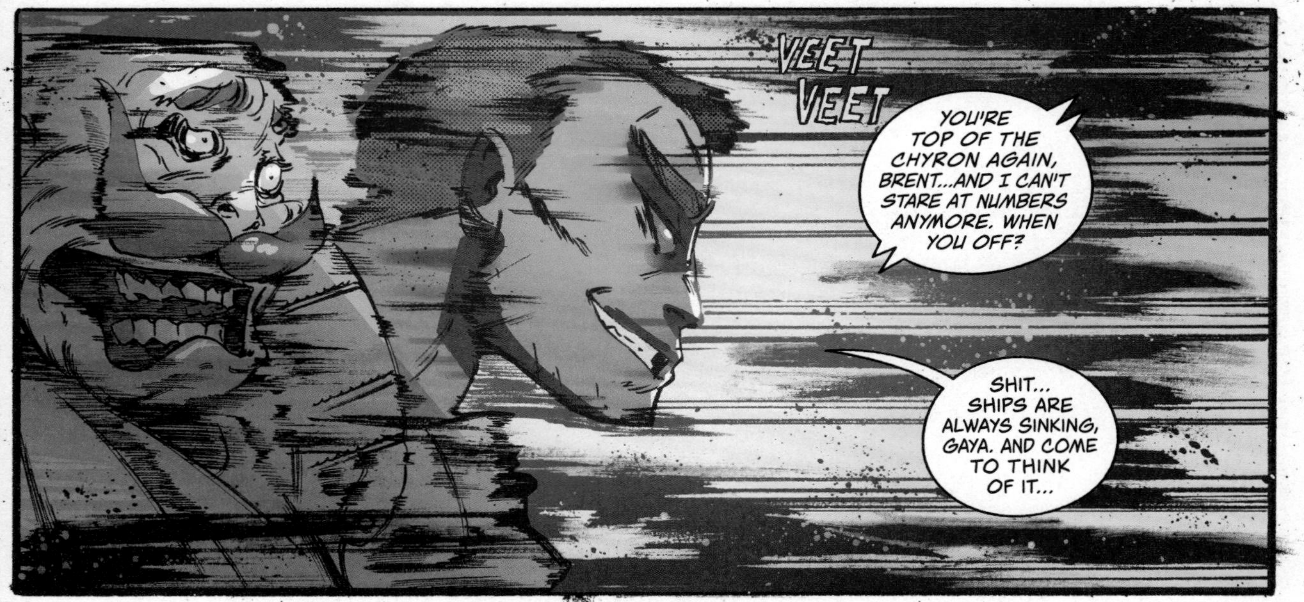
VEET VEET
YOU'RE TOP OF THE CHYRON AGAIN, BRENT...AND I CAN'T STARE AT NUMBERS ANYMORE. WHEN YOU OFF?
SHIT... SHIPS ARE ALWAYS SINKING, GAYA. AND COME TO THINK OF IT...

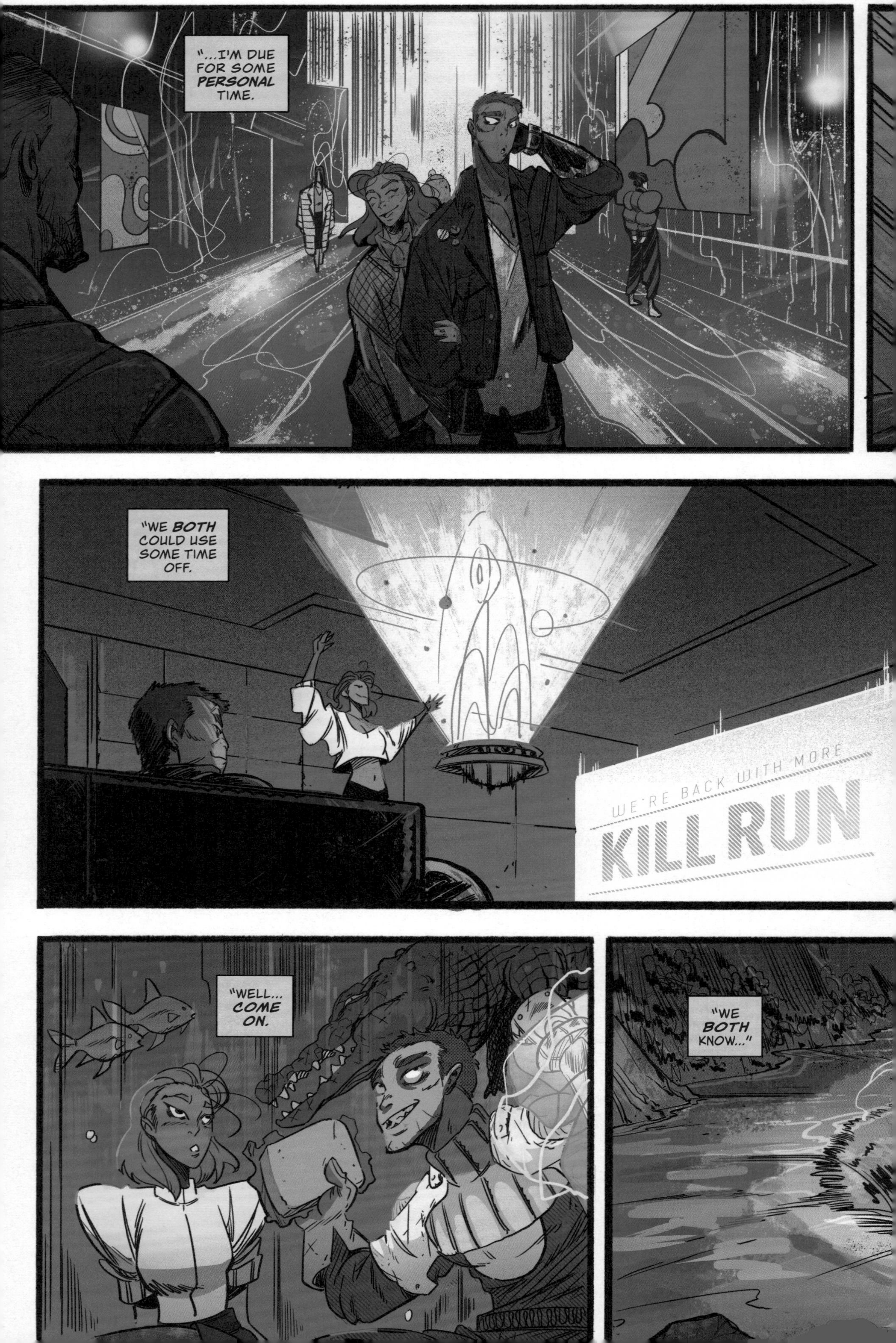
"...I'M DUE FOR SOME PERSONAL TIME.
"WE BOTH COULD USE SOME TIME OFF.
WE'RE BACK WITH MORE
KILL RUN
"WELL... COME ON.
"WE BOTH KNOW..."

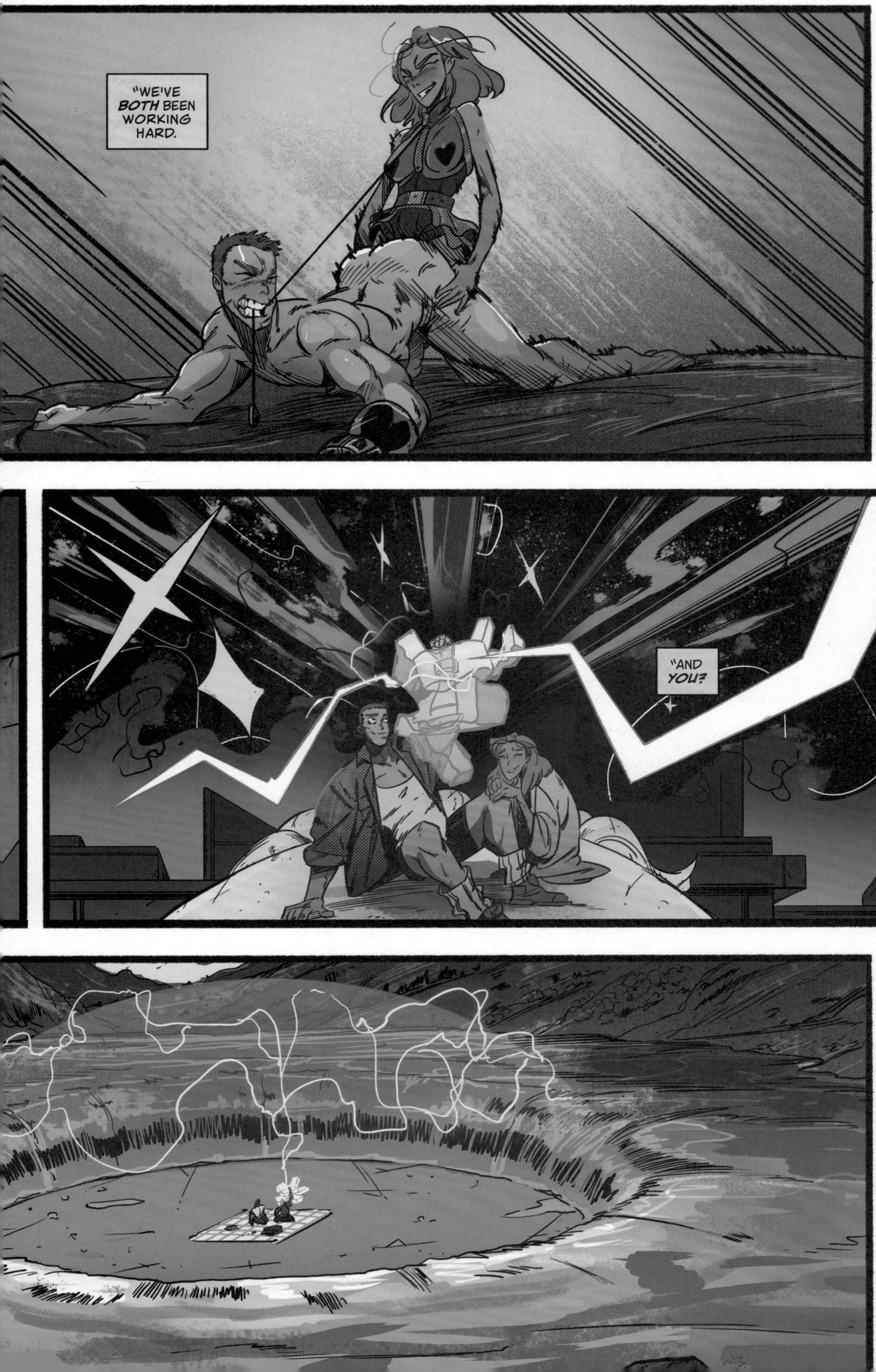
"WE'VE BOTH BEEN WORKING HARD.
"AND YOU?

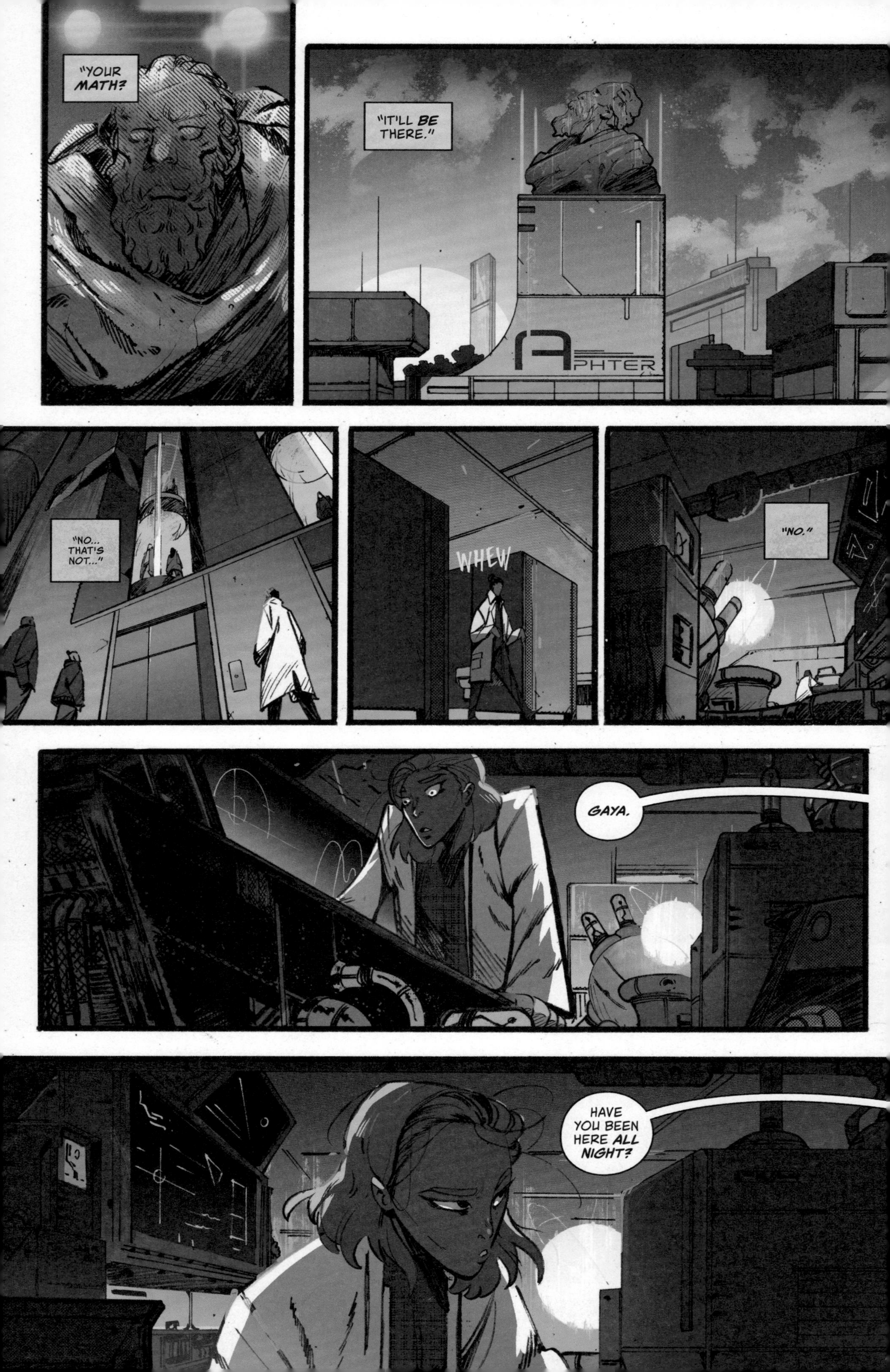
"YOUR MATH?
"IT'LL BE THERE."
APHTER
"NO... THAT'S NOT..."
WHEW
"NO."
GAYA.
HAVE YOU BEEN HERE ALL NIGHT?

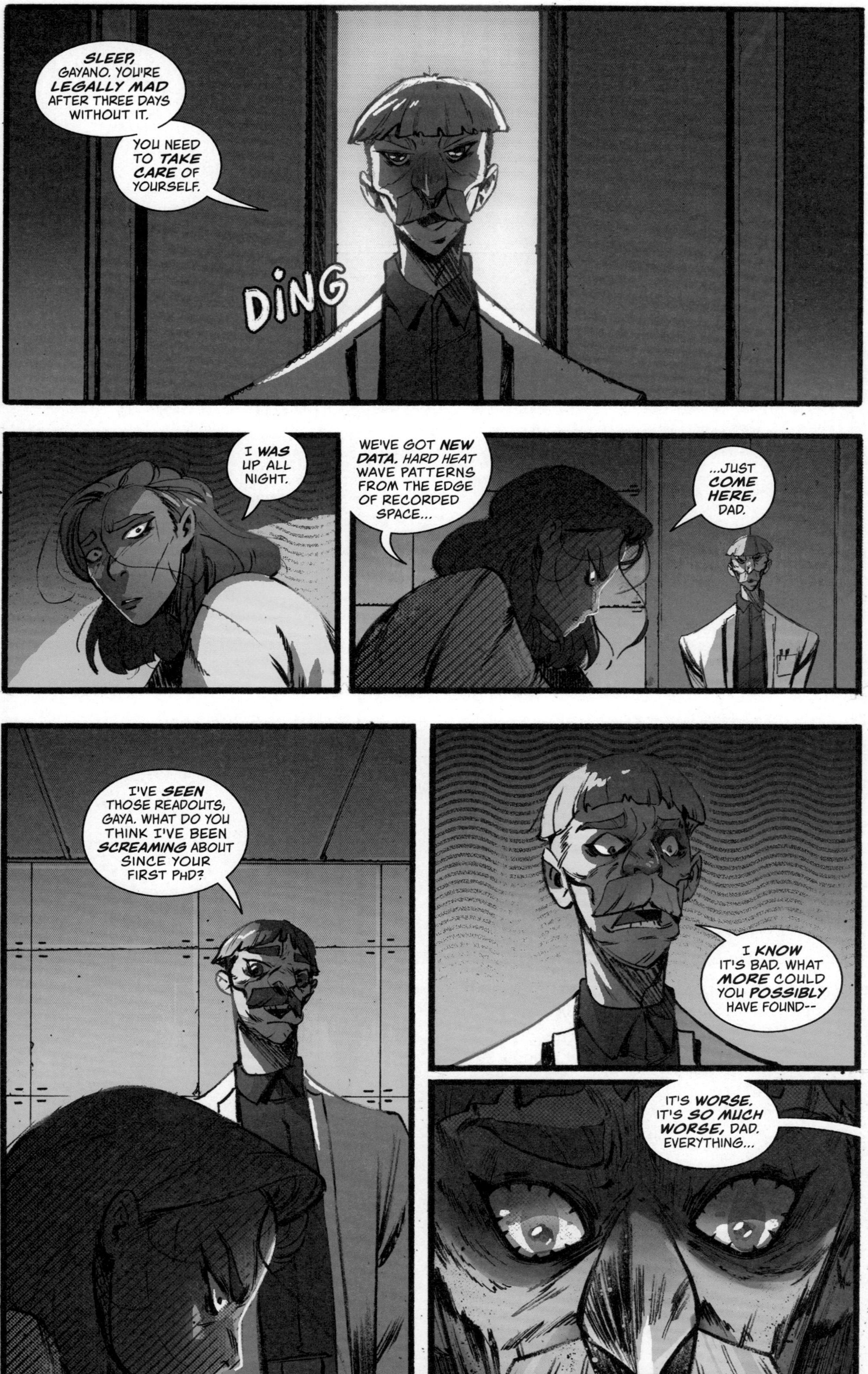
SLEEP, GAYANO. YOU'RE LEGALLY MAD AFTER THREE DAYS WITHOUT IT.
YOU NEED TO TAKE CARE OF YOURSELF.
DING
I WAS UP ALL NIGHT.
WE'VE GOT NEW DATA. HARD HEAT WAVE PATTERNS FROM THE EDGE OF RECORDED SPACE...
...JUST COME HERE, DAD.
I'VE SEEN THOSE READOUTS, GAYA. WHAT DO YOU THINK I'VE BEEN SCREAMING ABOUT SINCE YOUR FIRST PHD?
I KNOW IT'S BAD. WHAT MORE COULD YOU POSSIBLY HAVE FOUND--
IT'S WORSE. IT'S SO MUCH WORSE, DAD. EVERYTHING...

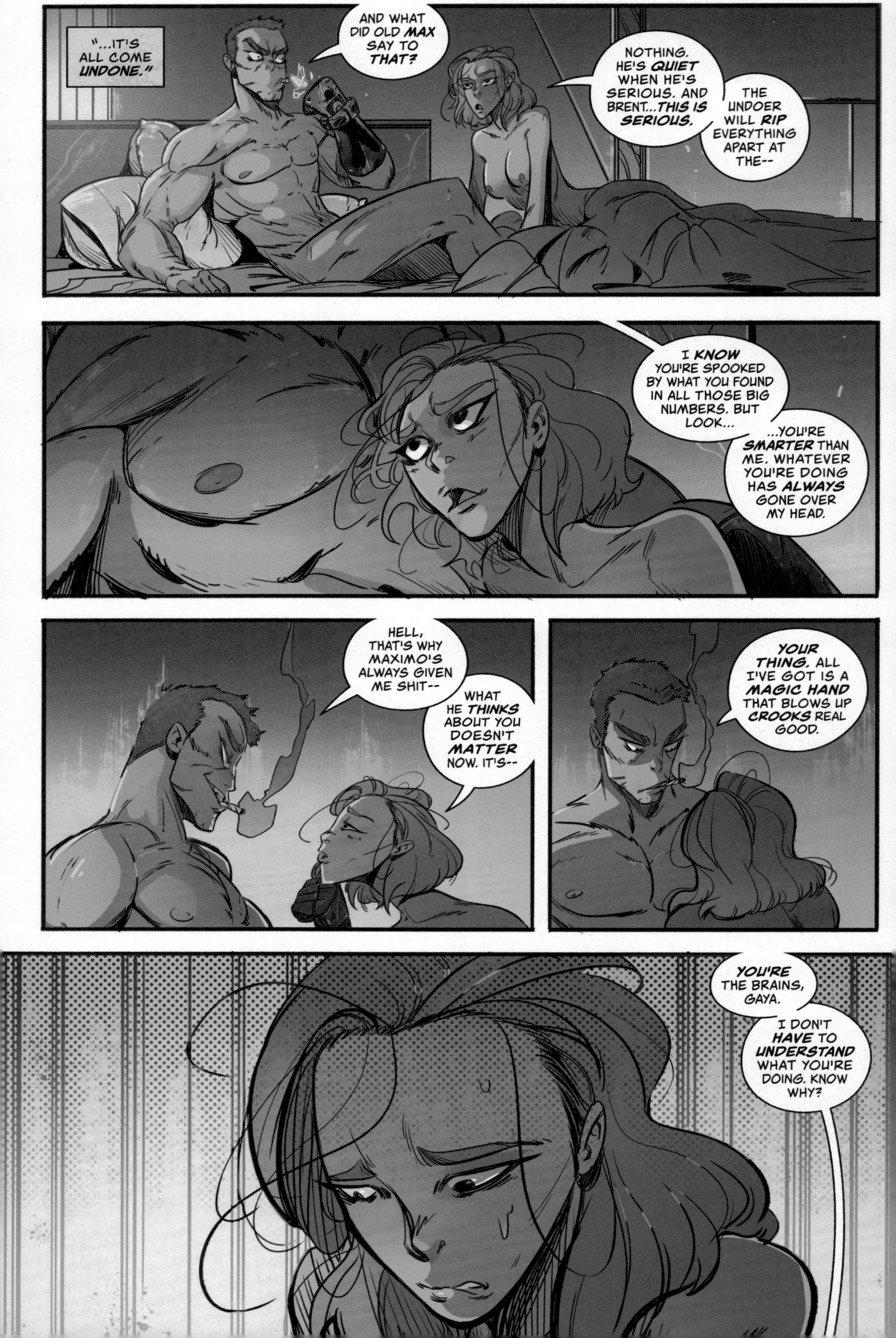
"...IT'S ALL COME UNDONE."
AND WHAT DID OLD MAX SAY TO THAT?
NOTHING. HE'S QUIET WHEN HE'S SERIOUS. AND BRENT...THIS IS SERIOUS.
THE UNDOER WILL RIP EVERYTHING APART AT THE--
I KNOW YOU'RE SPOOKED BY WHAT YOU FOUND IN ALL THOSE BIG NUMBERS. BUT LOOK...
...YOU'RE SMARTER THAN ME. WHATEVER YOU'RE DOING HAS ALWAYS GONE OVER MY HEAD.
HELL, THAT'S WHY MAXIMO'S ALWAYS GIVEN ME SHIT--
WHAT HE THINKS ABOUT YOU DOESN'T MATTER NOW. IT'S--
YOUR THING. ALL I'VE GOT IS A MAGIC HAND THAT BLOWS UP CROOKS REAL GOOD.
YOU'RE THE BRAINS, GAYA.
I DON'T HAVE TO UNDERSTAND WHAT YOU'RE DOING. KNOW WHY?

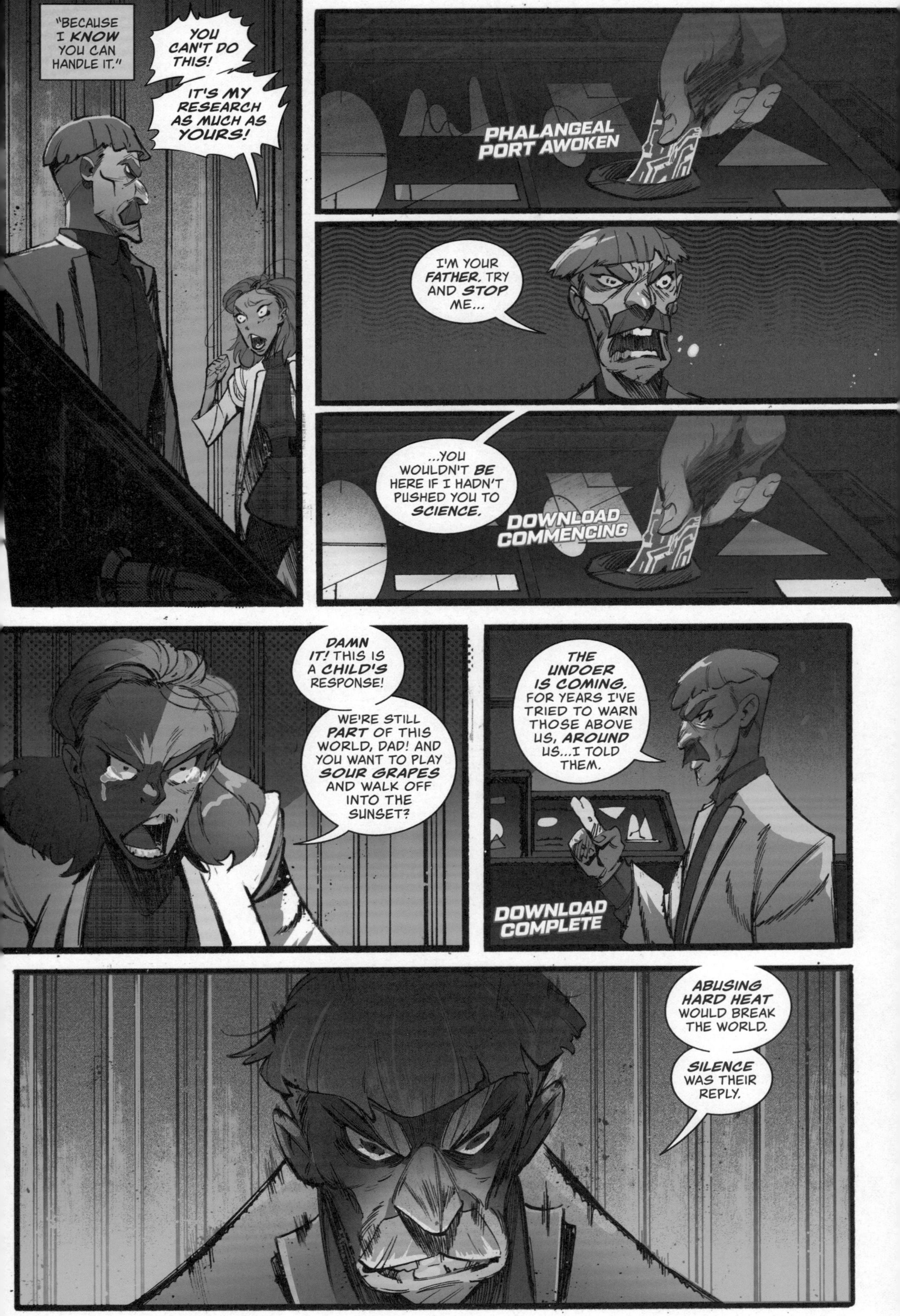
"BECAUSE I KNOW YOU CAN HANDLE IT."
YOU CAN'T DO THIS!
IT'S MY RESEARCH AS MUCH AS YOURS!
PHALANGEAL PORT AWOKEN
I'M YOUR FATHER. TRY AND STOP ME...
...YOU WOULDN'T BE HERE IF I HADN'T PUSHED YOU TO SCIENCE.
DOWNLOAD COMMENCING
DAMN IT! THIS IS A CHILD'S RESPONSE!
WE'RE STILL PART OF THIS WORLD, DAD! AND YOU WANT TO PLAY SOUR GRAPES AND WALK OFF INTO THE SUNSET?
THE UNDOER IS COMING. FOR YEARS I'VE TRIED TO WARN THOSE ABOVE US, AROUND US...I TOLD THEM.
DOWNLOAD COMPLETE
ABUSING HARD HEAT WOULD BREAK THE WORLD.
SILENCE WAS THEIR REPLY.

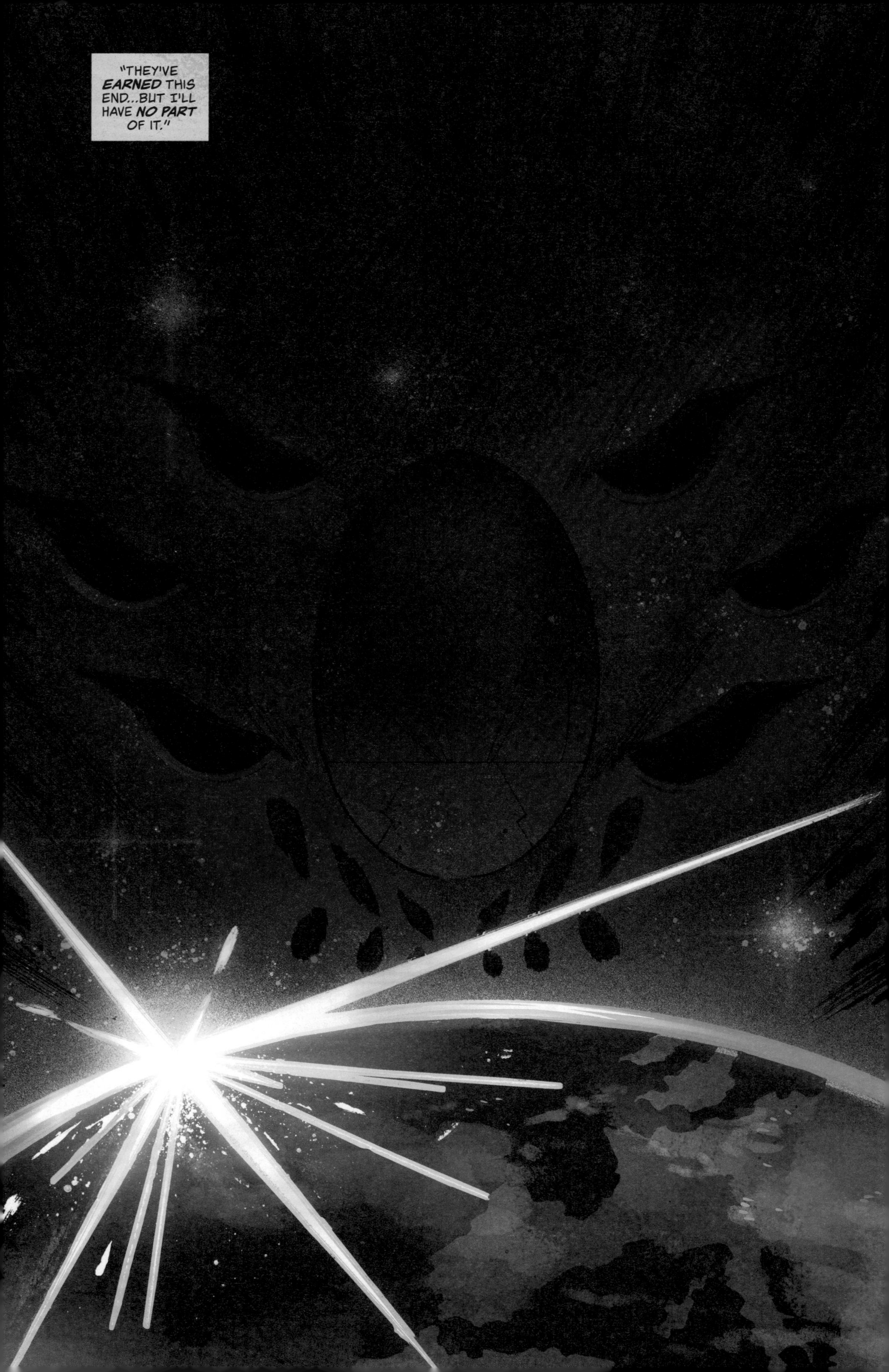
"THEY'VE EARNED THIS END...BUT I'LL HAVE NO PART OF IT."

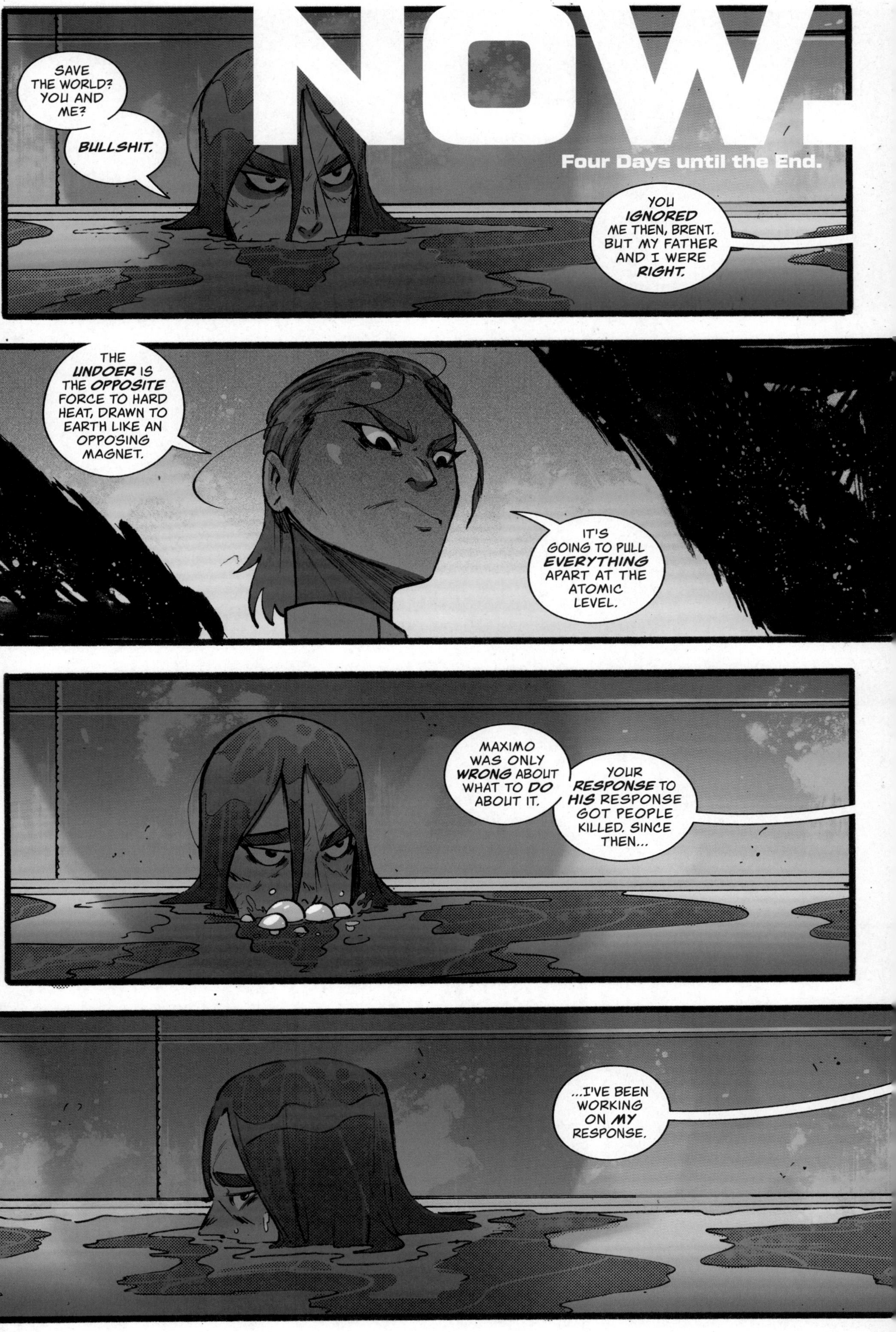
NOW.
Four Days until the End.
SAVE THE WORLD? YOU AND ME?
BULLSHIT.
YOU IGNORED ME THEN, BRENT. BUT MY FATHER AND I WERE RIGHT.
THE UNDOER IS THE OPPOSITE FORCE TO HARD HEAT, DRAWN TO EARTH LIKE AN OPPOSING MAGNET.
IT'S GOING TO PULL EVERYTHING APART AT THE ATOMIC LEVEL.
MAXIMO WAS ONLY WRONG ABOUT WHAT TO DO ABOUT IT.
YOUR RESPONSE TO HIS RESPONSE GOT PEOPLE KILLED. SINCE THEN...
...I'VE BEEN WORKING ON MY RESPONSE.

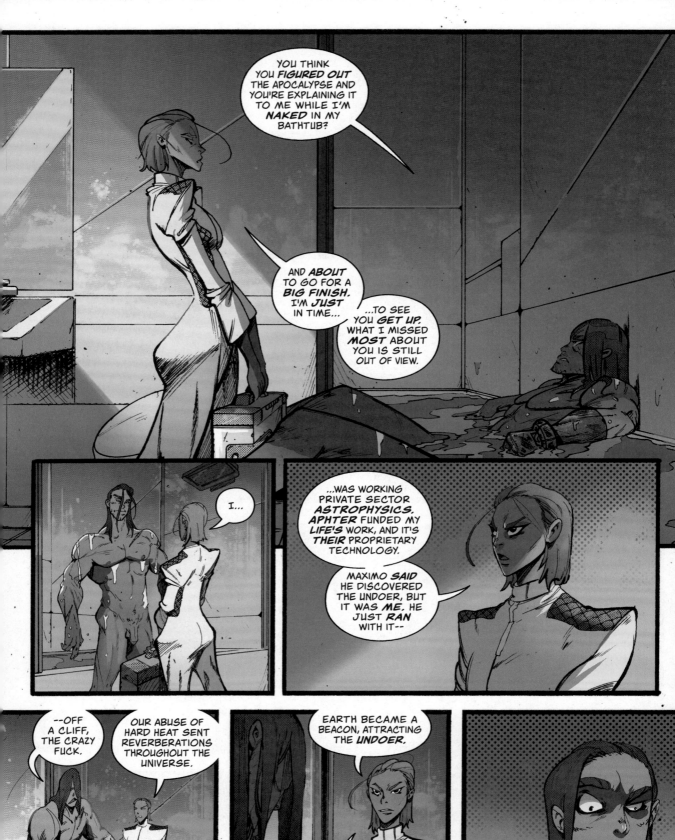

YOU THINK YOU *FIGURED OUT* THE APOCALYPSE AND YOU'RE EXPLAINING IT TO ME WHILE I'M *NAKED* IN MY BATHTUB?

AND *ABOUT* TO GO FOR A *BIG FINISH.* I'M *JUST* IN TIME...

...TO SEE YOU *GET UP.* WHAT I MISSED *MOST* ABOUT YOU IS STILL OUT OF VIEW.

I...

...WAS WORKING PRIVATE SECTOR *ASTROPHYSICS.* APHTER FUNDED MY LIFE'S WORK, AND IT'S *THEIR* PROPRIETARY TECHNOLOGY.

MAXIMO *SAID* HE DISCOVERED THE UNDOER, BUT IT WAS *ME.* HE JUST *RAN* WITH IT--

--OFF A CLIFF, THE CRAZY FUCK.

OUR ABUSE OF HARD HEAT SENT REVERBERATIONS THROUGHOUT THE UNIVERSE.

EARTH BECAME A BEACON, ATTRACTING THE *UNDOER.*

I TOLD YOU, APOCALYPTIC MAGNETS.

BUT I CAN STOP IT...WITH *THIS.*

IF YOU CAN KEEP ME ALIVE *LONG* ENOUGH TO GATHER THE FINAL COMPONENTS.

YOU WANT...*MY MUSCLE?*

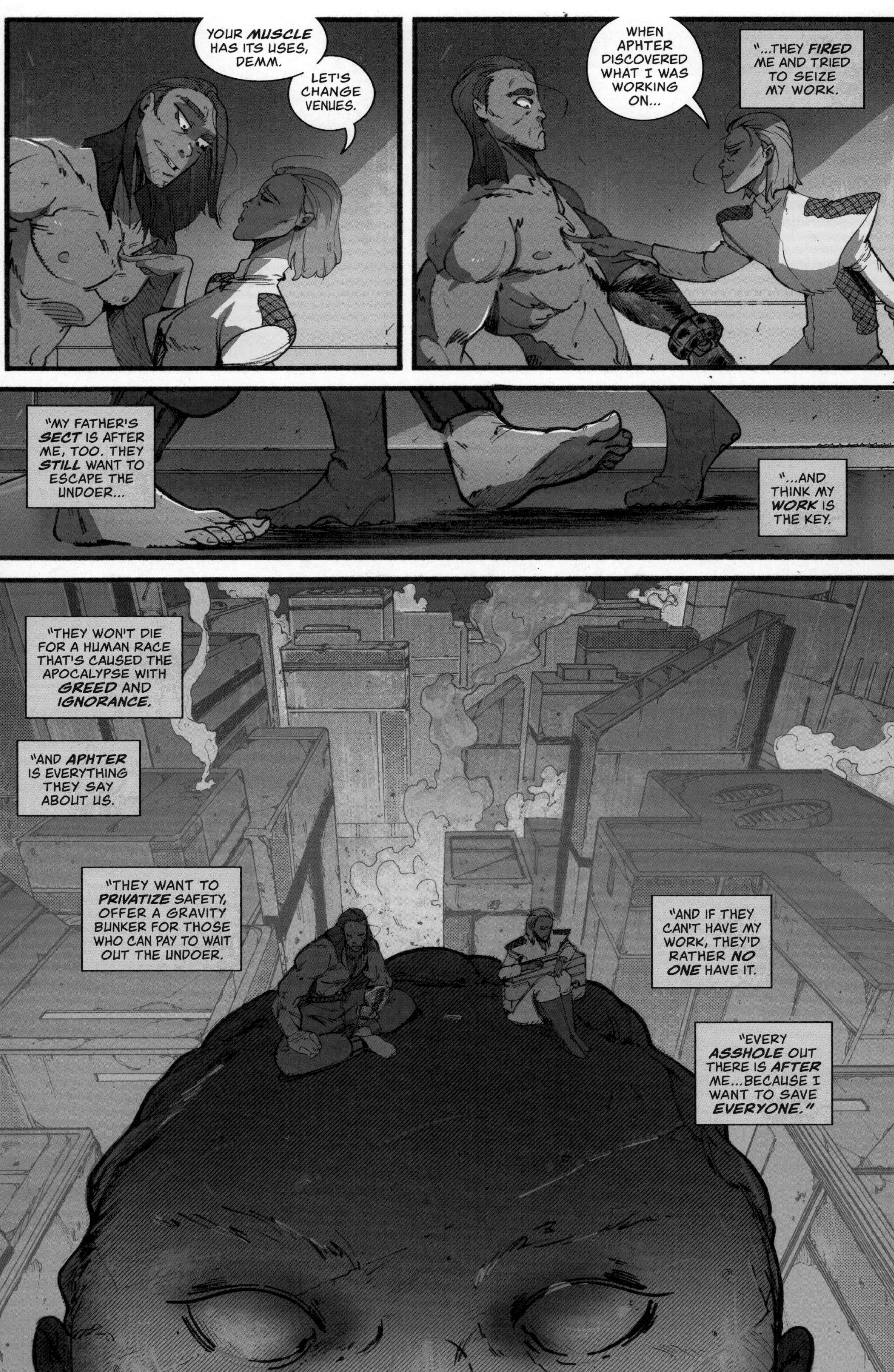
YOUR MUSCLE HAS ITS USES, DEMM.
LET'S CHANGE VENUES.
WHEN APHTER DISCOVERED WHAT I WAS WORKING ON...
"...THEY FIRED ME AND TRIED TO SEIZE MY WORK.
"MY FATHER'S SECT IS AFTER ME, TOO. THEY STILL WANT TO ESCAPE THE UNDOER...
"...AND THINK MY WORK IS THE KEY.
"THEY WON'T DIE FOR A HUMAN RACE THAT'S CAUSED THE APOCALYPSE WITH GREED AND IGNORANCE.
"AND APHTER IS EVERYTHING THEY SAY ABOUT US.
"THEY WANT TO PRIVATIZE SAFETY, OFFER A GRAVITY BUNKER FOR THOSE WHO CAN PAY TO WAIT OUT THE UNDOER.
"AND IF THEY CAN'T HAVE MY WORK, THEY'D RATHER NO ONE HAVE IT.
"EVERY ASSHOLE OUT THERE IS AFTER ME...BECAUSE I WANT TO SAVE EVERYONE."

≠FWHEW≠

SO *YOU* WANT A BIGGER ASSHOLE TO *STOP* THEM.

YOU'RE *RESPONSIBLE* FOR MAXIMO'S DEATH. *YOU* LET HIS SECT OFF THE LEASH.

MAXIMO GOT HIMSELF KILLED. THE OTHER PEOPLE WERE *IDIOTS*... BUT THAT'S NOT A CAPITAL FUCKING OFFENSE.

THERE'S *PLENTY* OF OTHER PIECES OF SHIT OUT THERE, GAYA.

LIFE AS WE KNOW IT IS ON THE LINE... I NEED SOMEONE WHO'LL DO *ANYTHING*.

I...CAN'T *TRUST* ANYONE ELSE. AND WHAT WE HAD...

...I HAVEN'T HAD *SINCE*.

YOUR *THING*... HOW'S A CAR BATTERY GOING TO SAVE THE WORLD?

LEAVE THAT TO *ME*. YOU DIDN'T *WANT* THE DETAILS *BEFORE*.

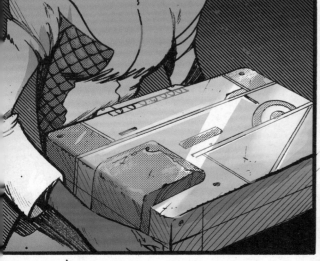

I...I *NEED* YOU TO HELP ME...AND I *KNOW* YOU'RE GOING TO.

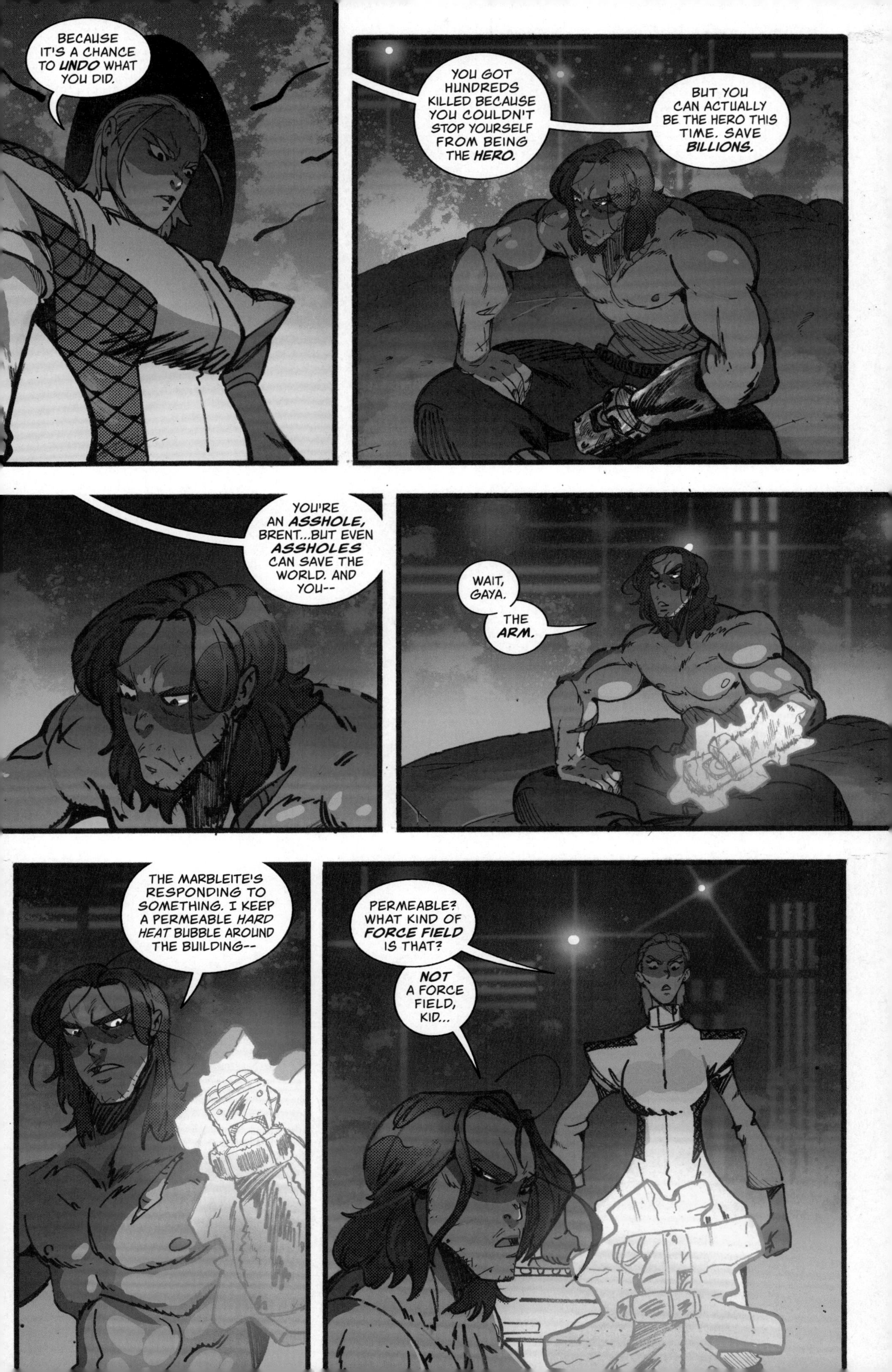
BECAUSE IT'S A CHANCE TO UNDO WHAT YOU DID.
YOU GOT HUNDREDS KILLED BECAUSE YOU COULDN'T STOP YOURSELF FROM BEING THE HERO.
BUT YOU CAN ACTUALLY BE THE HERO THIS TIME. SAVE BILLIONS.
YOU'RE AN ASSHOLE, BRENT...BUT EVEN ASSHOLES CAN SAVE THE WORLD. AND YOU--
WAIT, GAYA.
THE ARM.
THE MARBLEITE'S RESPONDING TO SOMETHING. I KEEP A PERMEABLE HARD HEAT BUBBLE AROUND THE BUILDING--
PERMEABLE? WHAT KIND OF FORCE FIELD IS THAT?
NOT A FORCE FIELD, KID...

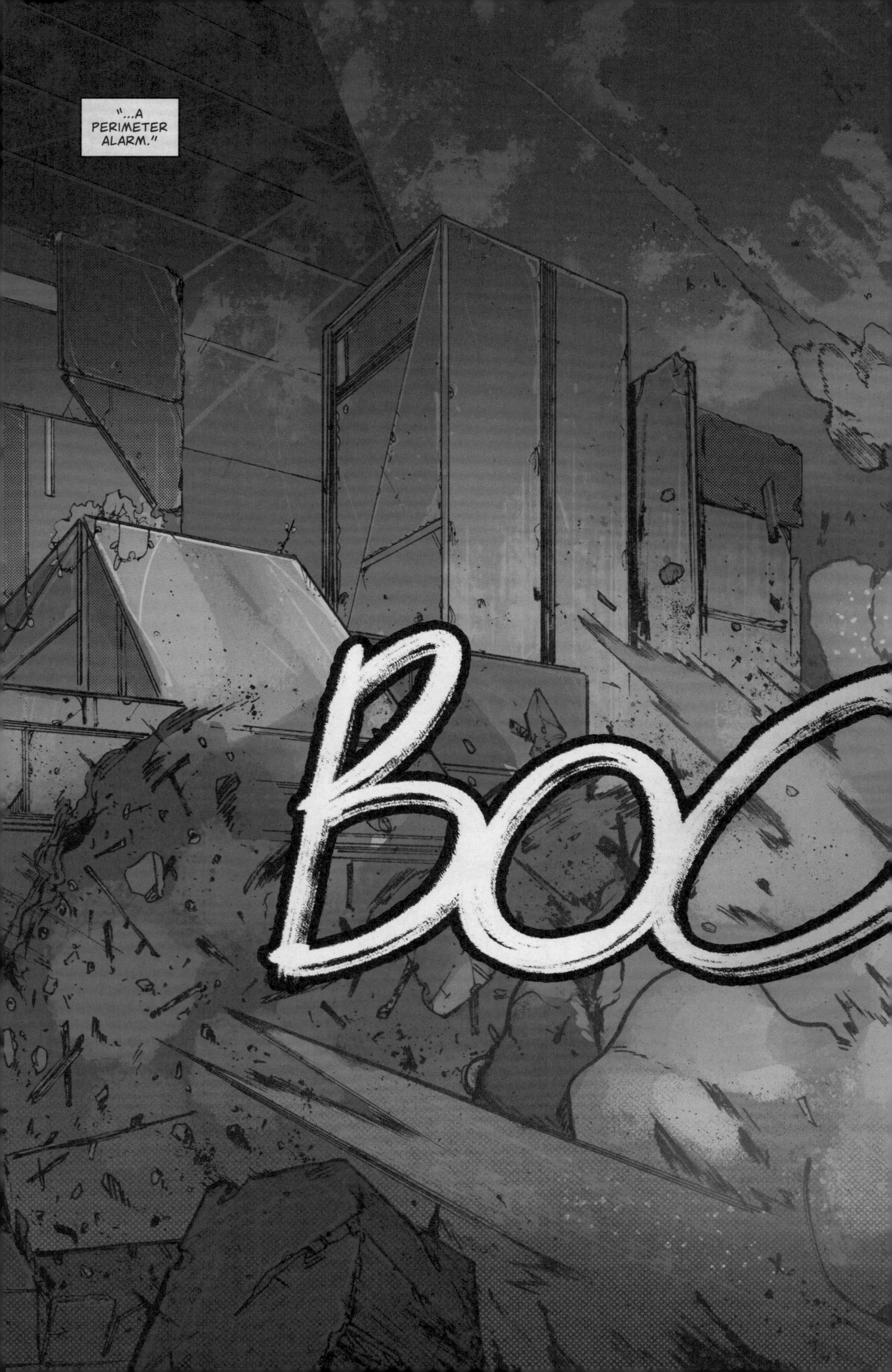
"...A PERIMETER ALARM."
BOO

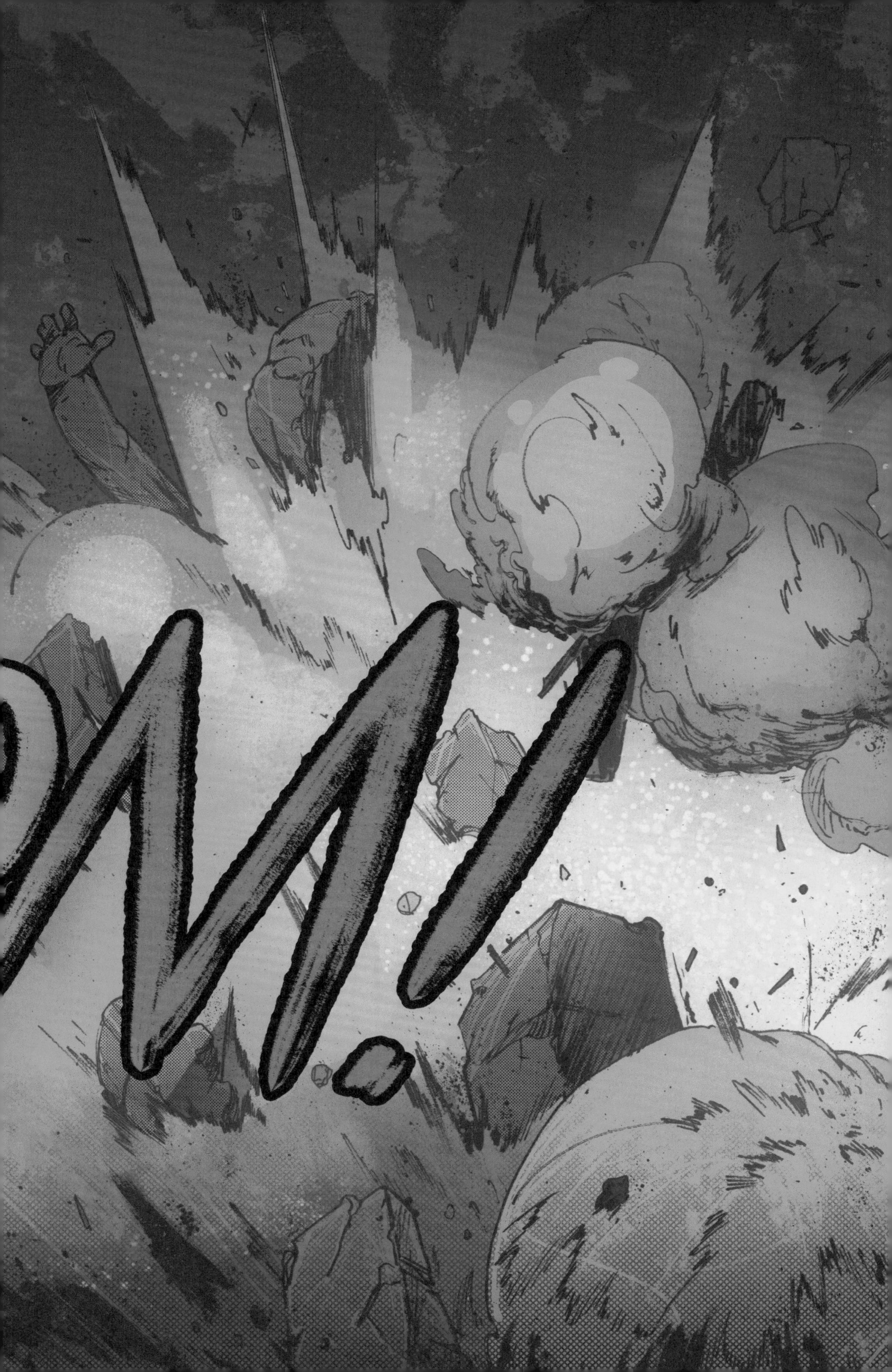

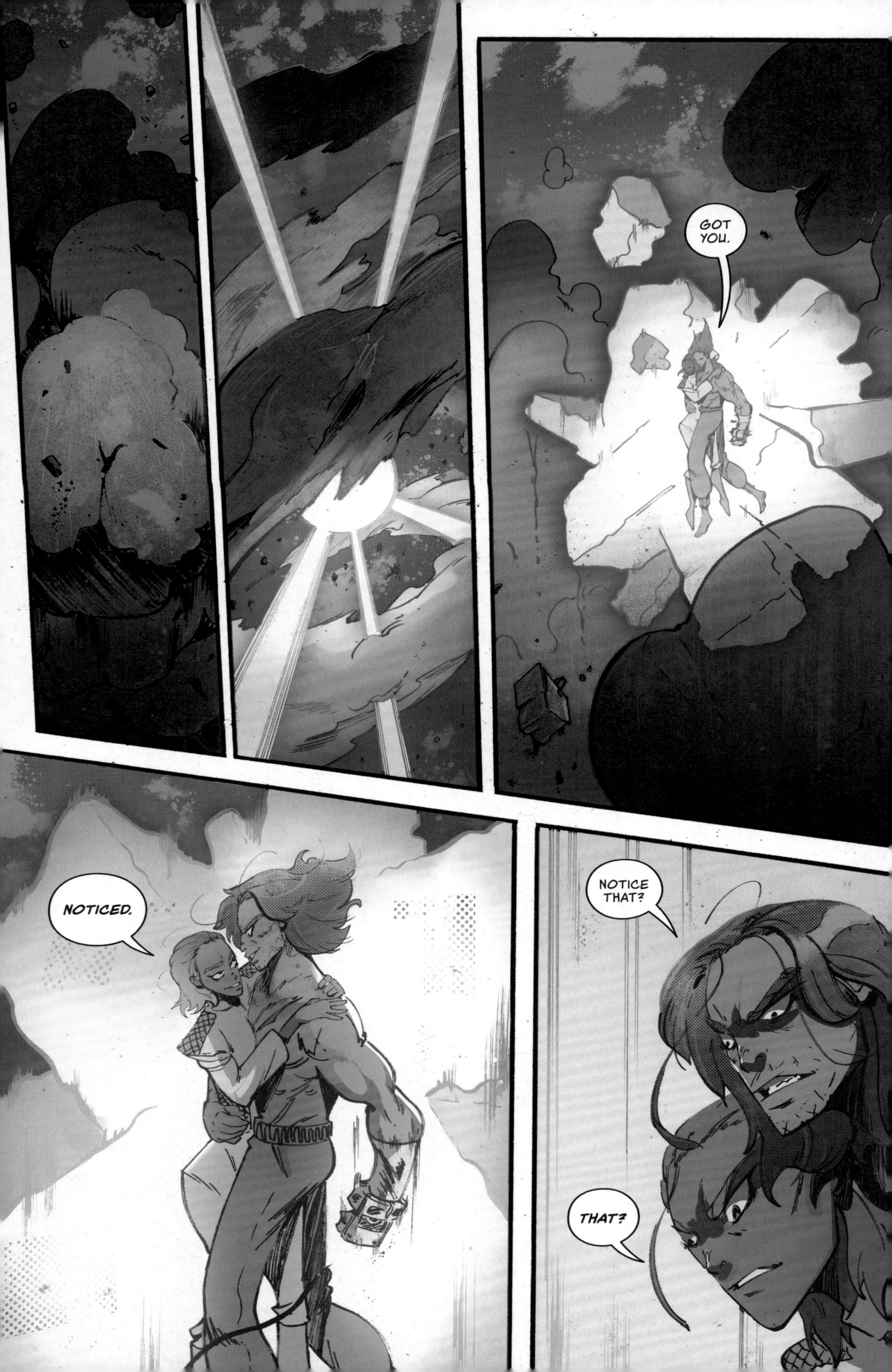
GOT YOU.
NOTICED.
NOTICE THAT?
THAT?

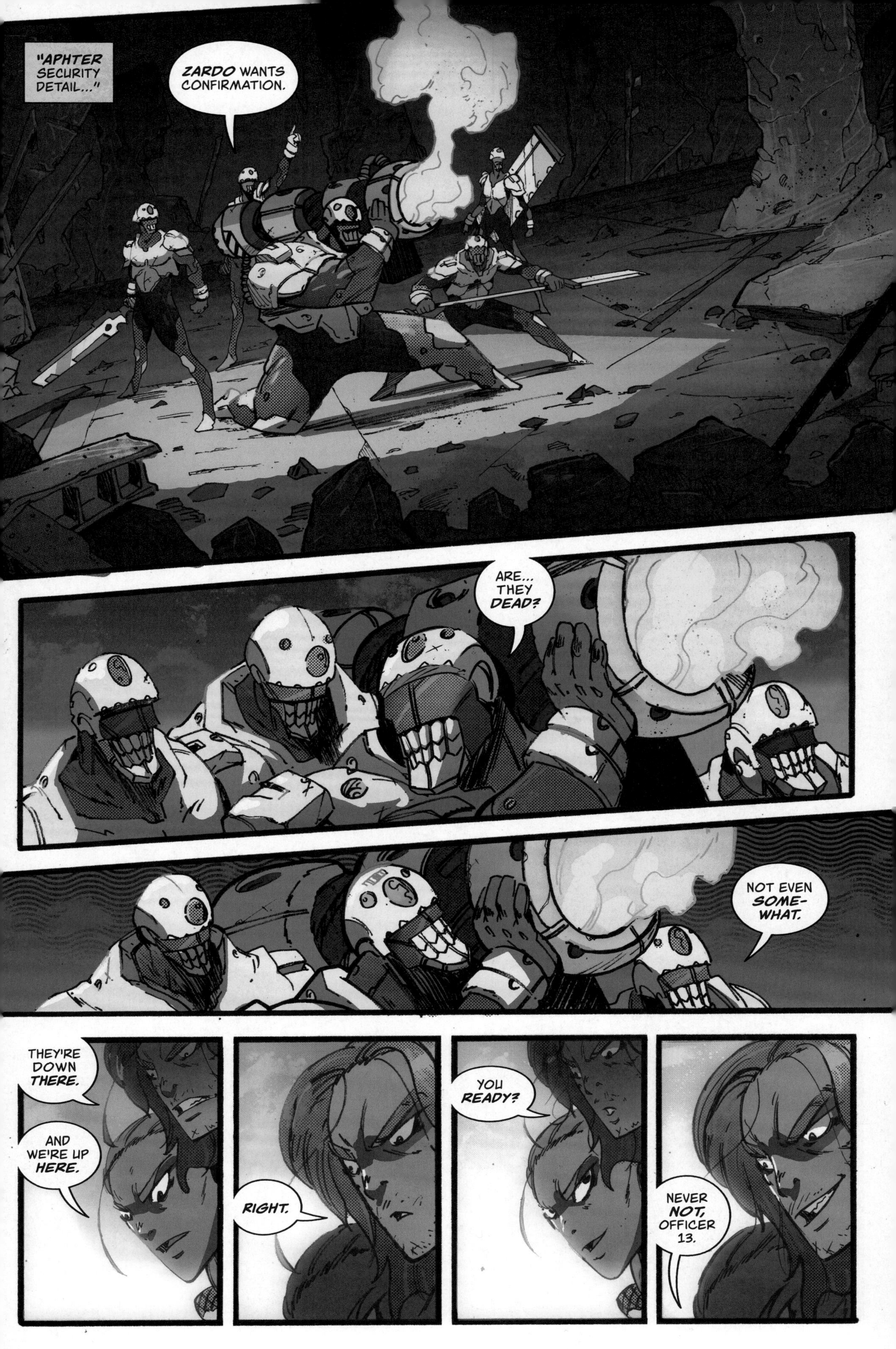
"APHTER SECURITY DETAIL..."
ZARDO WANTS CONFIRMATION.
ARE... THEY DEAD?
NOT EVEN SOME-WHAT.
THEY'RE DOWN THERE.
AND WE'RE UP HERE.
RIGHT.
YOU READY?
NEVER NOT, OFFICER 13.

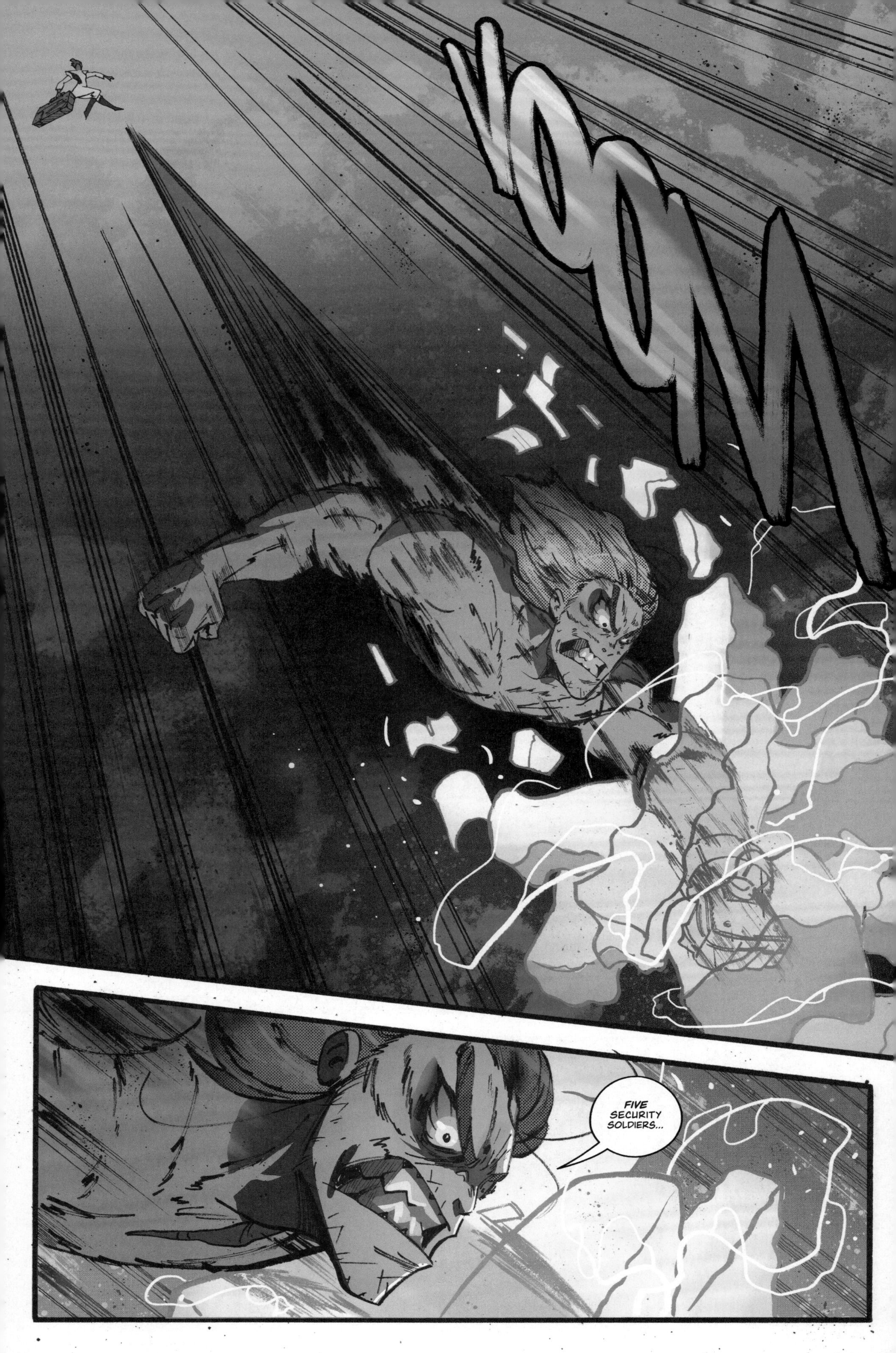
VOOM
FIVE SECURITY SOLDIERS...

"...SIX SECONDS UNTIL SHE HITS THE GROUND."

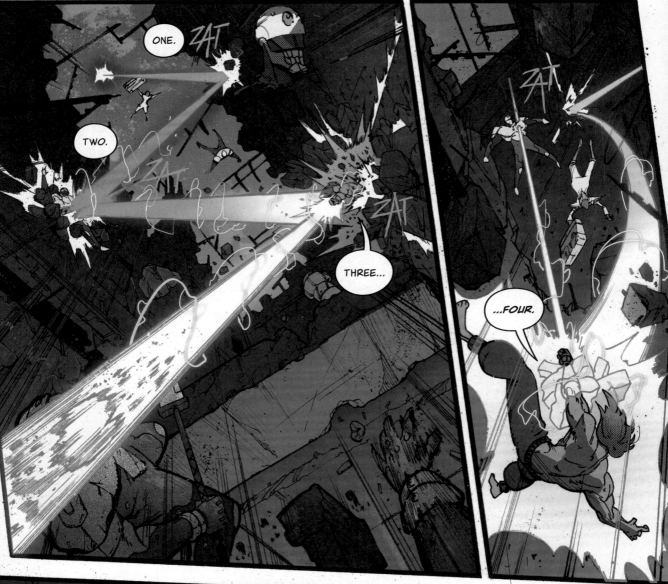

ONE.

ZAT

TWO.

ZAT

THREE...

ZAT

ZAT

...FOUR.

FIVE--

ZSCOT

=HRNGGH=

SI--
FUCK!

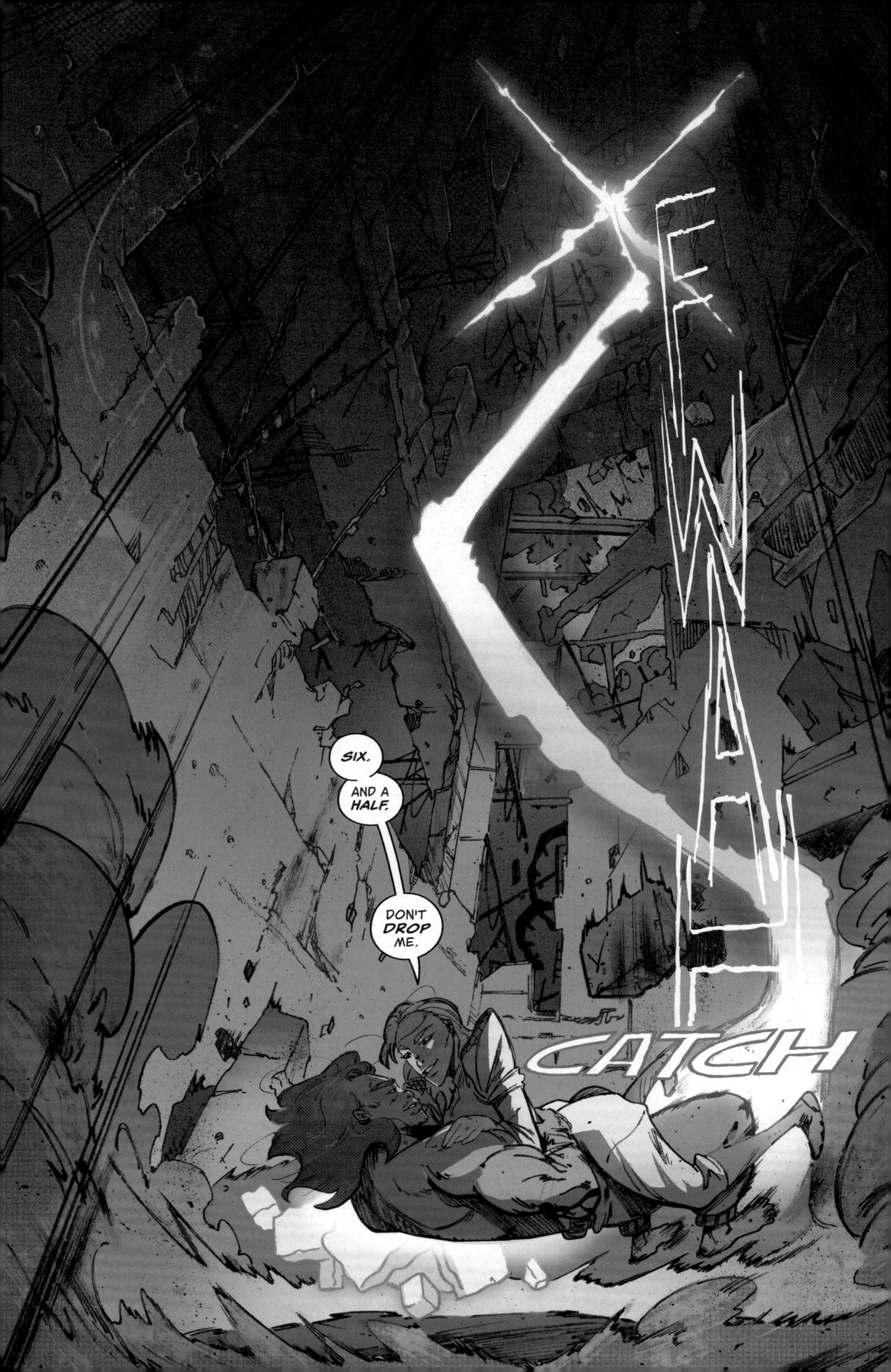
SIX.
AND A HALF.
DON'T DROP ME.
FWAP
CATCH

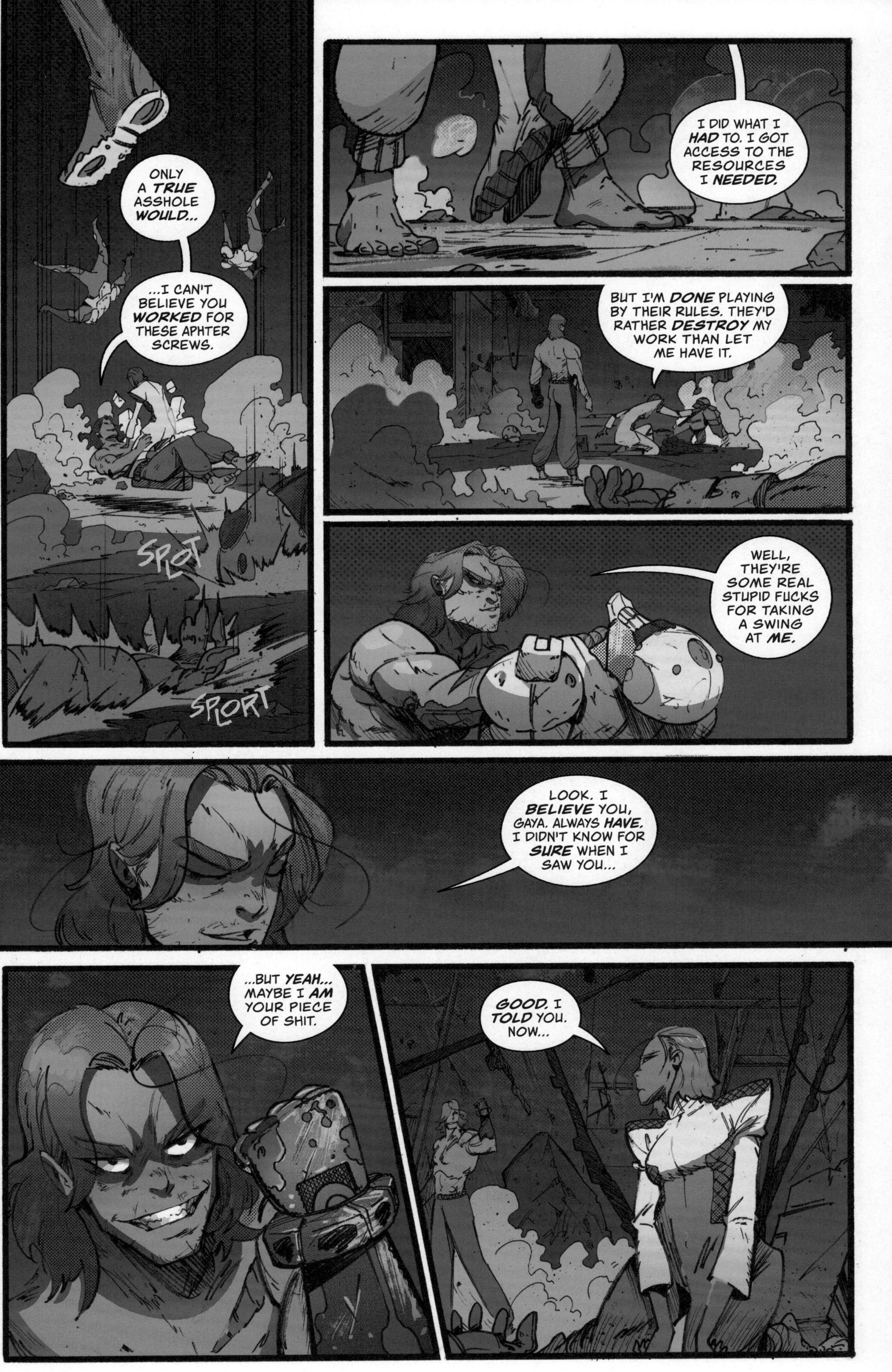
ONLY A **TRUE** ASSHOLE **WOULD...**
...I CAN'T BELIEVE YOU **WORKED** FOR THESE APHTER SCREWS.
SPLOT
SPLORT
I DID WHAT I **HAD** TO. I GOT ACCESS TO THE RESOURCES I **NEEDED.**
BUT I'M **DONE** PLAYING BY THEIR RULES. THEY'D RATHER **DESTROY** MY WORK THAN LET ME HAVE IT.
WELL, THEY'RE SOME REAL STUPID FUCKS FOR TAKING A SWING AT **ME.**
LOOK. I **BELIEVE** YOU, GAYA. ALWAYS **HAVE.** I DIDN'T KNOW FOR **SURE** WHEN I SAW YOU...
...BUT **YEAH...** MAYBE I **AM** YOUR PIECE OF SHIT.
GOOD. I **TOLD** YOU. NOW...

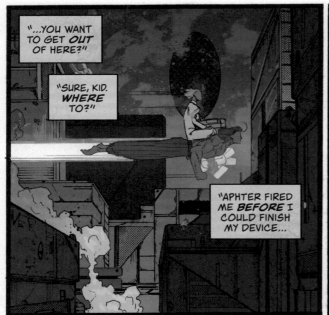

"...YOU WANT TO GET *OUT* OF HERE?"

"SURE, KID. *WHERE* TO?"

"APHTER FIRED ME *BEFORE* I COULD FINISH MY DEVICE..."

"...AND IT CAN *ONLY* STOP THE *UNDOER* IF IT'S *COMPLETE*.

"THE *NEXT* PART I NEED IS TRADEMARKED *APHTER* TECH. A DIFFERENT DEPARTMENT FROM MINE.

"AN ASTRO-METEOROLOGY COMPUTER. IT'S HOW WE *AIM* THIS *RIFLE*...

"...APHTER WANTS TO USE IT TO PREDICT THE FLOW OF COSMIC RAYS.

"BUT IT'LL *ALSO* GIVE US A FULL SPECTRUM READOUT ON THE UNDOER'S COMPOSITION.

"APHTER KEEPS IT AT THE MOST SECURE *R & D* SITE THEY'VE GOT..."

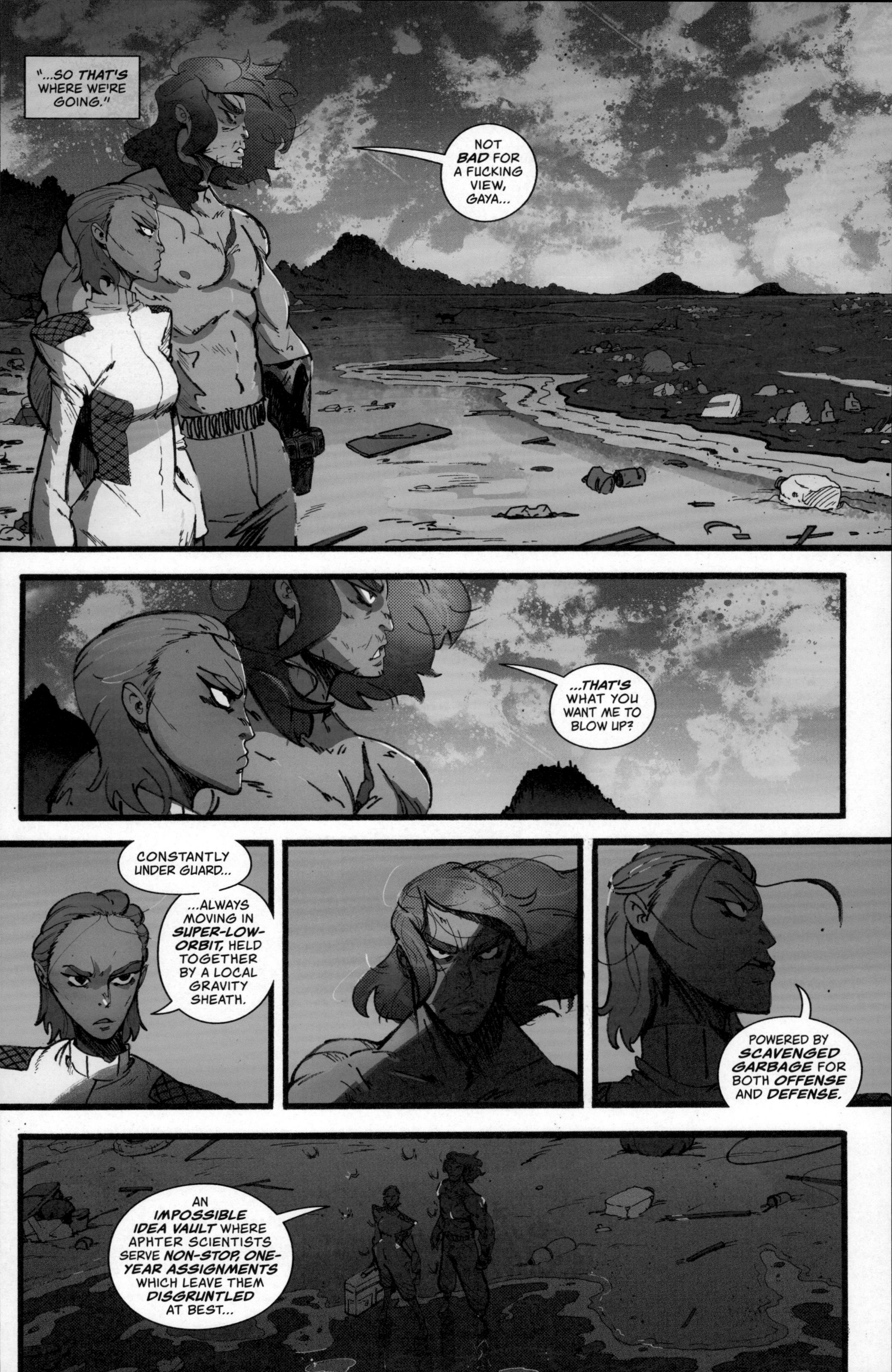
"...SO THAT'S WHERE WE'RE GOING."
NOT BAD FOR A FUCKING VIEW, GAYA...
...THAT'S WHAT YOU WANT ME TO BLOW UP?
CONSTANTLY UNDER GUARD...
...ALWAYS MOVING IN SUPER-LOW-ORBIT, HELD TOGETHER BY A LOCAL GRAVITY SHEATH.
POWERED BY SCAVENGED GARBAGE FOR BOTH OFFENSE AND DEFENSE.
AN IMPOSSIBLE IDEA VAULT WHERE APHTER SCIENTISTS SERVE NON-STOP, ONE-YEAR ASSIGNMENTS WHICH LEAVE THEM DISGRUNTLED AT BEST...

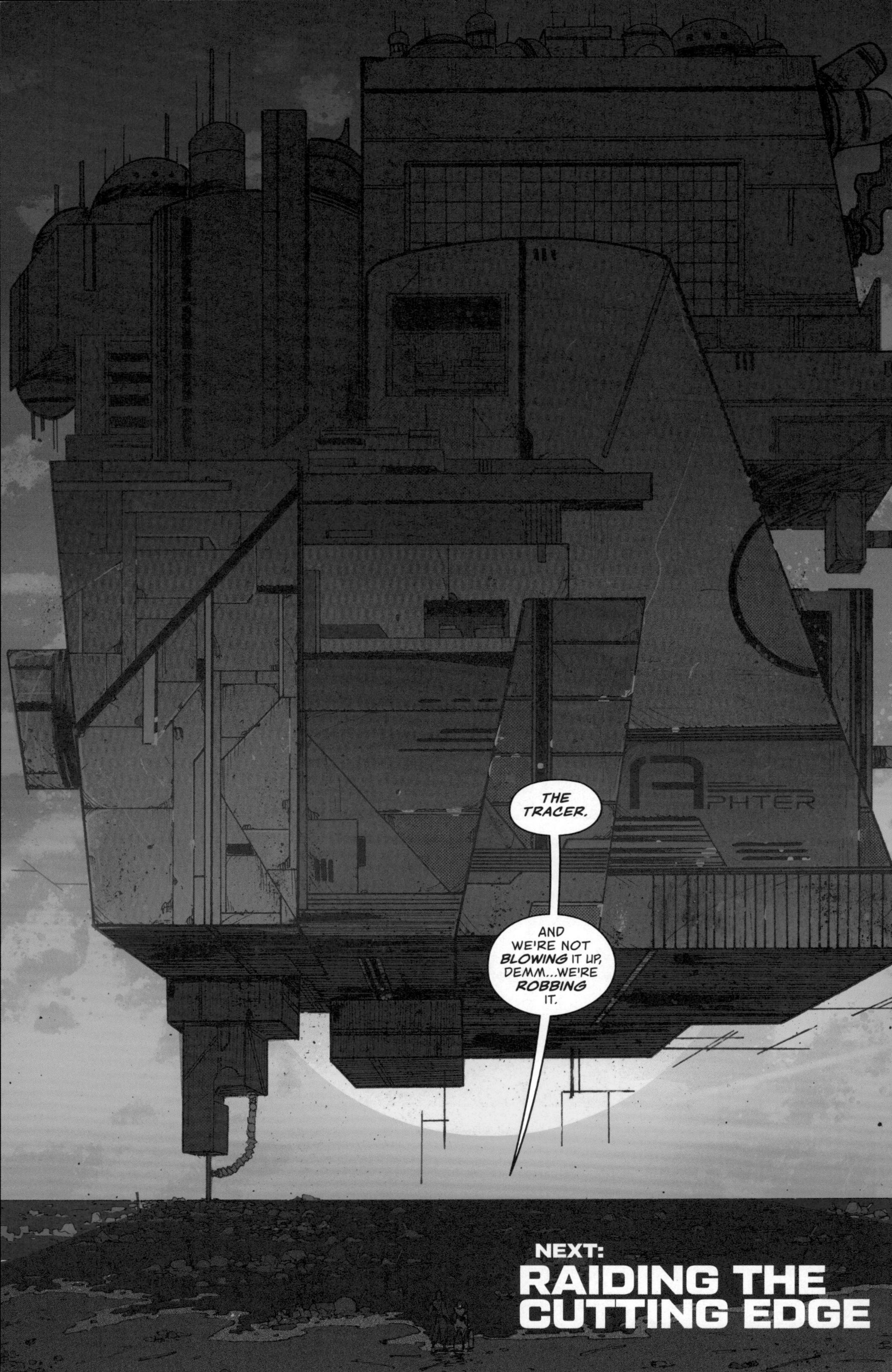
APHTER
THE TRACER.
AND WE'RE NOT BLOWING IT UP, DEMM...WE'RE ROBBING IT.
NEXT:
RAIDING THE CUTTING EDGE

CHAPTER 3

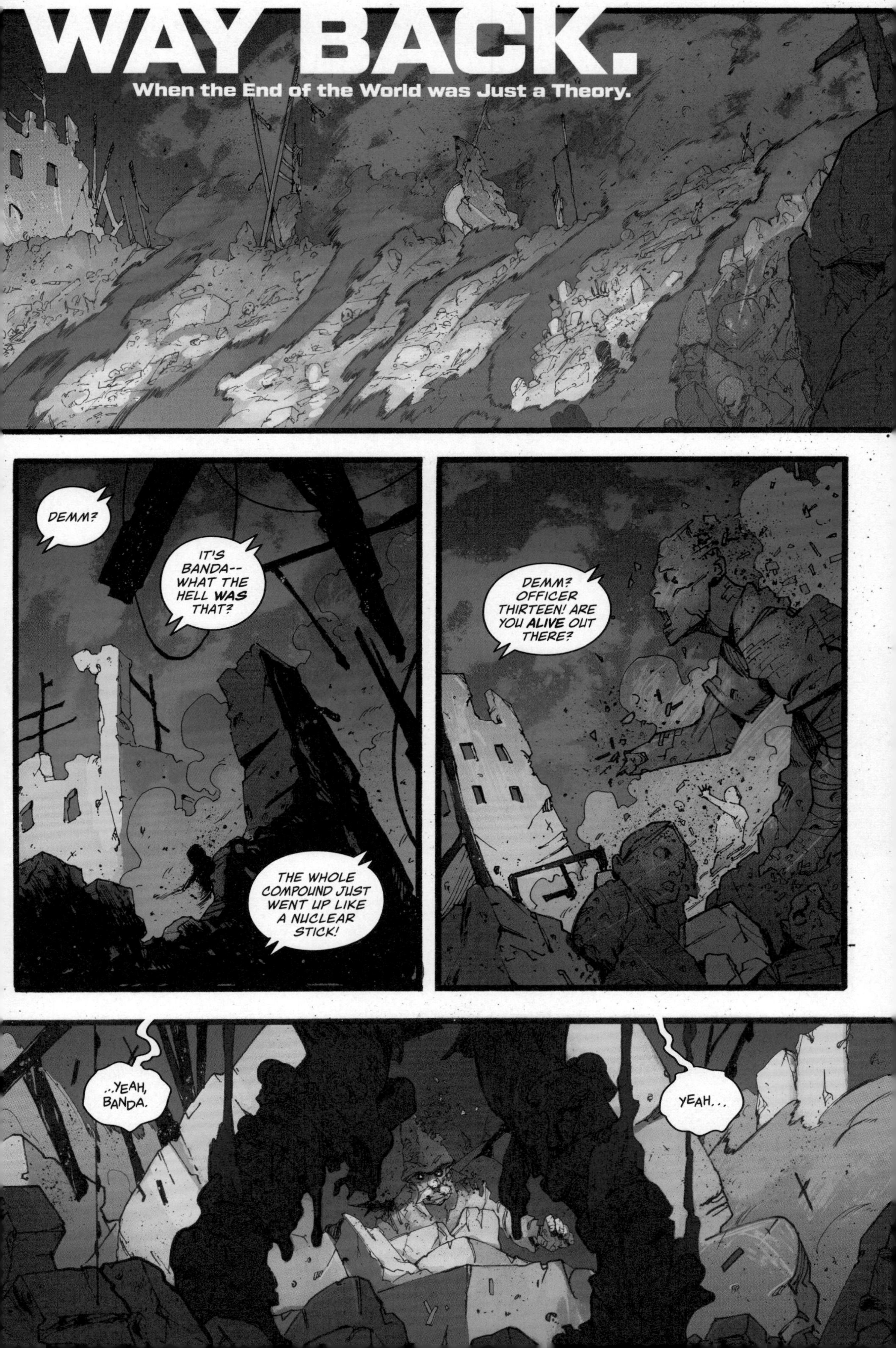
WAY BACK.
When the End of the World was Just a Theory.
DEMM?
IT'S BANDA-- WHAT THE HELL WAS THAT?
THE WHOLE COMPOUND JUST WENT UP LIKE A NUCLEAR STICK!
DEMM? OFFICER THIRTEEN! ARE YOU ALIVE OUT THERE?
...YEAH, BANDA.
YEAH...

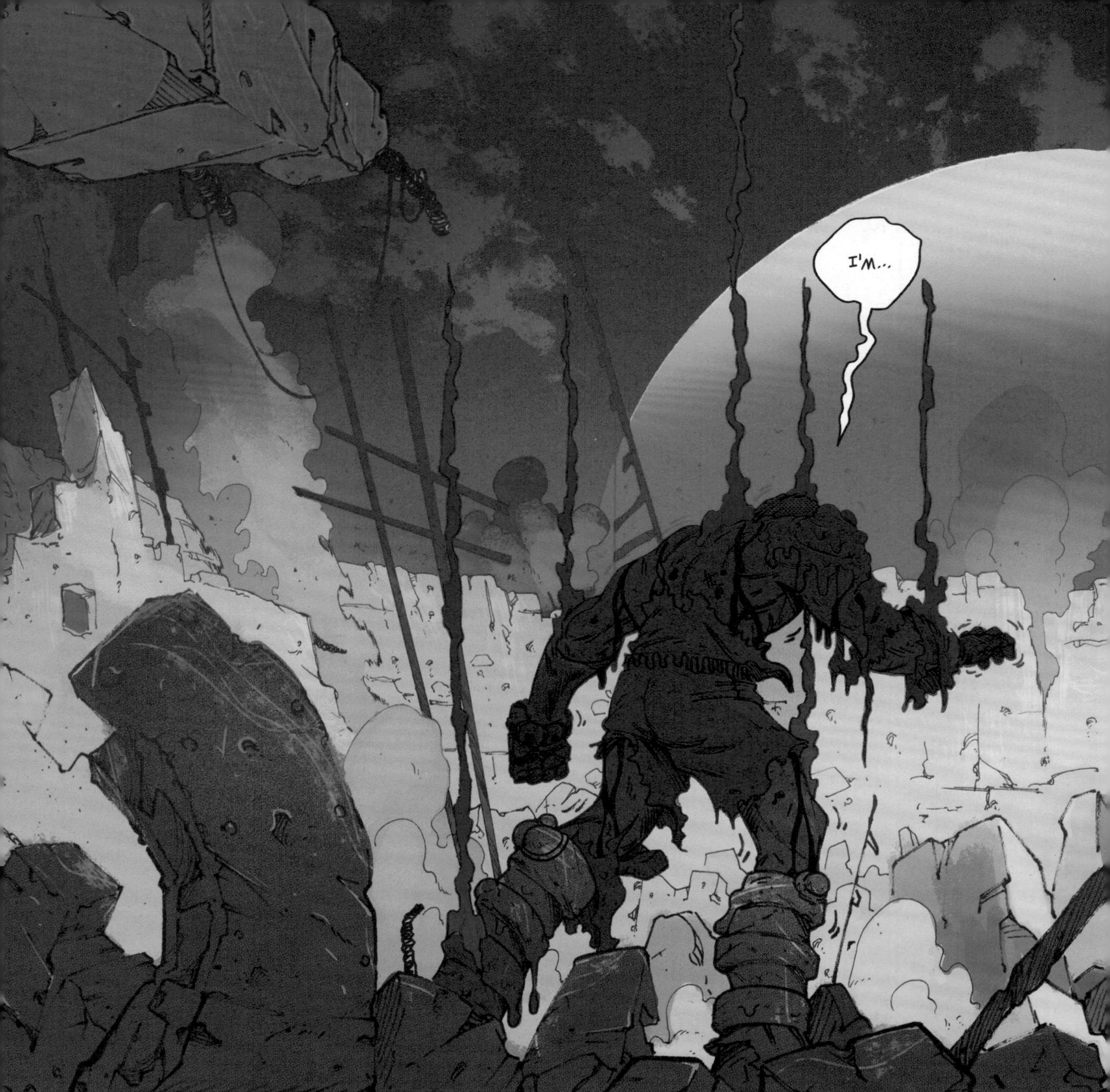
I'M...
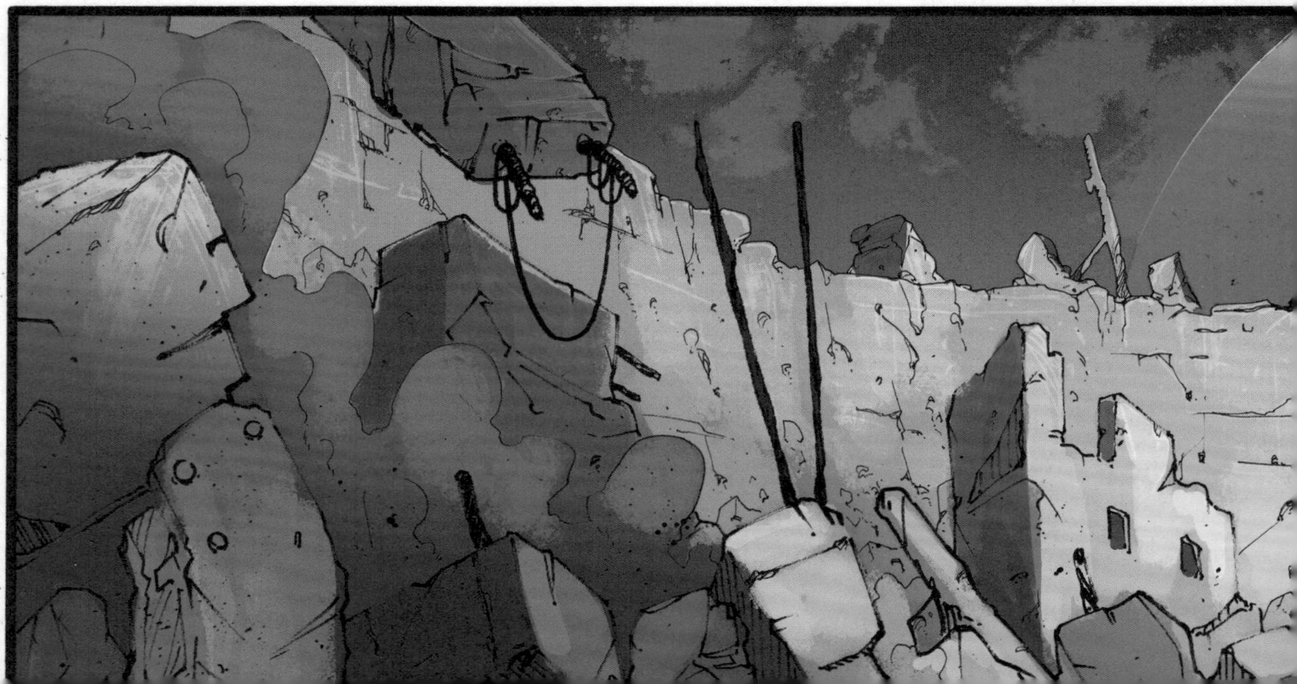

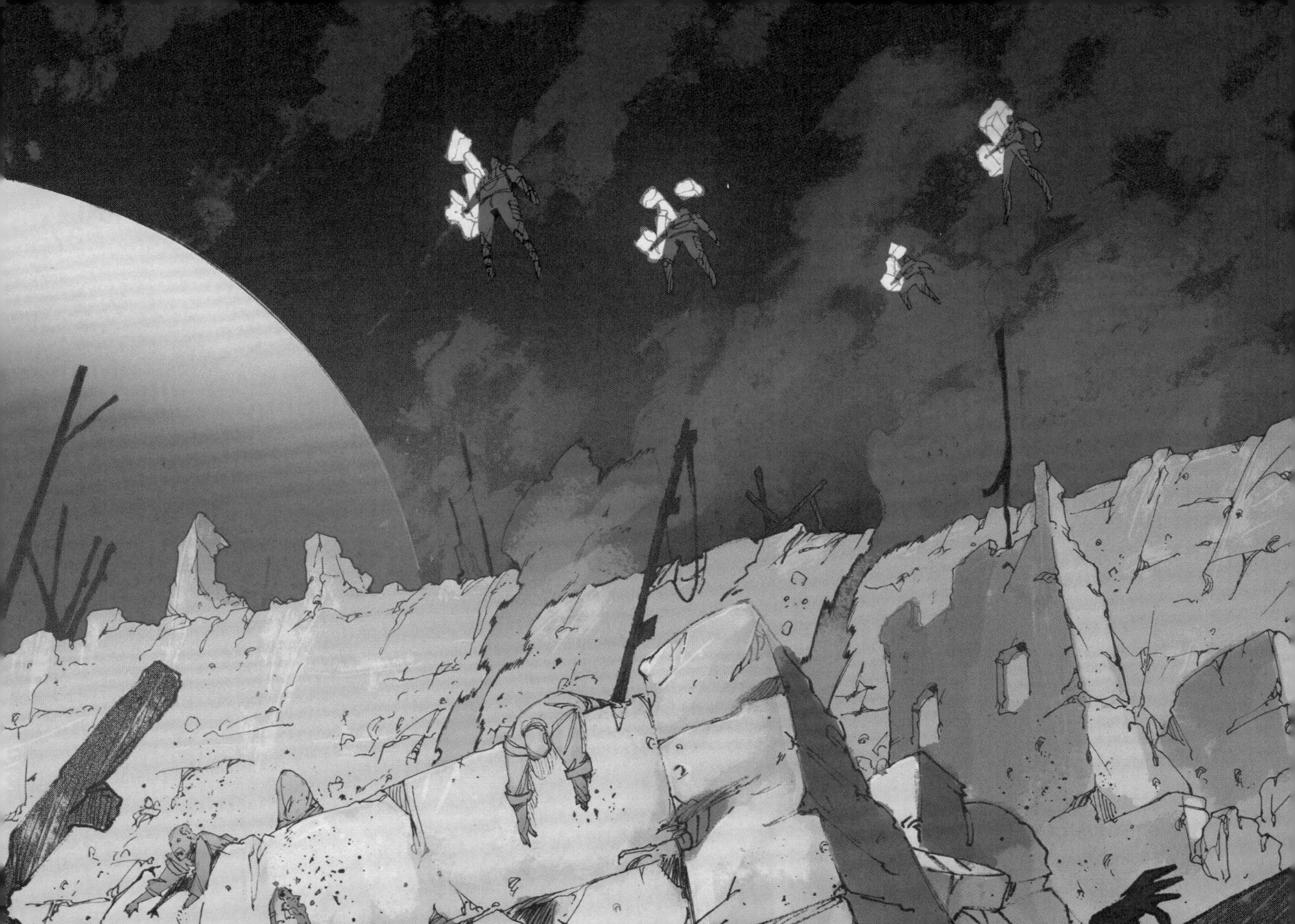

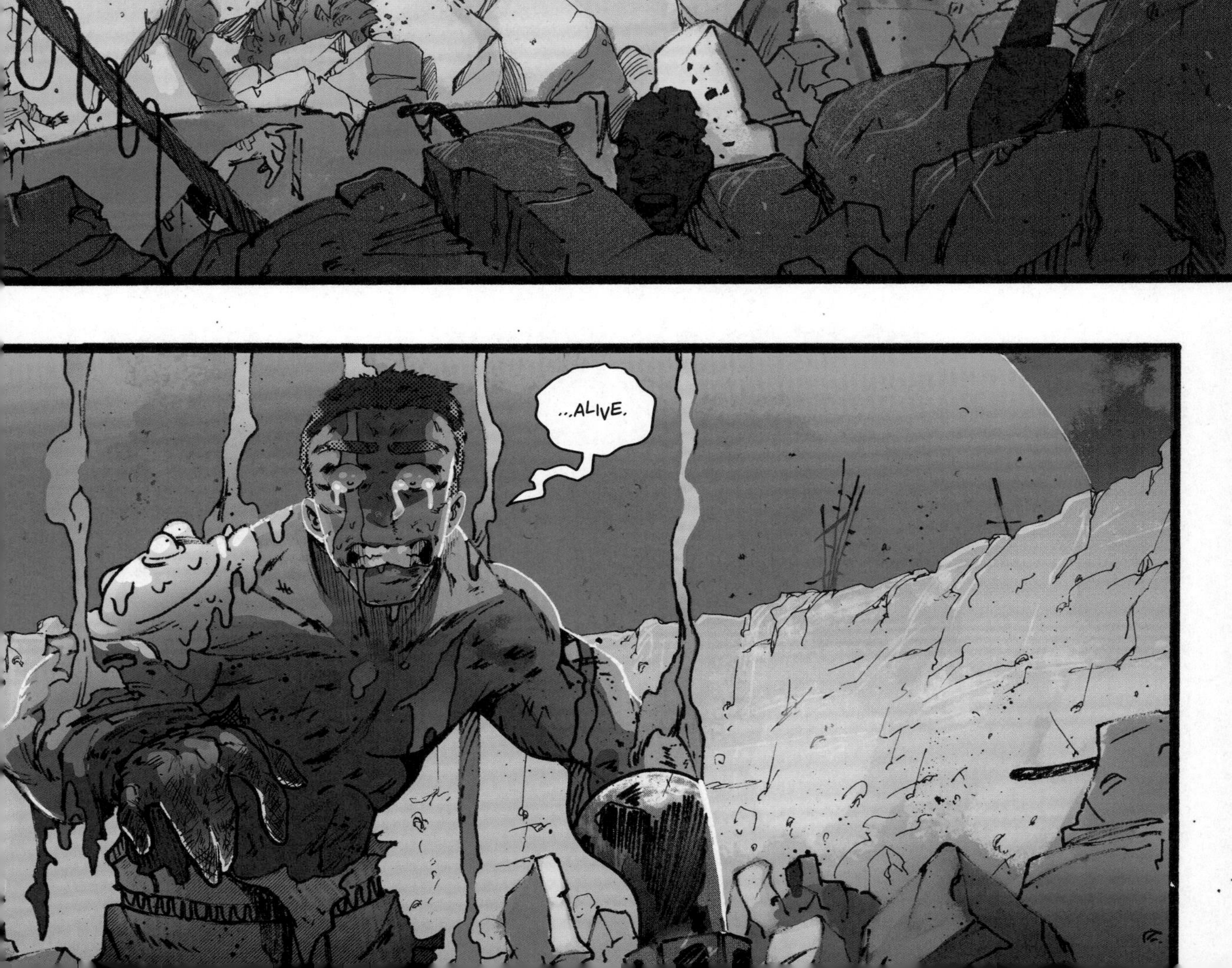
...ALIVE.

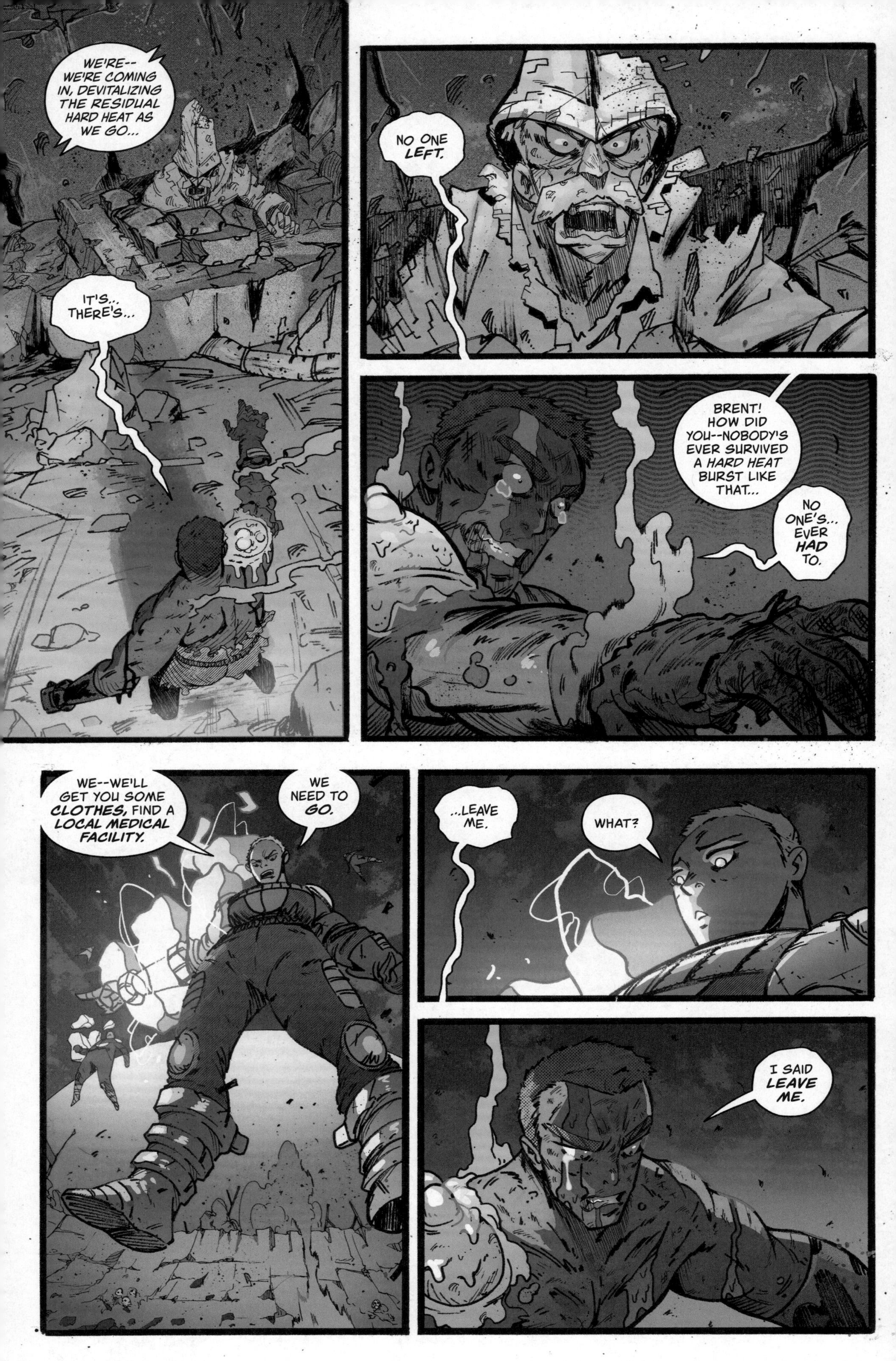

WE'RE-- WE'RE COMING IN, DEVITALIZING THE RESIDUAL HARD HEAT AS WE GO...
IT'S... THERE'S...
NO ONE LEFT.
BRENT! HOW DID YOU--NOBODY'S EVER SURVIVED A HARD HEAT BURST LIKE THAT...
NO ONE'S... EVER HAD TO.
WE--WE'LL GET YOU SOME CLOTHES, FIND A LOCAL MEDICAL FACILITY.
WE NEED TO GO.
...LEAVE ME.
WHAT?
I SAID LEAVE ME.

NOT A **CHANCE**. **YOU** HOTSHOTTED IN THERE, DEMM. SO I'M PATCHING YOU UP, GETTING YOU **HEALTHY**...

...THEN YOU'RE GOING TO **OWN** THIS.

BANDA, I...I **DID** IT.

I PANICKED WHEN I SAW MAXIMO...HE WAS SO **SURE**.

I DIDN'T EXPECT IT BUT...THERE'S A CHANCE...HE'S RIGHT.

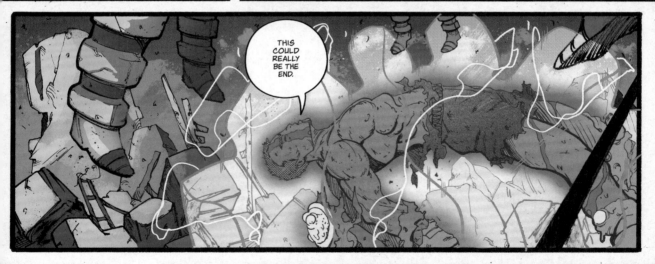

THIS COULD REALLY BE THE END.

HEY, IS THAT A... HEY!

WAIT! GET A MED TEAM IN HERE!

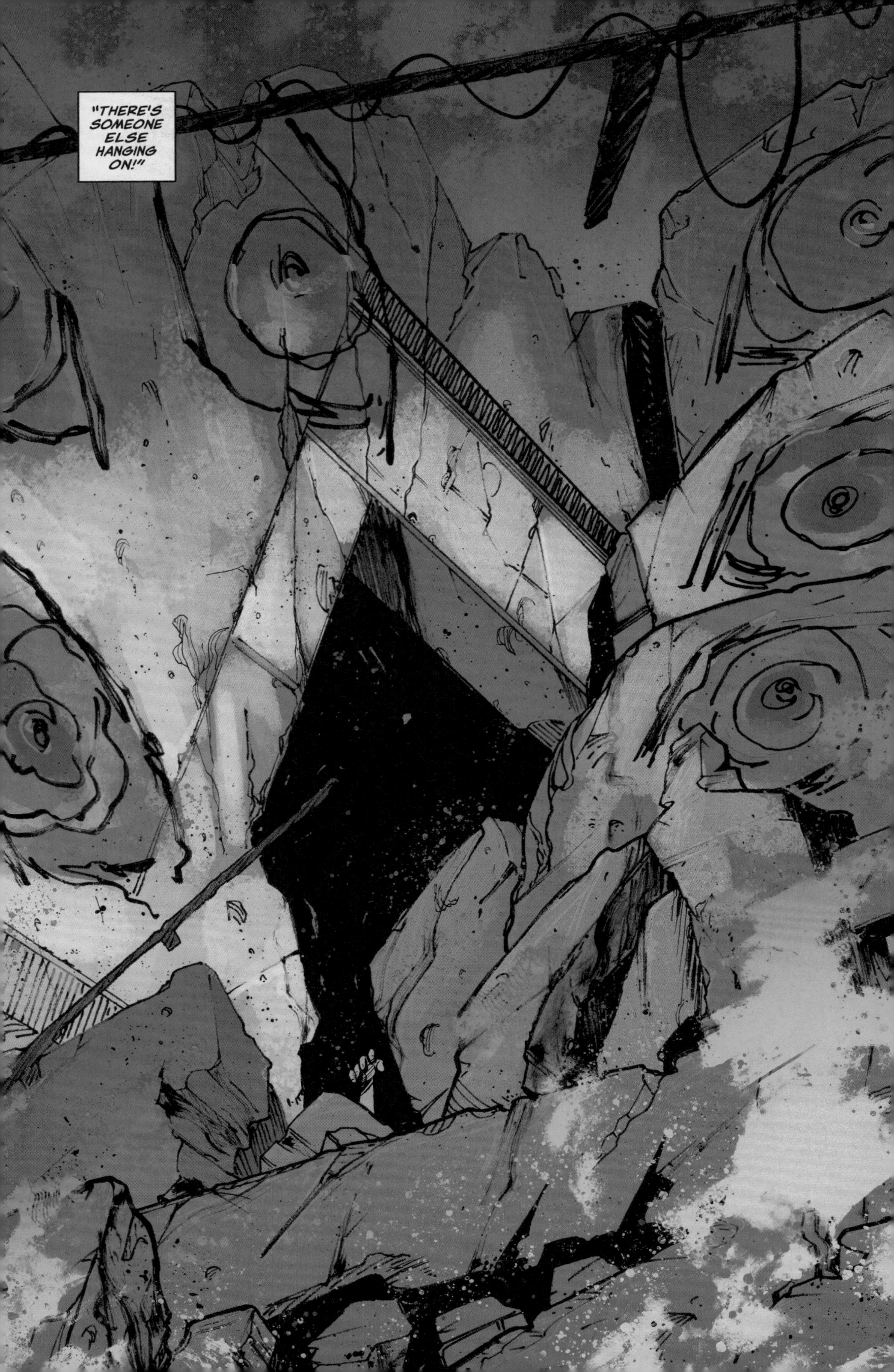
"THERE'S SOMEONE ELSE HANGING ON!"

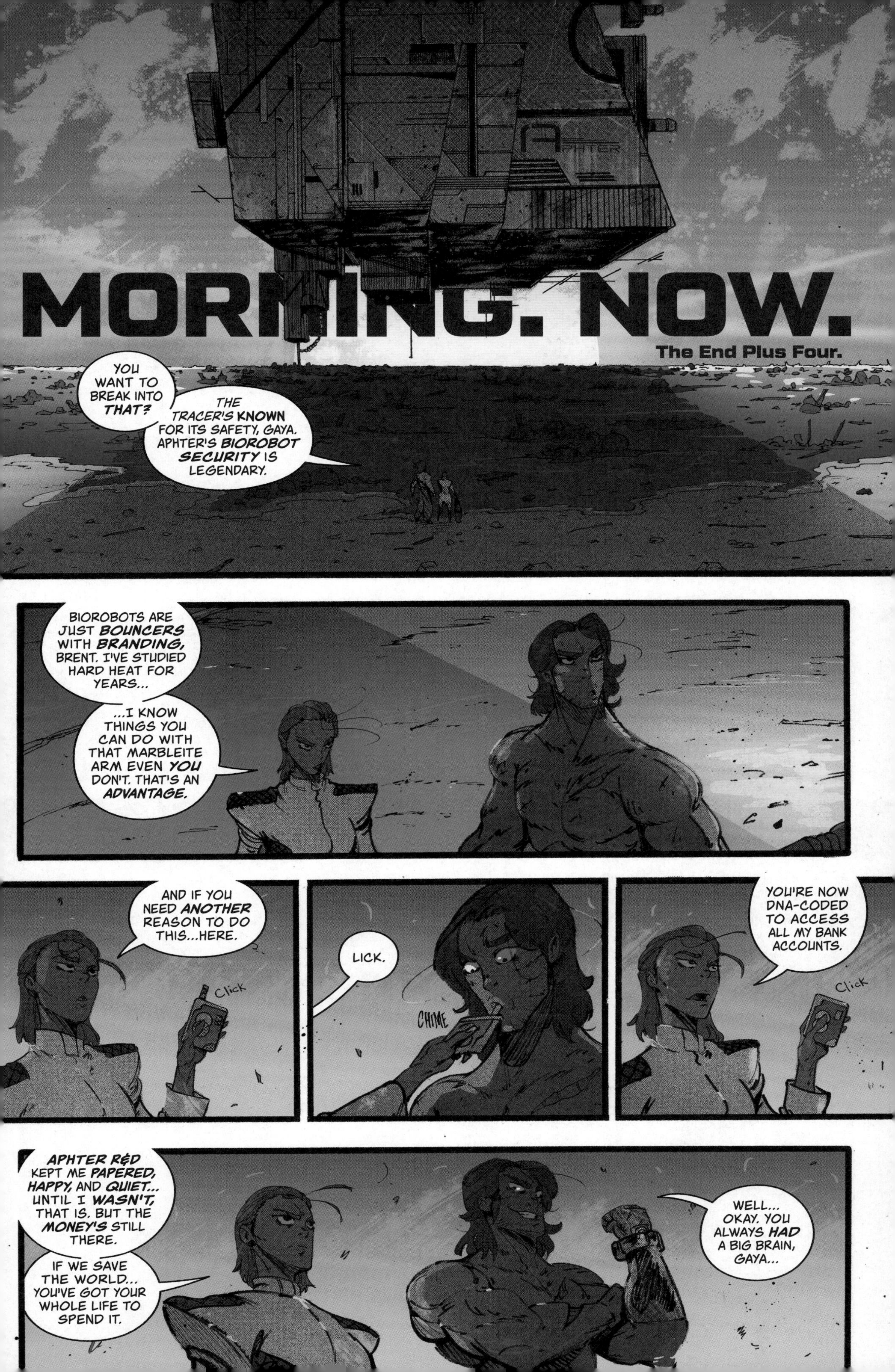

MORNING. NOW.
The End Plus Four.
YOU WANT TO BREAK INTO *THAT?*
THE TRACER'S **KNOWN** FOR ITS SAFETY, GAYA. APHTER'S ***BIOROBOT SECURITY*** IS LEGENDARY.
APHTER
BIOROBOTS ARE JUST ***BOUNCERS*** WITH ***BRANDING,*** BRENT. I'VE STUDIED HARD HEAT FOR YEARS...
...I KNOW THINGS YOU CAN DO WITH THAT MARBLEITE ARM EVEN ***YOU*** DON'T. THAT'S AN ***ADVANTAGE.***
AND IF YOU NEED ***ANOTHER*** REASON TO DO THIS...HERE.
Click
LICK.
CHIME
YOU'RE NOW DNA-CODED TO ACCESS ALL MY BANK ACCOUNTS.
Click
APHTER R&D KEPT ME ***PAPERED, HAPPY,*** AND ***QUIET...*** UNTIL I ***WASN'T,*** THAT IS. BUT THE ***MONEY'S*** STILL THERE.
IF WE SAVE THE WORLD... YOU'VE GOT YOUR WHOLE LIFE TO SPEND IT.
WELL... OKAY. YOU ALWAYS ***HAD*** A BIG BRAIN, GAYA...

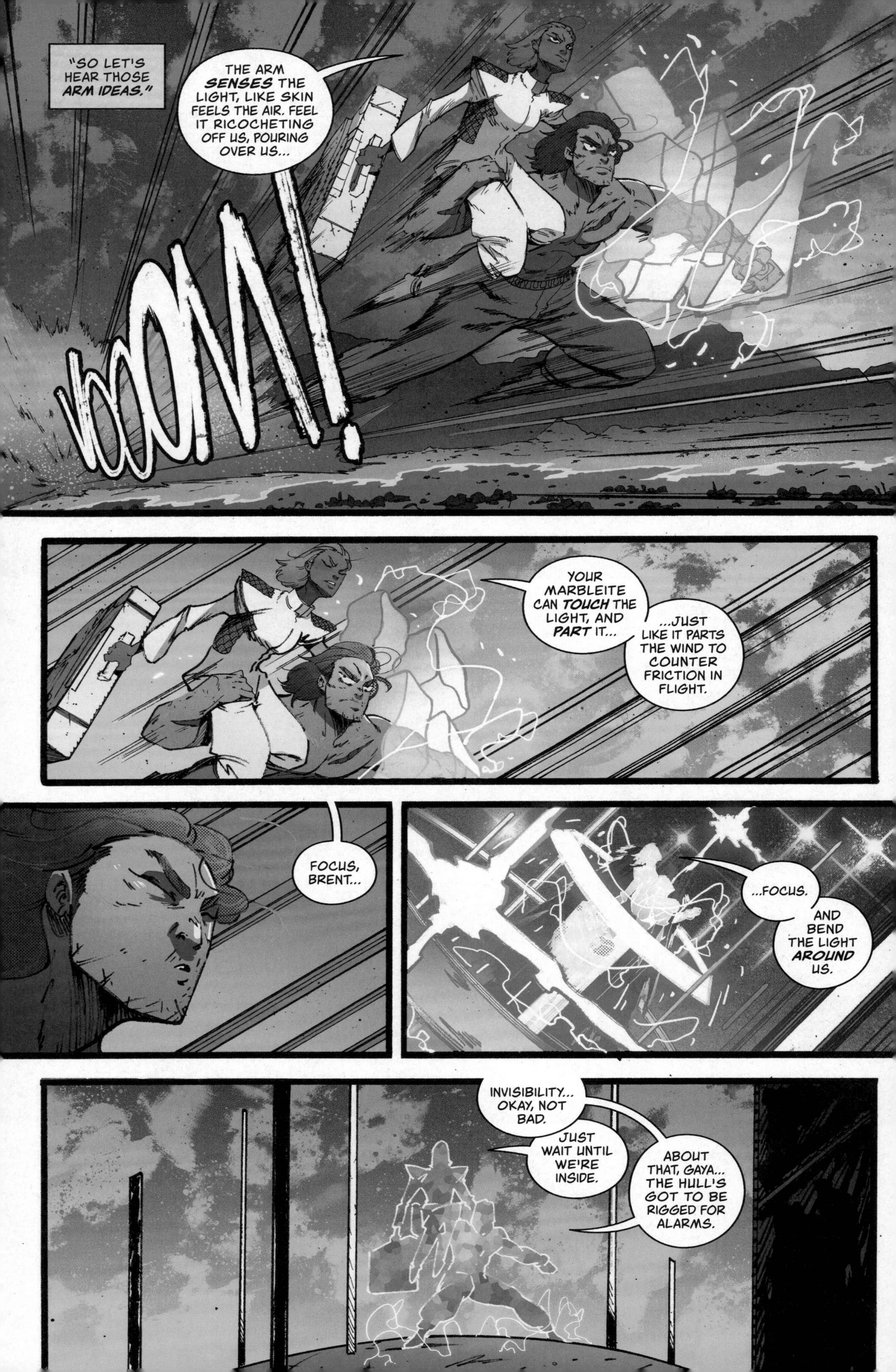
"SO LET'S HEAR THOSE ARM IDEAS."
THE ARM SENSES THE LIGHT, LIKE SKIN FEELS THE AIR. FEEL IT RICOCHETING OFF US, POURING OVER US...
VOOOM!
YOUR MARBLEITE CAN TOUCH THE LIGHT, AND PART IT...
...JUST LIKE IT PARTS THE WIND TO COUNTER FRICTION IN FLIGHT.
FOCUS, BRENT...
...FOCUS.
AND BEND THE LIGHT AROUND US.
INVISIBILITY... OKAY, NOT BAD.
JUST WAIT UNTIL WE'RE INSIDE.
ABOUT THAT, GAYA... THE HULL'S GOT TO BE RIGGED FOR ALARMS.

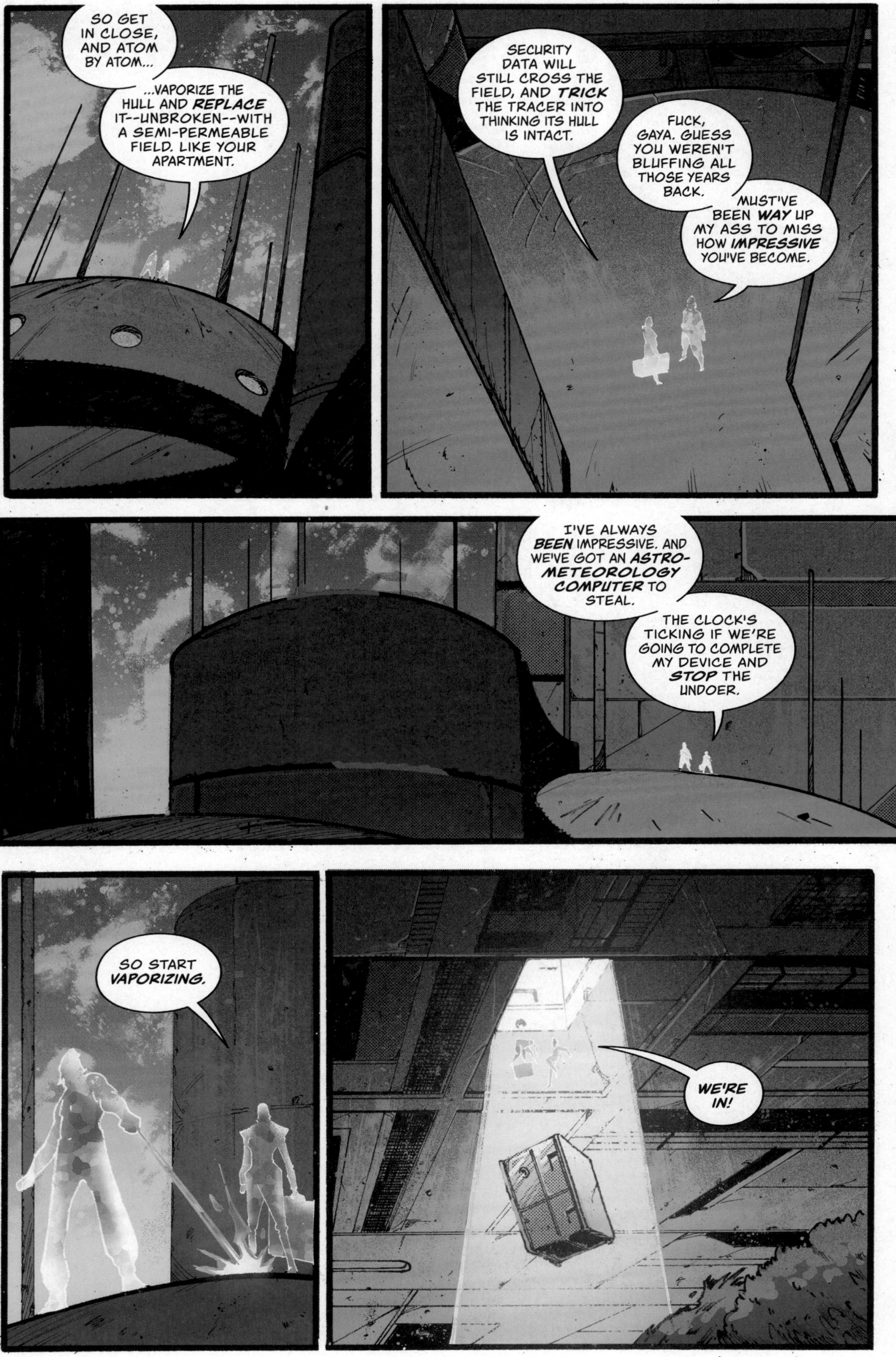
SO GET IN CLOSE, AND ATOM BY ATOM...
...VAPORIZE THE HULL AND REPLACE IT--UNBROKEN--WITH A SEMI-PERMEABLE FIELD. LIKE YOUR APARTMENT.
SECURITY DATA WILL STILL CROSS THE FIELD, AND TRICK THE TRACER INTO THINKING ITS HULL IS INTACT.
FUCK, GAYA. GUESS YOU WEREN'T BLUFFING ALL THOSE YEARS BACK.
MUST'VE BEEN WAY UP MY ASS TO MISS HOW IMPRESSIVE YOU'VE BECOME.
I'VE ALWAYS BEEN IMPRESSIVE. AND WE'VE GOT AN ASTRO-METEOROLOGY COMPUTER TO STEAL.
THE CLOCK'S TICKING IF WE'RE GOING TO COMPLETE MY DEVICE AND STOP THE UNDOER.
SO START VAPORIZING.
WE'RE IN!

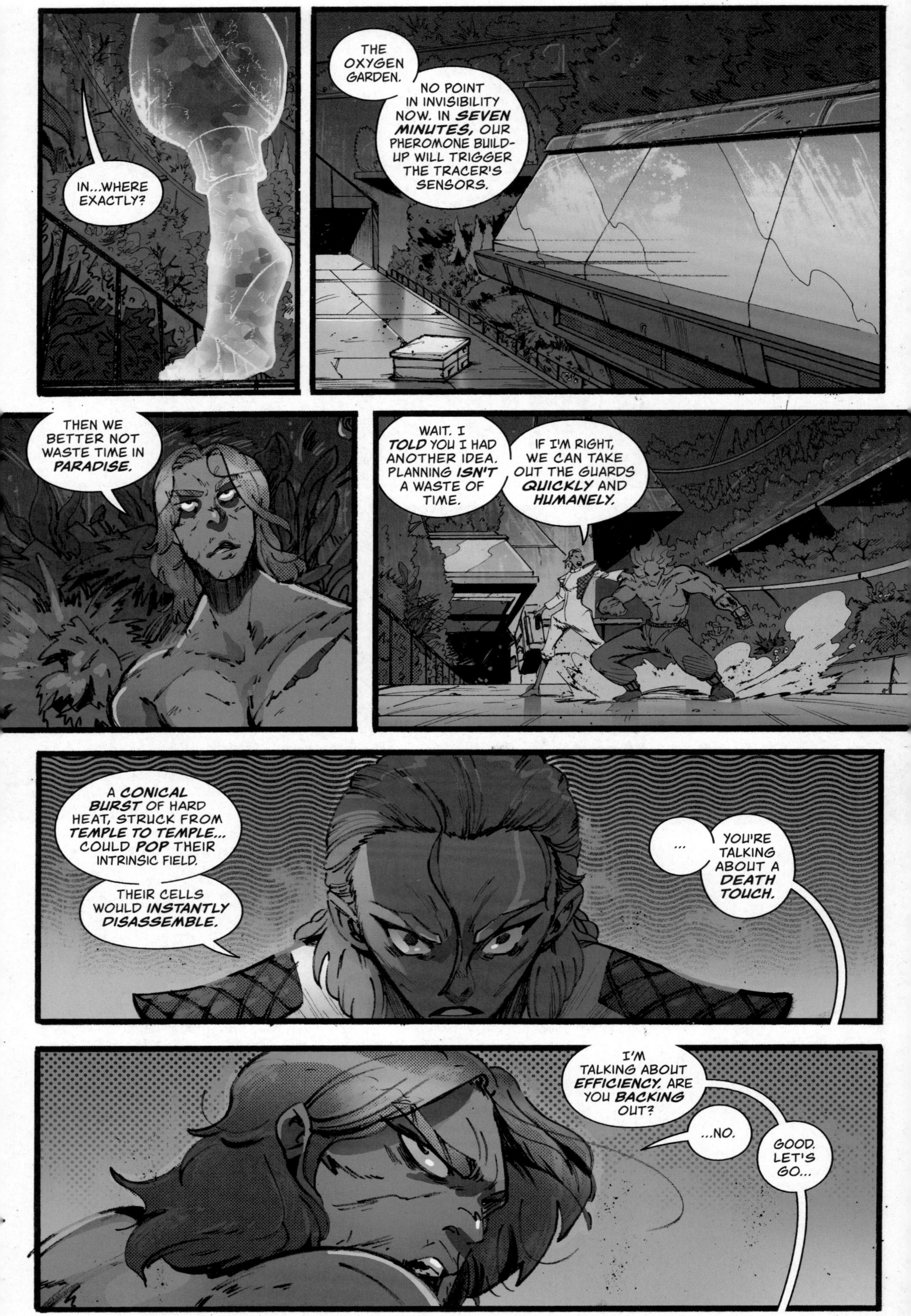
IN...WHERE EXACTLY?
THE OXYGEN GARDEN.
NO POINT IN INVISIBILITY NOW. IN SEVEN MINUTES, OUR PHEROMONE BUILD-UP WILL TRIGGER THE TRACER'S SENSORS.
THEN WE BETTER NOT WASTE TIME IN PARADISE.
WAIT. I TOLD YOU I HAD ANOTHER IDEA. PLANNING ISN'T A WASTE OF TIME.
IF I'M RIGHT, WE CAN TAKE OUT THE GUARDS QUICKLY AND HUMANELY.
A CONICAL BURST OF HARD HEAT, STRUCK FROM TEMPLE TO TEMPLE... COULD POP THEIR INTRINSIC FIELD.
THEIR CELLS WOULD INSTANTLY DISASSEMBLE.
...
YOU'RE TALKING ABOUT A DEATH TOUCH.
I'M TALKING ABOUT EFFICIENCY. ARE YOU BACKING OUT?
...NO.
GOOD. LET'S GO...

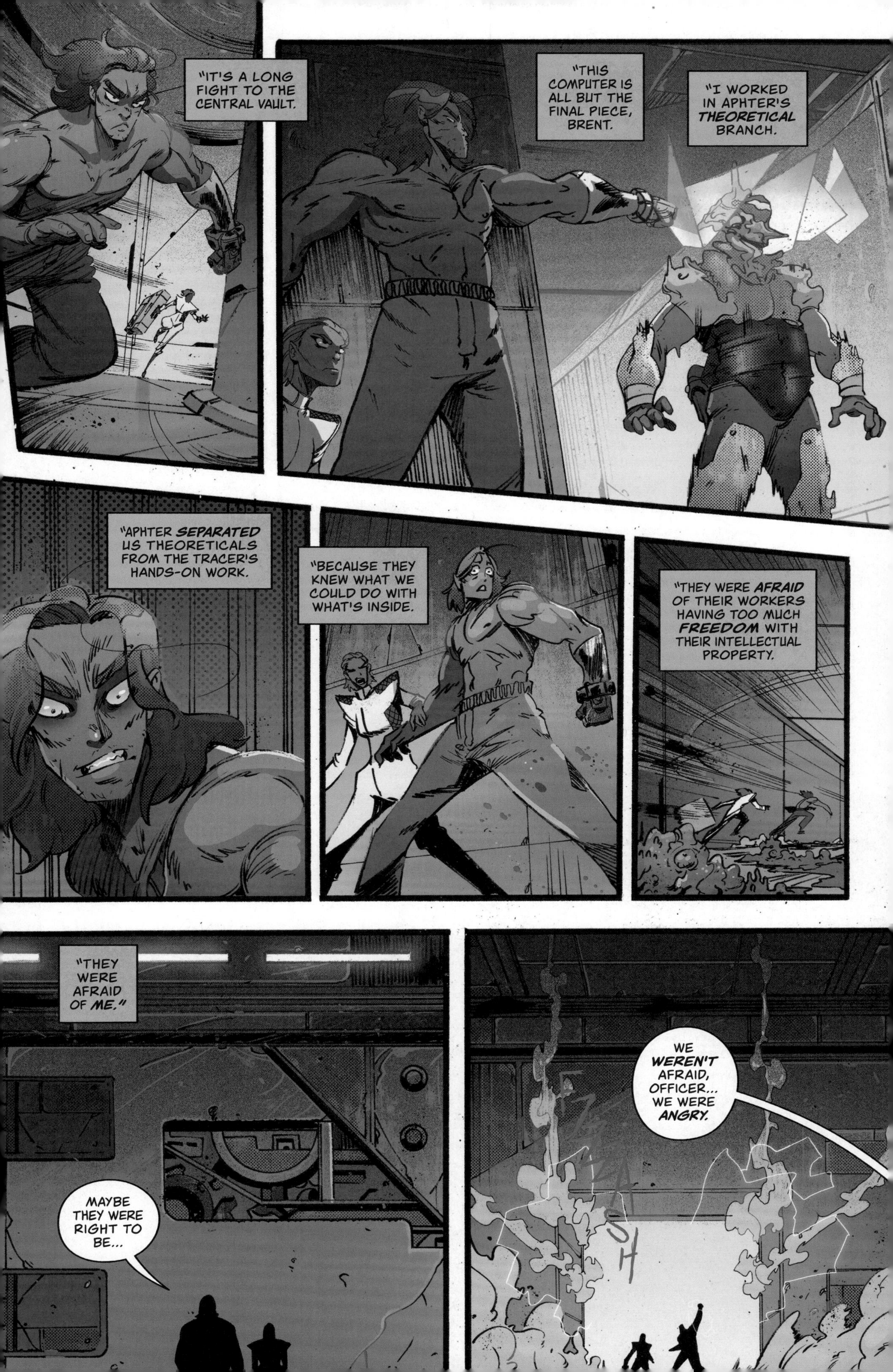

"IT'S A LONG FIGHT TO THE CENTRAL VAULT.
"THIS COMPUTER IS ALL BUT THE FINAL PIECE, BRENT.
"I WORKED IN APHTER'S *THEORETICAL* BRANCH.
"APHTER *SEPARATED* US THEORETICALS FROM THE TRACER'S HANDS-ON WORK.
"BECAUSE THEY KNEW WHAT WE COULD DO WITH WHAT'S INSIDE.
"THEY WERE *AFRAID* OF THEIR WORKERS HAVING TOO MUCH *FREEDOM* WITH THEIR INTELLECTUAL PROPERTY.
"THEY WERE AFRAID OF *ME.*"
MAYBE THEY WERE RIGHT TO BE...
WE *WEREN'T* AFRAID, OFFICER... WE WERE *ANGRY.*

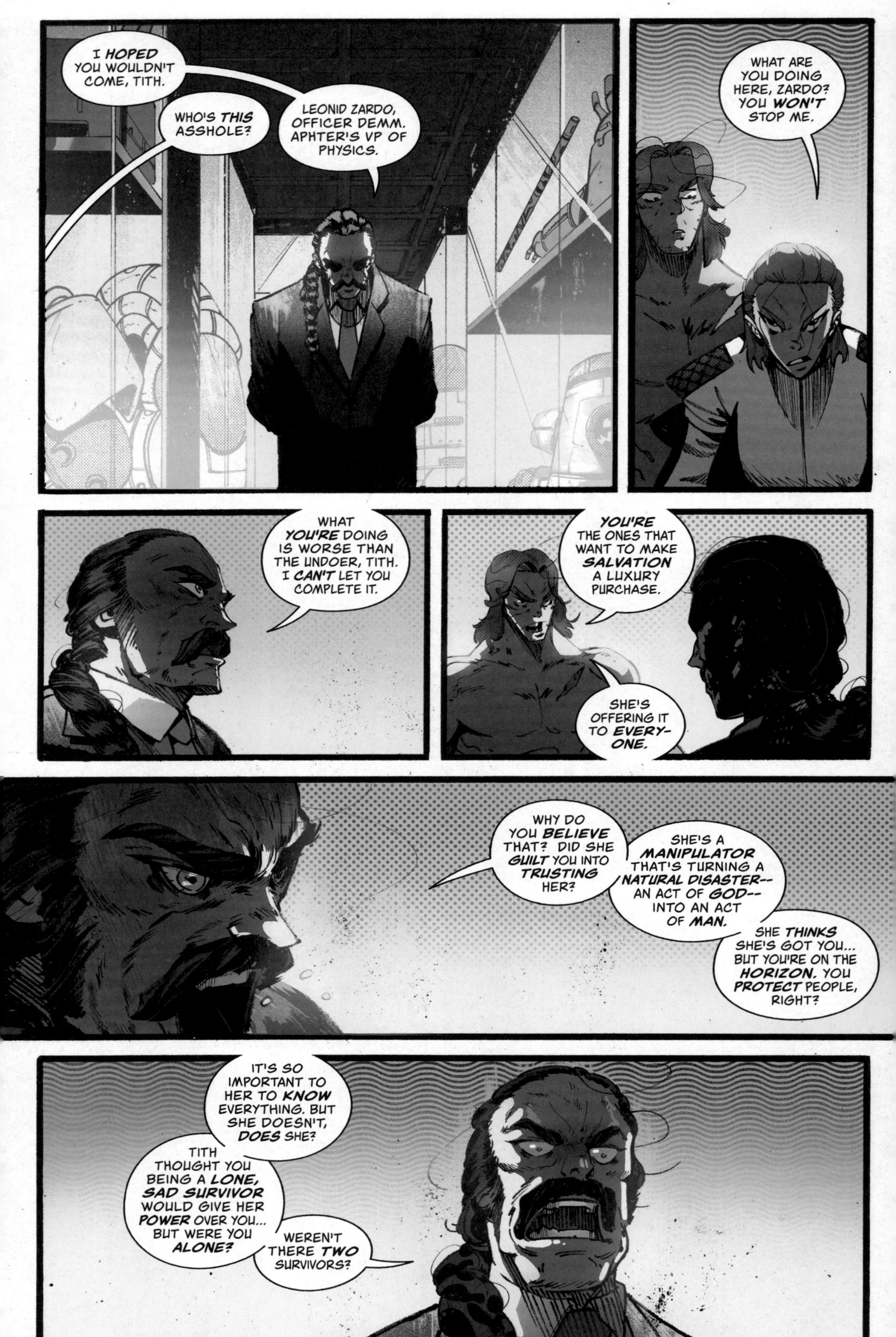
I HOPED YOU WOULDN'T COME, TITH.
WHO'S THIS ASSHOLE?
LEONID ZARDO, OFFICER DEMM. APHTER'S VP OF PHYSICS.
WHAT ARE YOU DOING HERE, ZARDO? YOU WON'T STOP ME.
WHAT YOU'RE DOING IS WORSE THAN THE UNDOER, TITH. I CAN'T LET YOU COMPLETE IT.
YOU'RE THE ONES THAT WANT TO MAKE SALVATION A LUXURY PURCHASE.
SHE'S OFFERING IT TO EVERY-ONE.
WHY DO YOU BELIEVE THAT? DID SHE GUILT YOU INTO TRUSTING HER?
SHE'S A MANIPULATOR THAT'S TURNING A NATURAL DISASTER-- AN ACT OF GOD-- INTO AN ACT OF MAN.
SHE THINKS SHE'S GOT YOU... BUT YOU'RE ON THE HORIZON. YOU PROTECT PEOPLE, RIGHT?
IT'S SO IMPORTANT TO HER TO KNOW EVERYTHING. BUT SHE DOESN'T, DOES SHE?
TITH THOUGHT YOU BEING A LONE, SAD SURVIVOR WOULD GIVE HER POWER OVER YOU... BUT WERE YOU ALONE?
WEREN'T THERE TWO SURVIVORS?

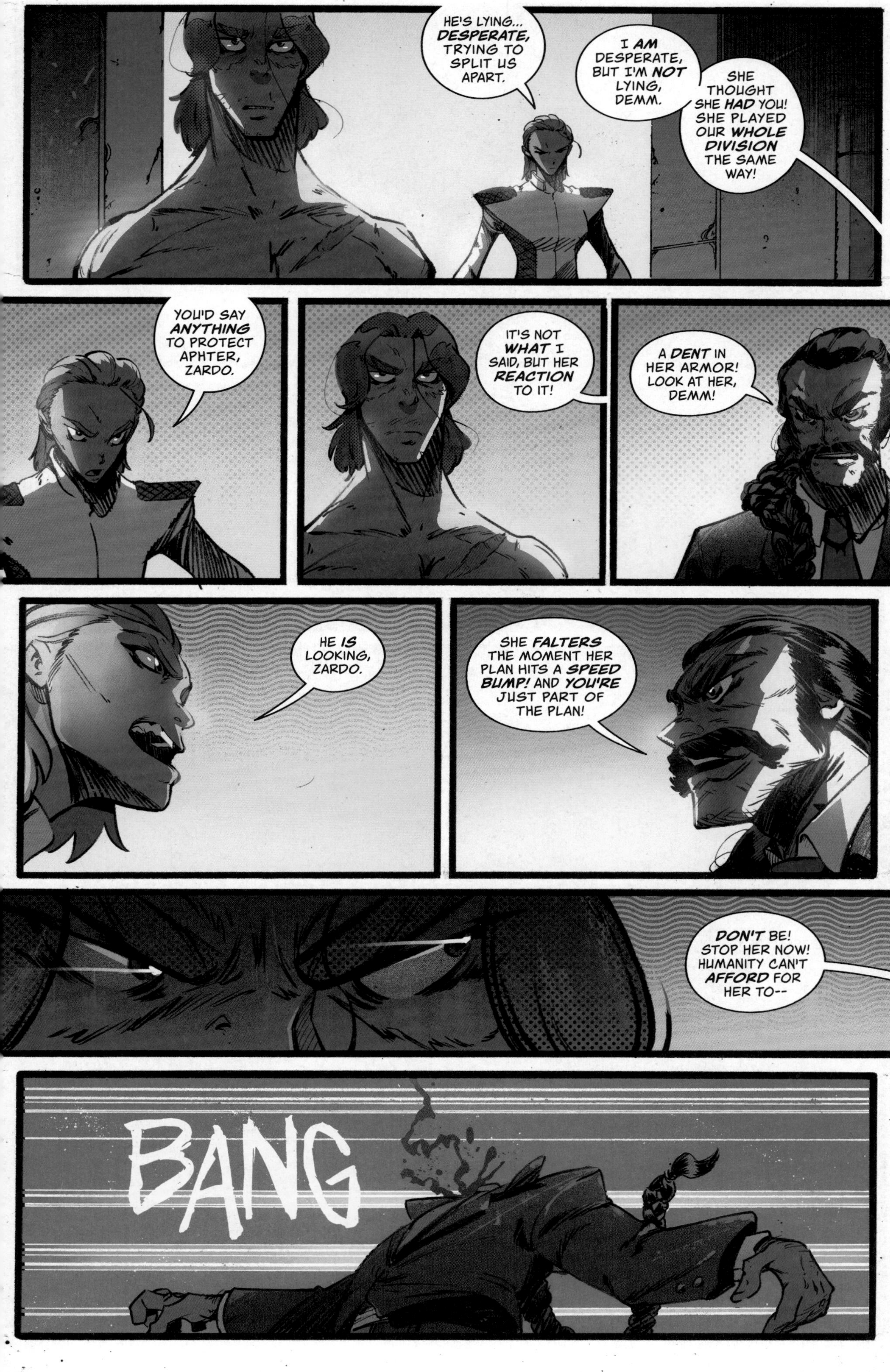
HE'S LYING... DESPERATE, TRYING TO SPLIT US APART.
I AM DESPERATE, BUT I'M NOT LYING, DEMM.
SHE THOUGHT SHE HAD YOU! SHE PLAYED OUR WHOLE DIVISION THE SAME WAY!
YOU'D SAY ANYTHING TO PROTECT APHTER, ZARDO.
IT'S NOT WHAT I SAID, BUT HER REACTION TO IT!
A DENT IN HER ARMOR! LOOK AT HER, DEMM!
HE IS LOOKING, ZARDO.
SHE FALTERS THE MOMENT HER PLAN HITS A SPEED BUMP! AND YOU'RE JUST PART OF THE PLAN!
DON'T BE! STOP HER NOW! HUMANITY CAN'T AFFORD FOR HER TO--
BANG

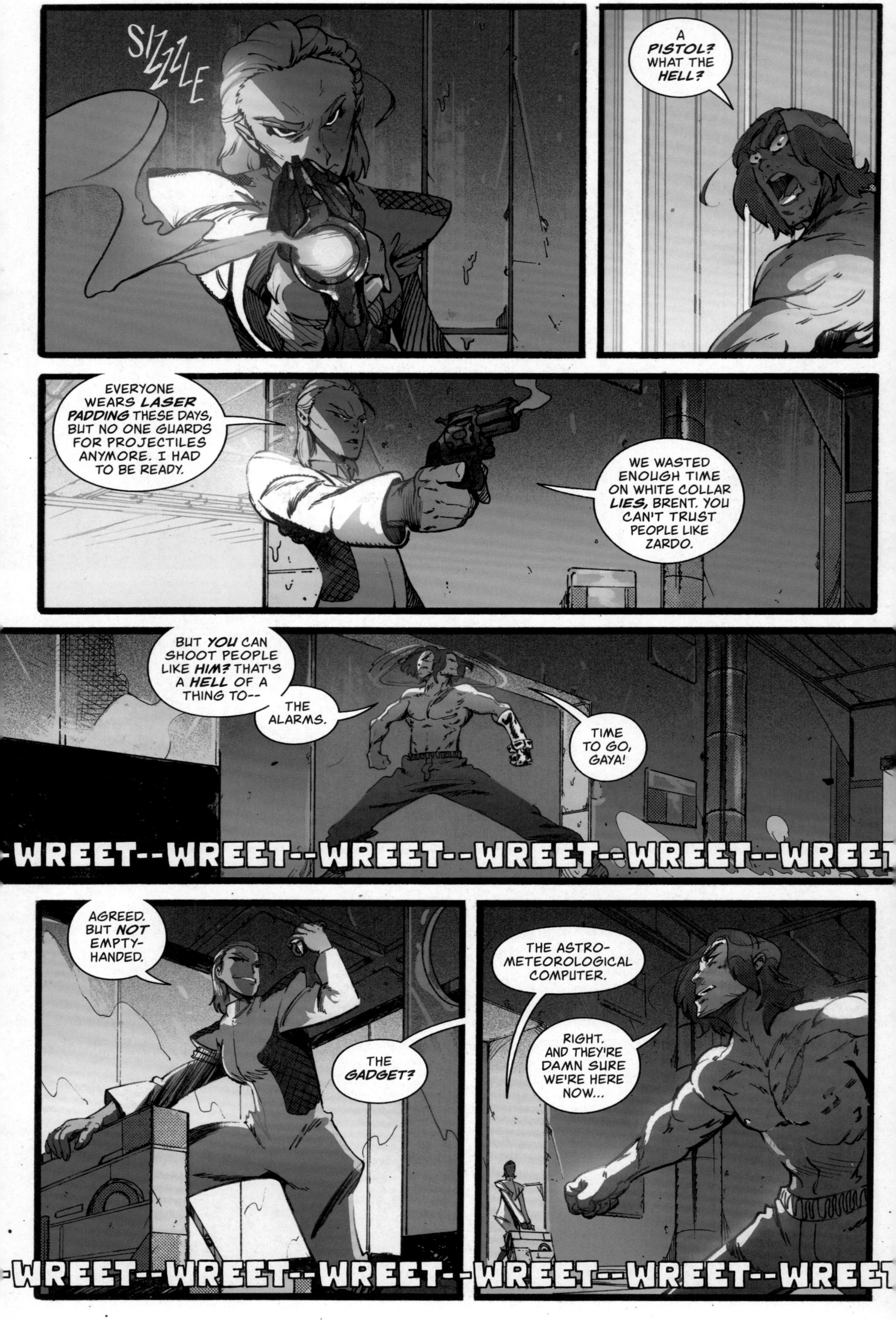
SIZZZLE
A PISTOL? WHAT THE HELL?
EVERYONE WEARS LASER PADDING THESE DAYS, BUT NO ONE GUARDS FOR PROJECTILES ANYMORE. I HAD TO BE READY.
WE WASTED ENOUGH TIME ON WHITE COLLAR LIES, BRENT. YOU CAN'T TRUST PEOPLE LIKE ZARDO.
BUT YOU CAN SHOOT PEOPLE LIKE HIM? THAT'S A HELL OF A THING TO--
THE ALARMS.
TIME TO GO, GAYA!
-WREET--WREET--WREET--WREET--WREET--WREET
AGREED. BUT NOT EMPTY-HANDED.
THE GADGET?
THE ASTRO-METEOROLOGICAL COMPUTER.
RIGHT. AND THEY'RE DAMN SURE WE'RE HERE NOW...
-WREET--WREET--WREET--WREET--WREET--WREET

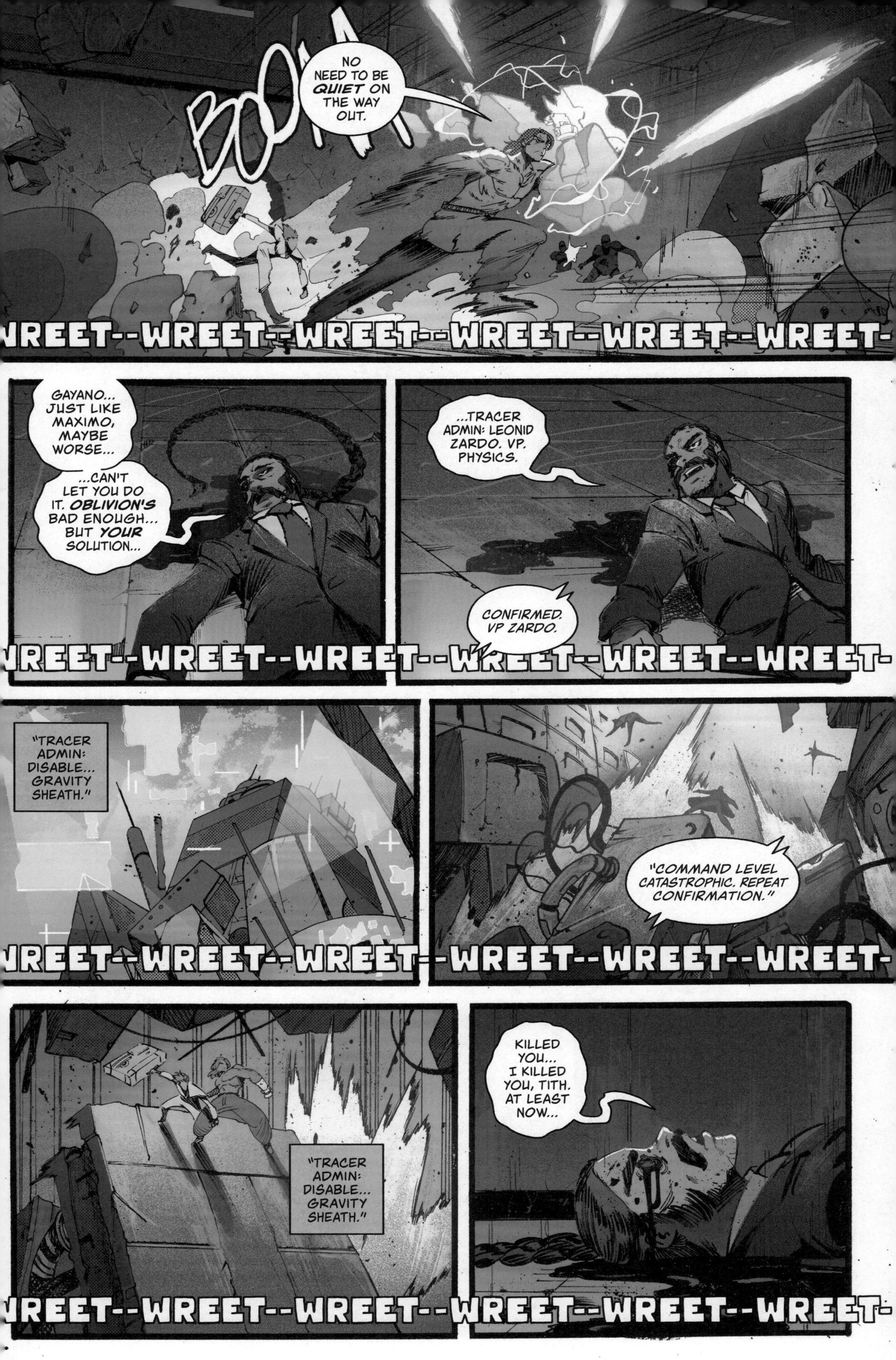
BOO
NO NEED TO BE **QUIET** ON THE WAY OUT.
REET--WREET--WREET--WREET--WREET--WREET-
GAYANO... JUST LIKE MAXIMO, MAYBE WORSE...
...CAN'T LET YOU DO IT. **OBLIVION'S** BAD ENOUGH... BUT **YOUR** SOLUTION...
...TRACER ADMIN: LEONID ZARDO. VP. PHYSICS.
CONFIRMED. VP ZARDO.
REET--WREET--WREET--WREET--WREET--WREET-
"TRACER ADMIN: DISABLE... GRAVITY SHEATH."
"COMMAND LEVEL CATASTROPHIC. REPEAT CONFIRMATION."
REET--WREET--WREET--WREET--WREET--WREET-
"TRACER ADMIN: DISABLE... GRAVITY SHEATH."
KILLED YOU... I KILLED YOU, TITH. AT LEAST NOW...
REET--WREET--WREET--WREET--WREET--WREET-

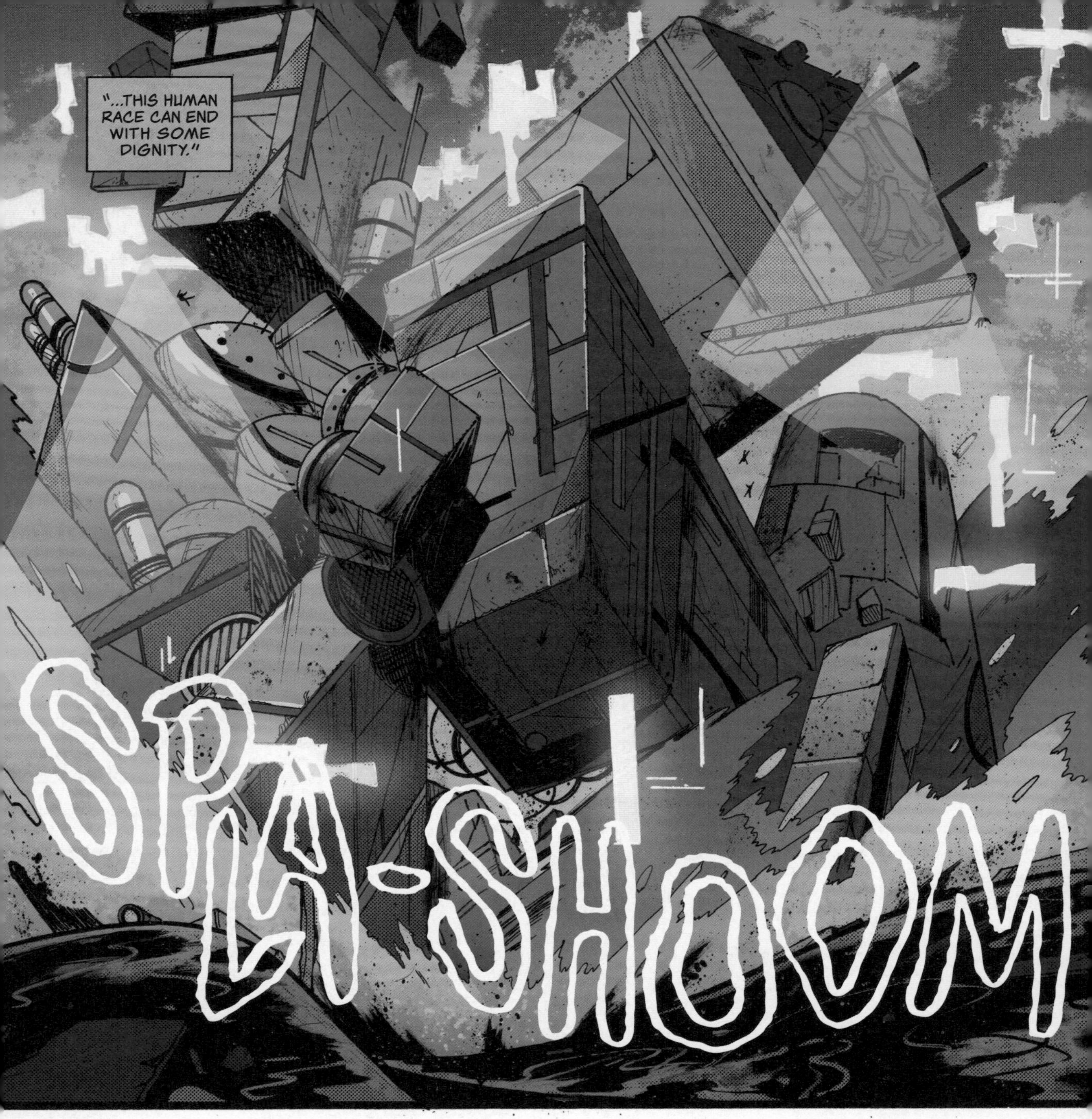
"...THIS HUMAN RACE CAN END WITH SOME DIGNITY."
SPA-SHOOM
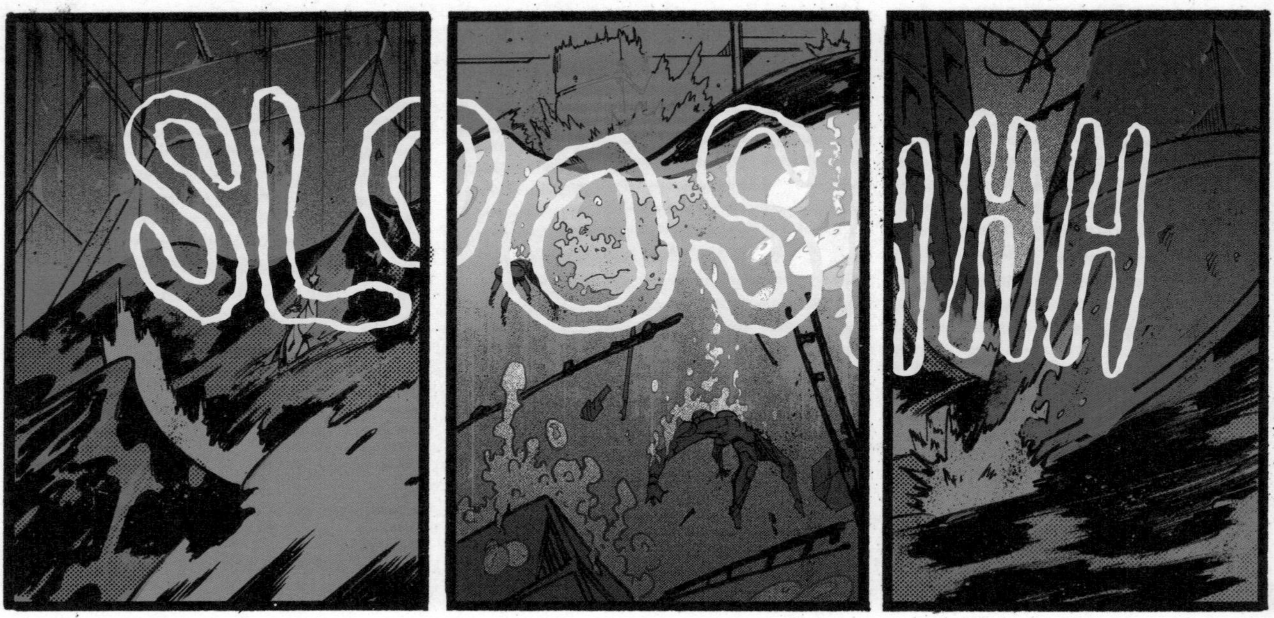
SLOOSHH

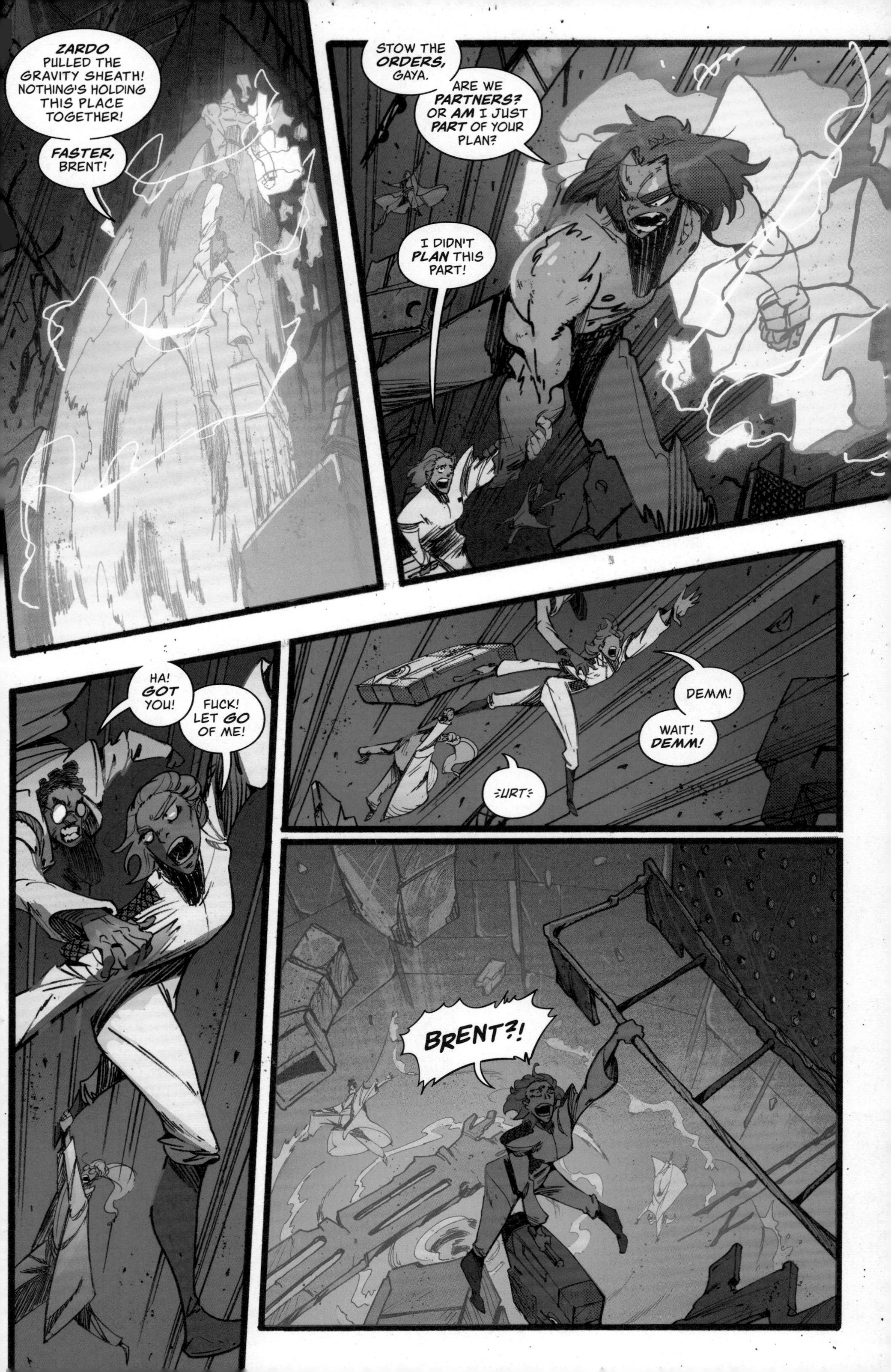
ZARDO PULLED THE GRAVITY SHEATH! NOTHING'S HOLDING THIS PLACE TOGETHER!
FASTER, BRENT!
STOW THE ORDERS, GAYA.
ARE WE PARTNERS? OR AM I JUST PART OF YOUR PLAN?
I DIDN'T PLAN THIS PART!
HA! GOT YOU!
FUCK! LET GO OF ME!
DEMM!
WAIT! DEMM!
URT
BRENT?!

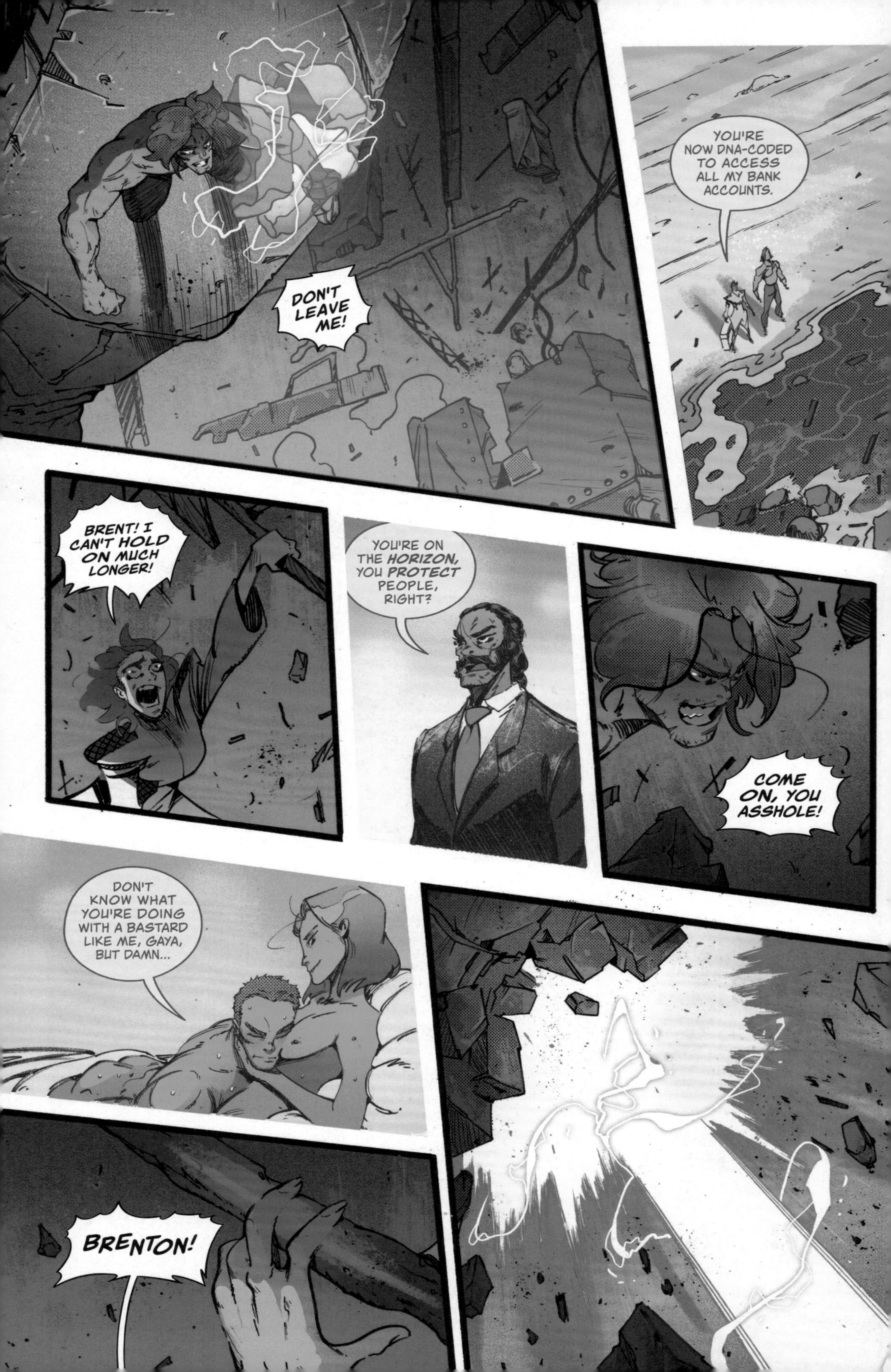
DON'T LEAVE ME!
YOU'RE NOW DNA-CODED TO ACCESS ALL MY BANK ACCOUNTS.
BRENT! I CAN'T HOLD ON MUCH LONGER!
YOU'RE ON THE *HORIZON*, YOU *PROTECT* PEOPLE, RIGHT?
COME ON, YOU ASSHOLE!
DON'T KNOW WHAT YOU'RE DOING WITH A BASTARD LIKE ME, GAYA, BUT DAMN...
BRENTON!

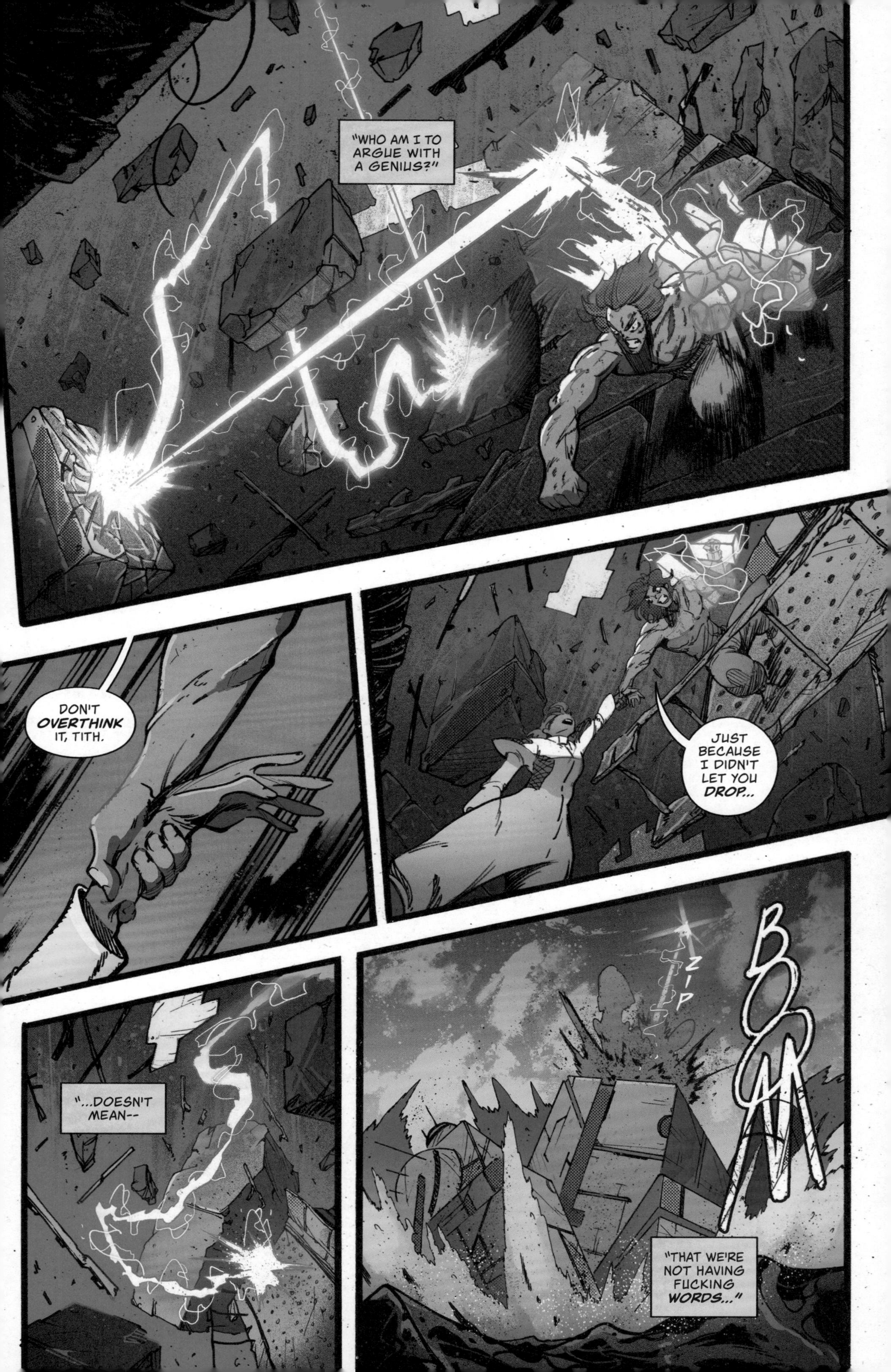
"WHO AM I TO ARGUE WITH A GENIUS?"
DON'T OVERTHINK IT, TITH.
JUST BECAUSE I DIDN'T LET YOU DROP...
"...DOESN'T MEAN--
ZIP
BOOM
"THAT WE'RE NOT HAVING FUCKING WORDS..."

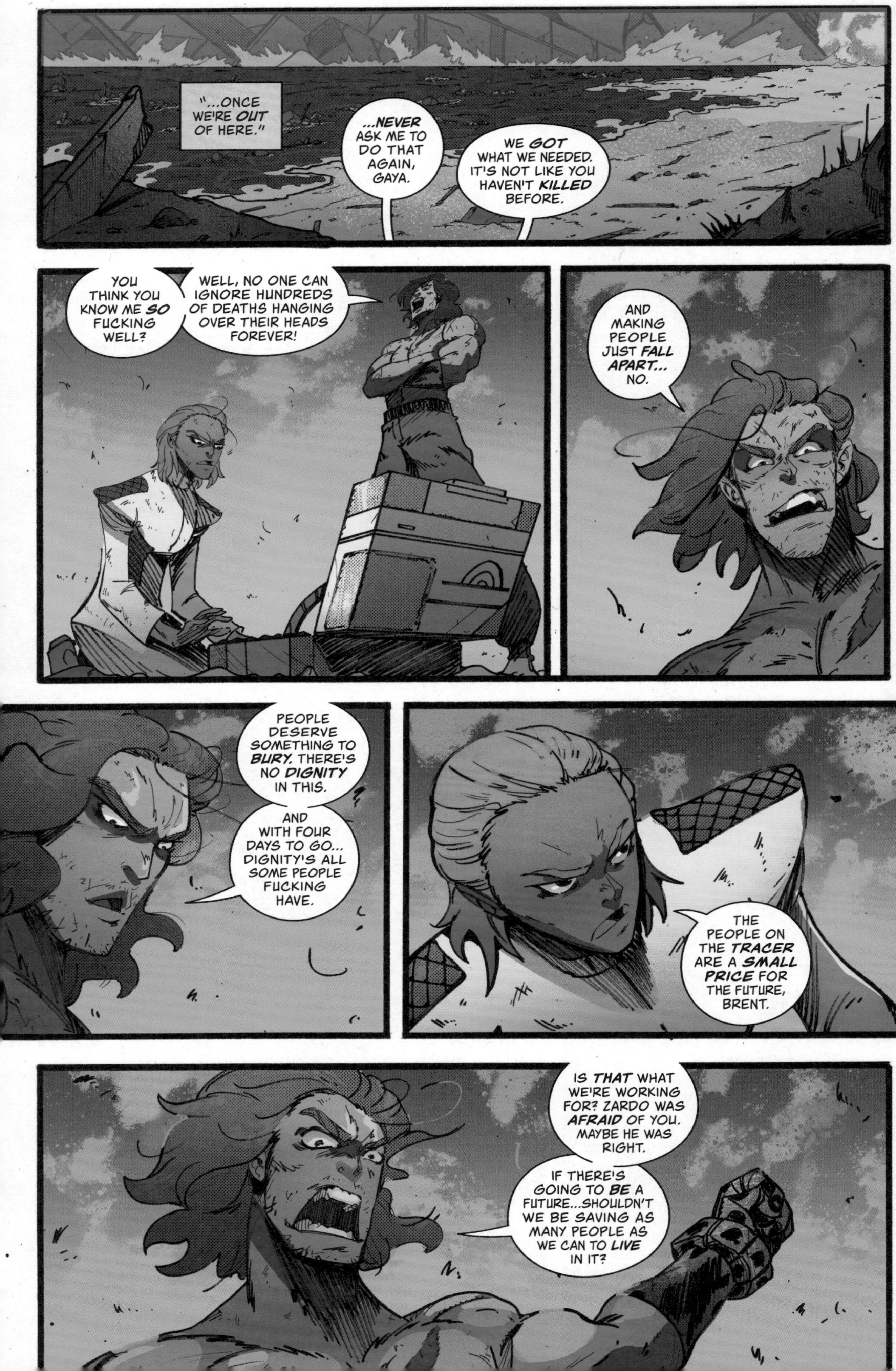
"...ONCE WE'RE *OUT* OF HERE."
...NEVER ASK ME TO DO THAT AGAIN, GAYA.
WE *GOT* WHAT WE NEEDED. IT'S NOT LIKE YOU HAVEN'T *KILLED* BEFORE.
YOU THINK YOU KNOW ME *SO* FUCKING WELL?
WELL, NO ONE CAN IGNORE HUNDREDS OF DEATHS HANGING OVER THEIR HEADS FOREVER!
AND MAKING PEOPLE JUST *FALL APART...* NO.
PEOPLE DESERVE SOMETHING TO *BURY.* THERE'S NO *DIGNITY* IN THIS.
AND WITH FOUR DAYS TO GO... DIGNITY'S ALL SOME PEOPLE FUCKING HAVE.
THE PEOPLE ON THE *TRACER* ARE A *SMALL PRICE* FOR THE FUTURE, BRENT.
IS *THAT* WHAT WE'RE WORKING FOR? ZARDO WAS *AFRAID* OF YOU. MAYBE HE WAS RIGHT.
IF THERE'S GOING TO *BE* A FUTURE...SHOULDN'T WE BE SAVING AS MANY PEOPLE AS WE CAN TO *LIVE* IN IT?

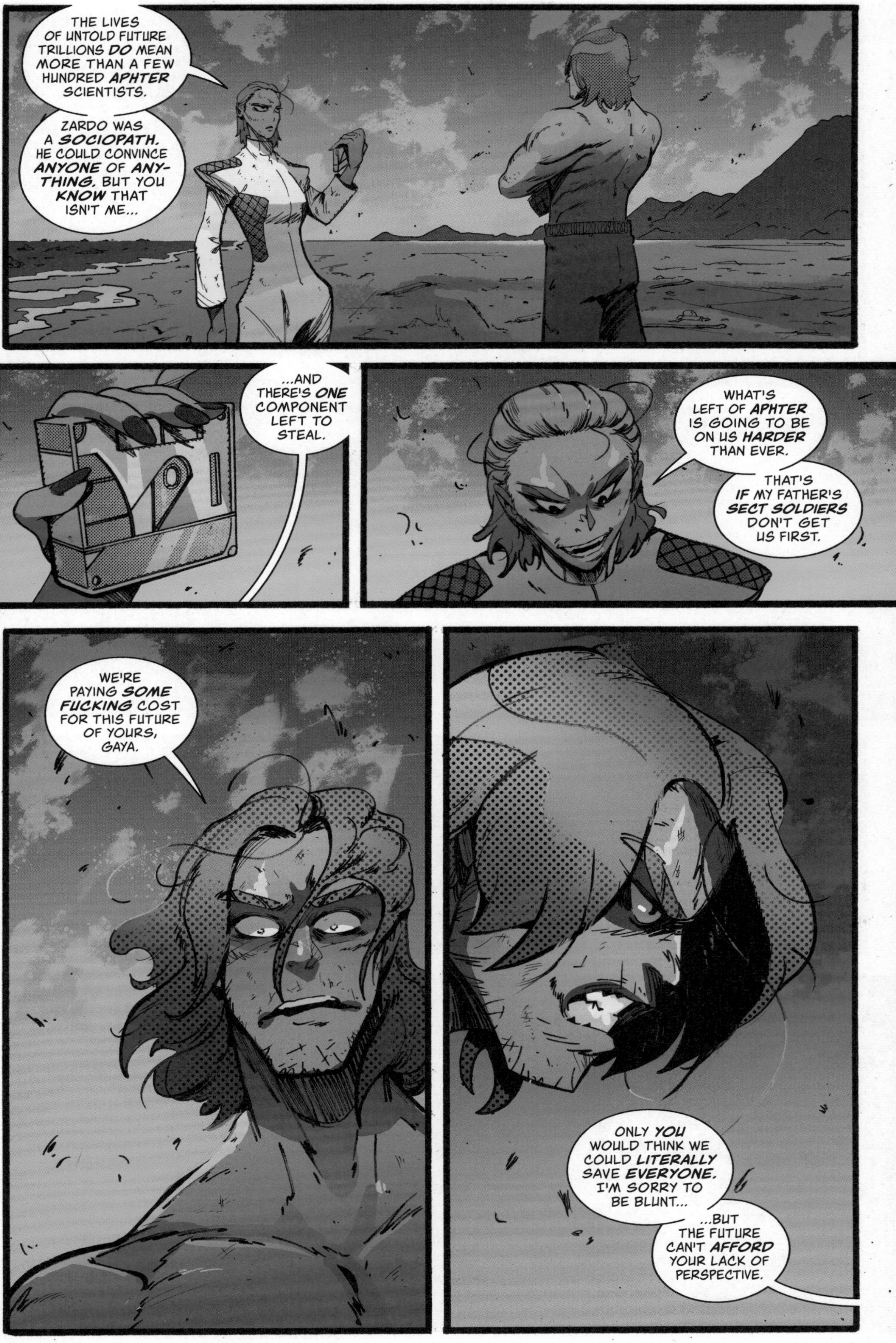
THE LIVES OF UNTOLD FUTURE TRILLIONS DO MEAN MORE THAN A FEW HUNDRED APHTER SCIENTISTS.
ZARDO WAS A SOCIOPATH. HE COULD CONVINCE ANYONE OF ANY-THING. BUT YOU KNOW THAT ISN'T ME...
...AND THERE'S ONE COMPONENT LEFT TO STEAL.
WHAT'S LEFT OF APHTER IS GOING TO BE ON US HARDER THAN EVER.
THAT'S IF MY FATHER'S SECT SOLDIERS DON'T GET US FIRST.
WE'RE PAYING SOME FUCKING COST FOR THIS FUTURE OF YOURS, GAYA.
ONLY YOU WOULD THINK WE COULD LITERALLY SAVE EVERYONE. I'M SORRY TO BE BLUNT...
...BUT THE FUTURE CAN'T AFFORD YOUR LACK OF PERSPECTIVE.

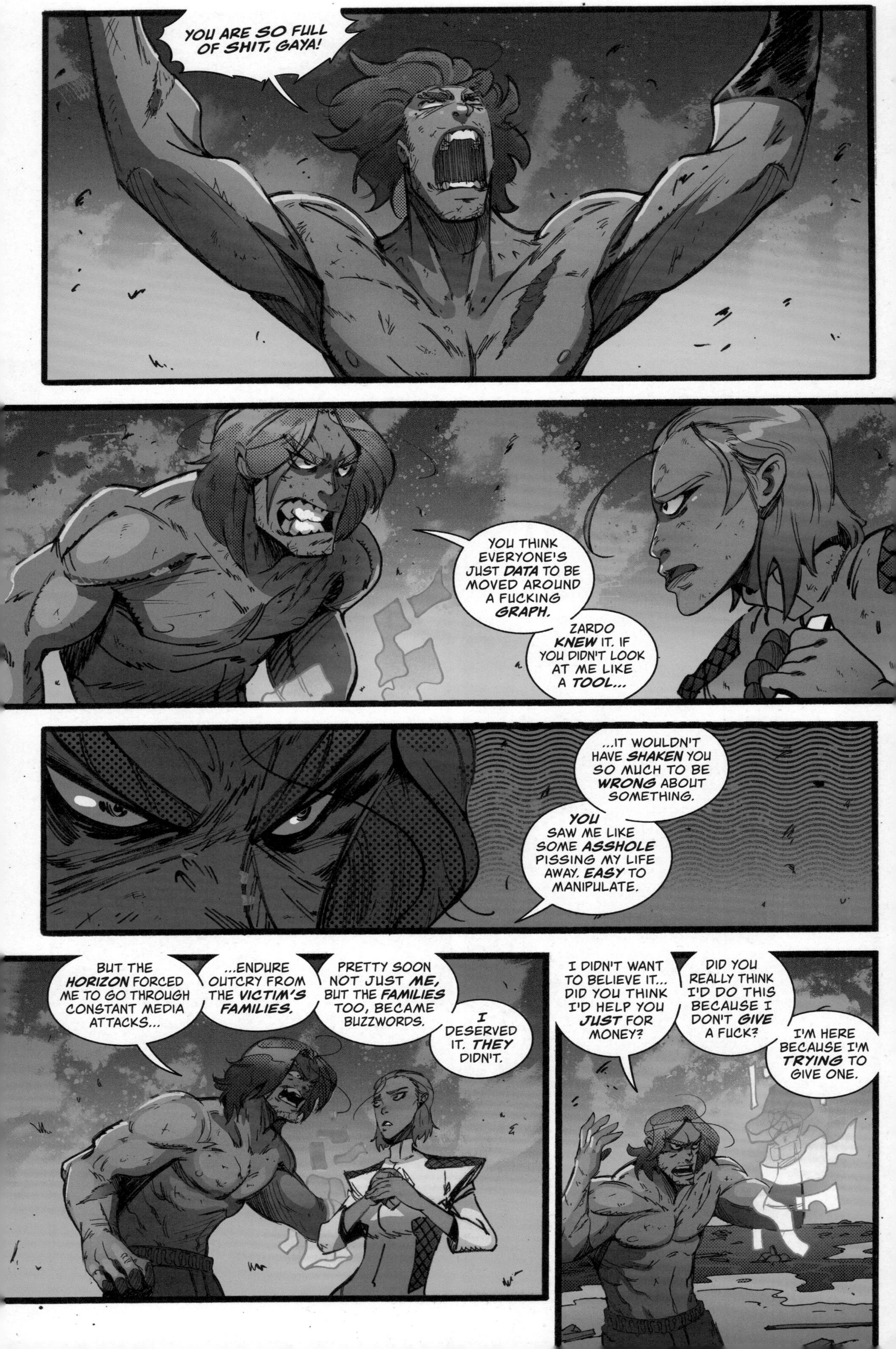
YOU ARE SO FULL OF SHIT, GAYA!
YOU THINK EVERYONE'S JUST DATA TO BE MOVED AROUND A FUCKING GRAPH.
ZARDO KNEW IT. IF YOU DIDN'T LOOK AT ME LIKE A TOOL...
...IT WOULDN'T HAVE SHAKEN YOU SO MUCH TO BE WRONG ABOUT SOMETHING.
YOU SAW ME LIKE SOME ASSHOLE PISSING MY LIFE AWAY. EASY TO MANIPULATE.
BUT THE HORIZON FORCED ME TO GO THROUGH CONSTANT MEDIA ATTACKS...
...ENDURE OUTCRY FROM THE VICTIM'S FAMILIES.
PRETTY SOON NOT JUST ME, BUT THE FAMILIES TOO, BECAME BUZZWORDS.
I DESERVED IT. THEY DIDN'T.
I DIDN'T WANT TO BELIEVE IT... DID YOU THINK I'D HELP YOU JUST FOR MONEY?
DID YOU REALLY THINK I'D DO THIS BECAUSE I DON'T GIVE A FUCK?
I'M HERE BECAUSE I'M TRYING TO GIVE ONE.

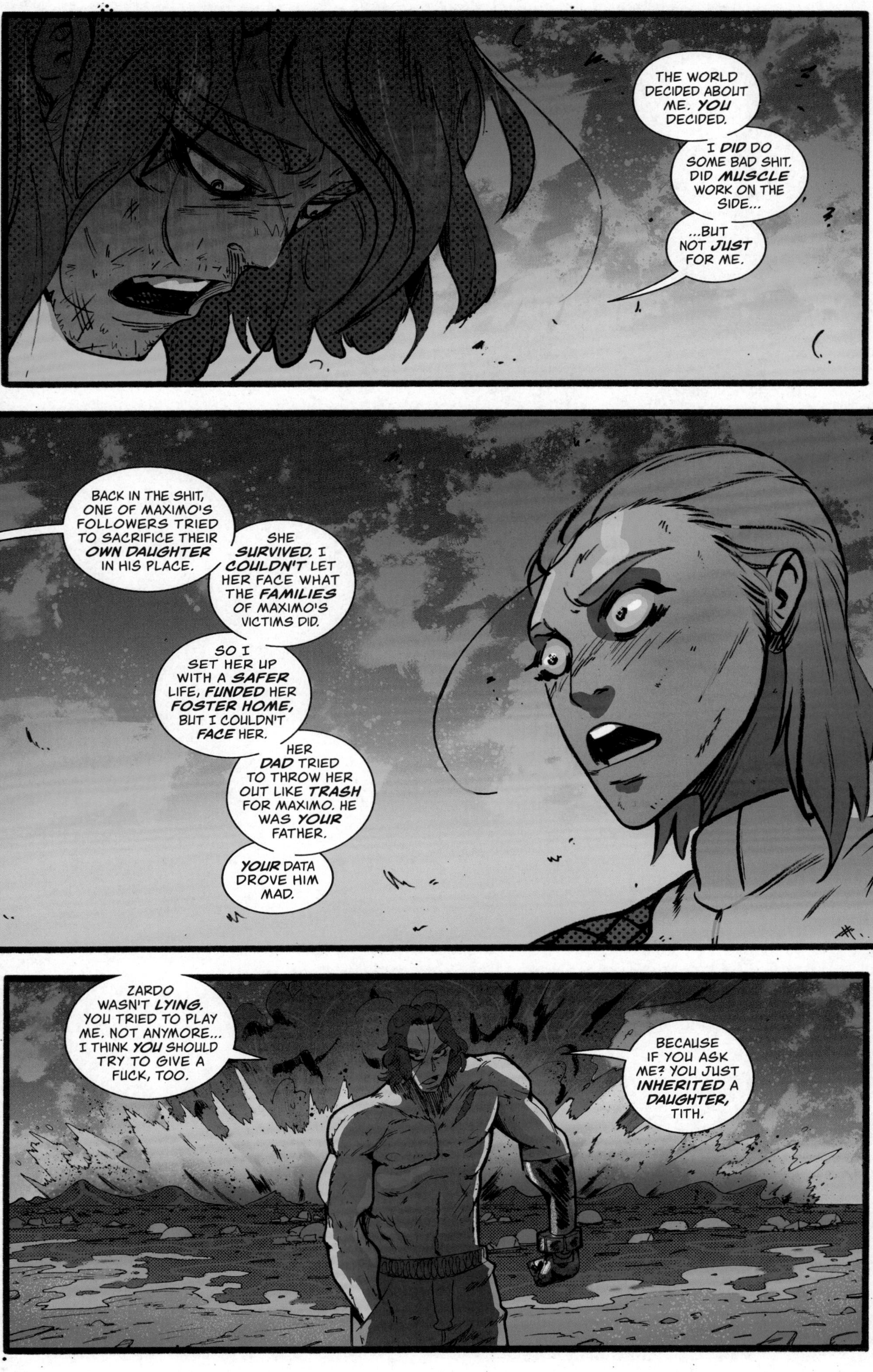
THE WORLD DECIDED ABOUT ME. YOU DECIDED.
I DID DO SOME BAD SHIT. DID MUSCLE WORK ON THE SIDE...
...BUT NOT JUST FOR ME.
BACK IN THE SHIT, ONE OF MAXIMO'S FOLLOWERS TRIED TO SACRIFICE THEIR OWN DAUGHTER IN HIS PLACE.
SHE SURVIVED. I COULDN'T LET HER FACE WHAT THE FAMILIES OF MAXIMO'S VICTIMS DID.
SO I SET HER UP WITH A SAFER LIFE, FUNDED HER FOSTER HOME, BUT I COULDN'T FACE HER.
HER DAD TRIED TO THROW HER OUT LIKE TRASH FOR MAXIMO. HE WAS YOUR FATHER.
YOUR DATA DROVE HIM MAD.
ZARDO WASN'T LYING. YOU TRIED TO PLAY ME. NOT ANYMORE... I THINK YOU SHOULD TRY TO GIVE A FUCK, TOO.
BECAUSE IF YOU ASK ME? YOU JUST INHERITED A DAUGHTER, TITH.

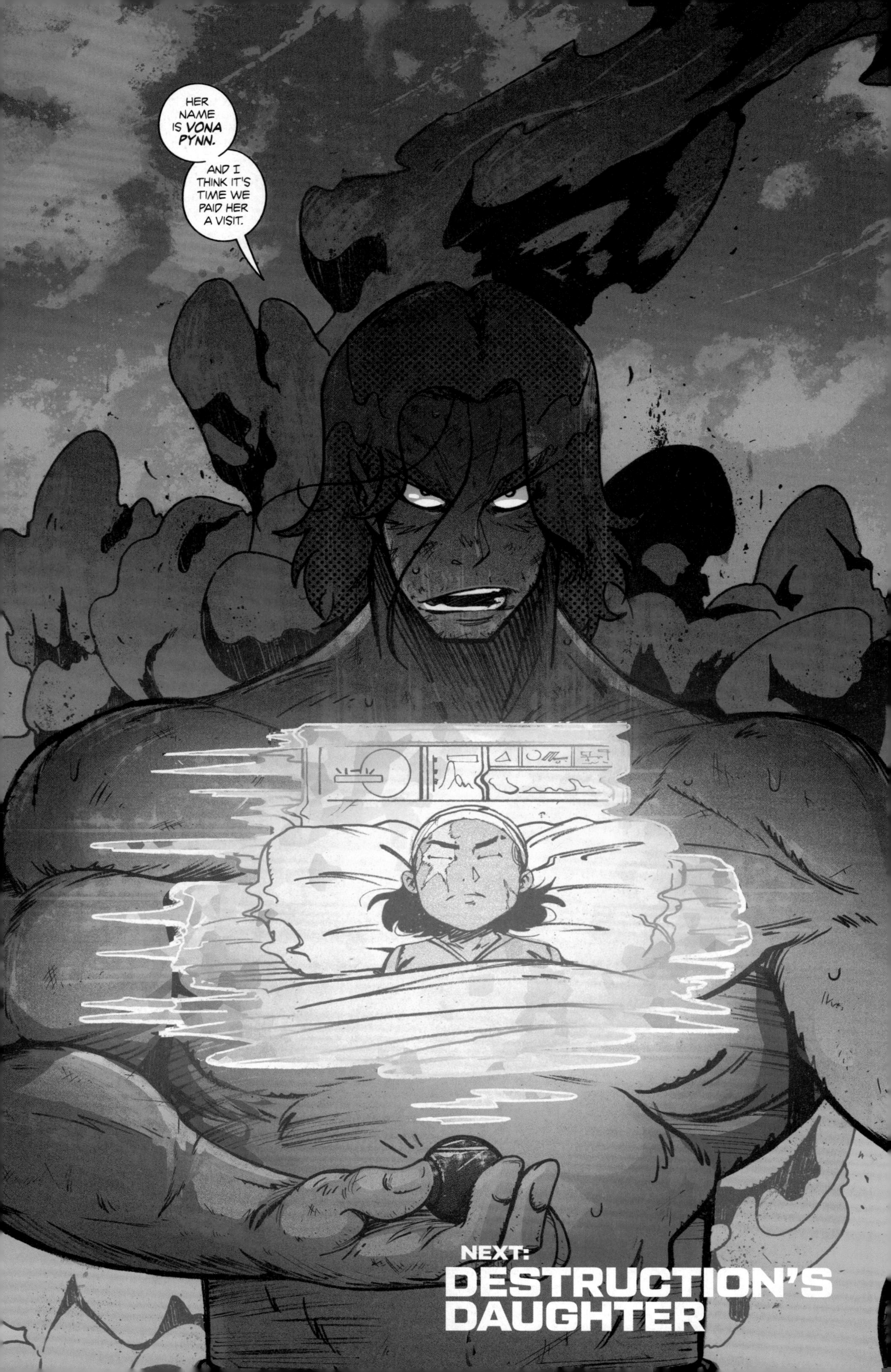
HER NAME IS VONA PYNN.
AND I THINK IT'S TIME WE PAID HER A VISIT.
NEXT:
DESTRUCTION'S DAUGHTER

CHAPTER 4

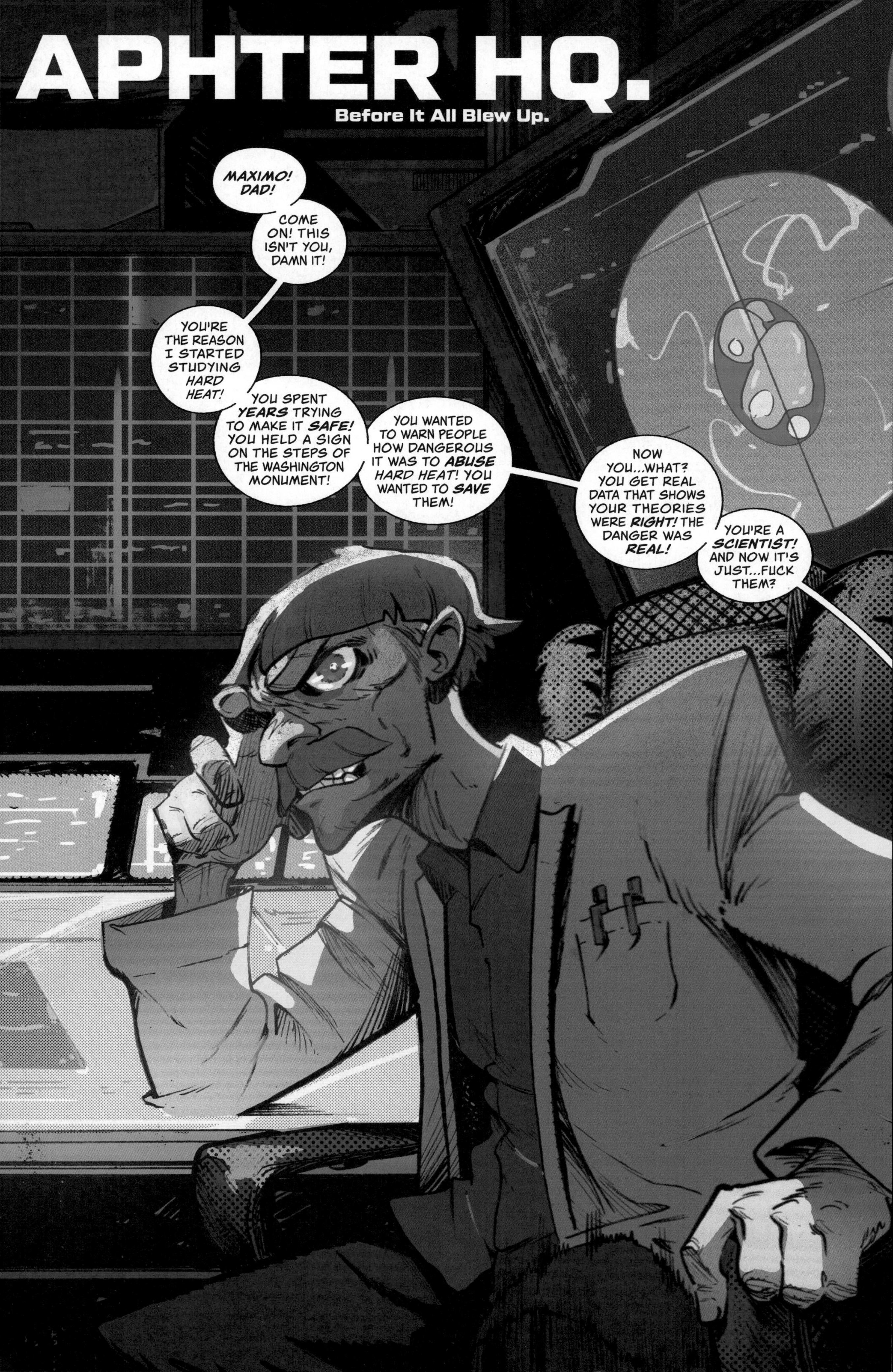
APHTER HQ.
Before It All Blew Up.
MAXIMO! DAD!
COME ON! THIS ISN'T YOU, DAMN IT!
YOU'RE THE REASON I STARTED STUDYING HARD HEAT!
YOU SPENT YEARS TRYING TO MAKE IT SAFE! YOU HELD A SIGN ON THE STEPS OF THE WASHINGTON MONUMENT!
YOU WANTED TO WARN PEOPLE HOW DANGEROUS IT WAS TO ABUSE HARD HEAT! YOU WANTED TO SAVE THEM!
NOW YOU...WHAT? YOU GET REAL DATA THAT SHOWS YOUR THEORIES WERE RIGHT! THE DANGER WAS REAL!
YOU'RE A SCIENTIST! AND NOW IT'S JUST...FUCK THEM?

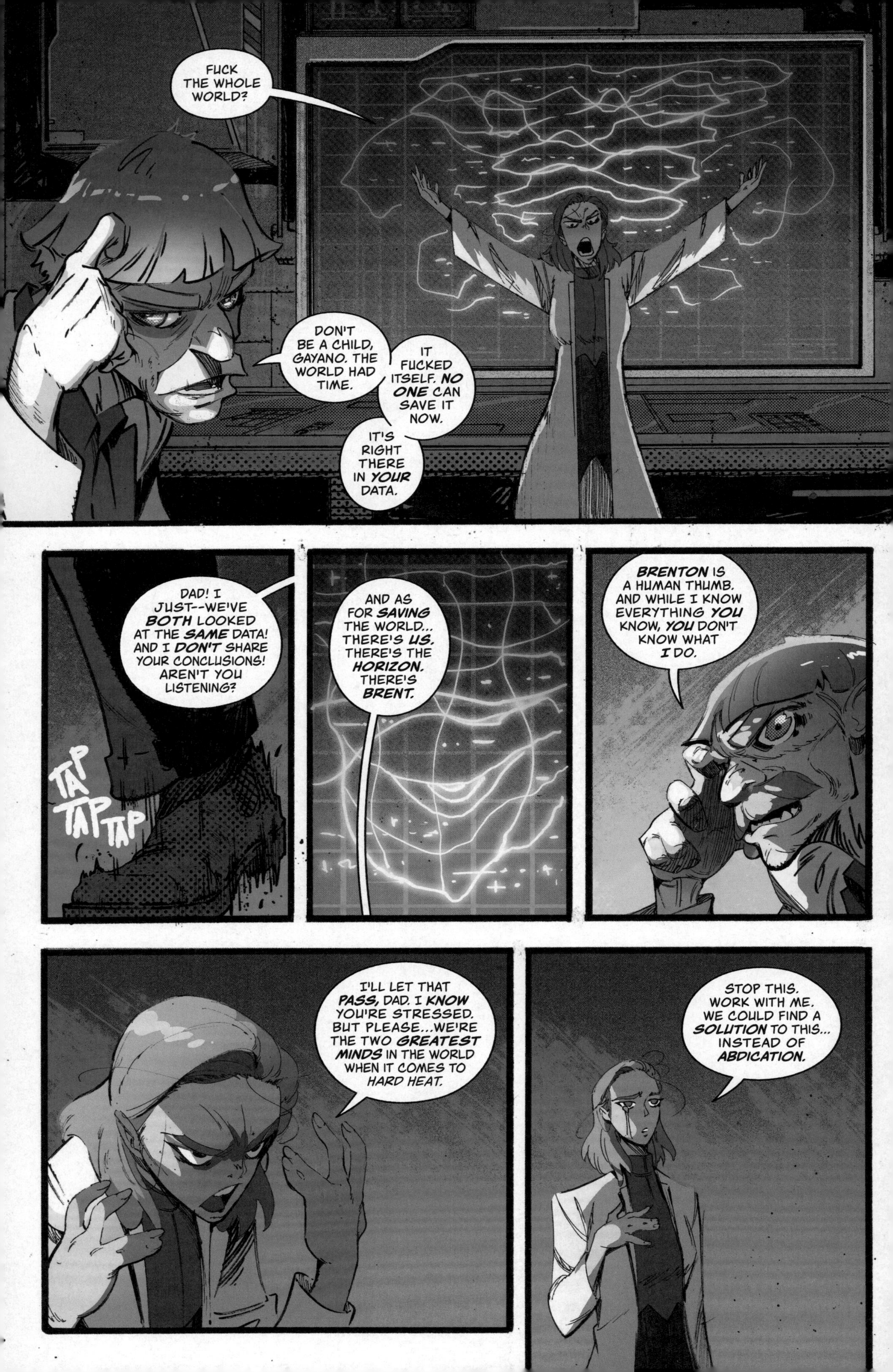
FUCK THE WHOLE WORLD?
DON'T BE A CHILD, GAYANO. THE WORLD HAD TIME.
IT FUCKED ITSELF. NO ONE CAN SAVE IT NOW.
IT'S RIGHT THERE IN YOUR DATA.
DAD! I JUST--WE'VE BOTH LOOKED AT THE SAME DATA! AND I DON'T SHARE YOUR CONCLUSIONS! AREN'T YOU LISTENING?
TAP TAP TAP TAP
AND AS FOR SAVING THE WORLD... THERE'S US. THERE'S THE HORIZON. THERE'S BRENT.
BRENTON IS A HUMAN THUMB. AND WHILE I KNOW EVERYTHING YOU KNOW, YOU DON'T KNOW WHAT I DO.
I'LL LET THAT PASS, DAD. I KNOW YOU'RE STRESSED. BUT PLEASE...WE'RE THE TWO GREATEST MINDS IN THE WORLD WHEN IT COMES TO HARD HEAT.
STOP THIS. WORK WITH ME. WE COULD FIND A SOLUTION TO THIS... INSTEAD OF ABDICATION.

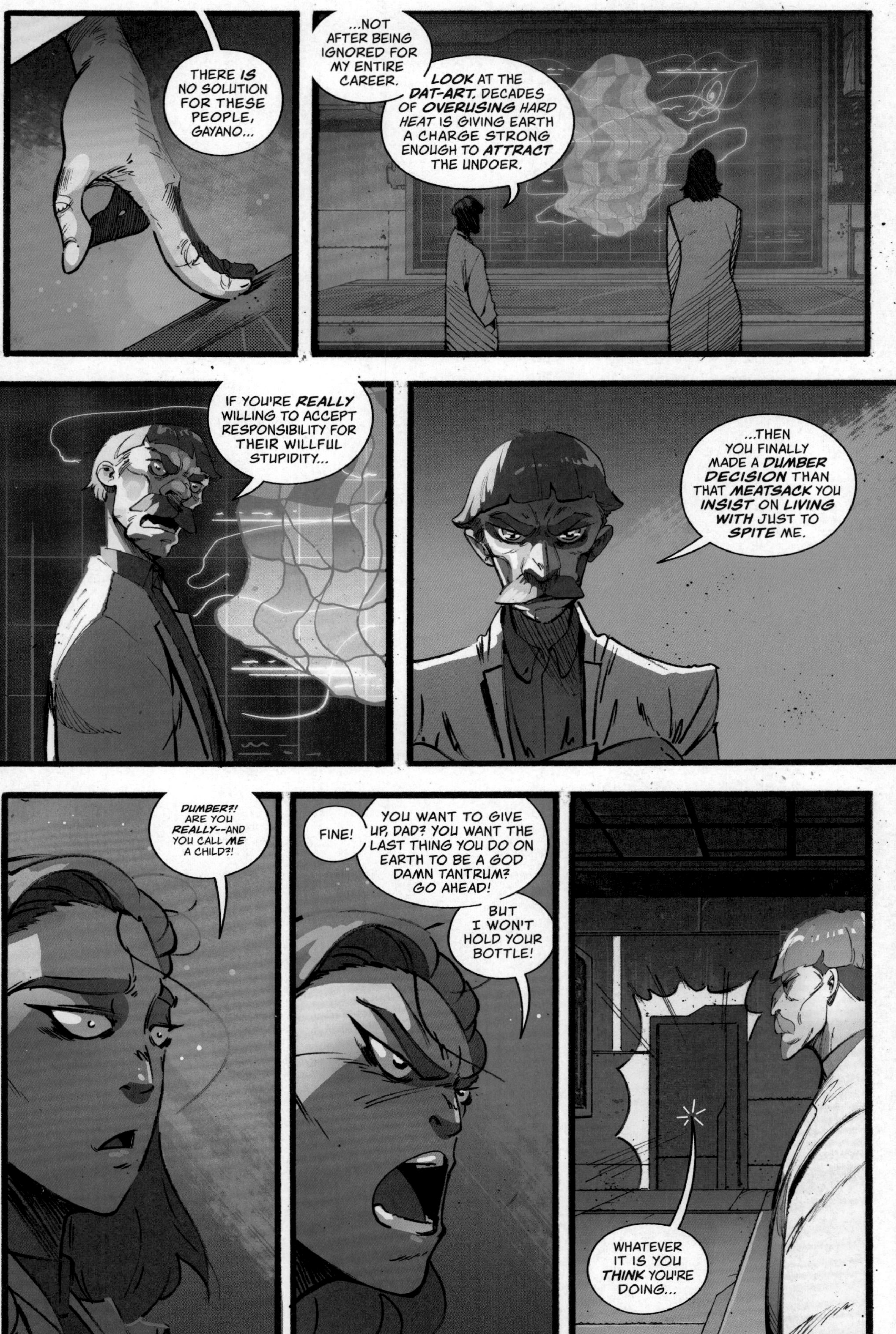
THERE IS NO SOLUTION FOR THESE PEOPLE, GAYANO...
...NOT AFTER BEING IGNORED FOR MY ENTIRE CAREER.
LOOK AT THE DAT-ART. DECADES OF OVERUSING HARD HEAT IS GIVING EARTH A CHARGE STRONG ENOUGH TO ATTRACT THE UNDOER.
IF YOU'RE REALLY WILLING TO ACCEPT RESPONSIBILITY FOR THEIR WILLFUL STUPIDITY...
...THEN YOU FINALLY MADE A DUMBER DECISION THAN THAT MEATSACK YOU INSIST ON LIVING WITH JUST TO SPITE ME.
DUMBER?! ARE YOU REALLY--AND YOU CALL ME A CHILD?!
FINE!
YOU WANT TO GIVE UP, DAD? YOU WANT THE LAST THING YOU DO ON EARTH TO BE A GOD DAMN TANTRUM? GO AHEAD!
BUT I WON'T HOLD YOUR BOTTLE!
WHATEVER IT IS YOU THINK YOU'RE DOING...

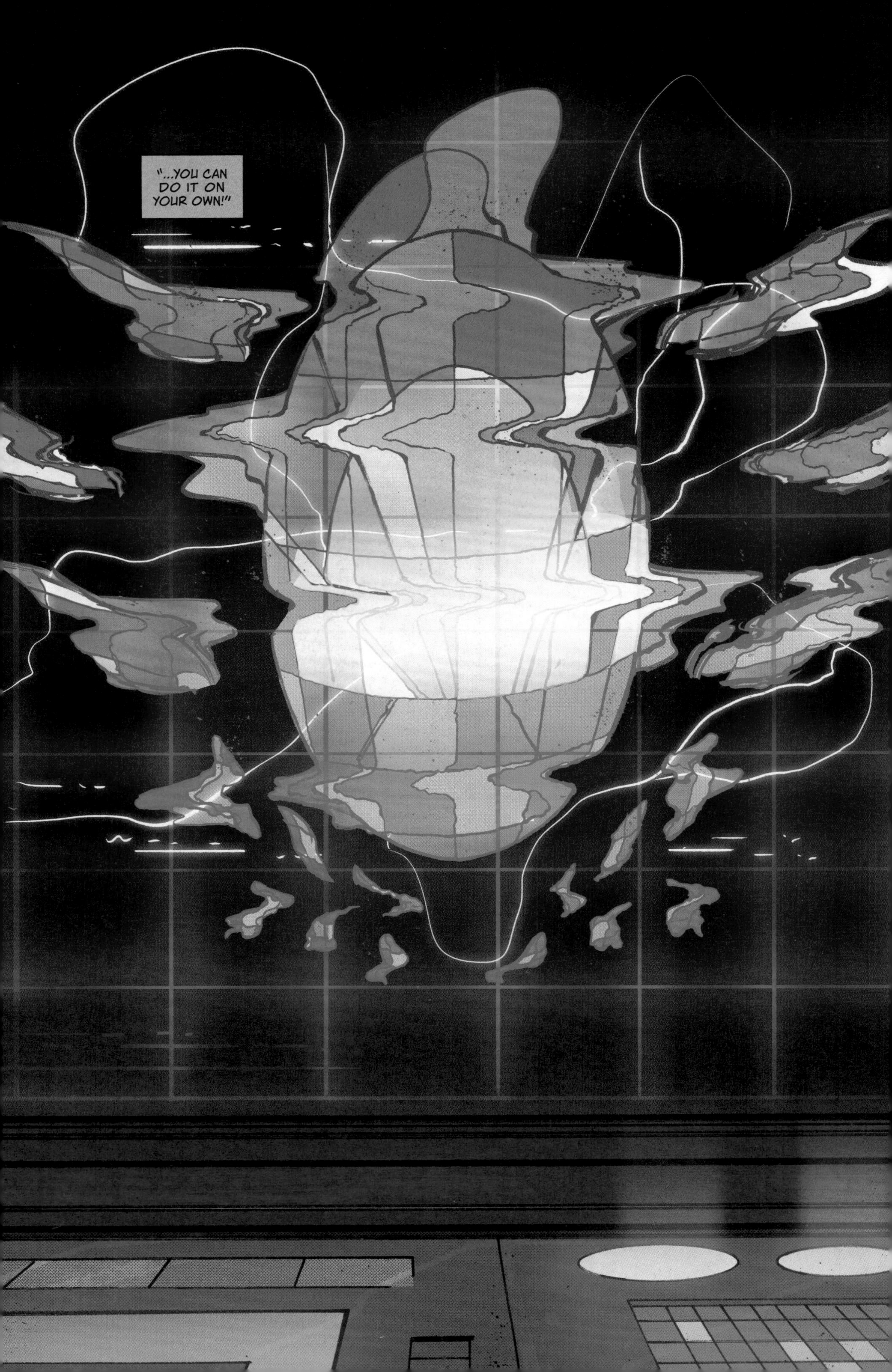
"...YOU CAN DO IT ON YOUR OWN!"

NOW.
Three Days Until the End.

I CAN'T BELIEVE YOU DIDN'T TELL ME, BRENT.

FUNNY. WHEN SOMEONE ACCUSES ME OF NEGLIGENT MASS MURDER AS A MEANS OF BREAKING UP WITH ME...

...I DON'T PRIORITIZE KEEPING THEM IN THE FUCKING LOOP, GAYA.

YOU *DID* FUCK UP.

I DIDN'T SAY I DIDN'T. WELL...I *DID*, BUT NOT FOR AS LONG AS YOU'D THINK. OR YOU'D KNOW... IF YOU STUCK AROUND.

MY FATHER WAS DEAD, BRENT. YOU WERE OFF THE RAILS.

WELL, GAYA... I *FOUND* THE FUCKING RAILS. JUST BARELY ENOUGH TO HOLD ON. BUT I DID... AND *SHE* WAS A BIG PART OF THAT.

YOU WEREN'T THERE. VONA'S PARENTS OFFERED HER UP LIKE *CAB FARE*. NO *KID* DESERVES THAT.

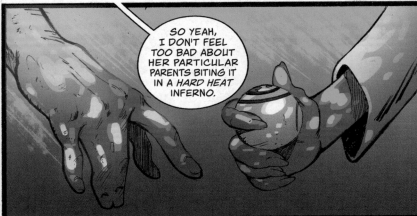

SO YEAH, I DON'T FEEL TOO BAD ABOUT HER PARTICULAR PARENTS BITING IT IN A *HARD HEAT* INFERNO.

AND YEAH, THE WORLD WAS ON A COLLISION COURSE...BUT UNTIL THEN, *SHE* DESERVED THE SMOOTHEST RIDE POSSIBLE.

SO I GAVE IT TO HER. AND I DIDN'T GIVE A SHIT HOW.

SHE'S *STILL* GOING TO DIE, BRENT. JUST LIKE *ALL* OF US...

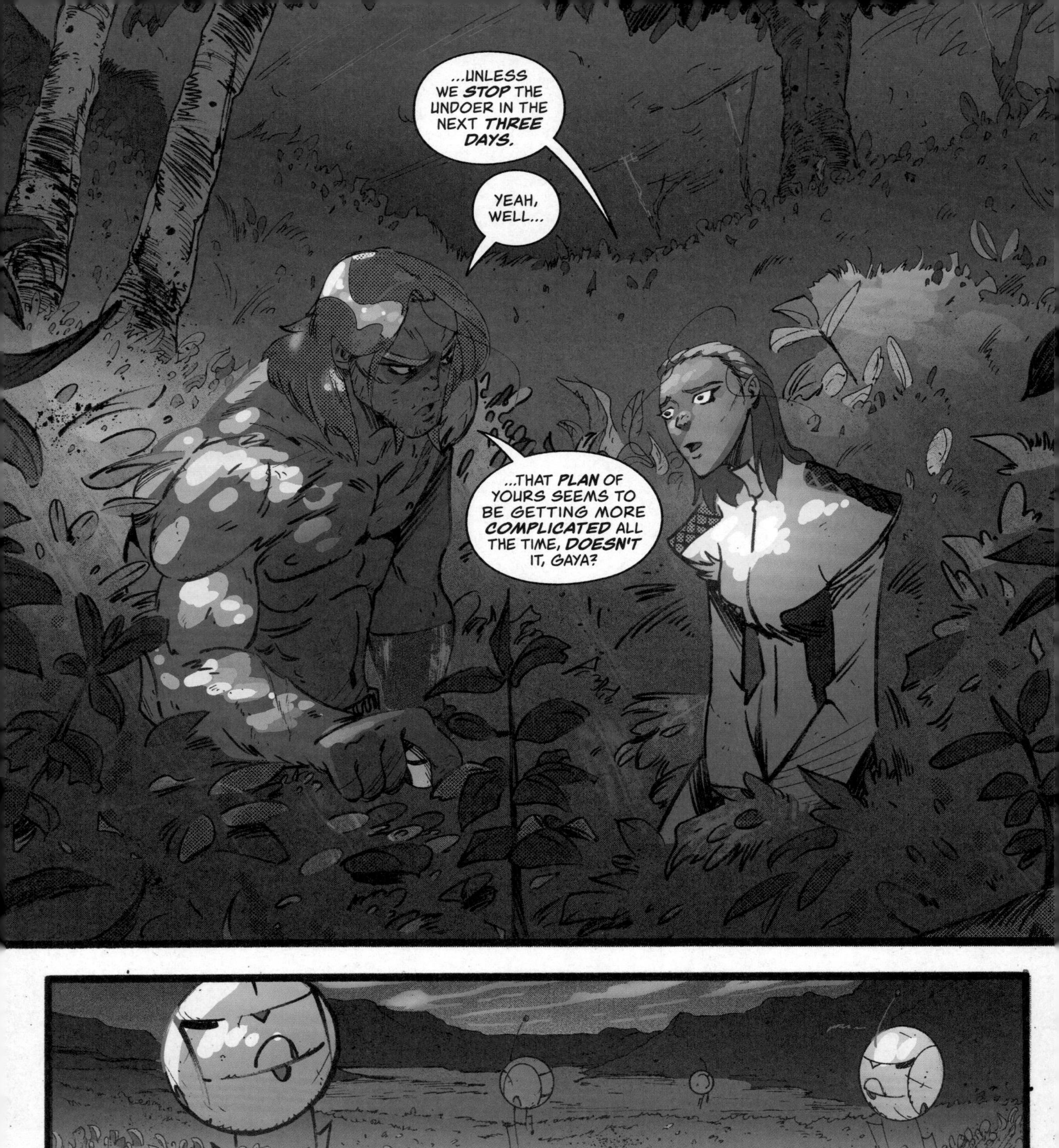
...UNLESS WE STOP THE UNDOER IN THE NEXT THREE DAYS.
YEAH, WELL...
...THAT PLAN OF YOURS SEEMS TO BE GETTING MORE COMPLICATED ALL THE TIME, DOESN'T IT, GAYA?

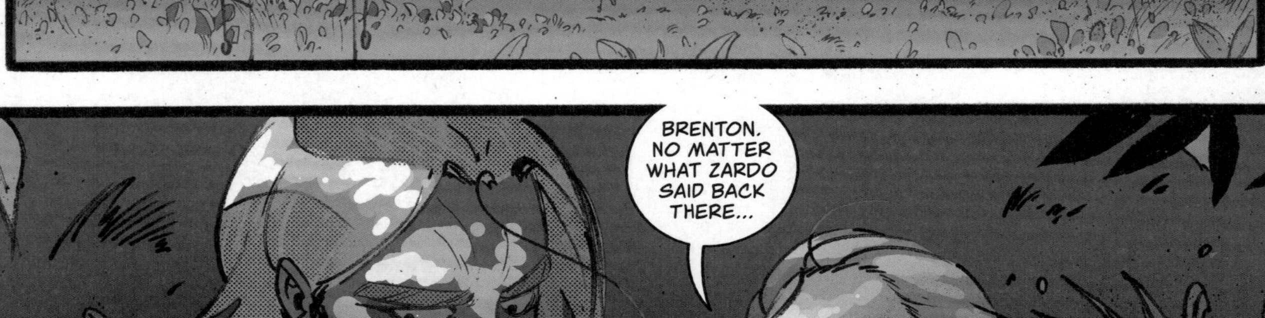

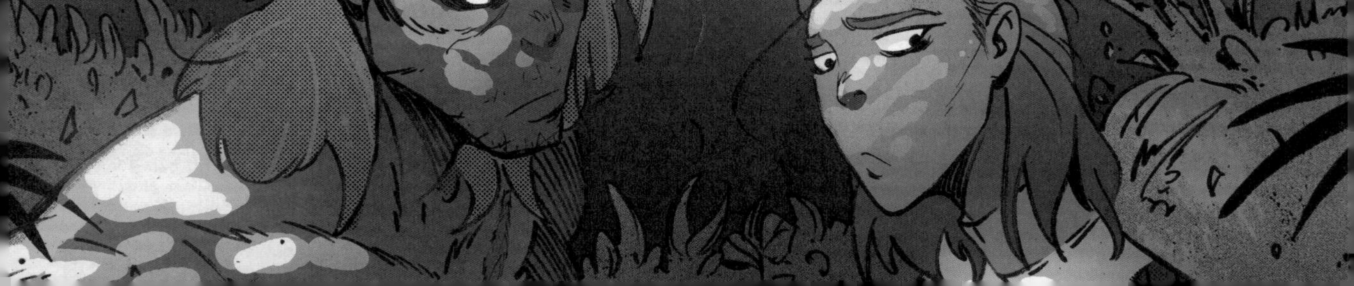
BRENTON. NO MATTER WHAT ZARDO SAID BACK THERE...

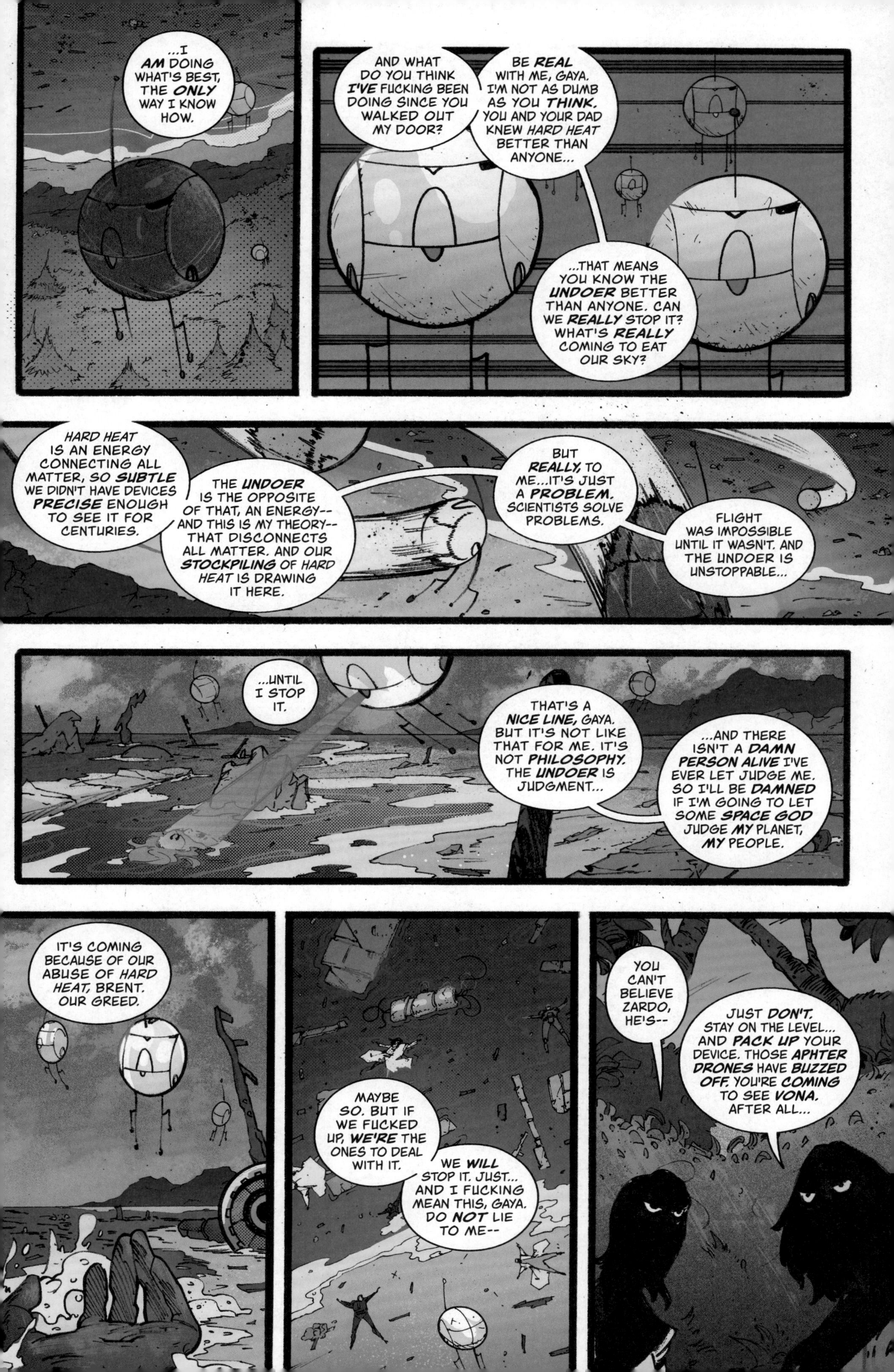
...I AM DOING WHAT'S BEST, THE ONLY WAY I KNOW HOW.
AND WHAT DO YOU THINK I'VE FUCKING BEEN DOING SINCE YOU WALKED OUT MY DOOR?
BE REAL WITH ME, GAYA. I'M NOT AS DUMB AS YOU THINK. YOU AND YOUR DAD KNEW HARD HEAT BETTER THAN ANYONE...
...THAT MEANS YOU KNOW THE UNDOER BETTER THAN ANYONE. CAN WE REALLY STOP IT? WHAT'S REALLY COMING TO EAT OUR SKY?
HARD HEAT IS AN ENERGY CONNECTING ALL MATTER, SO SUBTLE WE DIDN'T HAVE DEVICES PRECISE ENOUGH TO SEE IT FOR CENTURIES.
THE UNDOER IS THE OPPOSITE OF THAT, AN ENERGY-- AND THIS IS MY THEORY-- THAT DISCONNECTS ALL MATTER. AND OUR STOCKPILING OF HARD HEAT IS DRAWING IT HERE.
BUT REALLY, TO ME...IT'S JUST A PROBLEM. SCIENTISTS SOLVE PROBLEMS.
FLIGHT WAS IMPOSSIBLE UNTIL IT WASN'T. AND THE UNDOER IS UNSTOPPABLE...
...UNTIL I STOP IT.
THAT'S A NICE LINE, GAYA. BUT IT'S NOT LIKE THAT FOR ME. IT'S NOT PHILOSOPHY. THE UNDOER IS JUDGMENT...
...AND THERE ISN'T A DAMN PERSON ALIVE I'VE EVER LET JUDGE ME. SO I'LL BE DAMNED IF I'M GOING TO LET SOME SPACE GOD JUDGE MY PLANET, MY PEOPLE.
IT'S COMING BECAUSE OF OUR ABUSE OF HARD HEAT, BRENT. OUR GREED.
MAYBE SO. BUT IF WE FUCKED UP, WE'RE THE ONES TO DEAL WITH IT.
WE WILL STOP IT. JUST... AND I FUCKING MEAN THIS, GAYA. DO NOT LIE TO ME--
YOU CAN'T BELIEVE ZARDO, HE'S--
JUST DON'T. STAY ON THE LEVEL... AND PACK UP YOUR DEVICE. THOSE APHTER DRONES HAVE BUZZED OFF. YOU'RE COMING TO SEE VONA. AFTER ALL...

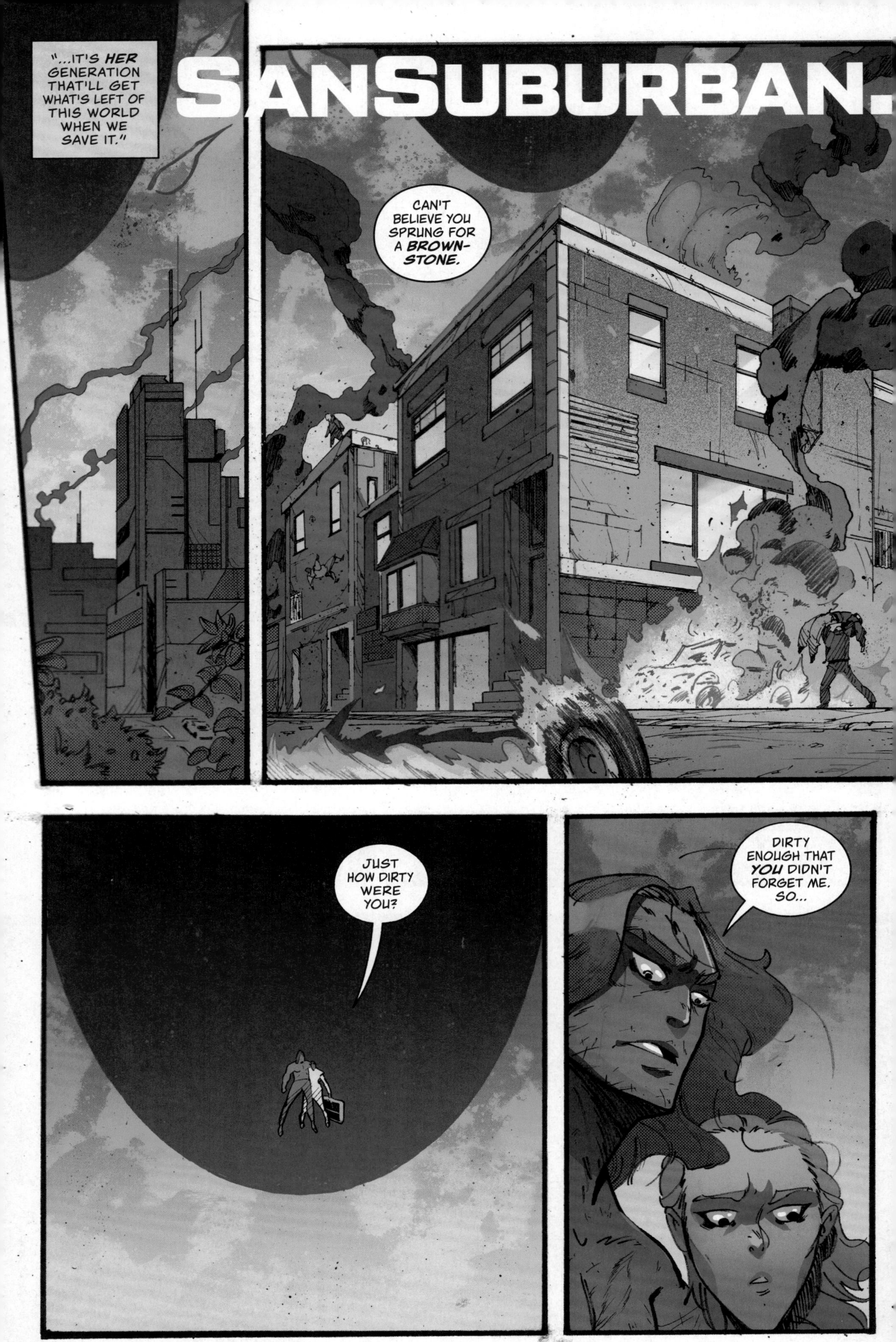
"...IT'S HER GENERATION THAT'LL GET WHAT'S LEFT OF THIS WORLD WHEN WE SAVE IT."
SANSUBURBAN.
CAN'T BELIEVE YOU SPRUNG FOR A BROWN-STONE.
JUST HOW DIRTY WERE YOU?
DIRTY ENOUGH THAT YOU DIDN'T FORGET ME. SO...

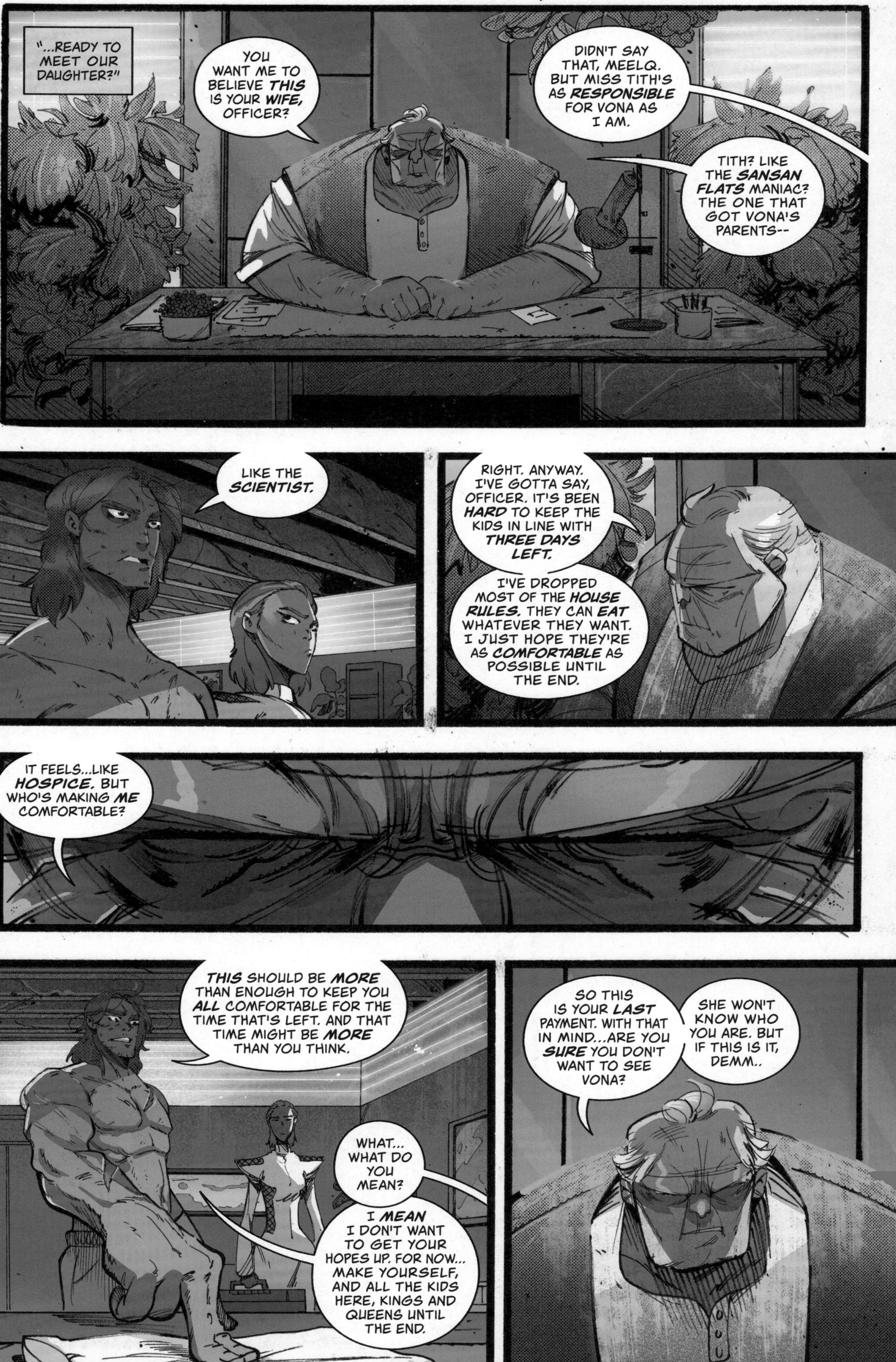
"...READY TO MEET OUR DAUGHTER?"
YOU WANT ME TO BELIEVE THIS IS YOUR WIFE, OFFICER?
DIDN'T SAY THAT, MEELQ. BUT MISS TITH'S AS RESPONSIBLE FOR VONA AS I AM.
TITH? LIKE THE SANSAN FLATS MANIAC? THE ONE THAT GOT VONA'S PARENTS--
LIKE THE SCIENTIST.
RIGHT. ANYWAY. I'VE GOTTA SAY, OFFICER. IT'S BEEN HARD TO KEEP THE KIDS IN LINE WITH THREE DAYS LEFT.
I'VE DROPPED MOST OF THE HOUSE RULES. THEY CAN EAT WHATEVER THEY WANT. I JUST HOPE THEY'RE AS COMFORTABLE AS POSSIBLE UNTIL THE END.
IT FEELS...LIKE HOSPICE. BUT WHO'S MAKING ME COMFORTABLE?
THIS SHOULD BE MORE THAN ENOUGH TO KEEP YOU ALL COMFORTABLE FOR THE TIME THAT'S LEFT. AND THAT TIME MIGHT BE MORE THAN YOU THINK.
WHAT... WHAT DO YOU MEAN?
I MEAN I DON'T WANT TO GET YOUR HOPES UP. FOR NOW... MAKE YOURSELF, AND ALL THE KIDS HERE, KINGS AND QUEENS UNTIL THE END.
SO THIS IS YOUR LAST PAYMENT. WITH THAT IN MIND...ARE YOU SURE YOU DON'T WANT TO SEE VONA?
SHE WON'T KNOW WHO YOU ARE. BUT IF THIS IS IT, DEMM..

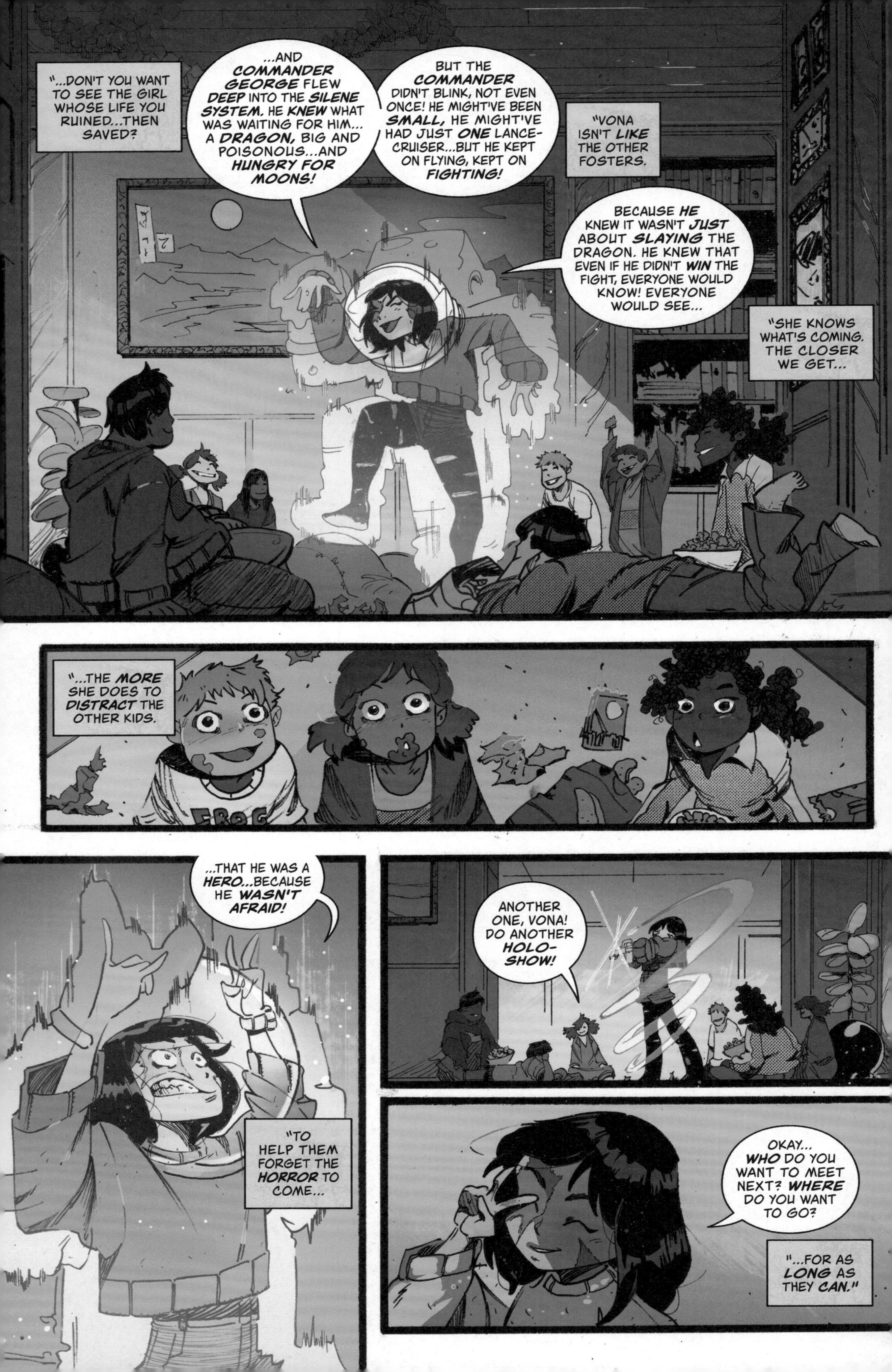
"...DON'T YOU WANT TO SEE THE GIRL WHOSE LIFE YOU RUINED...THEN SAVED?
...AND COMMANDER GEORGE FLEW DEEP INTO THE SILENE SYSTEM. HE KNEW WHAT WAS WAITING FOR HIM... A DRAGON, BIG AND POISONOUS...AND HUNGRY FOR MOONS!
BUT THE COMMANDER DIDN'T BLINK, NOT EVEN ONCE! HE MIGHT'VE BEEN SMALL, HE MIGHT'VE HAD JUST ONE LANCE-CRUISER...BUT HE KEPT ON FLYING, KEPT ON FIGHTING!
"VONA ISN'T LIKE THE OTHER FOSTERS.
BECAUSE HE KNEW IT WASN'T JUST ABOUT SLAYING THE DRAGON. HE KNEW THAT EVEN IF HE DIDN'T WIN THE FIGHT, EVERYONE WOULD KNOW! EVERYONE WOULD SEE...
"SHE KNOWS WHAT'S COMING. THE CLOSER WE GET...
"...THE MORE SHE DOES TO DISTRACT THE OTHER KIDS.
FROG
...THAT HE WAS A HERO...BECAUSE HE WASN'T AFRAID!
"TO HELP THEM FORGET THE HORROR TO COME...
ANOTHER ONE, VONA! DO ANOTHER HOLO-SHOW!
OKAY... WHO DO YOU WANT TO MEET NEXT? WHERE DO YOU WANT TO GO?
"...FOR AS LONG AS THEY CAN."

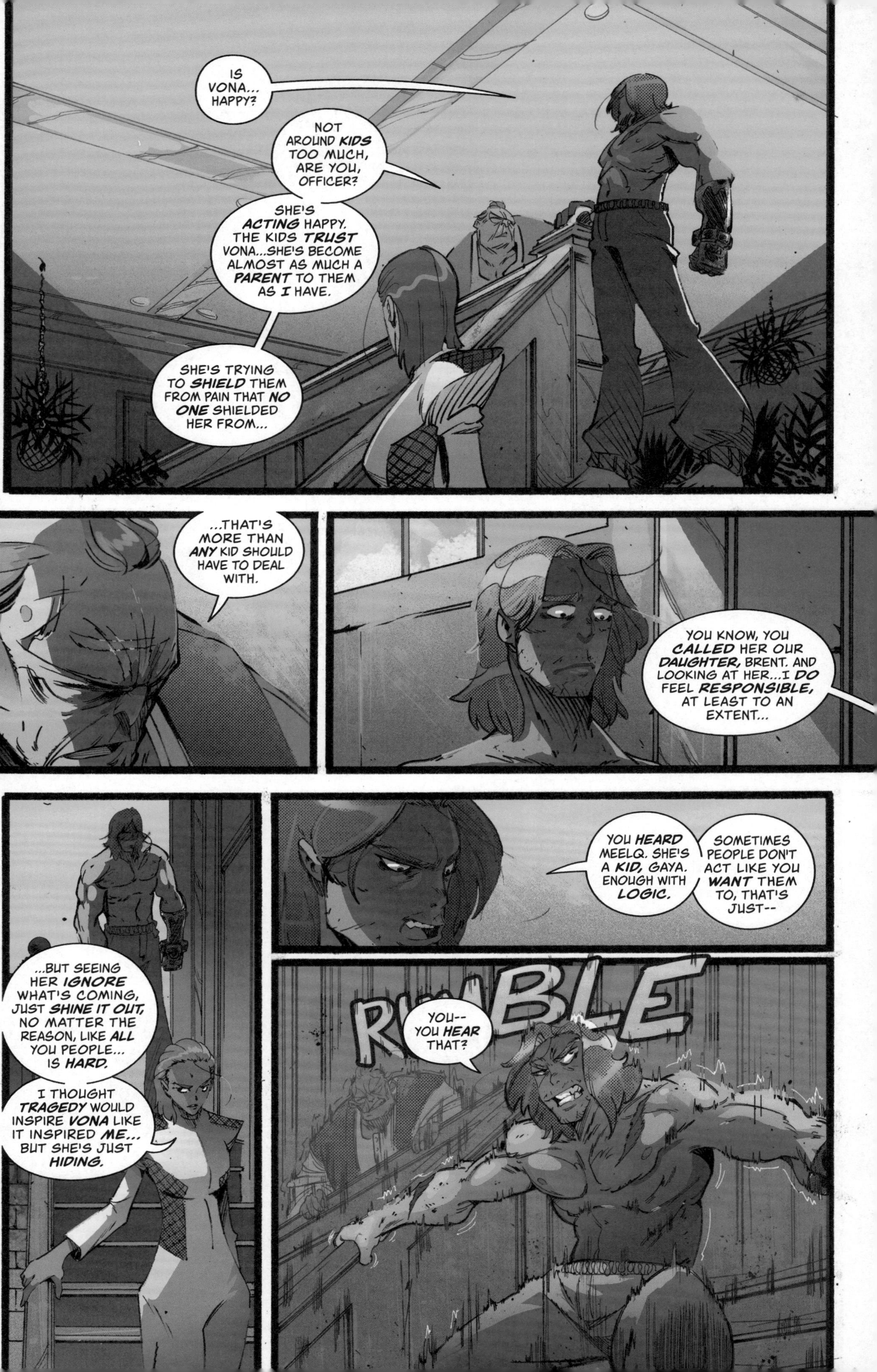
IS VONA... HAPPY?
NOT AROUND KIDS TOO MUCH, ARE YOU, OFFICER?
SHE'S ACTING HAPPY. THE KIDS TRUST VONA...SHE'S BECOME ALMOST AS MUCH A PARENT TO THEM AS I HAVE.
SHE'S TRYING TO SHIELD THEM FROM PAIN THAT NO ONE SHIELDED HER FROM...
...THAT'S MORE THAN ANY KID SHOULD HAVE TO DEAL WITH.
YOU KNOW, YOU CALLED HER OUR DAUGHTER, BRENT. AND LOOKING AT HER...I DO FEEL RESPONSIBLE, AT LEAST TO AN EXTENT...
...BUT SEEING HER IGNORE WHAT'S COMING, JUST SHINE IT OUT, NO MATTER THE REASON, LIKE ALL YOU PEOPLE... IS HARD.
I THOUGHT TRAGEDY WOULD INSPIRE VONA LIKE IT INSPIRED ME... BUT SHE'S JUST HIDING.
YOU HEARD MEELQ. SHE'S A KID, GAYA. ENOUGH WITH LOGIC.
SOMETIMES PEOPLE DON'T ACT LIKE YOU WANT THEM TO, THAT'S JUST--
YOU-- YOU HEAR THAT?

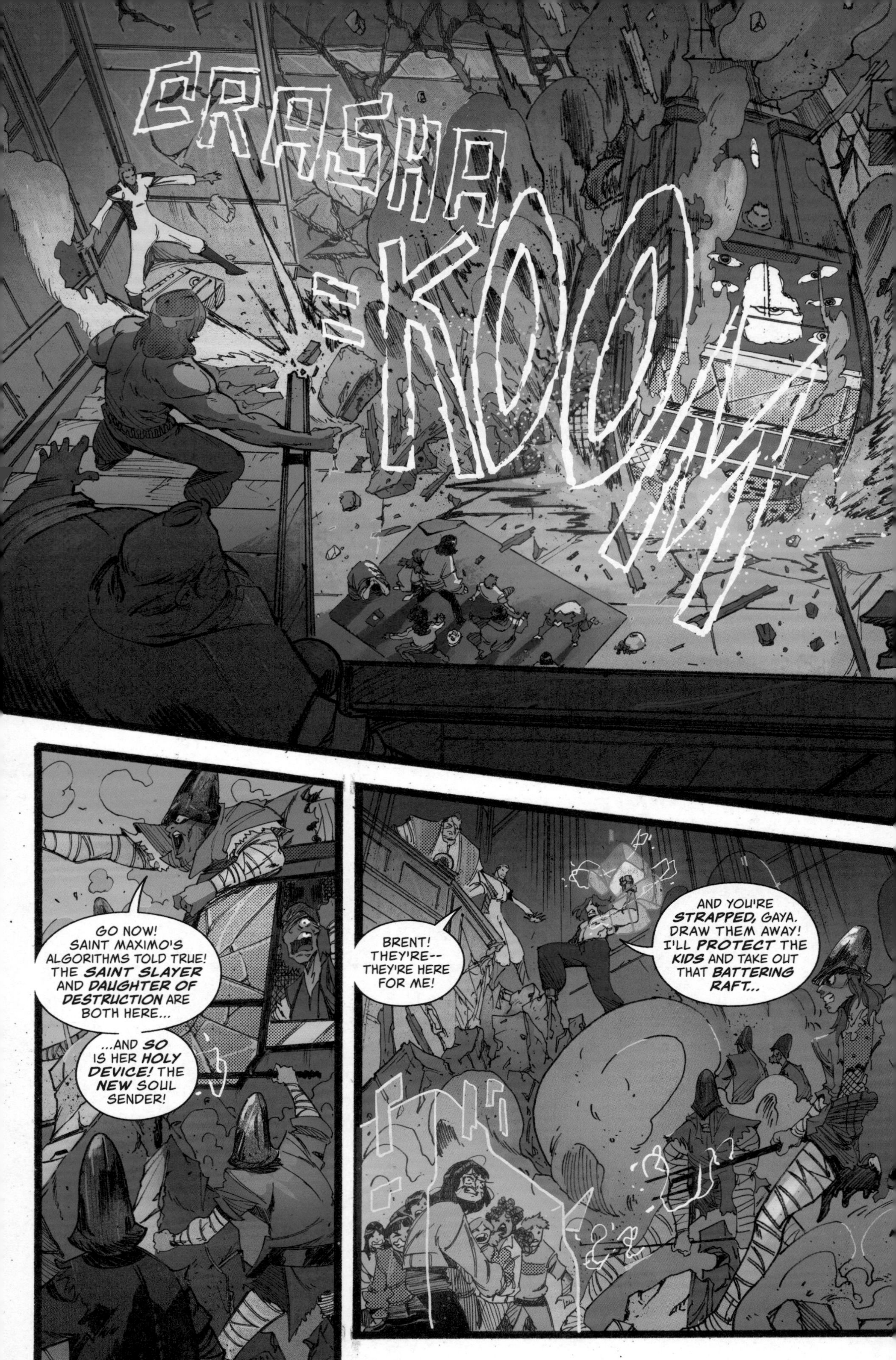
CRASHA-KOOM!
GO NOW! SAINT MAXIMO'S ALGORITHMS TOLD TRUE! THE SAINT SLAYER AND DAUGHTER OF DESTRUCTION ARE BOTH HERE...
...AND SO IS HER HOLY DEVICE! THE NEW SOUL SENDER!
BRENT! THEY'RE-- THEY'RE HERE FOR ME!
AND YOU'RE STRAPPED, GAYA. DRAW THEM AWAY! I'LL PROTECT THE KIDS AND TAKE OUT THAT BATTERING RAFT...

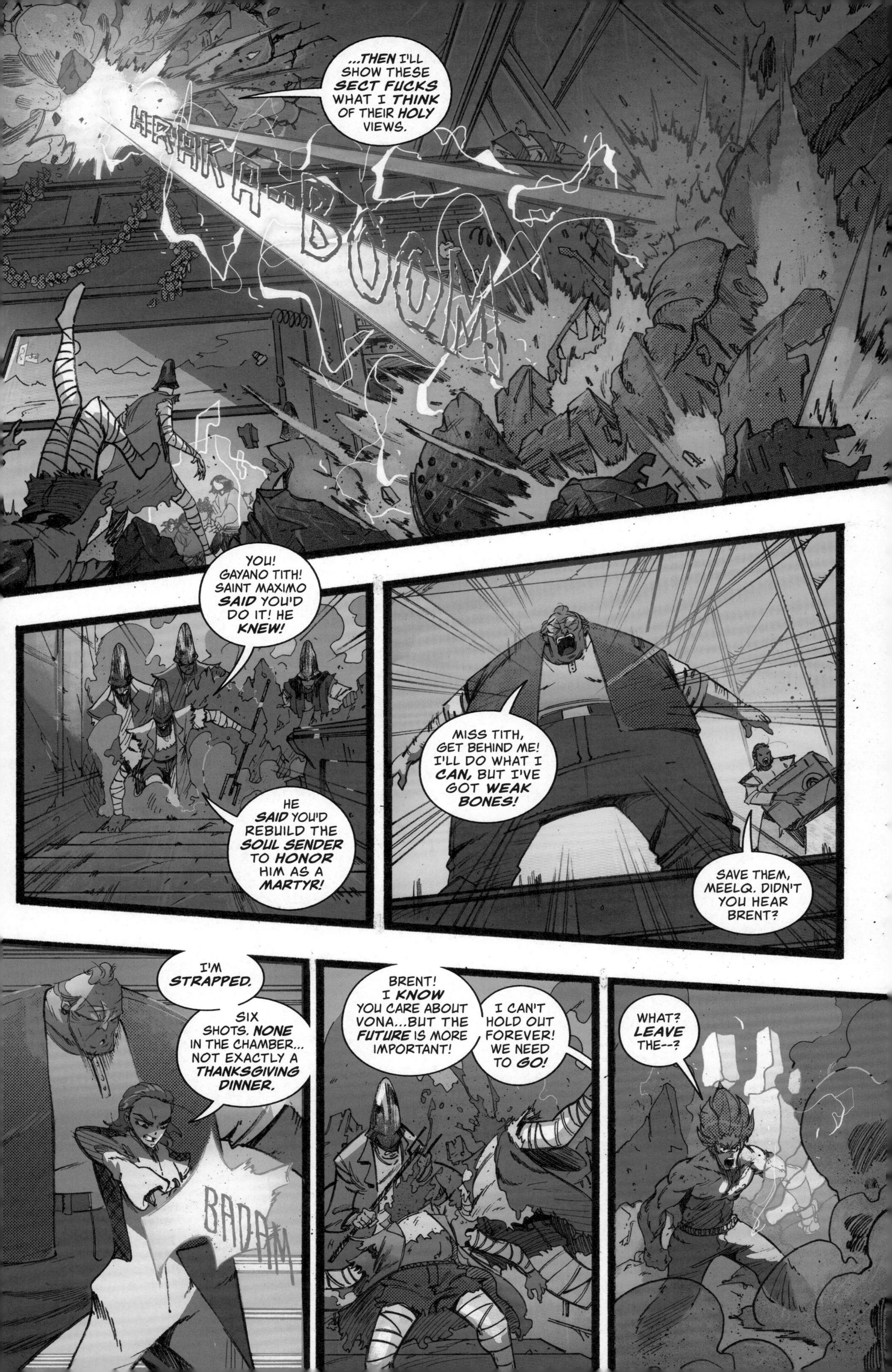
...THEN I'LL SHOW THESE SECT FUCKS WHAT I THINK OF THEIR HOLY VIEWS.
HRAKA-BOOM
YOU! GAYANO TITH! SAINT MAXIMO SAID YOU'D DO IT! HE KNEW!
HE SAID YOU'D REBUILD THE SOUL SENDER TO HONOR HIM AS A MARTYR!
MISS TITH, GET BEHIND ME! I'LL DO WHAT I CAN, BUT I'VE GOT WEAK BONES!
SAVE THEM, MEELQ. DIDN'T YOU HEAR BRENT?
I'M STRAPPED.
SIX SHOTS. NONE IN THE CHAMBER... NOT EXACTLY A THANKSGIVING DINNER.
BADAAM
BRENT! I KNOW YOU CARE ABOUT VONA...BUT THE FUTURE IS MORE IMPORTANT!
I CAN'T HOLD OUT FOREVER! WE NEED TO GO!
WHAT? LEAVE THE--?

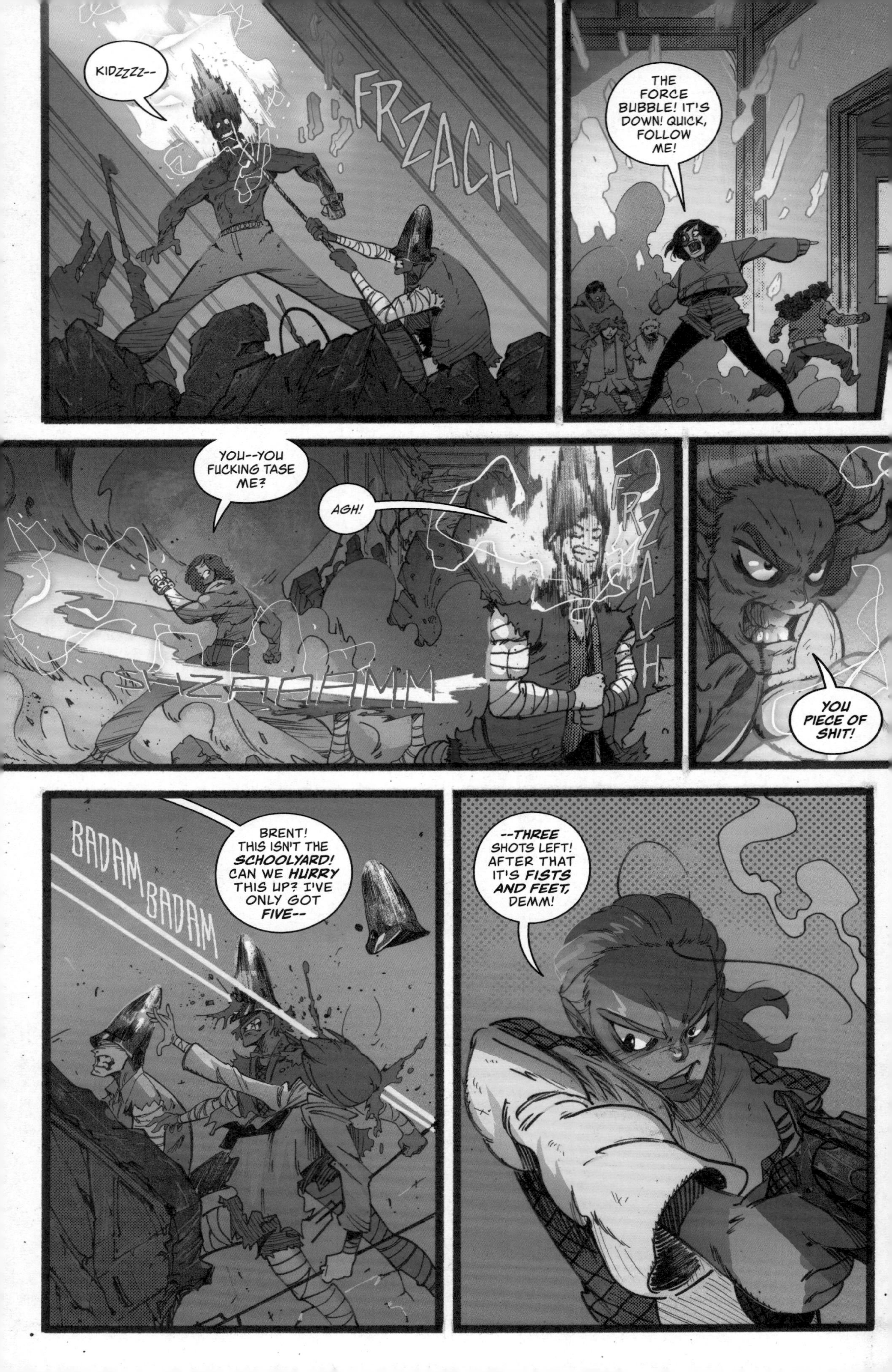
KIDZZZZ--
FRZACH
THE FORCE BUBBLE! IT'S DOWN! QUICK, FOLLOW ME!
YOU--YOU FUCKING TASE ME?
AGH!
FRZACH
SHZAAAAMM
YOU PIECE OF SHIT!
BADAM BADAM
BRENT! THIS ISN'T THE SCHOOLYARD! CAN WE HURRY THIS UP? I'VE ONLY GOT FIVE--
--THREE SHOTS LEFT! AFTER THAT IT'S FISTS AND FEET, DEMM!

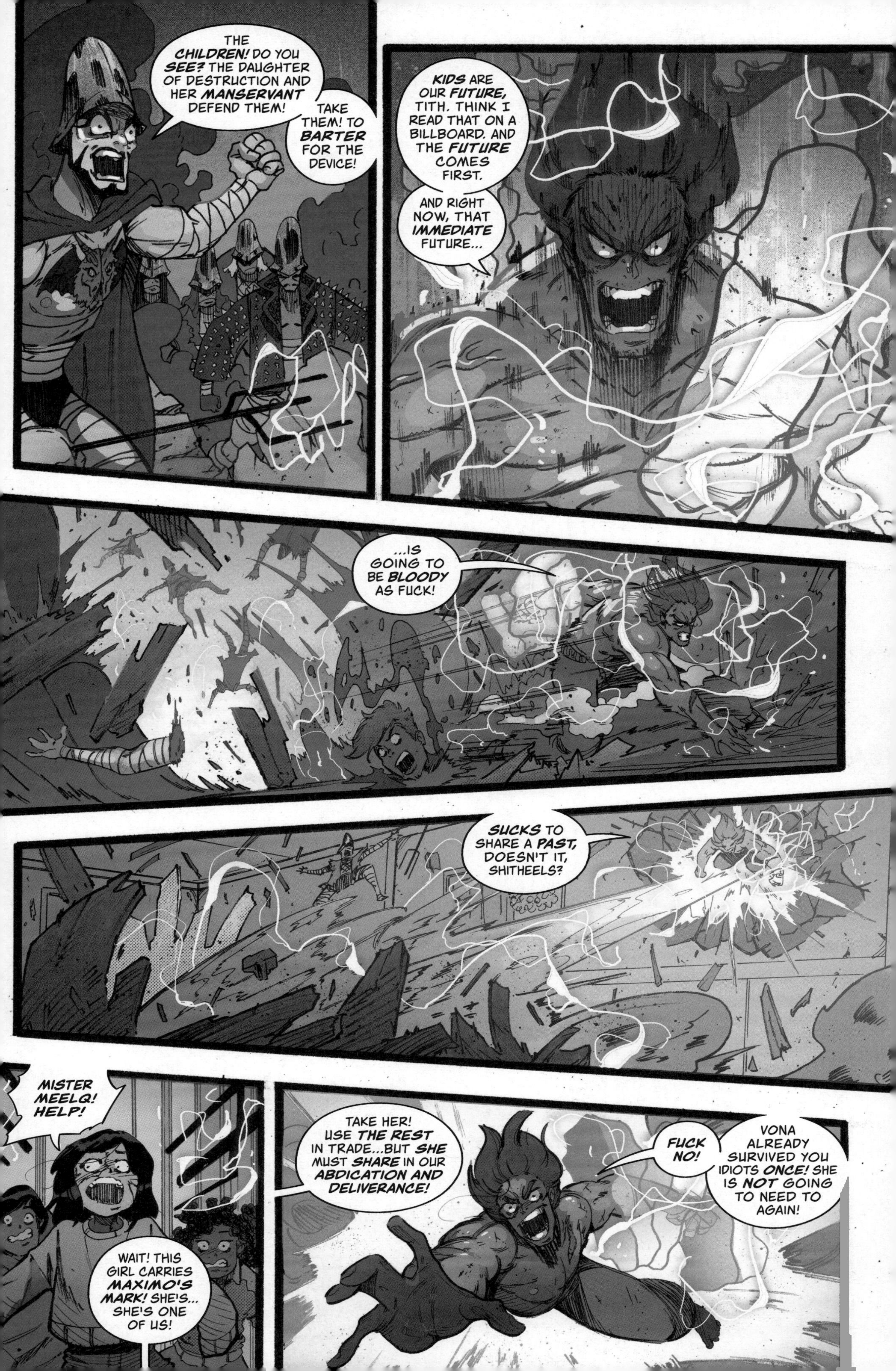
THE CHILDREN! DO YOU SEE? THE DAUGHTER OF DESTRUCTION AND HER MANSERVANT DEFEND THEM!
TAKE THEM! TO BARTER FOR THE DEVICE!
KIDS ARE OUR FUTURE, TITH. THINK I READ THAT ON A BILLBOARD. AND THE FUTURE COMES FIRST.
AND RIGHT NOW, THAT IMMEDIATE FUTURE...
...IS GOING TO BE BLOODY AS FUCK!
SUCKS TO SHARE A PAST, DOESN'T IT, SHITHEELS?
MISTER MEELQ! HELP!
WAIT! THIS GIRL CARRIES MAXIMO'S MARK! SHE'S... SHE'S ONE OF US!
TAKE HER! USE THE REST IN TRADE...BUT SHE MUST SHARE IN OUR ABDICATION AND DELIVERANCE!
FUCK NO!
VONA ALREADY SURVIVED YOU IDIOTS ONCE! SHE IS NOT GOING TO NEED TO AGAIN!

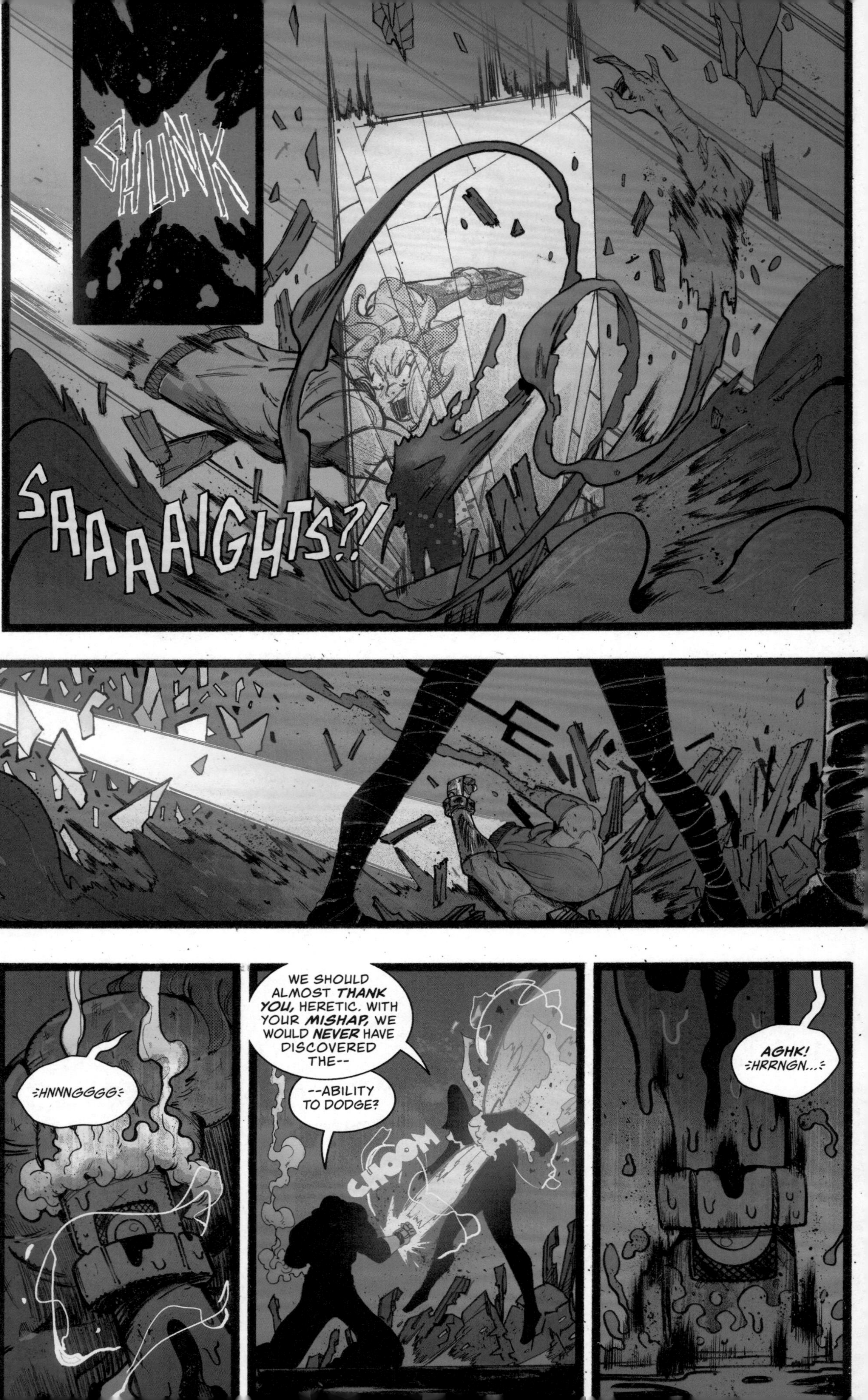
SHUNK
SRAAAIGHTS?!
HNNNGGGG
WE SHOULD ALMOST THANK YOU, HERETIC. WITH YOUR MISHAP, WE WOULD NEVER HAVE DISCOVERED THE--
--ABILITY TO DODGE?
CHOOM
AGHK! HRRNGN...

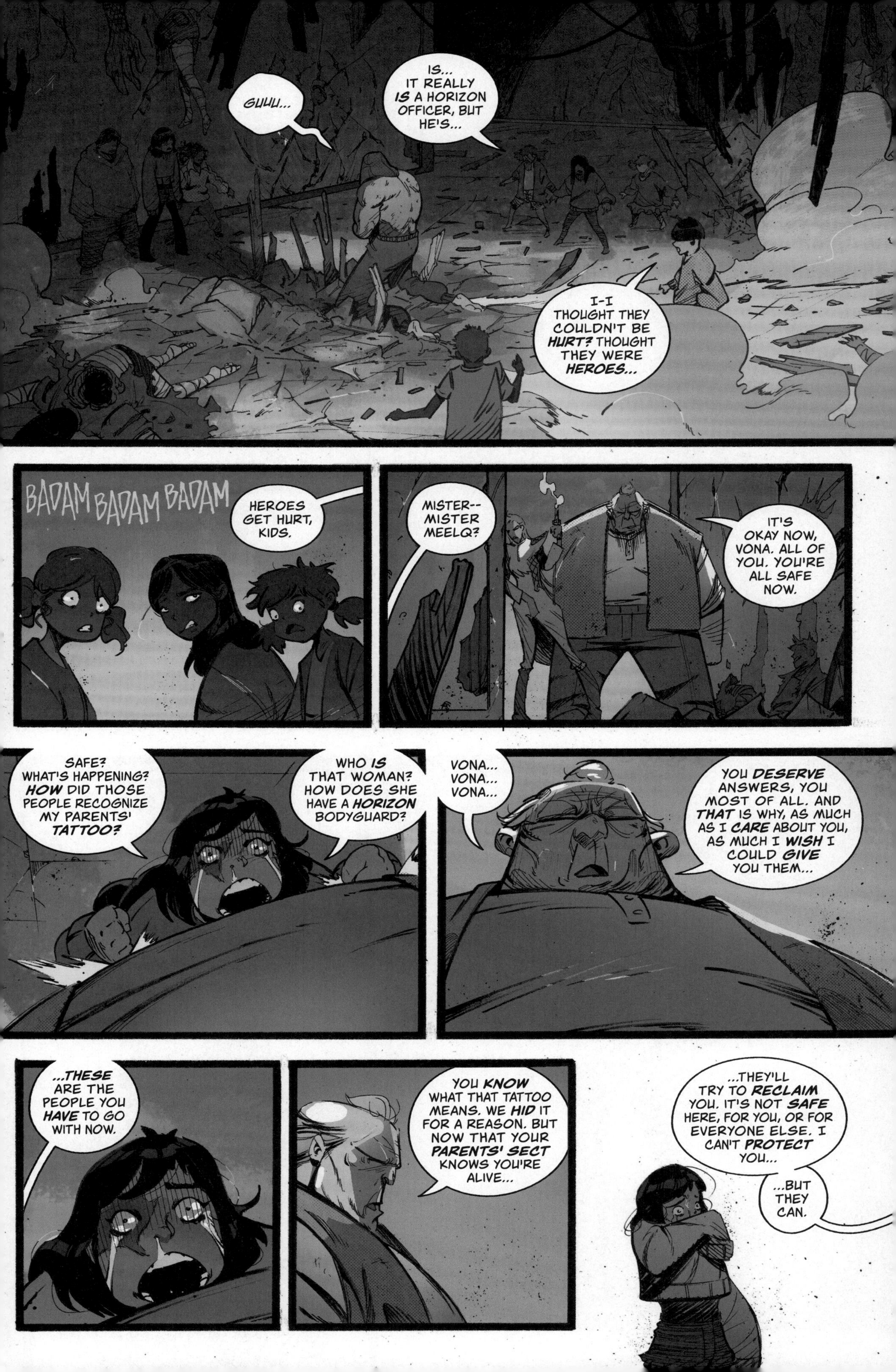
GUUU...
IS... IT REALLY IS A HORIZON OFFICER, BUT HE'S...
I-I THOUGHT THEY COULDN'T BE HURT? THOUGHT THEY WERE HEROES...
BADAM BADAM BADAM
HEROES GET HURT, KIDS.
MISTER-- MISTER MEELQ?
IT'S OKAY NOW, VONA. ALL OF YOU. YOU'RE ALL SAFE NOW.
SAFE? WHAT'S HAPPENING? HOW DID THOSE PEOPLE RECOGNIZE MY PARENTS' TATTOO?
WHO IS THAT WOMAN? HOW DOES SHE HAVE A HORIZON BODYGUARD?
VONA... VONA... VONA...
YOU DESERVE ANSWERS, YOU MOST OF ALL. AND THAT IS WHY, AS MUCH AS I CARE ABOUT YOU, AS MUCH I WISH I COULD GIVE YOU THEM...
...THESE ARE THE PEOPLE YOU HAVE TO GO WITH NOW.
YOU KNOW WHAT THAT TATTOO MEANS. WE HID IT FOR A REASON. BUT NOW THAT YOUR PARENTS' SECT KNOWS YOU'RE ALIVE...
...THEY'LL TRY TO RECLAIM YOU. IT'S NOT SAFE HERE, FOR YOU, OR FOR EVERYONE ELSE. I CAN'T PROTECT YOU...
...BUT THEY CAN.

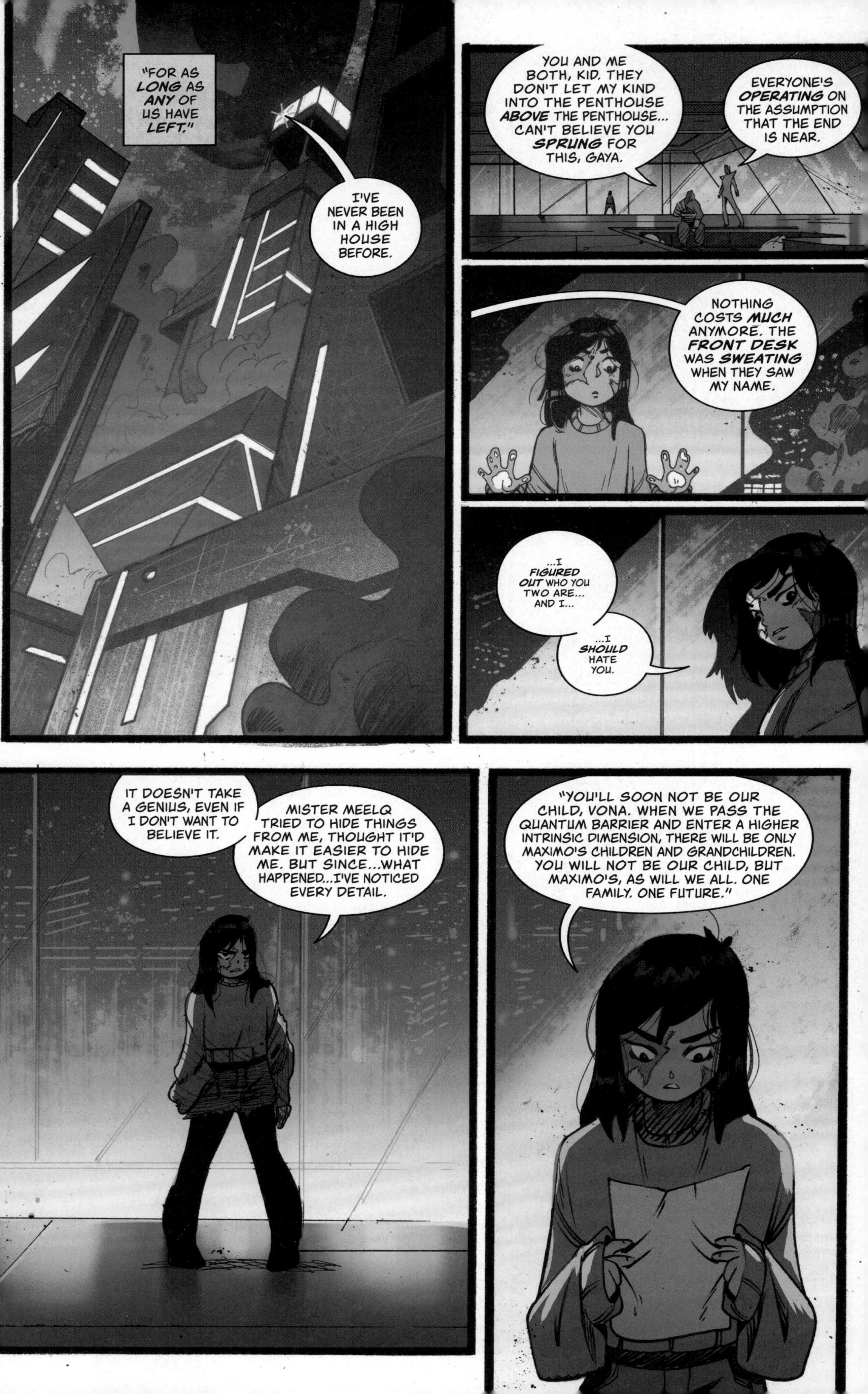
"FOR AS LONG AS ANY OF US HAVE LEFT."
I'VE NEVER BEEN IN A HIGH HOUSE BEFORE.
YOU AND ME BOTH, KID. THEY DON'T LET MY KIND INTO THE PENTHOUSE ABOVE THE PENTHOUSE... CAN'T BELIEVE YOU SPRUNG FOR THIS, GAYA.
EVERYONE'S OPERATING ON THE ASSUMPTION THAT THE END IS NEAR.
NOTHING COSTS MUCH ANYMORE. THE FRONT DESK WAS SWEATING WHEN THEY SAW MY NAME.
...I FIGURED OUT WHO YOU TWO ARE... AND I...
...I SHOULD HATE YOU.
IT DOESN'T TAKE A GENIUS, EVEN IF I DON'T WANT TO BELIEVE IT.
MISTER MEELQ TRIED TO HIDE THINGS FROM ME, THOUGHT IT'D MAKE IT EASIER TO HIDE ME. BUT SINCE...WHAT HAPPENED...I'VE NOTICED EVERY DETAIL.
"YOU'LL SOON NOT BE OUR CHILD, VONA. WHEN WE PASS THE QUANTUM BARRIER AND ENTER A HIGHER INTRINSIC DIMENSION, THERE WILL BE ONLY MAXIMO'S CHILDREN AND GRANDCHILDREN. YOU WILL NOT BE OUR CHILD, BUT MAXIMO'S, AS WILL WE ALL. ONE FAMILY. ONE FUTURE."

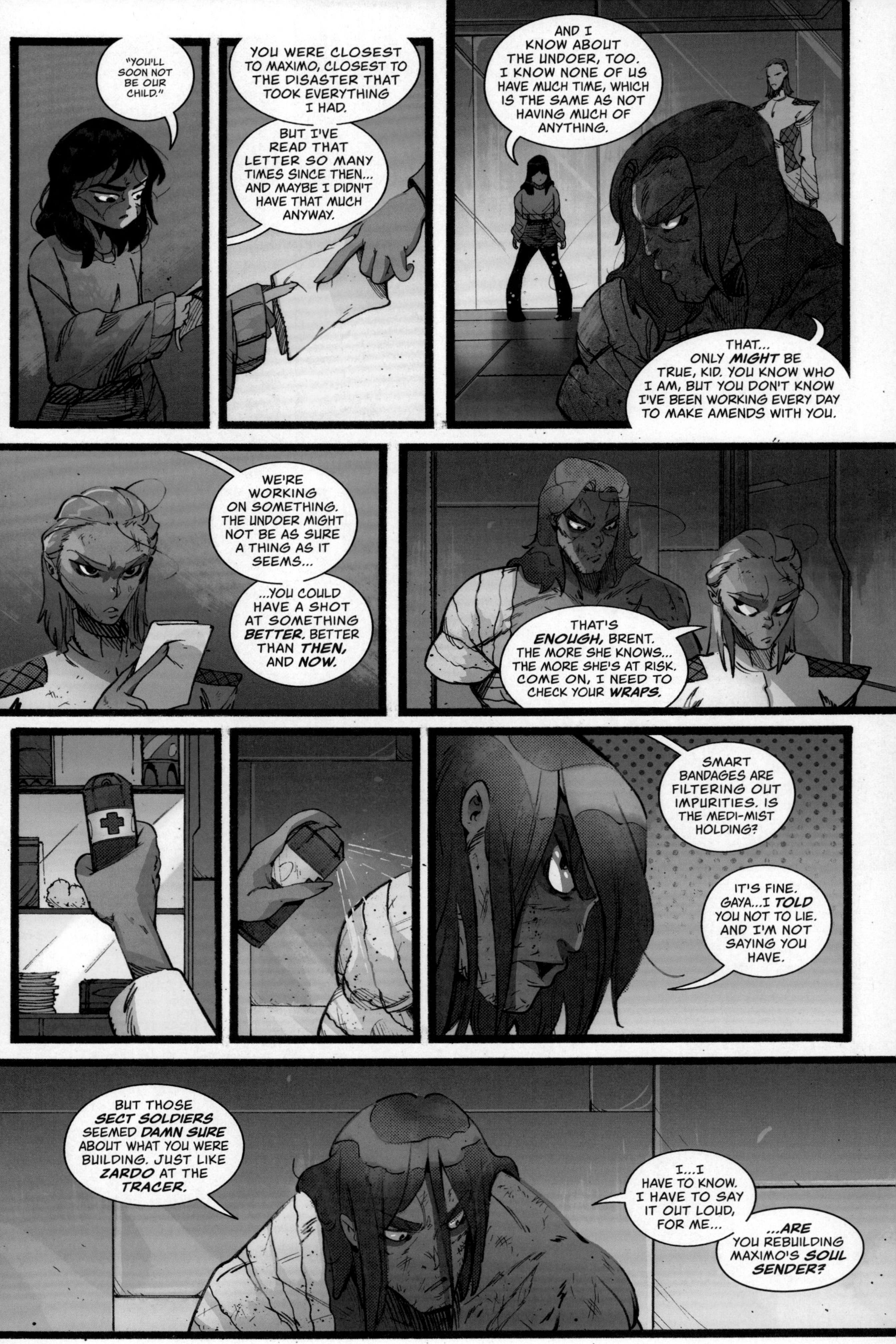
"YOU'LL SOON NOT BE OUR CHILD."
YOU WERE CLOSEST TO MAXIMO, CLOSEST TO THE DISASTER THAT TOOK EVERYTHING I HAD.
BUT I'VE READ THAT LETTER SO MANY TIMES SINCE THEN... AND MAYBE I DIDN'T HAVE THAT MUCH ANYWAY.
AND I KNOW ABOUT THE UNDOER, TOO. I KNOW NONE OF US HAVE MUCH TIME, WHICH IS THE SAME AS NOT HAVING MUCH OF ANYTHING.
THAT... ONLY MIGHT BE TRUE, KID. YOU KNOW WHO I AM, BUT YOU DON'T KNOW I'VE BEEN WORKING EVERY DAY TO MAKE AMENDS WITH YOU.
WE'RE WORKING ON SOMETHING. THE UNDOER MIGHT NOT BE AS SURE A THING AS IT SEEMS...
...YOU COULD HAVE A SHOT AT SOMETHING BETTER. BETTER THAN THEN, AND NOW.
THAT'S ENOUGH, BRENT. THE MORE SHE KNOWS... THE MORE SHE'S AT RISK. COME ON, I NEED TO CHECK YOUR WRAPS.
SMART BANDAGES ARE FILTERING OUT IMPURITIES. IS THE MEDI-MIST HOLDING?
IT'S FINE. GAYA...I TOLD YOU NOT TO LIE. AND I'M NOT SAYING YOU HAVE.
BUT THOSE SECT SOLDIERS SEEMED DAMN SURE ABOUT WHAT YOU WERE BUILDING. JUST LIKE ZARDO AT THE TRACER.
I...I HAVE TO KNOW. I HAVE TO SAY IT OUT LOUD, FOR ME...
...ARE YOU REBUILDING MAXIMO'S SOUL SENDER?

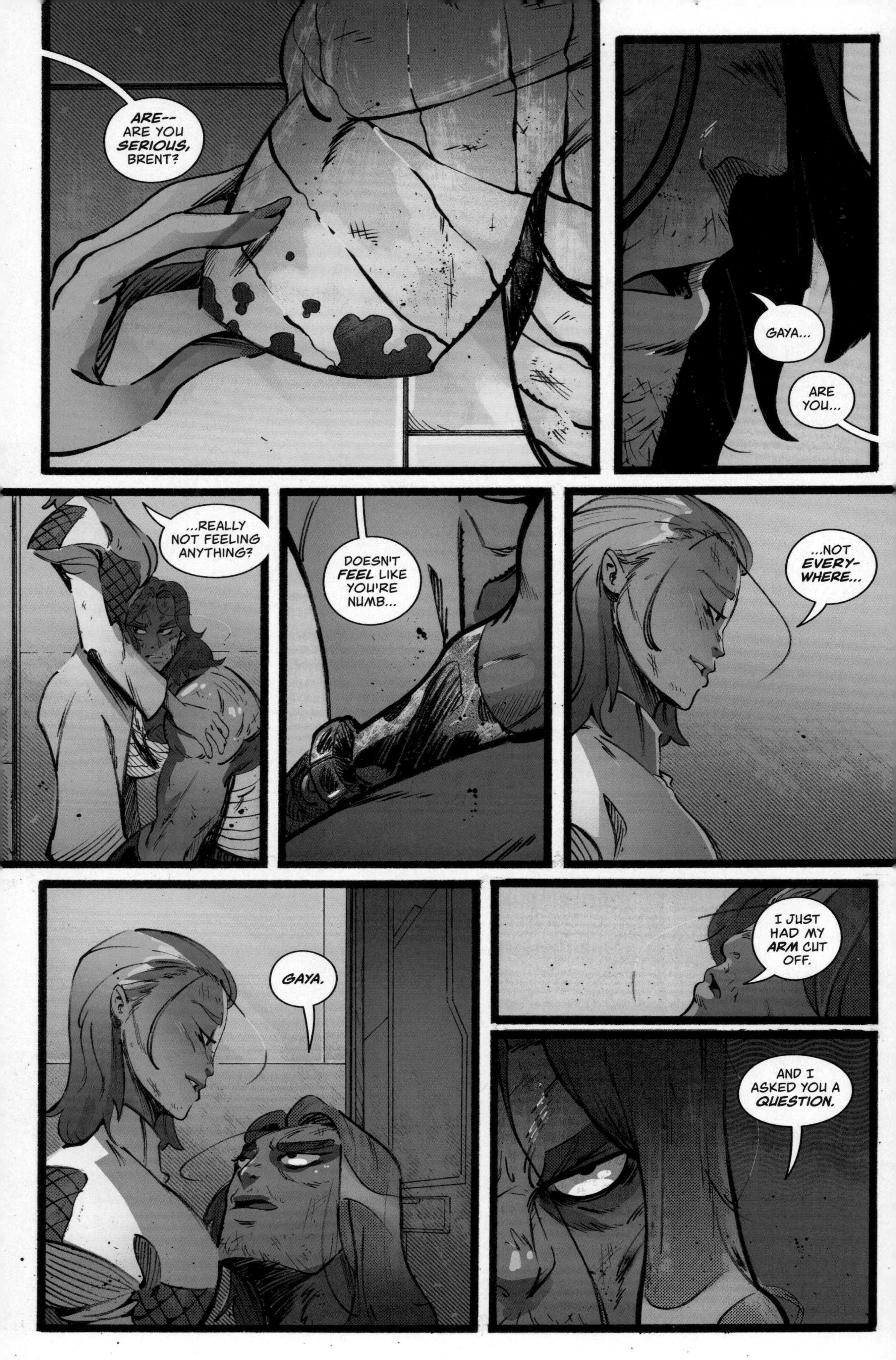
ARE--
ARE YOU SERIOUS, BRENT?
GAYA...
ARE YOU...
...REALLY NOT FEELING ANYTHING?
DOESN'T FEEL LIKE YOU'RE NUMB...
...NOT EVERY-WHERE...
GAYA.
I JUST HAD MY ARM CUT OFF.
AND I ASKED YOU A QUESTION.

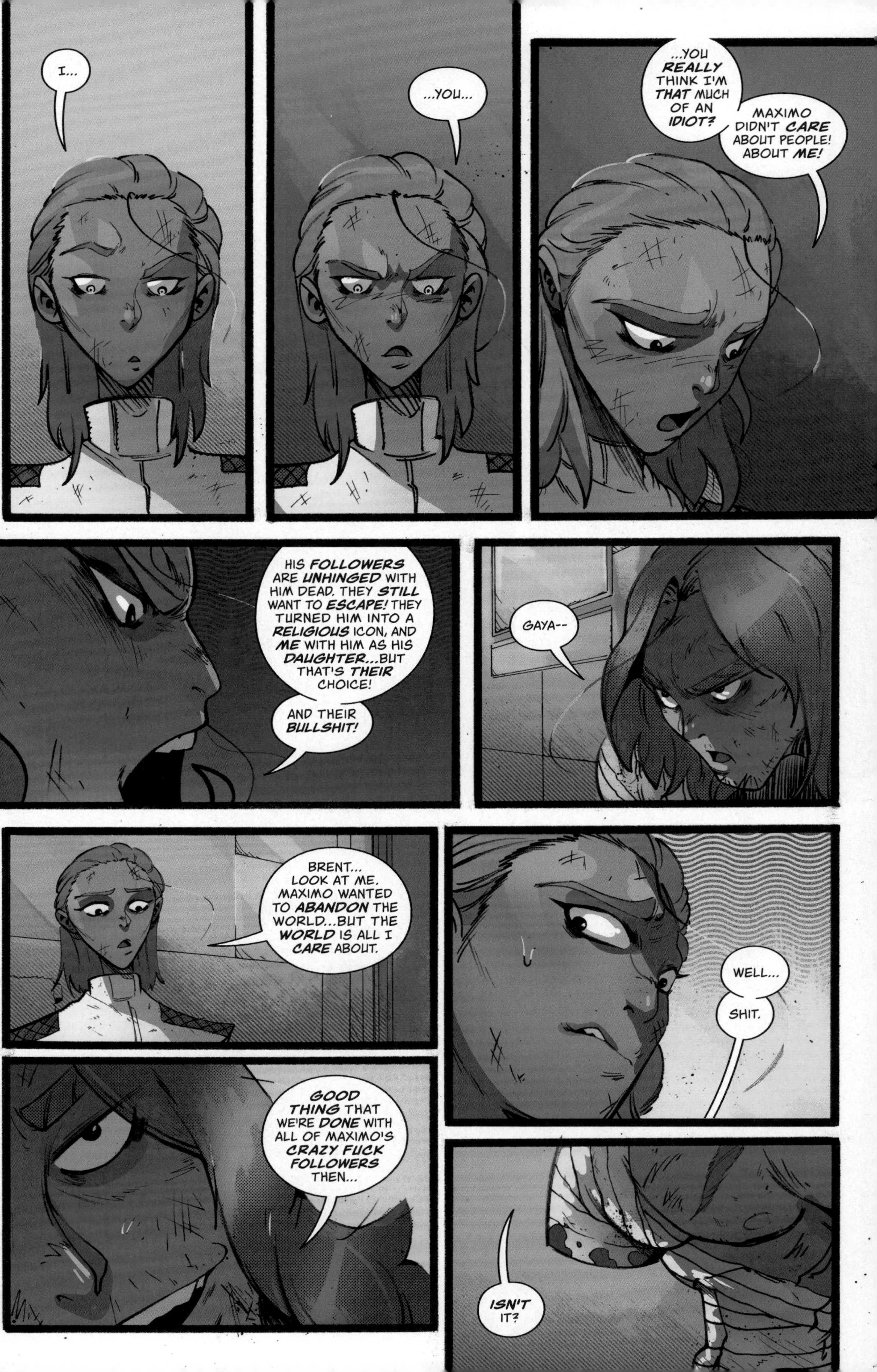
I...
...YOU...
...YOU REALLY THINK I'M THAT MUCH OF AN IDIOT?
MAXIMO DIDN'T CARE ABOUT PEOPLE! ABOUT ME!
HIS FOLLOWERS ARE UNHINGED WITH HIM DEAD. THEY STILL WANT TO ESCAPE! THEY TURNED HIM INTO A RELIGIOUS ICON, AND ME WITH HIM AS HIS DAUGHTER...BUT THAT'S THEIR CHOICE!
AND THEIR BULLSHIT!
GAYA--
BRENT... LOOK AT ME. MAXIMO WANTED TO ABANDON THE WORLD...BUT THE WORLD IS ALL I CARE ABOUT.
WELL...
SHIT.
GOOD THING THAT WE'RE DONE WITH ALL OF MAXIMO'S CRAZY FUCK FOLLOWERS THEN...
ISN'T IT?

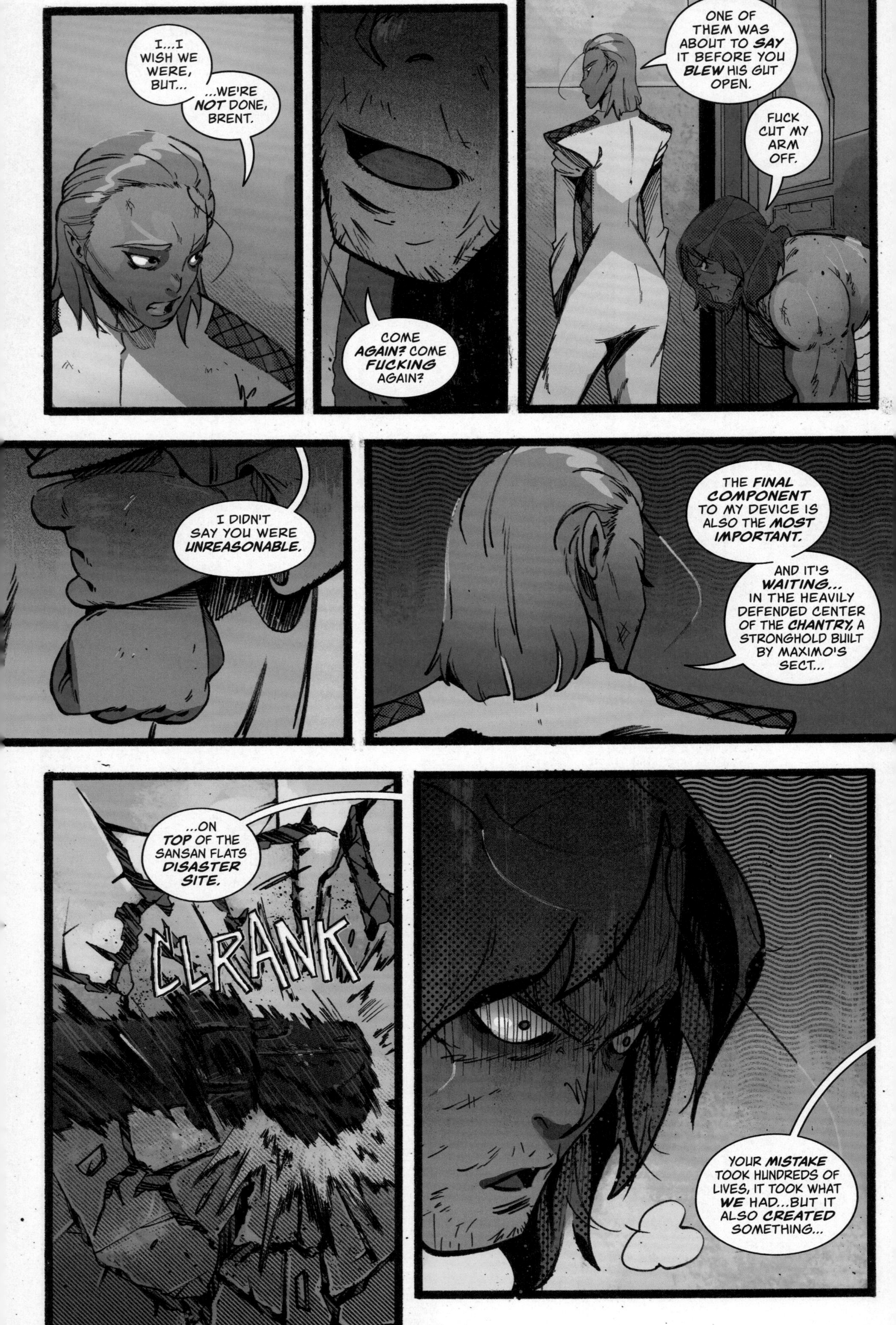
I...I WISH WE WERE, BUT...
...WE'RE NOT DONE, BRENT.
COME AGAIN? COME FUCKING AGAIN?
ONE OF THEM WAS ABOUT TO SAY IT BEFORE YOU BLEW HIS GUT OPEN.
FUCK CUT MY ARM OFF.
I DIDN'T SAY YOU WERE UNREASONABLE.
THE FINAL COMPONENT TO MY DEVICE IS ALSO THE MOST IMPORTANT.
AND IT'S WAITING... IN THE HEAVILY DEFENDED CENTER OF THE CHANTRY, A STRONGHOLD BUILT BY MAXIMO'S SECT...
...ON TOP OF THE SANSAN FLATS DISASTER SITE.
CLRANK
YOUR MISTAKE TOOK HUNDREDS OF LIVES, IT TOOK WHAT WE HAD...BUT IT ALSO CREATED SOMETHING...

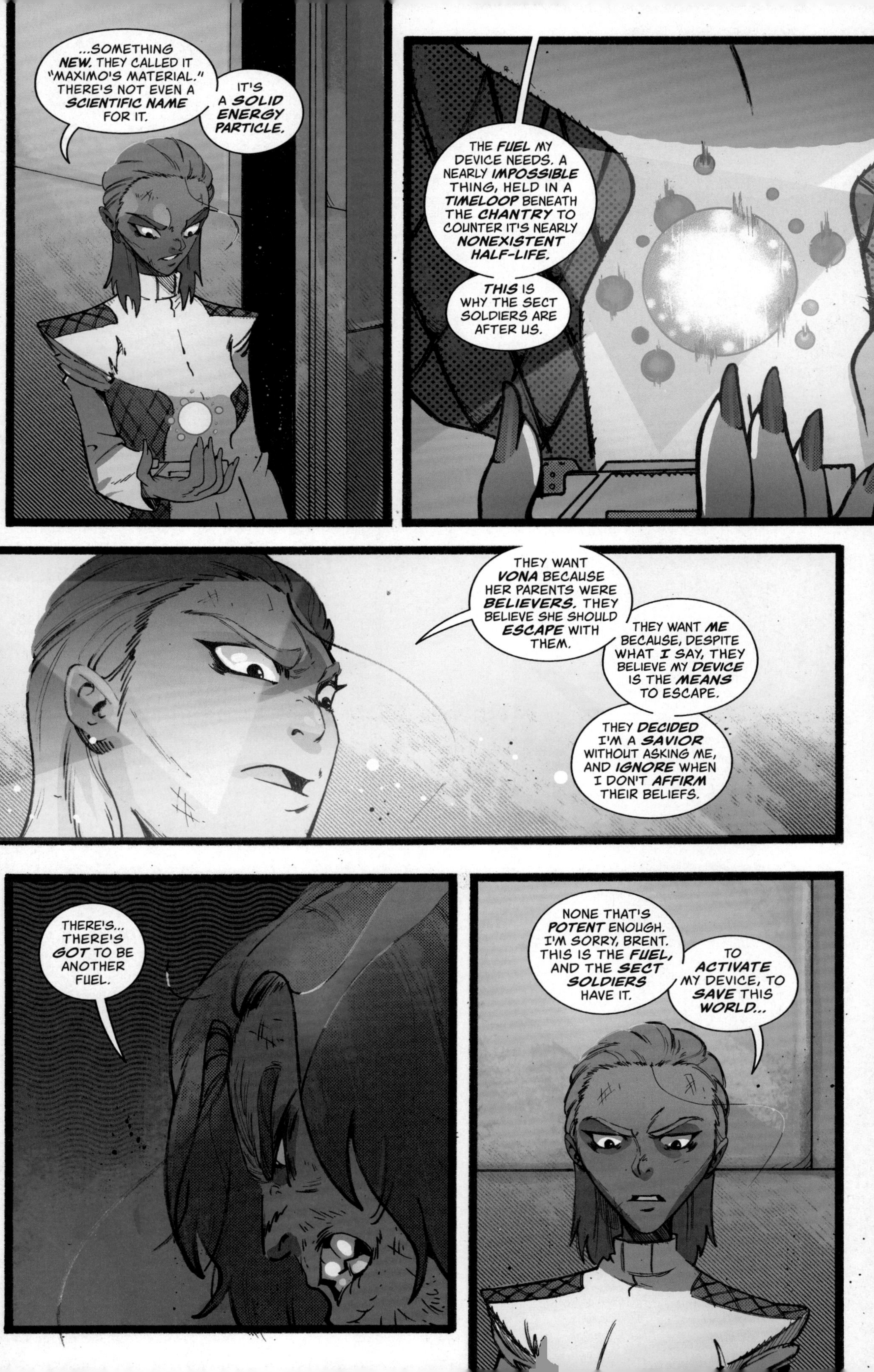
...SOMETHING NEW. THEY CALLED IT "MAXIMO'S MATERIAL." THERE'S NOT EVEN A SCIENTIFIC NAME FOR IT.
IT'S A SOLID ENERGY PARTICLE.
THE FUEL MY DEVICE NEEDS. A NEARLY IMPOSSIBLE THING, HELD IN A TIMELOOP BENEATH THE CHANTRY TO COUNTER IT'S NEARLY NONEXISTENT HALF-LIFE.
THIS IS WHY THE SECT SOLDIERS ARE AFTER US.
THEY WANT VONA BECAUSE HER PARENTS WERE BELIEVERS. THEY BELIEVE SHE SHOULD ESCAPE WITH THEM.
THEY WANT ME BECAUSE, DESPITE WHAT I SAY, THEY BELIEVE MY DEVICE IS THE MEANS TO ESCAPE.
THEY DECIDED I'M A SAVIOR WITHOUT ASKING ME, AND IGNORE WHEN I DON'T AFFIRM THEIR BELIEFS.
THERE'S... THERE'S GOT TO BE ANOTHER FUEL.
NONE THAT'S POTENT ENOUGH. I'M SORRY, BRENT. THIS IS THE FUEL, AND THE SECT SOLDIERS HAVE IT.
TO ACTIVATE MY DEVICE, TO SAVE THIS WORLD...

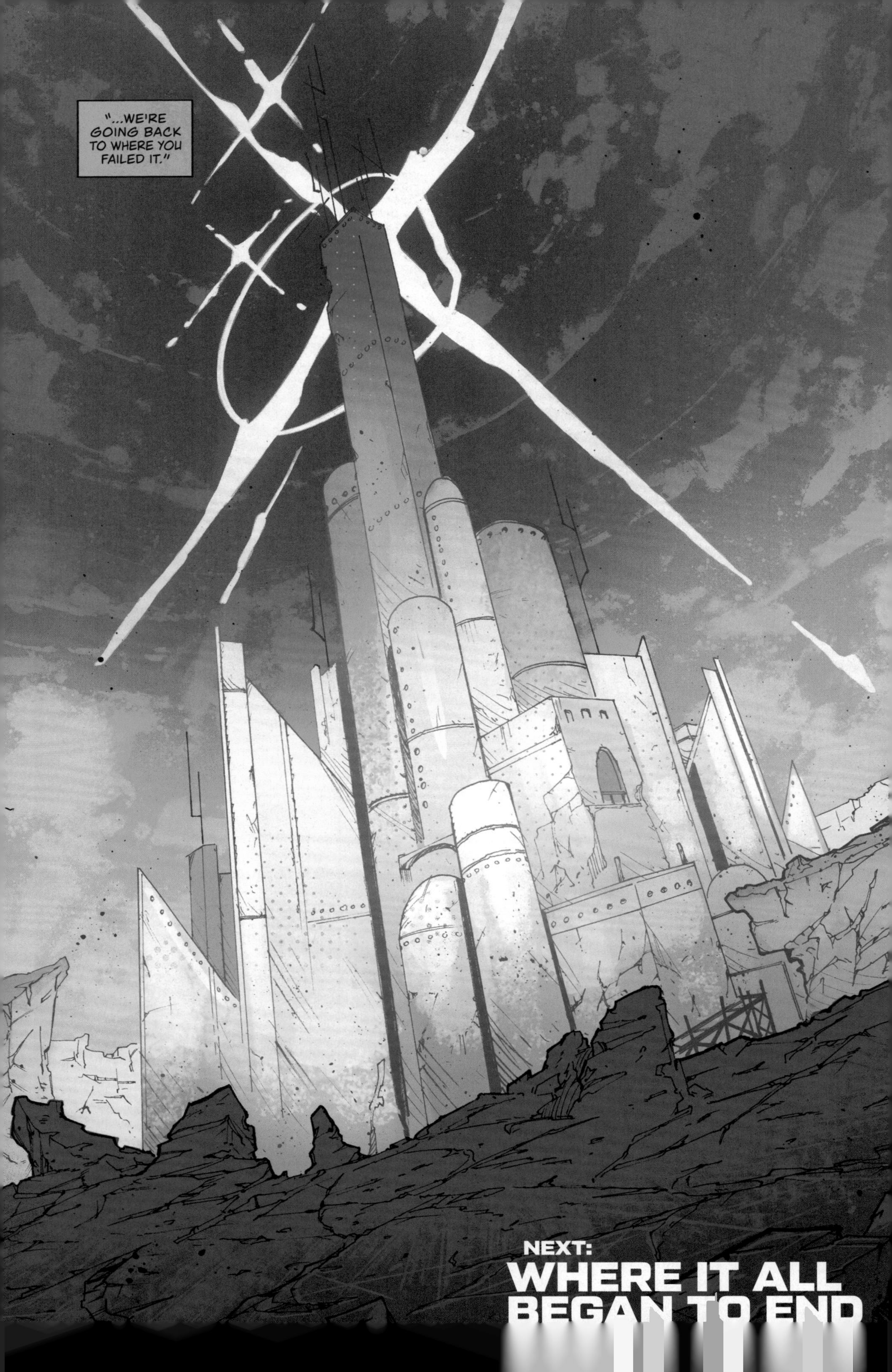
"...WE'RE GOING BACK TO WHERE YOU FAILED IT."
NEXT:
WHERE IT ALL BEGAN TO END

CHAPTER 5

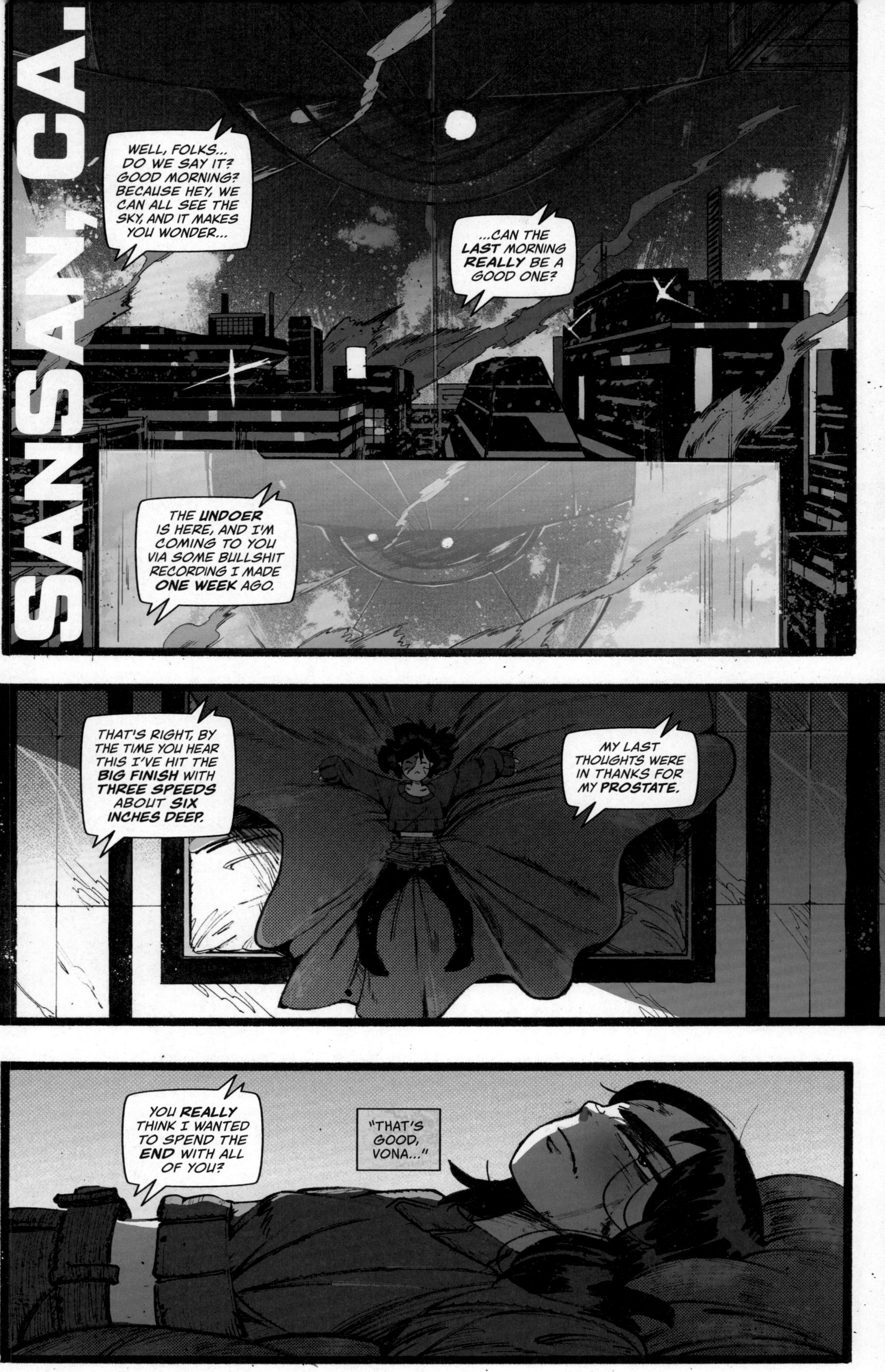
SAN, CA.
WELL, FOLKS... DO WE SAY IT? GOOD MORNING? BECAUSE HEY, WE CAN ALL SEE THE SKY, AND IT MAKES YOU WONDER...
...CAN THE LAST MORNING REALLY BE A GOOD ONE?
THE UNDOER IS HERE, AND I'M COMING TO YOU VIA SOME BULLSHIT RECORDING I MADE ONE WEEK AGO.
THAT'S RIGHT, BY THE TIME YOU HEAR THIS I'VE HIT THE BIG FINISH WITH THREE SPEEDS ABOUT SIX INCHES DEEP.
MY LAST THOUGHTS WERE IN THANKS FOR MY PROSTATE.
YOU REALLY THINK I WANTED TO SPEND THE END WITH ALL OF YOU?
"THAT'S GOOD, VONA..."

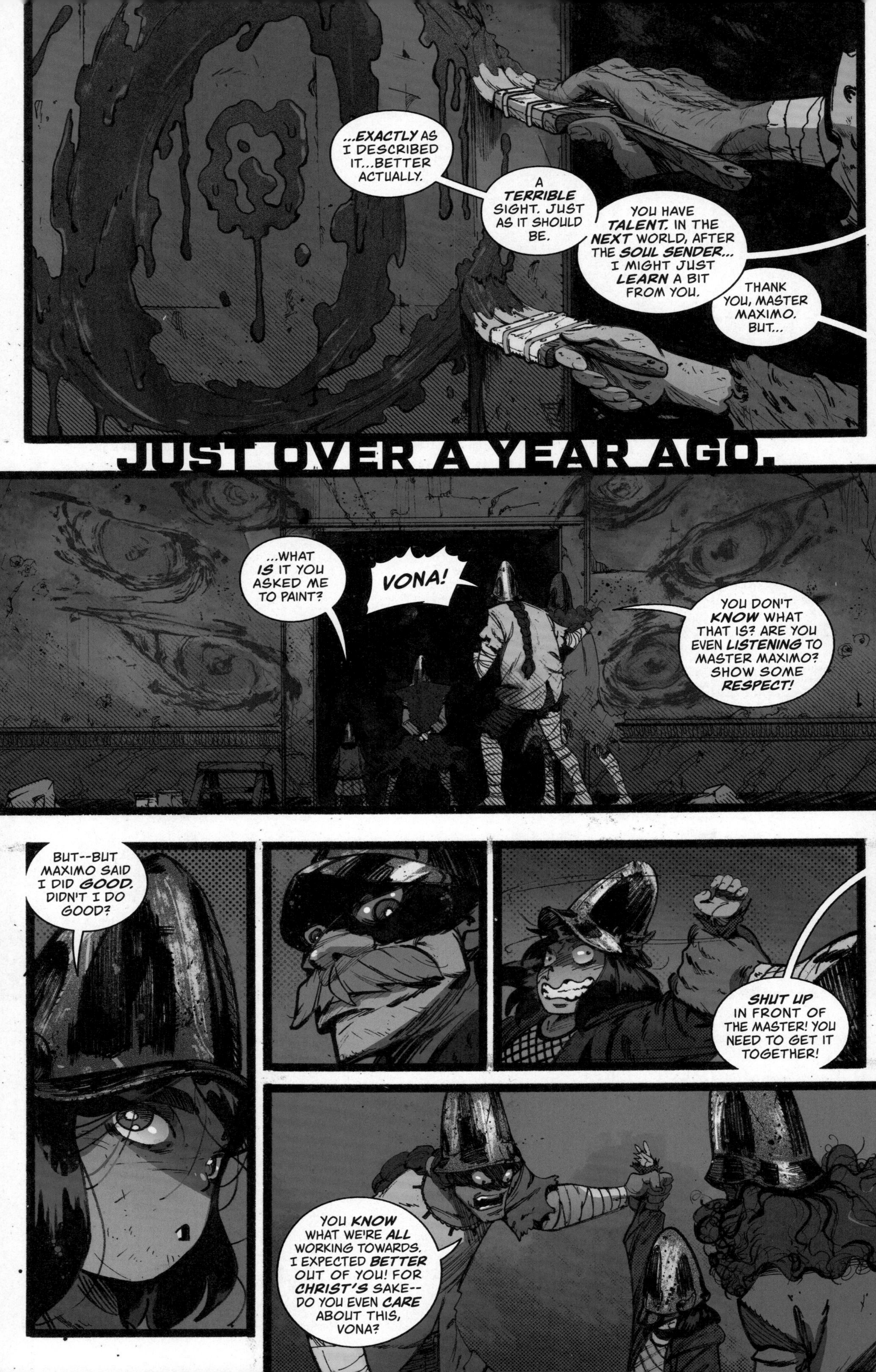
...EXACTLY AS I DESCRIBED IT...BETTER ACTUALLY.
A TERRIBLE SIGHT. JUST AS IT SHOULD BE.
YOU HAVE TALENT. IN THE NEXT WORLD, AFTER THE SOUL SENDER... I MIGHT JUST LEARN A BIT FROM YOU.
THANK YOU, MASTER MAXIMO. BUT...
JUST OVER A YEAR AGO.
...WHAT IS IT YOU ASKED ME TO PAINT?
VONA!
YOU DON'T KNOW WHAT THAT IS? ARE YOU EVEN LISTENING TO MASTER MAXIMO? SHOW SOME RESPECT!
BUT--BUT MAXIMO SAID I DID GOOD. DIDN'T I DO GOOD?
SHUT UP IN FRONT OF THE MASTER! YOU NEED TO GET IT TOGETHER!
YOU KNOW WHAT WE'RE ALL WORKING TOWARDS. I EXPECTED BETTER OUT OF YOU! FOR CHRIST'S SAKE-- DO YOU EVEN CARE ABOUT THIS, VONA?

STOP.

YOU *KNOW* THE RULES ABOUT MENTIONING *FALSE PROPHETS* IN OUR HOUSE.

WE-- WE'RE *SORRY,* MASTER! WE DO! WE *KNOW!*

ENOUGH. YOU SHOULDN'T BE *YELLING* AT VONA.

SHE SHOULDN'T *MATTER* TO YOU AT ALL.

YOU ARE BOTH YOUR OWN PEOPLE NOW. *YOU* ARE NOT TO BLAME FOR HER STUPIDITY.

IF SHE WILL NOT BE *TAUGHT* BEFORE OUR *GREAT MIGRATION*... SHE HAS NO RIGHT TO ESCAPE WHAT'S COMING.

REMEMBER THE TEACHINGS...

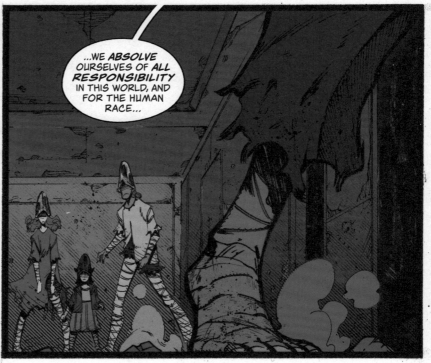

...WE *ABSOLVE* OURSELVES OF *ALL RESPONSIBILITY* IN THIS WORLD, AND FOR THE HUMAN RACE...

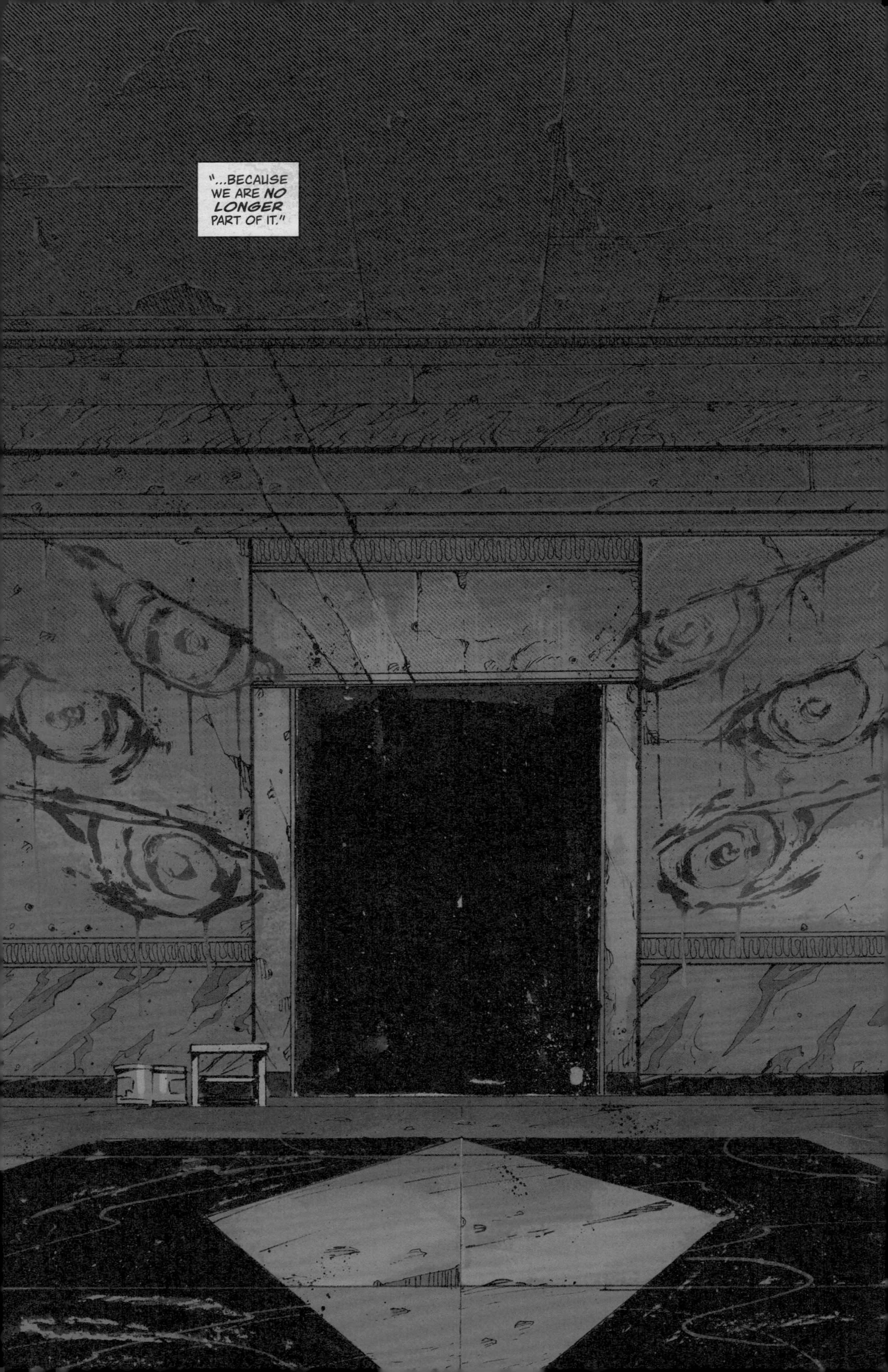
"...BECAUSE WE ARE *NO LONGER* PART OF IT."

The Last Day Left.

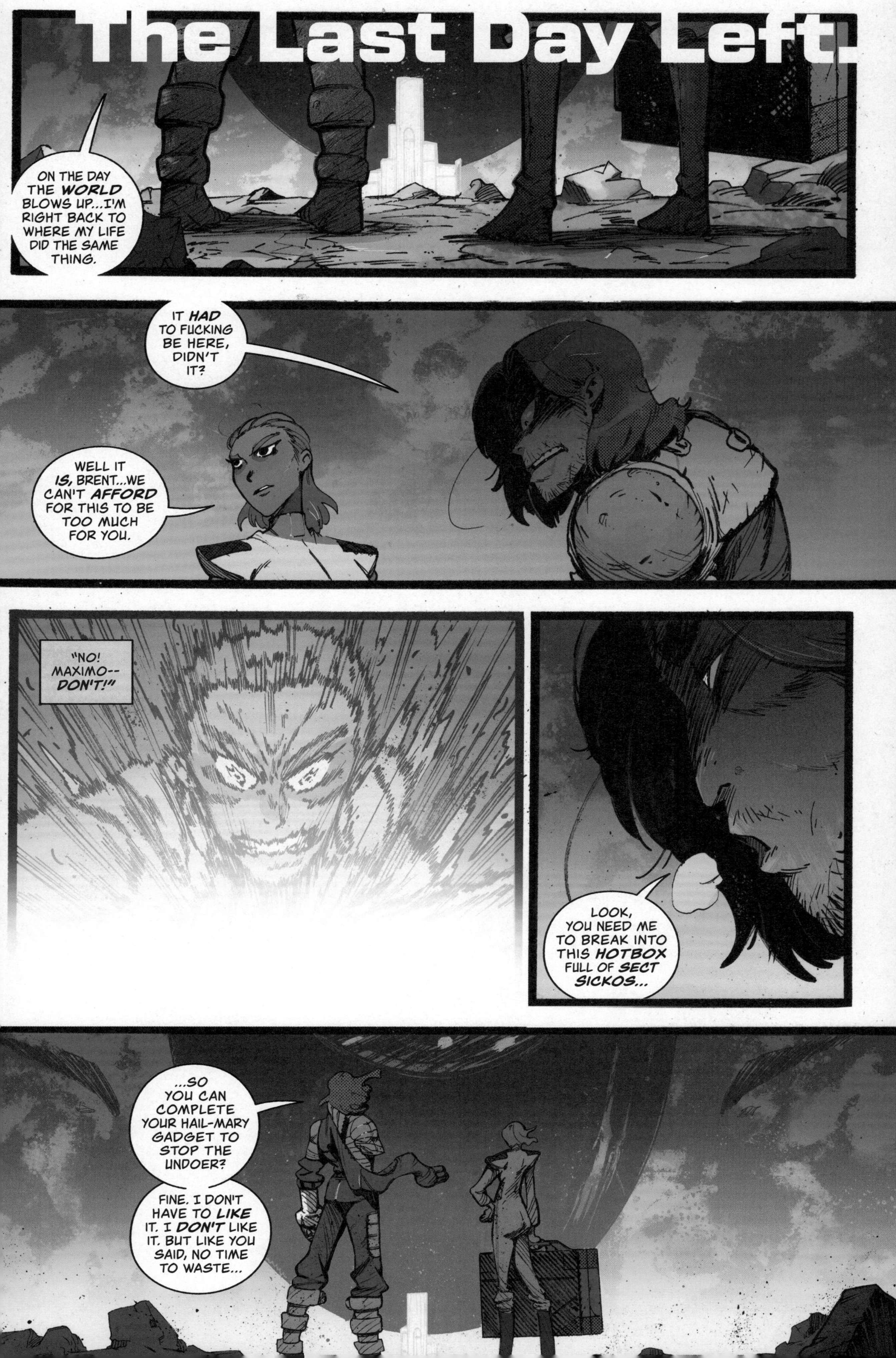

ON THE DAY THE WORLD BLOWS UP...I'M RIGHT BACK TO WHERE MY LIFE DID THE SAME THING.
IT HAD TO FUCKING BE HERE, DIDN'T IT?
WELL IT IS, BRENT...WE CAN'T AFFORD FOR THIS TO BE TOO MUCH FOR YOU.
"NO! MAXIMO-- DON'T!"
LOOK, YOU NEED ME TO BREAK INTO THIS HOTBOX FULL OF SECT SICKOS...
...SO YOU CAN COMPLETE YOUR HAIL-MARY GADGET TO STOP THE UNDOER?
FINE. I DON'T HAVE TO LIKE IT. I DON'T LIKE IT. BUT LIKE YOU SAID, NO TIME TO WASTE...

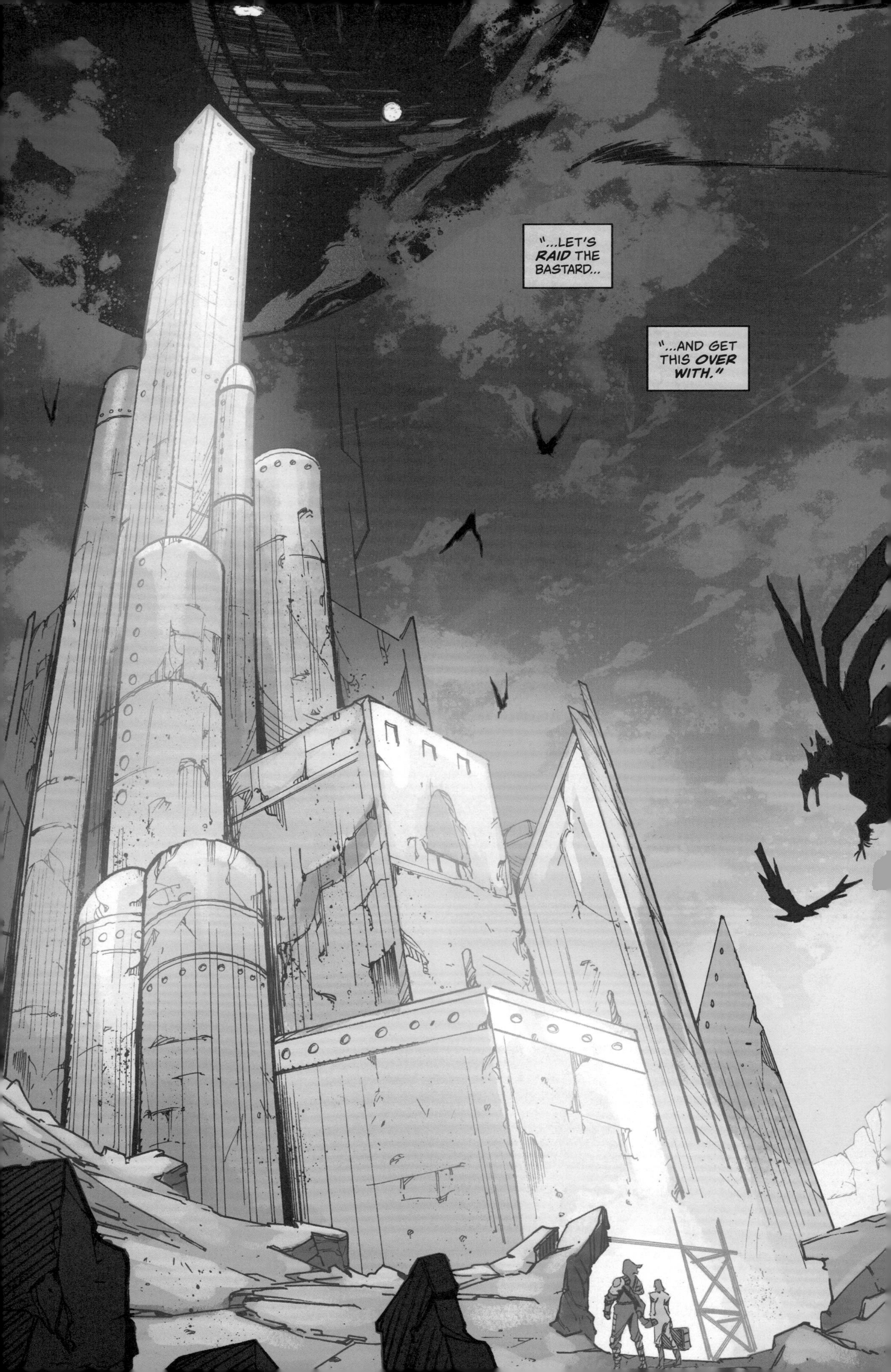
"...LET'S RAID THE BASTARD...
"...AND GET THIS OVER WITH."

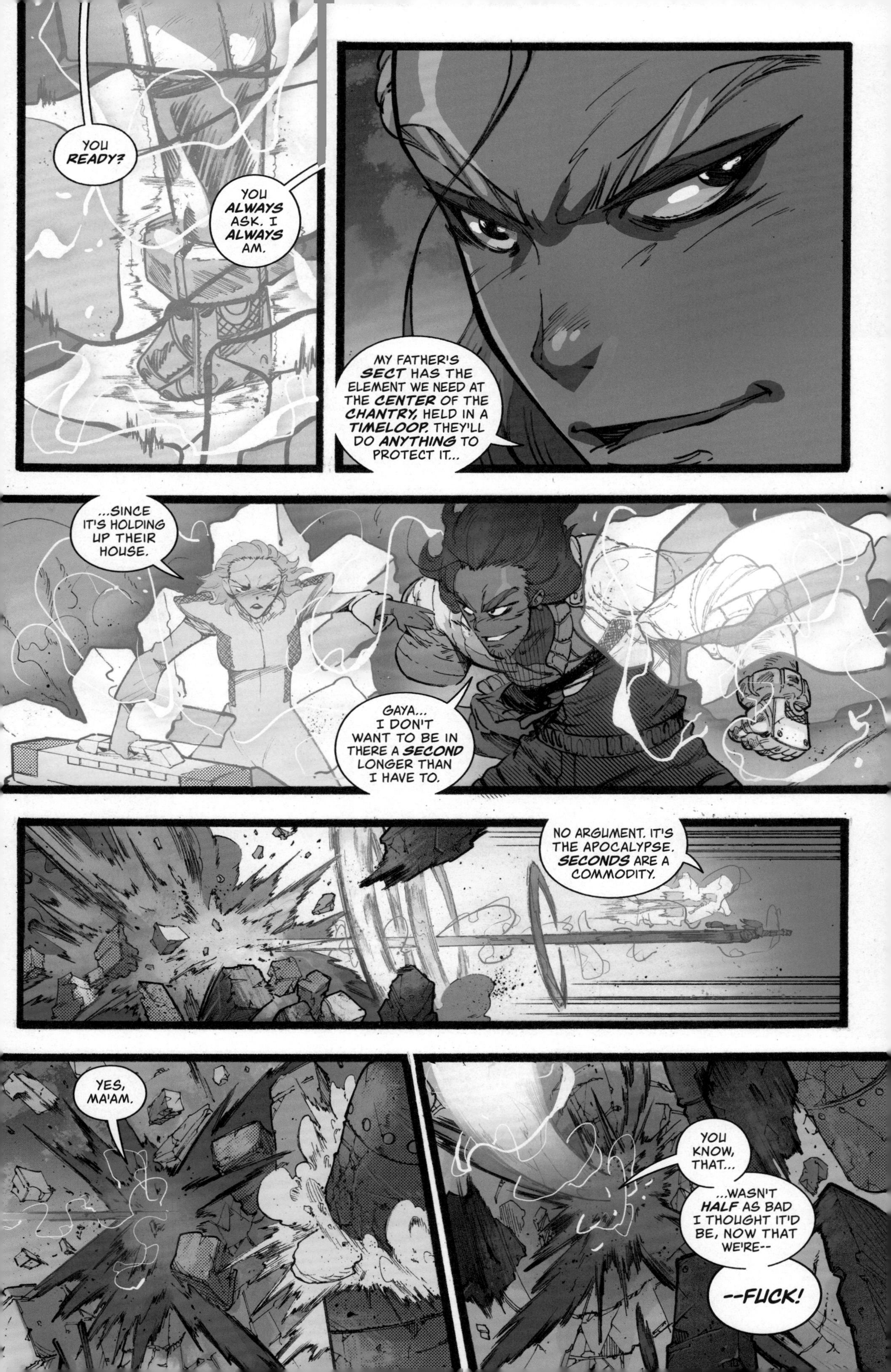
YOU READY?
YOU ALWAYS ASK. I ALWAYS AM.
MY FATHER'S SECT HAS THE ELEMENT WE NEED AT THE CENTER OF THE CHANTRY, HELD IN A TIMELOOP. THEY'LL DO ANYTHING TO PROTECT IT...
...SINCE IT'S HOLDING UP THEIR HOUSE.
GAYA... I DON'T WANT TO BE IN THERE A SECOND LONGER THAN I HAVE TO.
NO ARGUMENT. IT'S THE APOCALYPSE. SECONDS ARE A COMMODITY.
YES, MA'AM.
YOU KNOW, THAT...
...WASN'T HALF AS BAD I THOUGHT IT'D BE, NOW THAT WE'RE--
--FUCK!

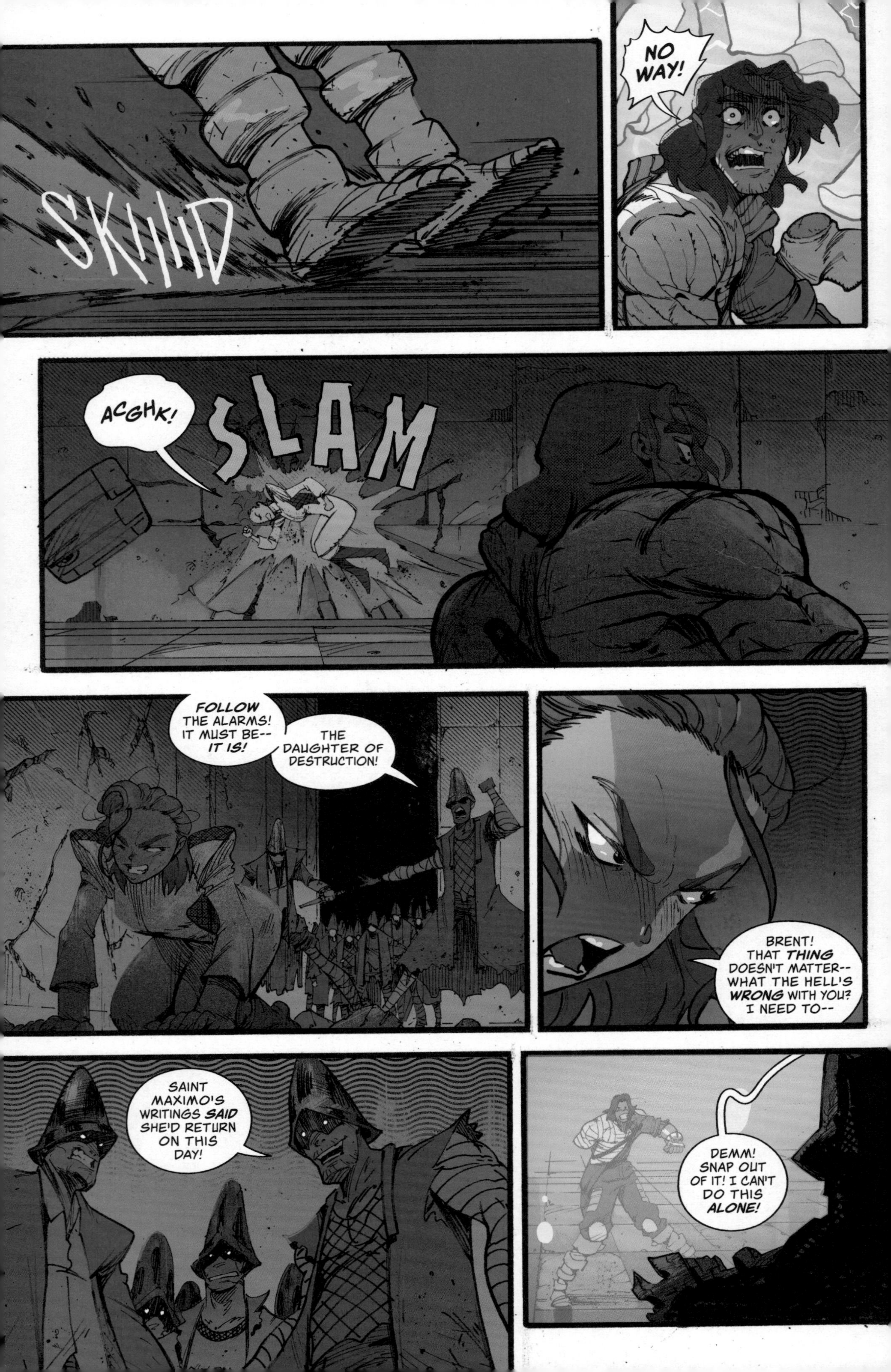
SKIIIID
NO WAY!
ACGHK!
SLAM
FOLLOW THE ALARMS! IT MUST BE-- IT IS!
THE DAUGHTER OF DESTRUCTION!
BRENT! THAT THING DOESN'T MATTER-- WHAT THE HELL'S WRONG WITH YOU? I NEED TO--
SAINT MAXIMO'S WRITINGS SAID SHE'D RETURN ON THIS DAY!
DEMM! SNAP OUT OF IT! I CAN'T DO THIS ALONE!

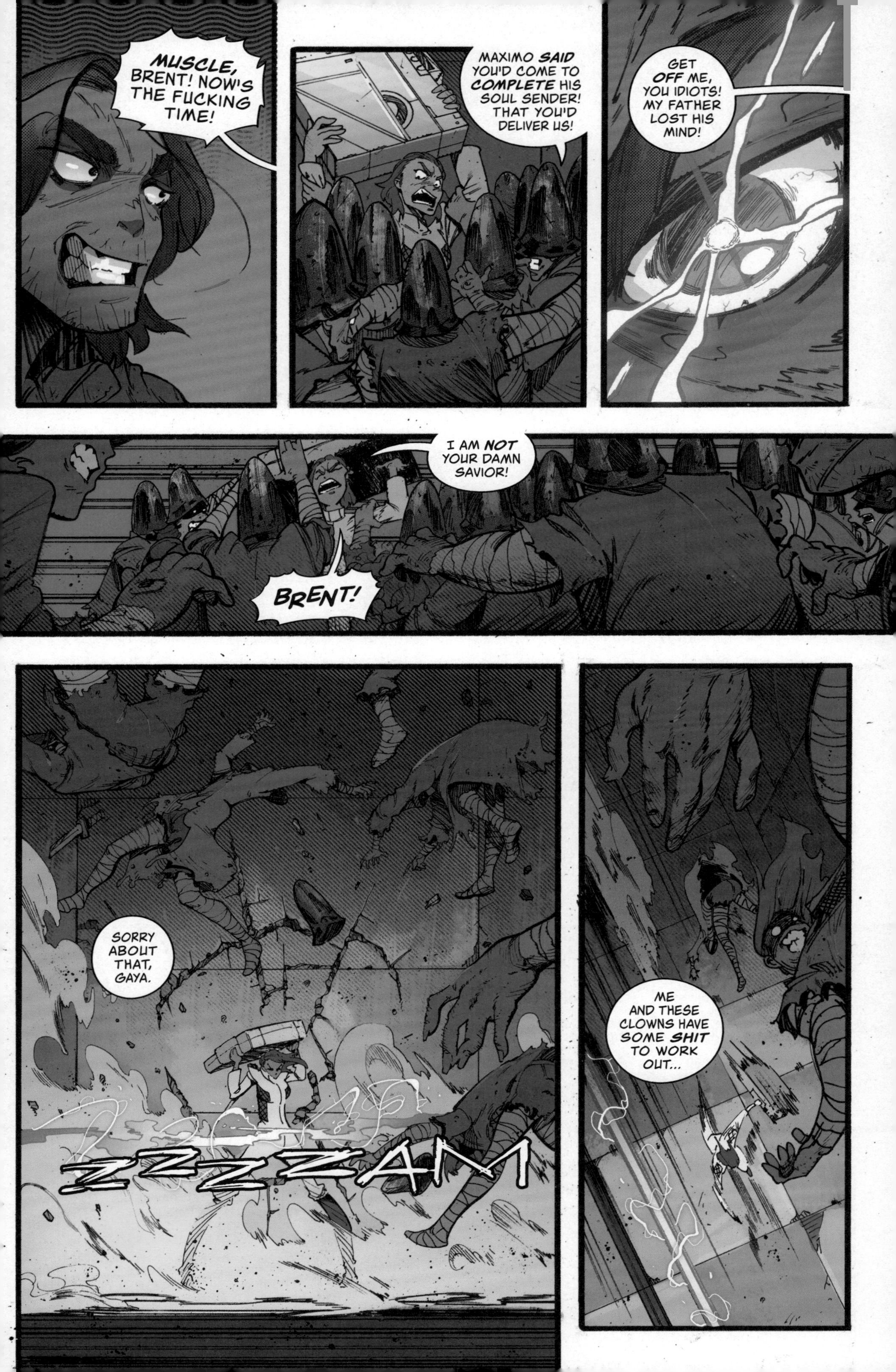
MUSCLE, BRENT! NOW'S THE FUCKING TIME!
MAXIMO SAID YOU'D COME TO COMPLETE HIS SOUL SENDER! THAT YOU'D DELIVER US!
GET OFF ME, YOU IDIOTS! MY FATHER LOST HIS MIND!
I AM NOT YOUR DAMN SAVIOR!
BRENT!
SORRY ABOUT THAT, GAYA.
ZZZZAM
ME AND THESE CLOWNS HAVE SOME SHIT TO WORK OUT...

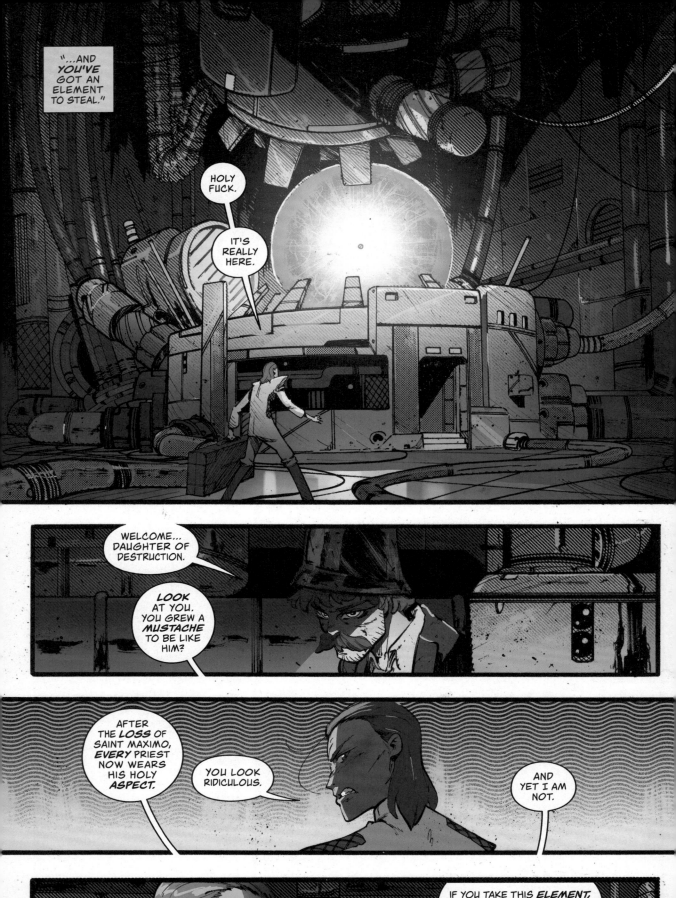

"...AND *YOU'VE* GOT AN ELEMENT TO STEAL."

HOLY FUCK.

IT'S REALLY HERE.

WELCOME... DAUGHTER OF DESTRUCTION.

LOOK AT YOU. YOU GREW A *MUSTACHE* TO BE LIKE HIM?

AFTER THE *LOSS* OF SAINT MAXIMO, *EVERY* PRIEST NOW WEARS HIS HOLY *ASPECT.*

YOU LOOK RIDICULOUS.

AND YET I AM NOT.

IF YOU TAKE THIS *ELEMENT*, YOU DOOM YOUR FATHER'S FOLLOWERS AND YOURSELF, AS THIS HOLY SITE COLLAPSES.

WE WOULD ALL *DIE* BY *DAY'S END* WITH THE REST OF HUMANITY...FOR SINS WE DIDN'T COMMIT.

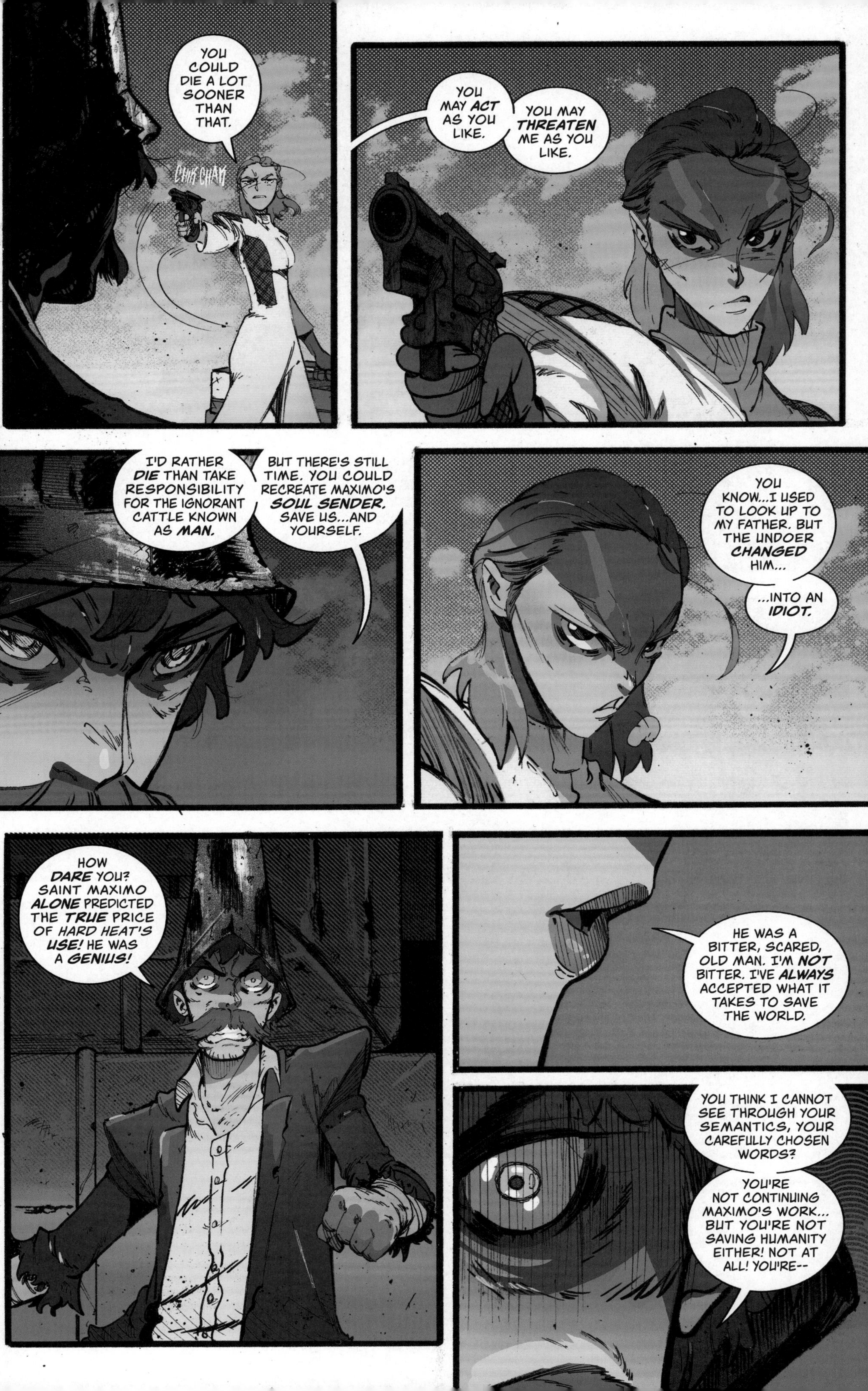
YOU COULD DIE A LOT SOONER THAN THAT.
CHIK CHAK
YOU MAY ACT AS YOU LIKE.
YOU MAY THREATEN ME AS YOU LIKE.
I'D RATHER DIE THAN TAKE RESPONSIBILITY FOR THE IGNORANT CATTLE KNOWN AS MAN.
BUT THERE'S STILL TIME. YOU COULD RECREATE MAXIMO'S SOUL SENDER. SAVE US...AND YOURSELF.
YOU KNOW...I USED TO LOOK UP TO MY FATHER. BUT THE UNDOER CHANGED HIM...
...INTO AN IDIOT.
HOW DARE YOU? SAINT MAXIMO ALONE PREDICTED THE TRUE PRICE OF HARD HEAT'S USE! HE WAS A GENIUS!
HE WAS A BITTER, SCARED, OLD MAN. I'M NOT BITTER. I'VE ALWAYS ACCEPTED WHAT IT TAKES TO SAVE THE WORLD.
YOU THINK I CANNOT SEE THROUGH YOUR SEMANTICS, YOUR CAREFULLY CHOSEN WORDS?
YOU'RE NOT CONTINUING MAXIMO'S WORK... BUT YOU'RE NOT SAVING HUMANITY EITHER! NOT AT ALL! YOU'RE--

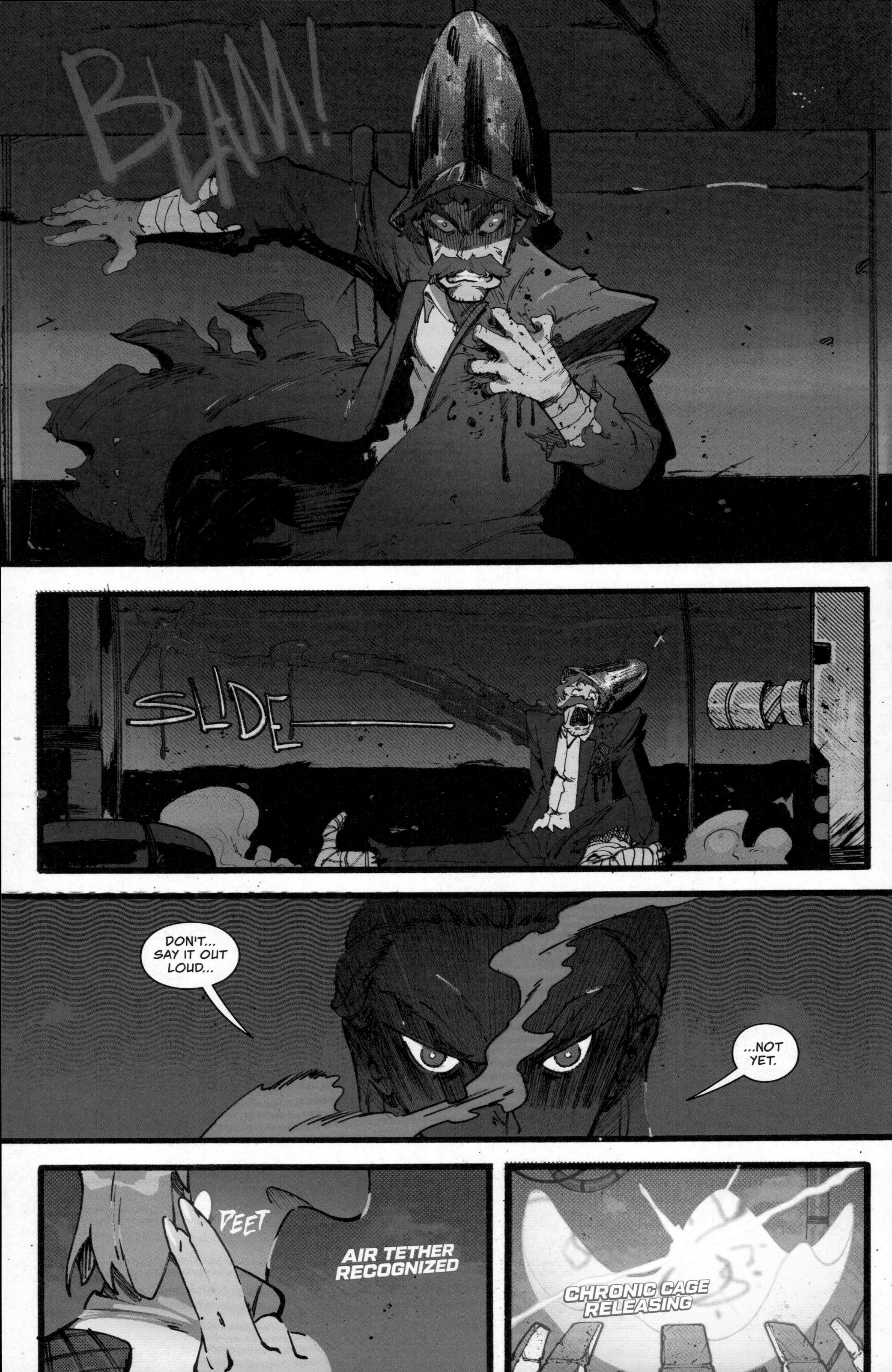
BLAM!
SLIDE
DON'T... SAY IT OUT LOUD...
...NOT YET.
DEET
AIR TETHER RECOGNIZED
CHRONIC CAGE RELEASING

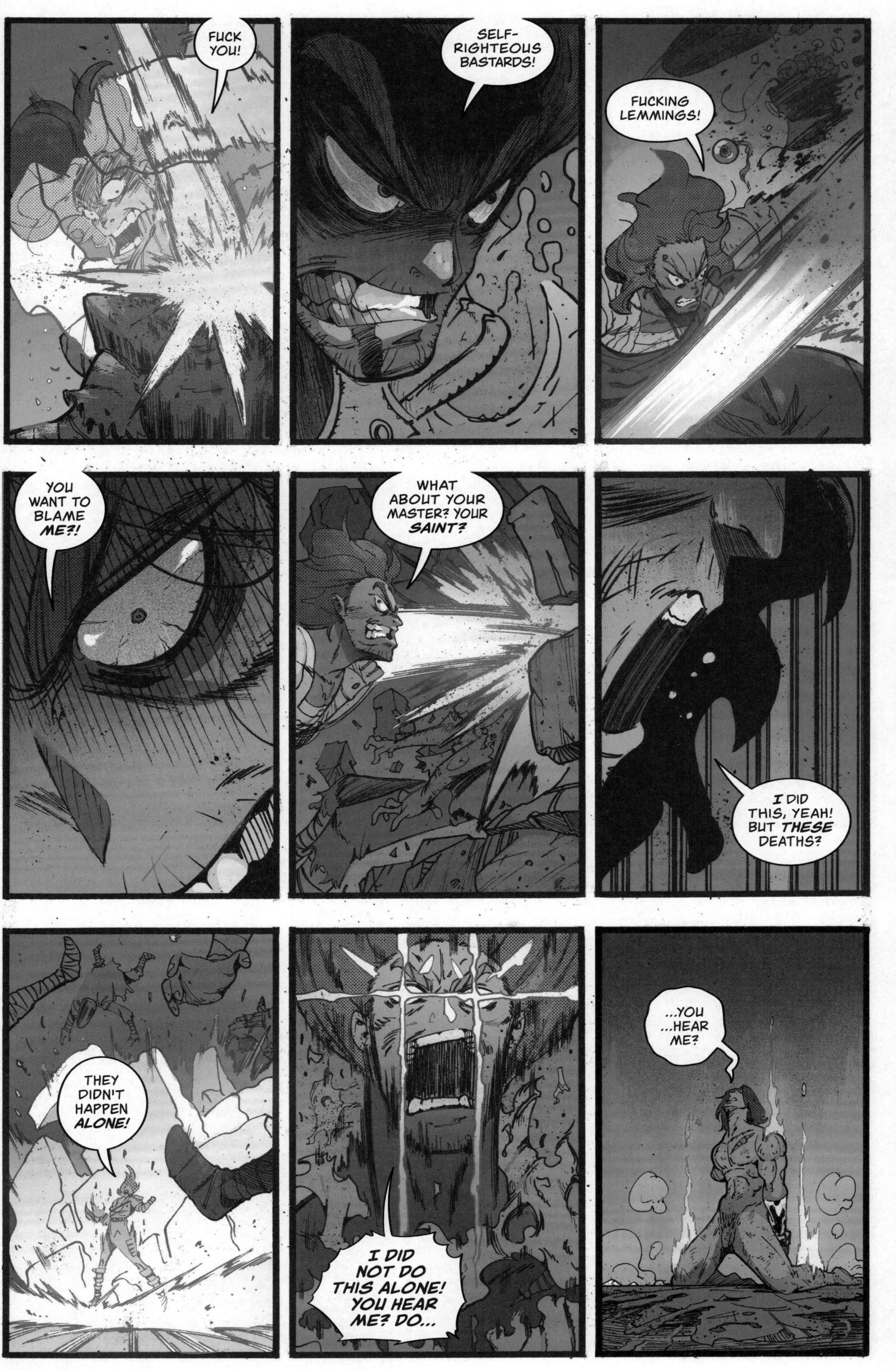
FUCK YOU!
SELF-RIGHTEOUS BASTARDS!
FUCKING LEMMINGS!
YOU WANT TO BLAME ME?!
WHAT ABOUT YOUR MASTER? YOUR SAINT?
I DID THIS, YEAH! BUT THESE DEATHS?
THEY DIDN'T HAPPEN ALONE!
I DID NOT DO THIS ALONE! YOU HEAR ME? DO...
...YOU ...HEAR ME?

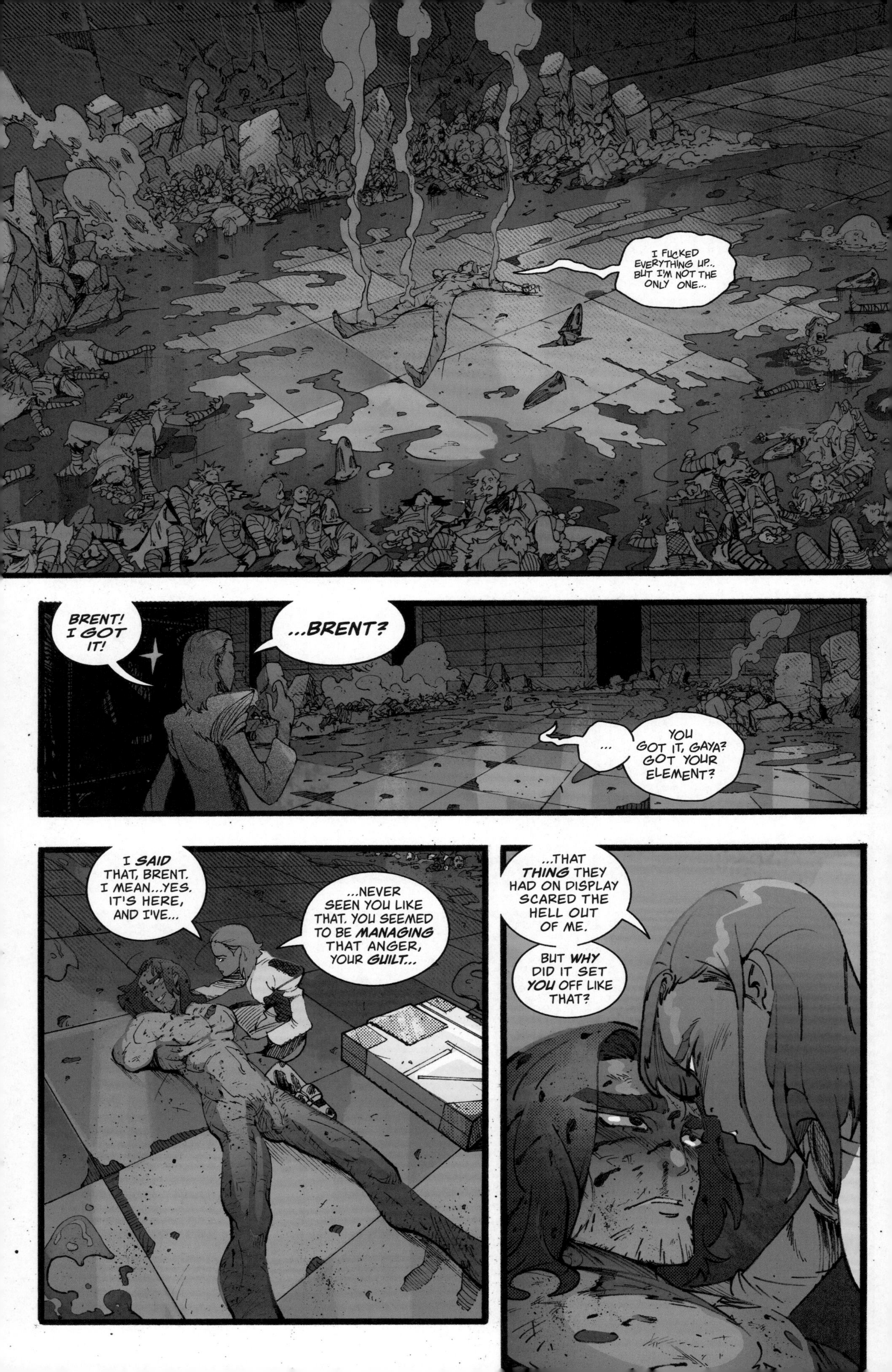
I FUCKED EVERYTHING UP.. BUT I'M NOT THE ONLY ONE...
BRENT! I GOT IT!
...BRENT?
...
YOU GOT IT, GAYA? GOT YOUR ELEMENT?
I SAID THAT, BRENT. I MEAN...YES. IT'S HERE, AND I'VE...
...NEVER SEEN YOU LIKE THAT. YOU SEEMED TO BE MANAGING THAT ANGER, YOUR GUILT...
...THAT THING THEY HAD ON DISPLAY SCARED THE HELL OUT OF ME.
BUT WHY DID IT SET YOU OFF LIKE THAT?

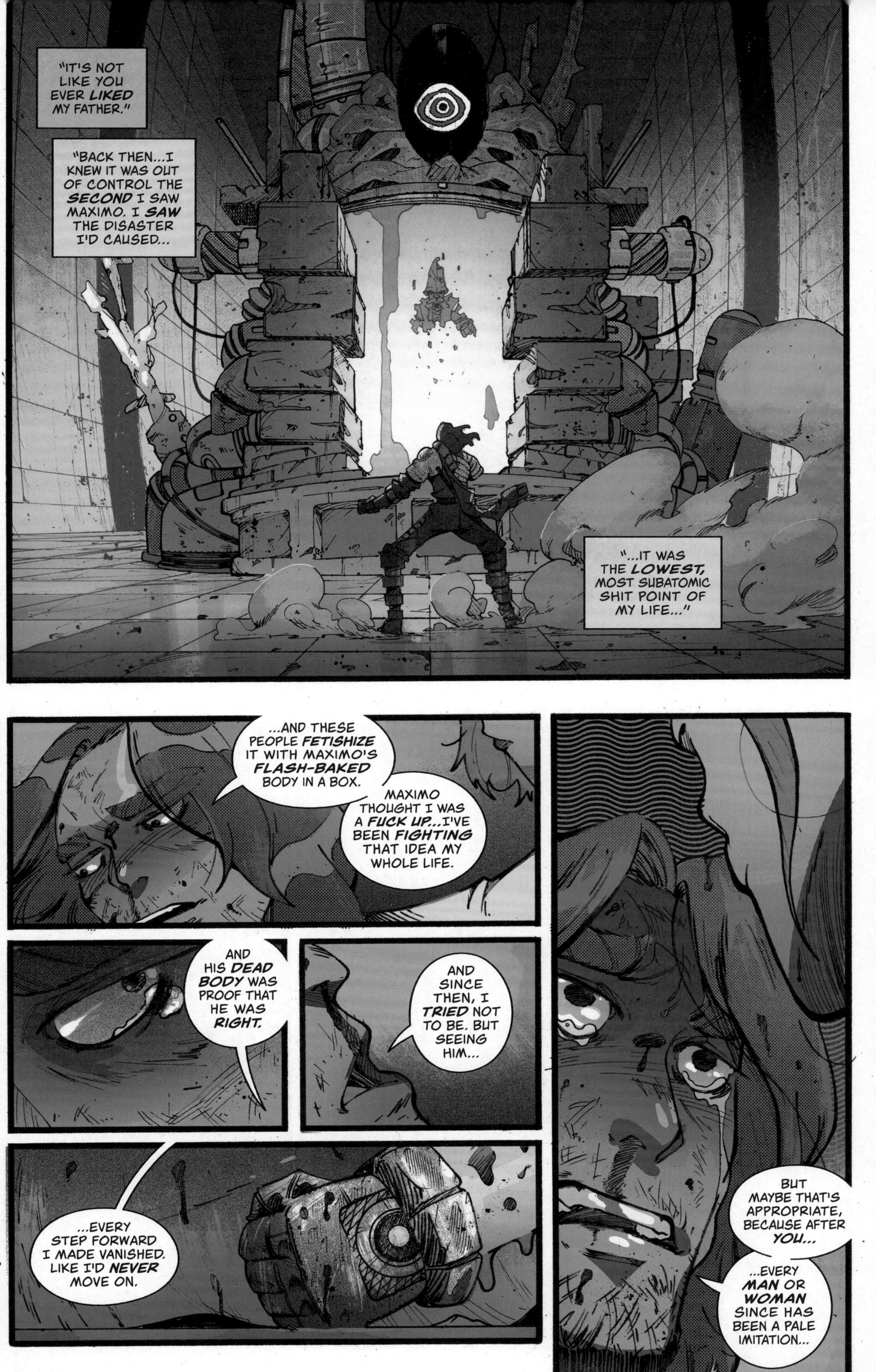
"IT'S NOT LIKE YOU EVER LIKED MY FATHER."
"BACK THEN... I KNEW IT WAS OUT OF CONTROL THE SECOND I SAW MAXIMO. I SAW THE DISASTER I'D CAUSED...
"...IT WAS THE LOWEST, MOST SUBATOMIC SHIT POINT OF MY LIFE..."
...AND THESE PEOPLE FETISHIZE IT WITH MAXIMO'S FLASH-BAKED BODY IN A BOX.
MAXIMO THOUGHT I WAS A FUCK UP... I'VE BEEN FIGHTING THAT IDEA MY WHOLE LIFE.
AND HIS DEAD BODY WAS PROOF THAT HE WAS RIGHT.
AND SINCE THEN, I TRIED NOT TO BE. BUT SEEING HIM...
...EVERY STEP FORWARD I MADE VANISHED. LIKE I'D NEVER MOVE ON.
BUT MAYBE THAT'S APPROPRIATE, BECAUSE AFTER YOU...
...EVERY MAN OR WOMAN SINCE HAS BEEN A PALE IMITATION...

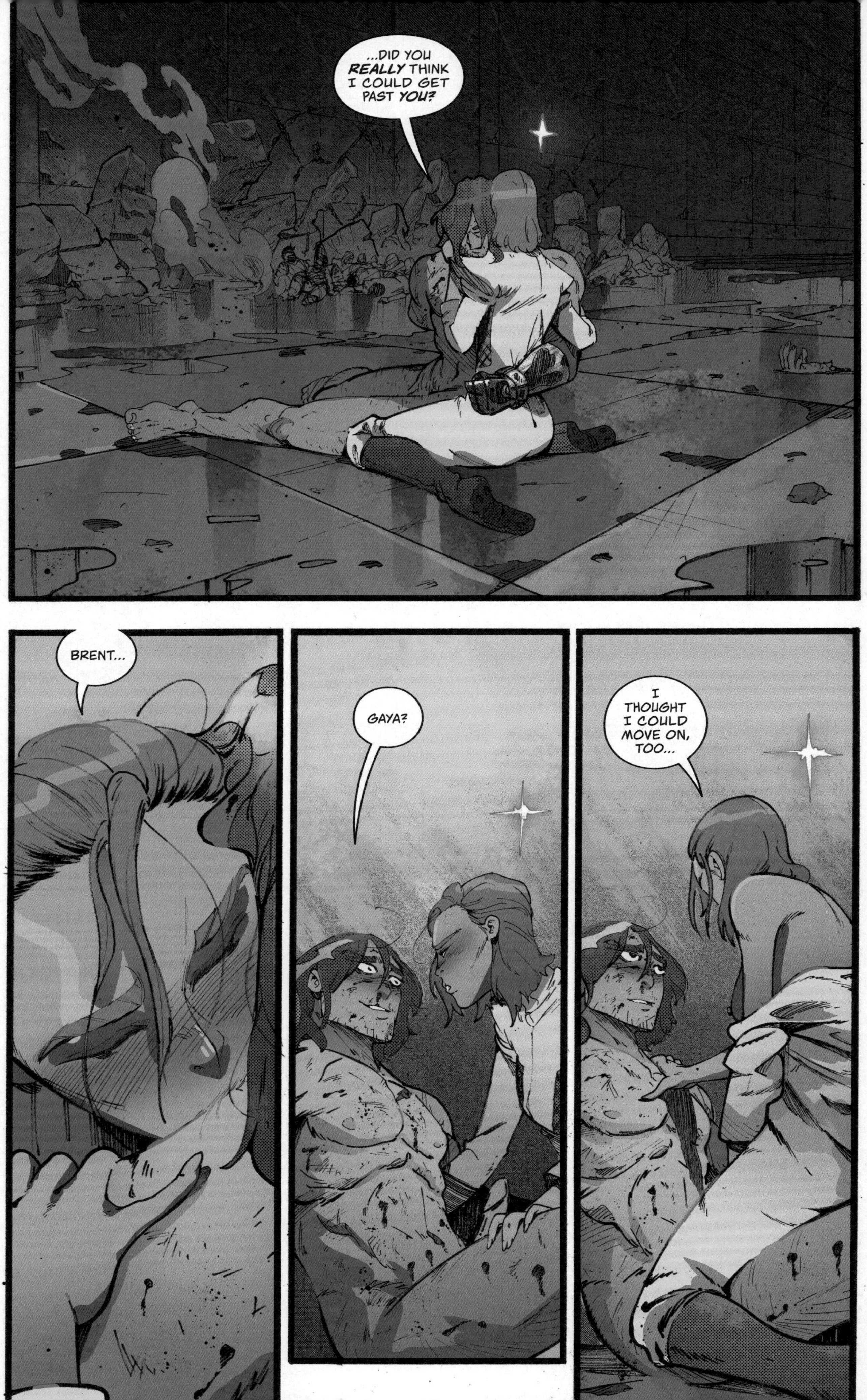
...DID YOU REALLY THINK I COULD GET PAST YOU?
BRENT...
GAYA?
I THOUGHT I COULD MOVE ON, TOO...

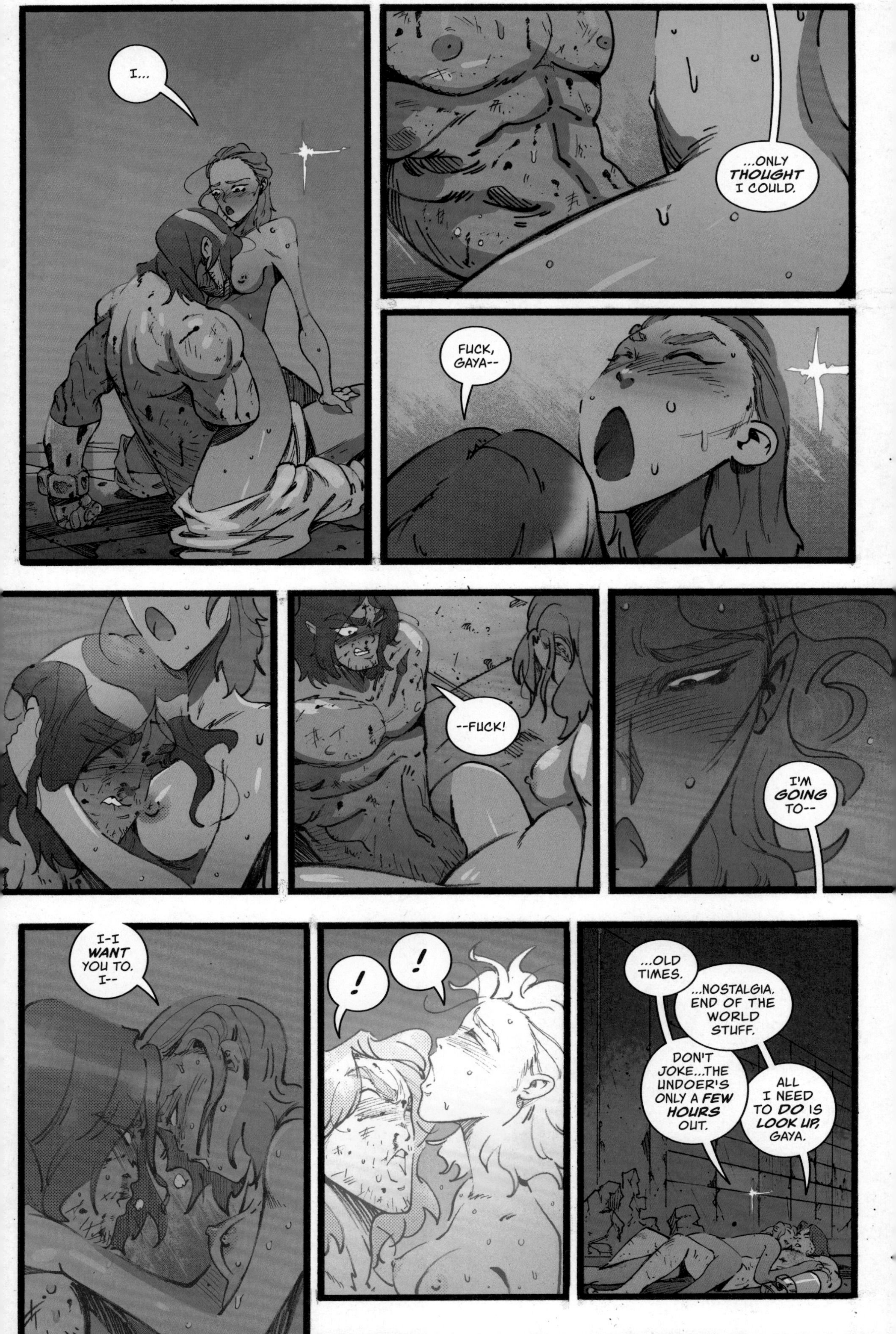

I...
...ONLY *THOUGHT* I COULD.
FUCK, GAYA--
--FUCK!
I'M *GOING* TO--
I-I *WANT* YOU TO. I--
!
!
...OLD TIMES.
...NOSTALGIA. END OF THE WORLD STUFF.
DON'T JOKE...THE UNDOER'S ONLY A *FEW HOURS* OUT.
ALL I NEED TO *DO* IS *LOOK UP,* GAYA.

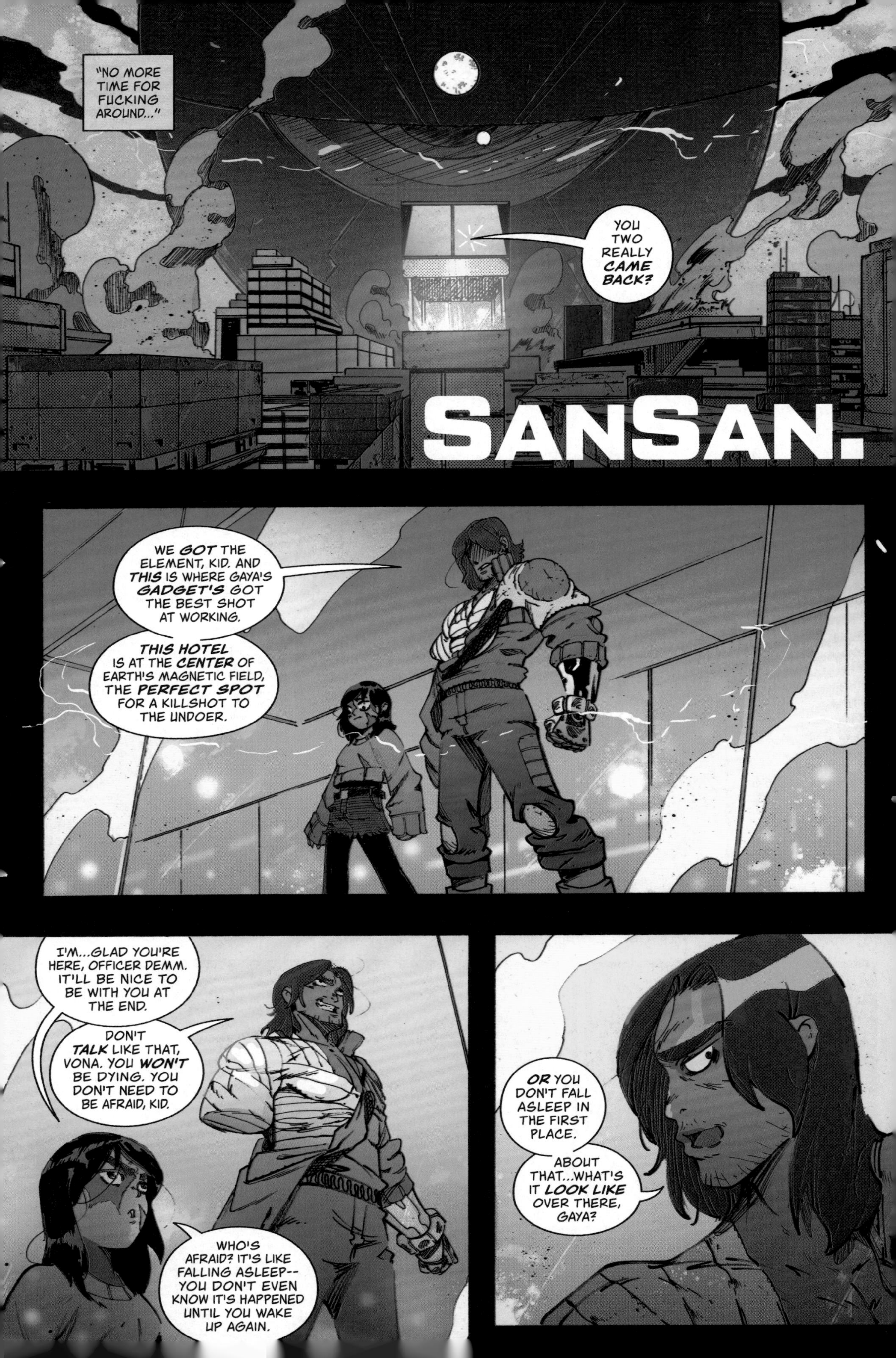
"NO MORE TIME FOR FUCKING AROUND..."
YOU TWO REALLY CAME BACK?
SANSAN.
WE GOT THE ELEMENT, KID. AND THIS IS WHERE GAYA'S GADGET'S GOT THE BEST SHOT AT WORKING.
THIS HOTEL IS AT THE CENTER OF EARTH'S MAGNETIC FIELD, THE PERFECT SPOT FOR A KILLSHOT TO THE UNDOER.
I'M...GLAD YOU'RE HERE, OFFICER DEMM. IT'LL BE NICE TO BE WITH YOU AT THE END.
DON'T TALK LIKE THAT, VONA. YOU WON'T BE DYING. YOU DON'T NEED TO BE AFRAID, KID.
WHO'S AFRAID? IT'S LIKE FALLING ASLEEP-- YOU DON'T EVEN KNOW IT'S HAPPENED UNTIL YOU WAKE UP AGAIN.
OR YOU DON'T FALL ASLEEP IN THE FIRST PLACE.
ABOUT THAT...WHAT'S IT LOOK LIKE OVER THERE, GAYA?

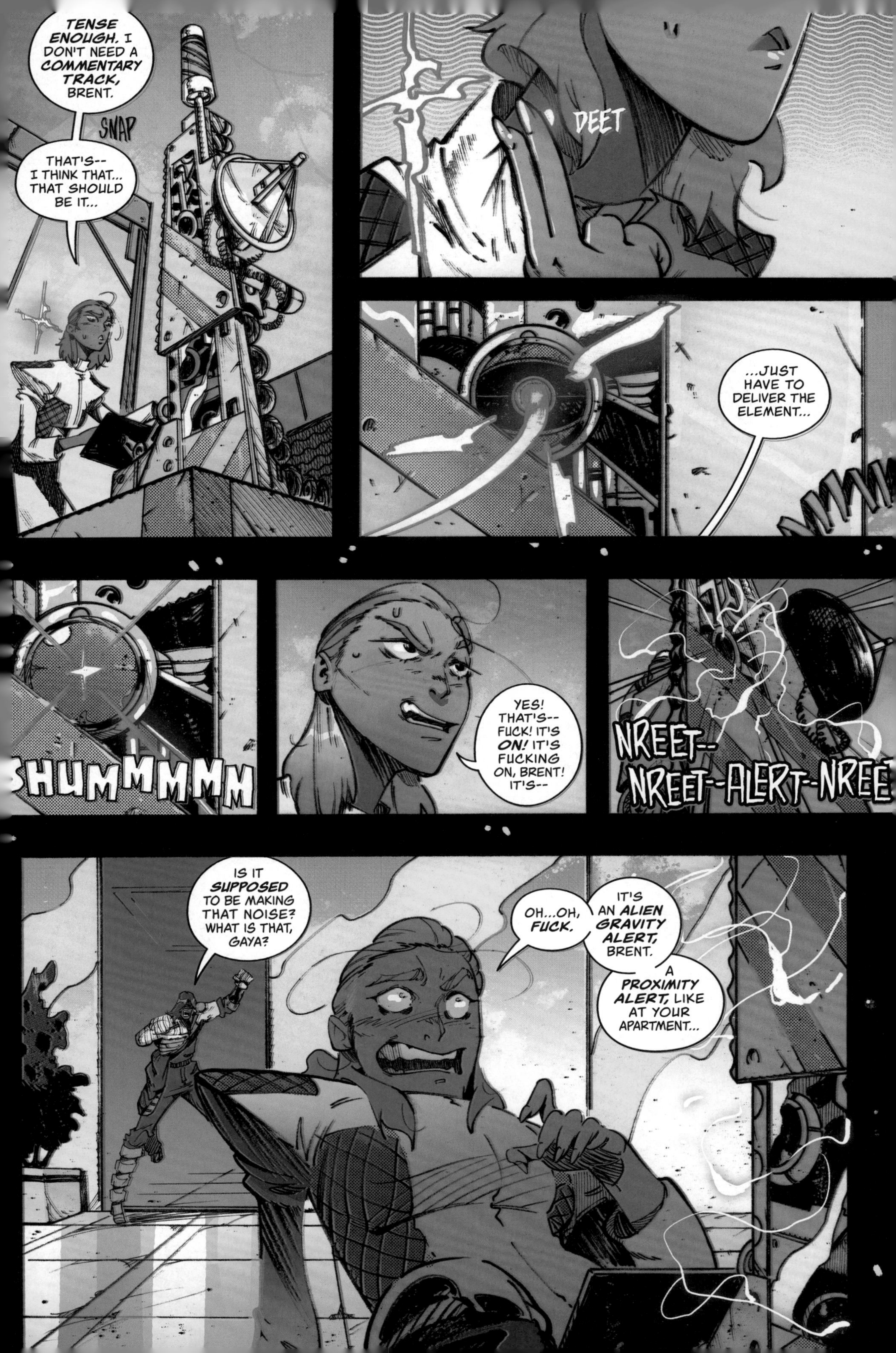
TENSE ENOUGH. I DON'T NEED A COMMENTARY TRACK, BRENT.
SNAP
THAT'S-- I THINK THAT... THAT SHOULD BE IT...
DEET
...JUST HAVE TO DELIVER THE ELEMENT...
SHUMMMMM
YES! THAT'S-- FUCK! IT'S ON! IT'S FUCKING ON, BRENT! IT'S--
NREET-- NREET--ALERT--NREE
IS IT SUPPOSED TO BE MAKING THAT NOISE? WHAT IS THAT, GAYA?
OH...OH, FUCK.
IT'S AN ALIEN GRAVITY ALERT, BRENT.
A PROXIMITY ALERT, LIKE AT YOUR APARTMENT...

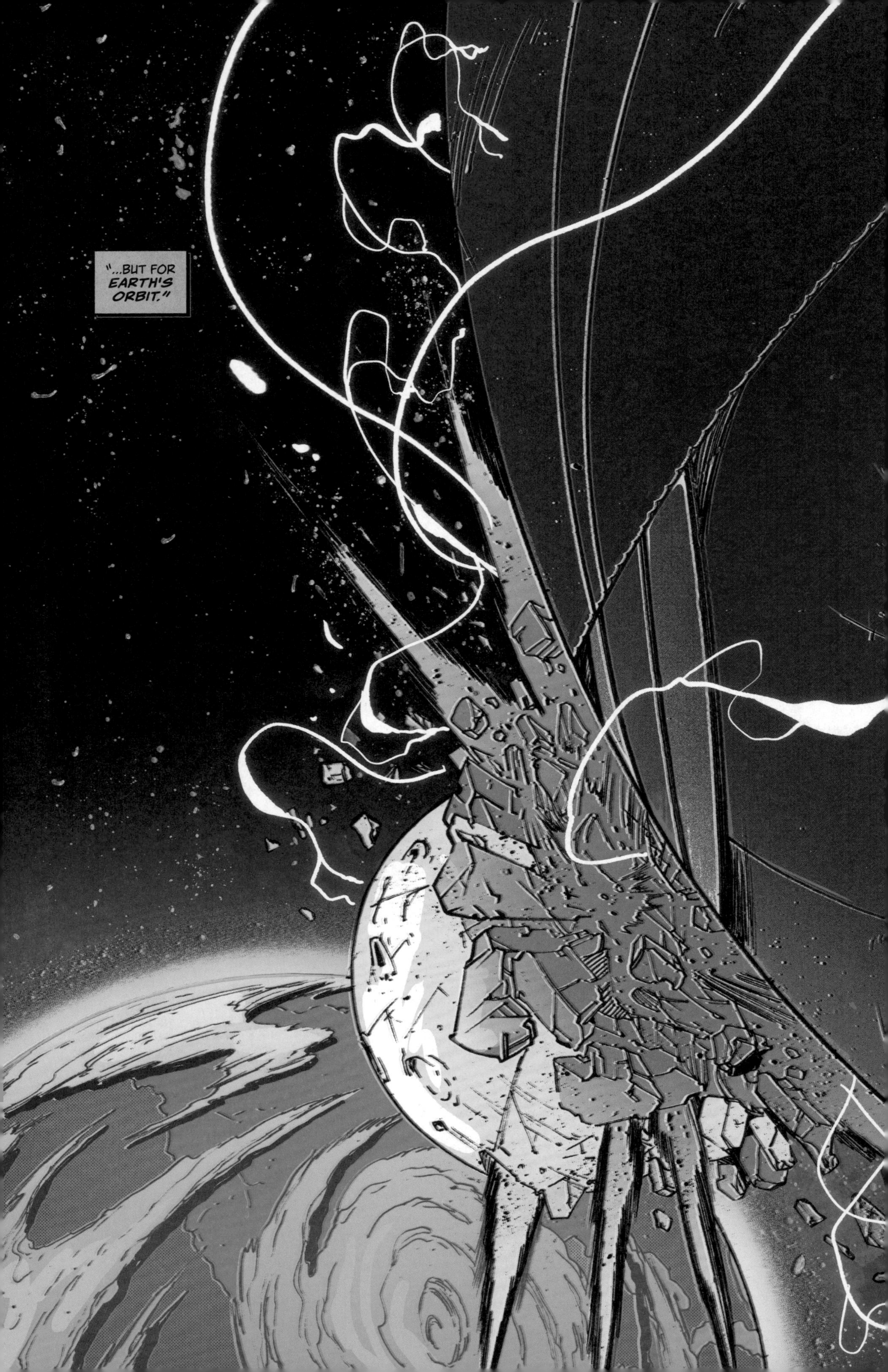
"...BUT FOR *EARTH'S ORBIT.*"

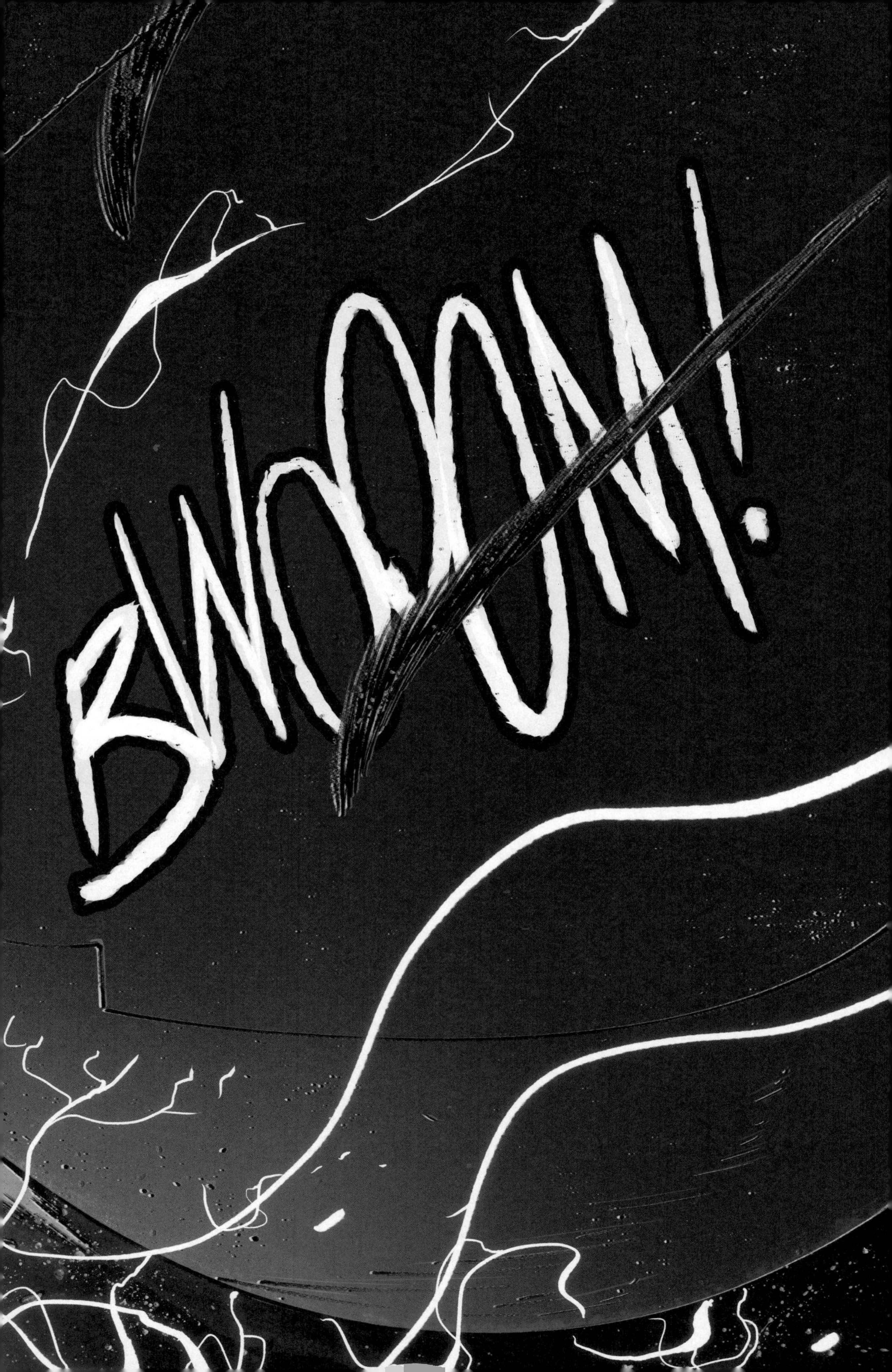
BWOOOM!

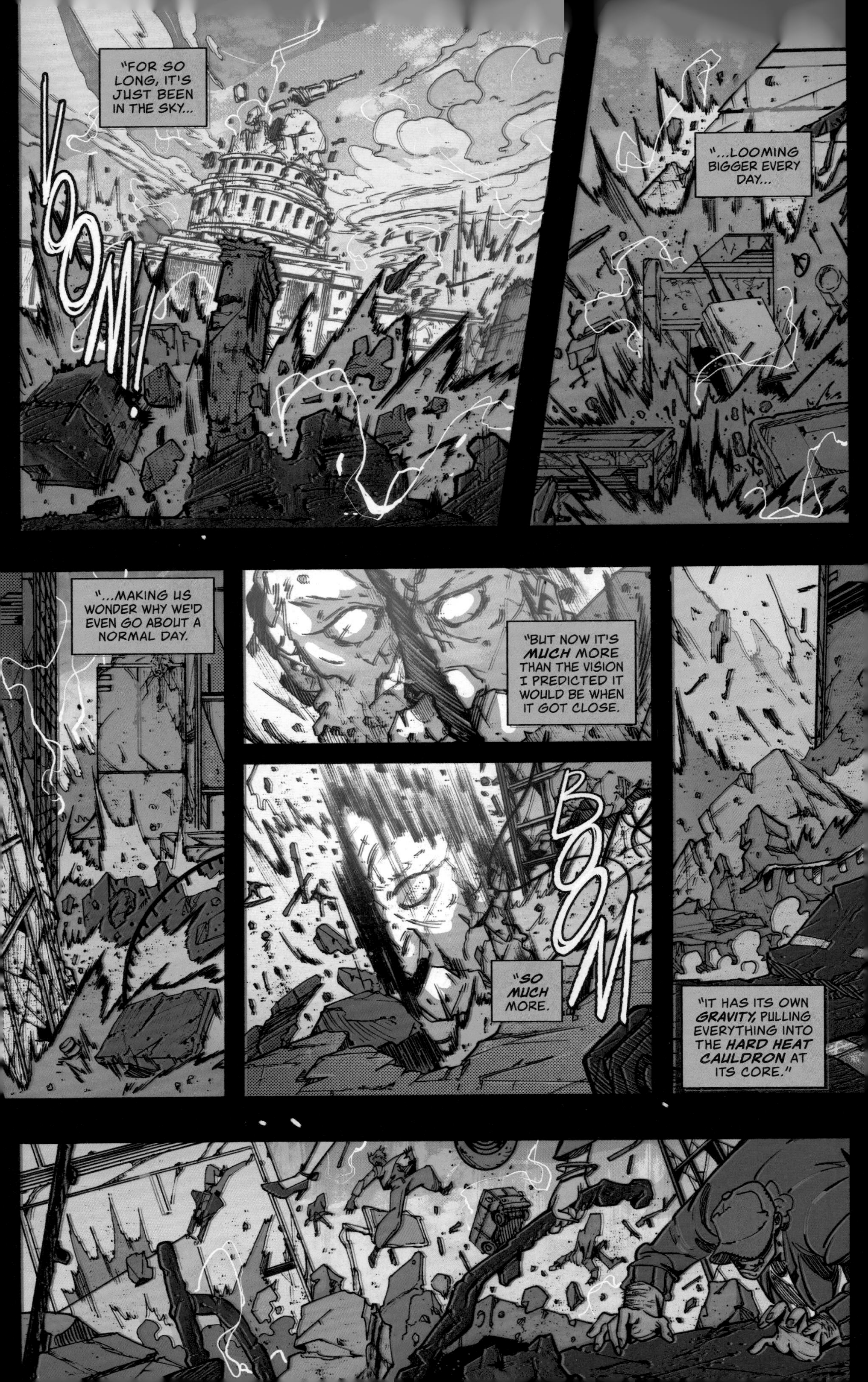
"FOR SO LONG, IT'S JUST BEEN IN THE SKY...
VOOM!!
"...LOOMING BIGGER EVERY DAY...
"...MAKING US WONDER WHY WE'D EVEN GO ABOUT A NORMAL DAY.
"BUT NOW IT'S MUCH MORE THAN THE VISION I PREDICTED IT WOULD BE WHEN IT GOT CLOSE.
BOOM
"SO MUCH MORE.
"IT HAS ITS OWN GRAVITY, PULLING EVERYTHING INTO THE HARD HEAT CAULDRON AT ITS CORE."

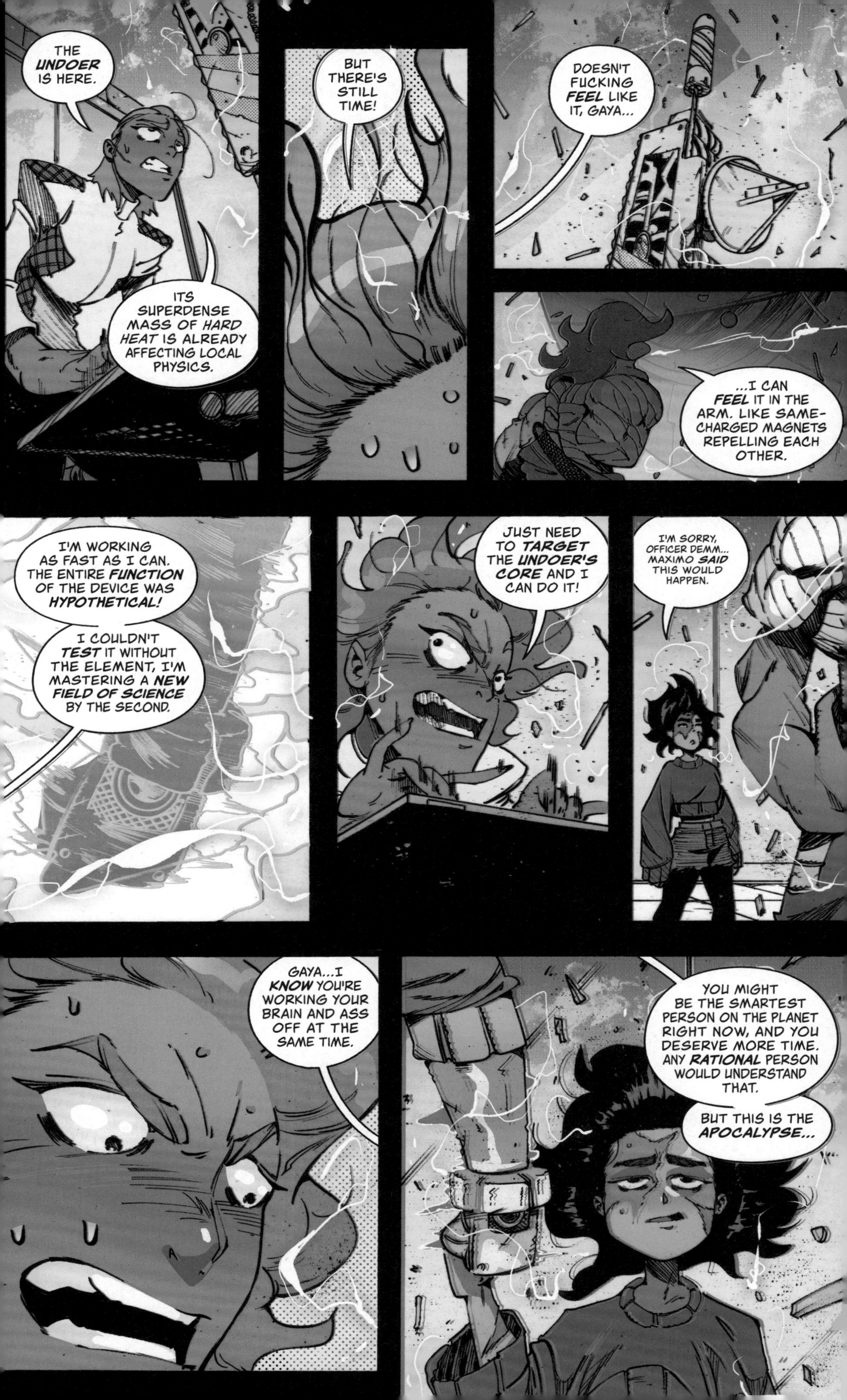
THE UNDOER IS HERE.
ITS SUPERDENSE MASS OF HARD HEAT IS ALREADY AFFECTING LOCAL PHYSICS.
BUT THERE'S STILL TIME!
DOESN'T FUCKING FEEL LIKE IT, GAYA...
...I CAN FEEL IT IN THE ARM. LIKE SAME-CHARGED MAGNETS REPELLING EACH OTHER.
I'M WORKING AS FAST AS I CAN. THE ENTIRE FUNCTION OF THE DEVICE WAS HYPOTHETICAL!
I COULDN'T TEST IT WITHOUT THE ELEMENT, I'M MASTERING A NEW FIELD OF SCIENCE BY THE SECOND.
JUST NEED TO TARGET THE UNDOER'S CORE AND I CAN DO IT!
I'M SORRY, OFFICER DEMM... MAXIMO SAID THIS WOULD HAPPEN.
GAYA...I KNOW YOU'RE WORKING YOUR BRAIN AND ASS OFF AT THE SAME TIME.
YOU MIGHT BE THE SMARTEST PERSON ON THE PLANET RIGHT NOW, AND YOU DESERVE MORE TIME. ANY RATIONAL PERSON WOULD UNDERSTAND THAT.
BUT THIS IS THE APOCALYPSE...

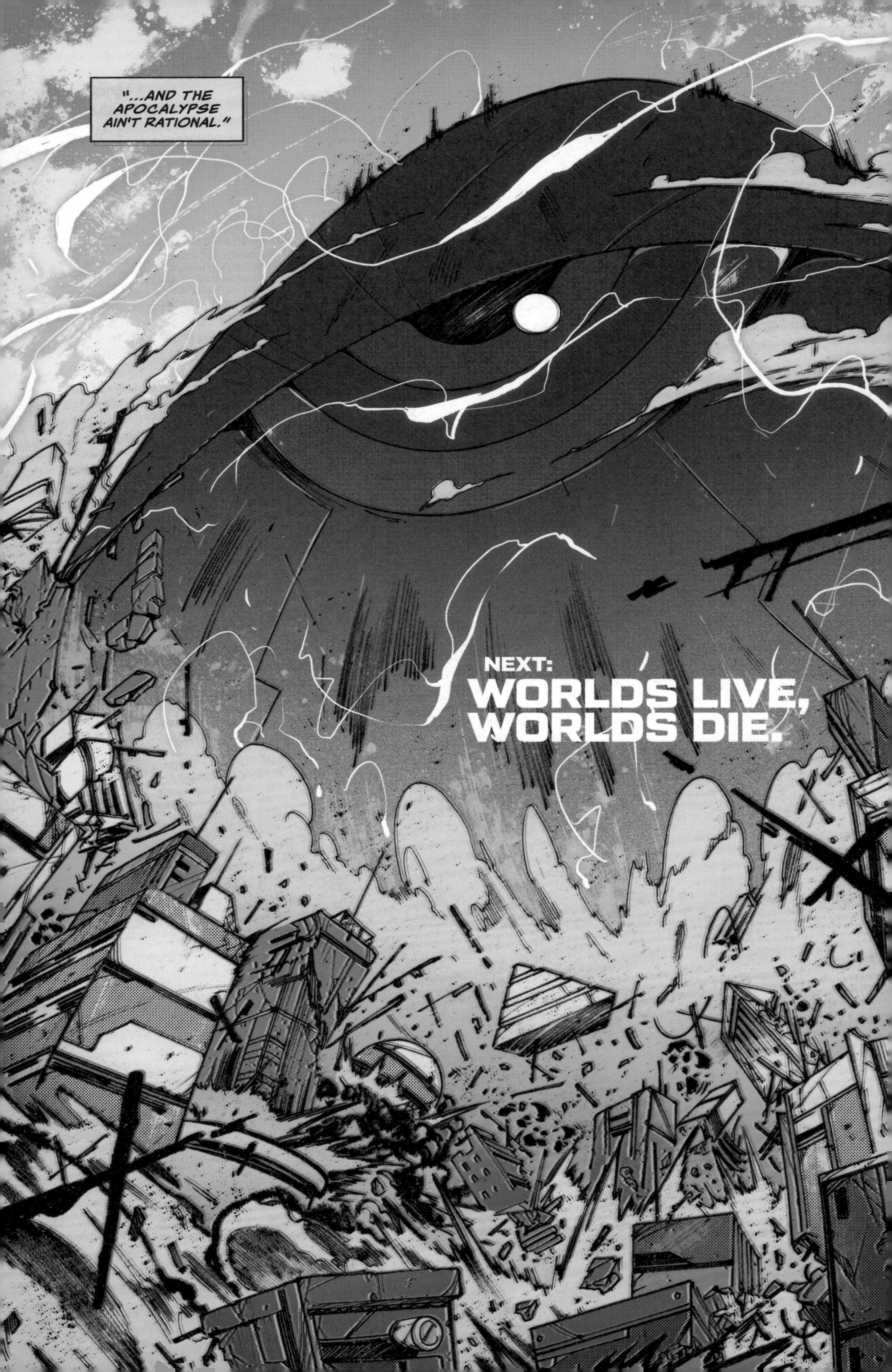
"...AND THE APOCALYPSE AIN'T RATIONAL."
NEXT:
WORLDS LIVE, WORLDS DIE.

CHAPTER 6

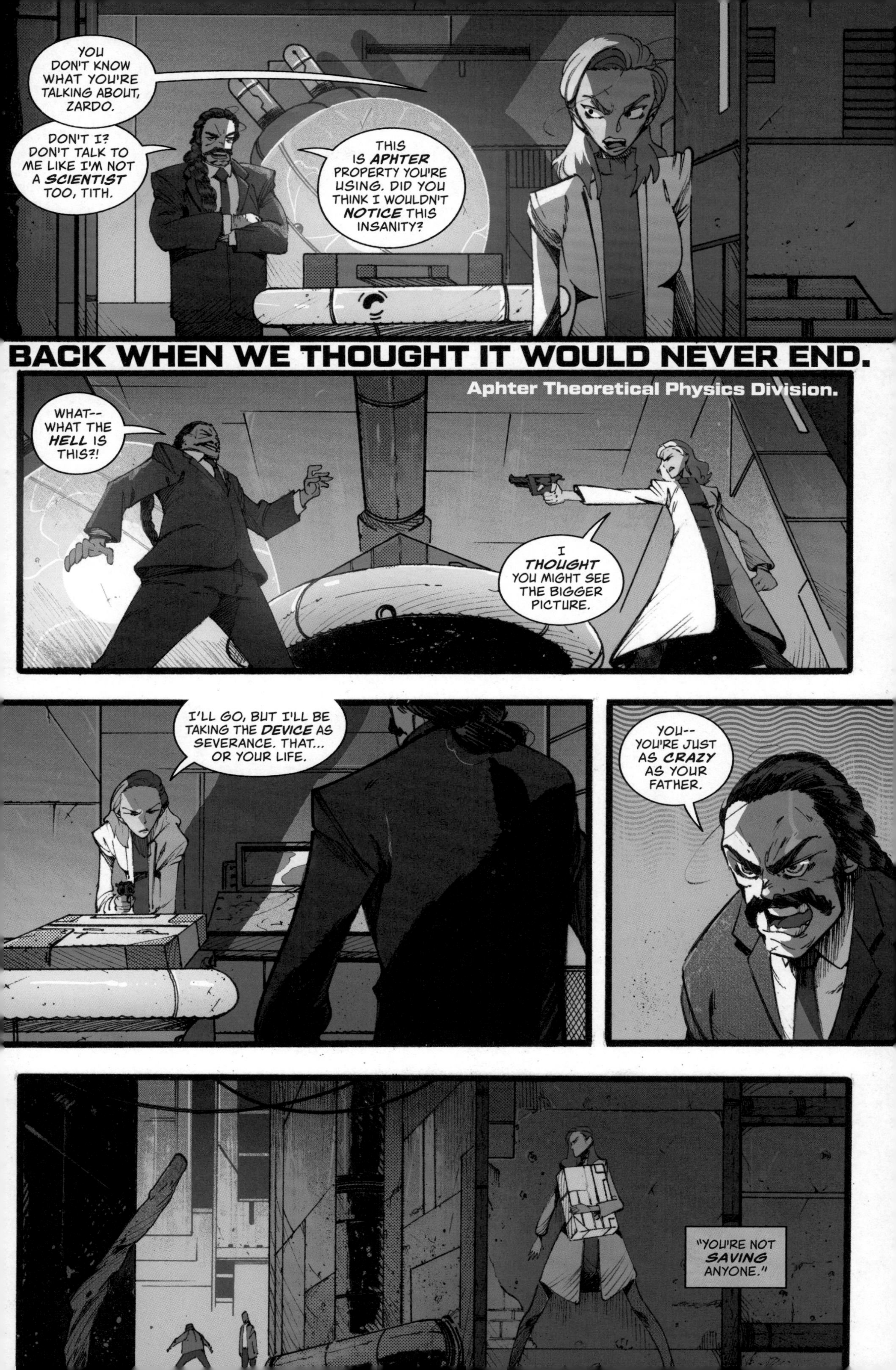
YOU DON'T KNOW WHAT YOU'RE TALKING ABOUT, ZARDO.
DON'T I? DON'T TALK TO ME LIKE I'M NOT A *SCIENTIST* TOO, TITH.
THIS IS *APHTER* PROPERTY YOU'RE USING. DID YOU THINK I WOULDN'T *NOTICE* THIS INSANITY?
BACK WHEN WE THOUGHT IT WOULD NEVER END.
Aphter Theoretical Physics Division.
WHAT-- WHAT THE *HELL* IS THIS?!
I *THOUGHT* YOU MIGHT SEE THE BIGGER PICTURE.
I'LL GO, BUT I'LL BE TAKING THE *DEVICE* AS SEVERANCE. THAT... OR YOUR LIFE.
YOU-- YOU'RE JUST AS *CRAZY* AS YOUR FATHER.
"YOU'RE NOT *SAVING* ANYONE."

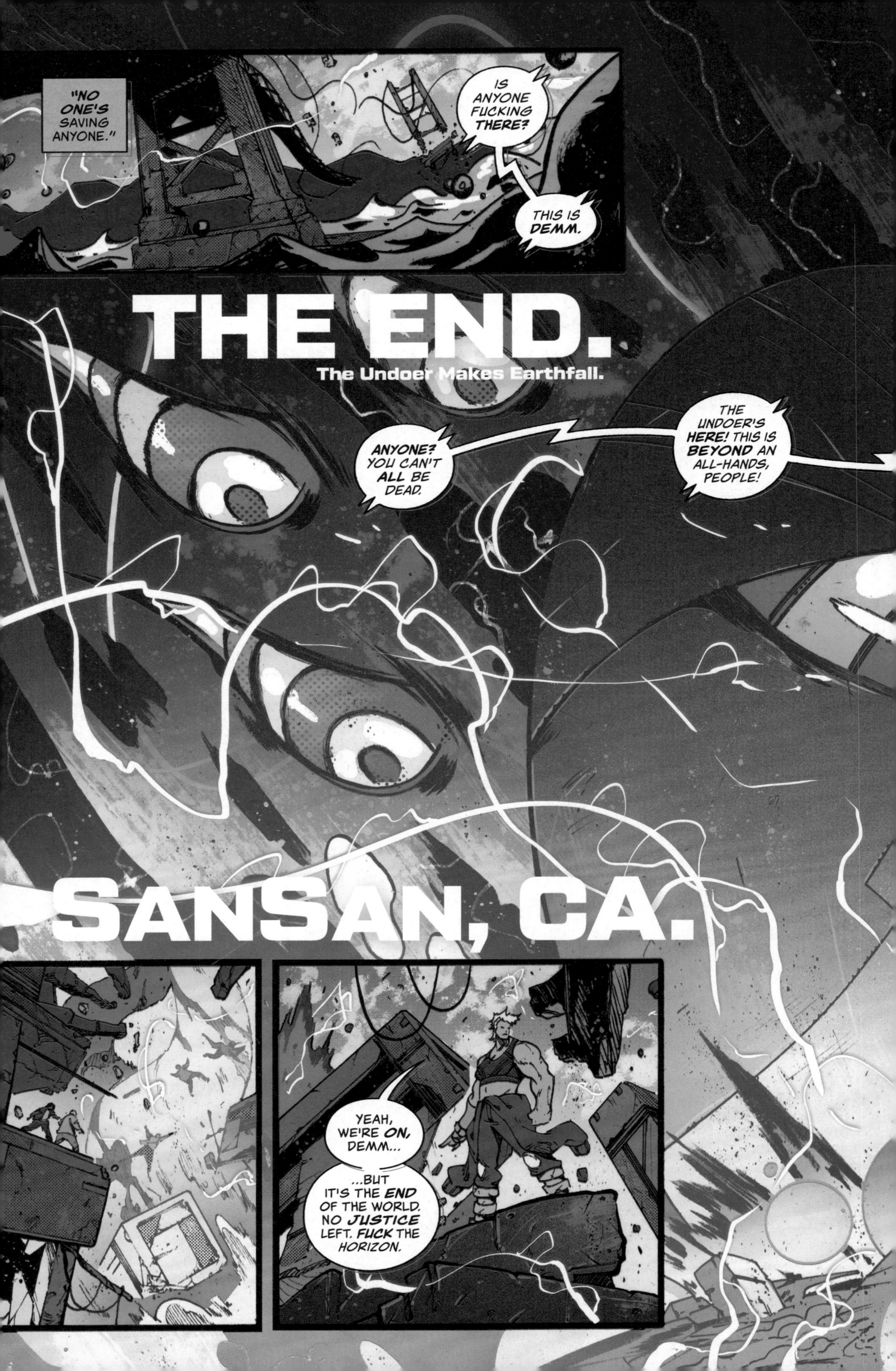
"NO ONE'S SAVING ANYONE."
IS ANYONE FUCKING THERE?
THIS IS DEMM.
THE END.
The Undoer Makes Earthfall.
ANYONE? YOU CAN'T ALL BE DEAD.
THE UNDOER'S HERE! THIS IS BEYOND AN ALL-HANDS, PEOPLE!
SANSAN, CA.
YEAH, WE'RE ON, DEMM...
...BUT IT'S THE END OF THE WORLD. NO JUSTICE LEFT. FUCK THE HORIZON.

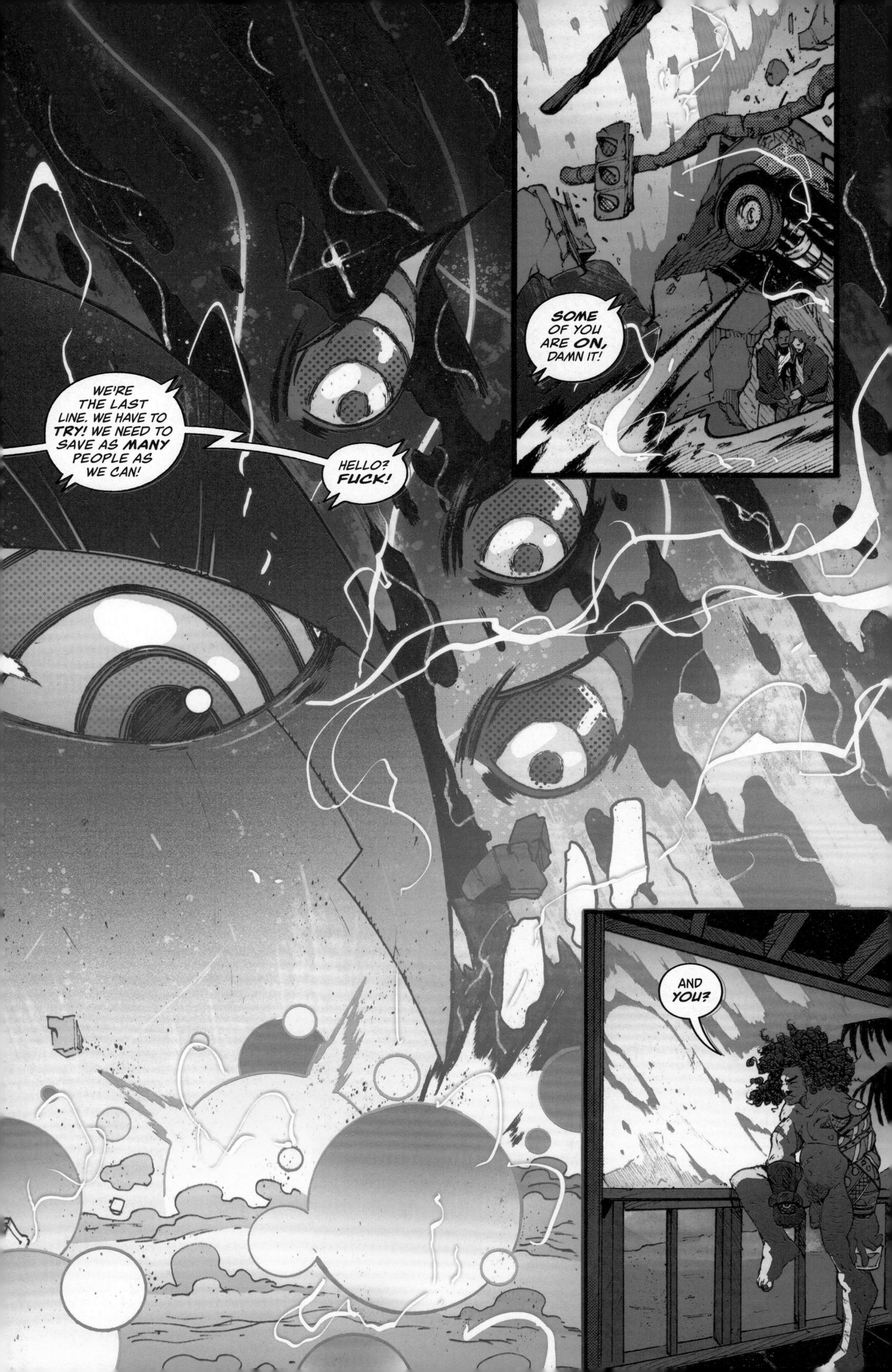

WE'RE THE LAST LINE. WE HAVE TO TRY! WE NEED TO SAVE AS MANY PEOPLE AS WE CAN!
HELLO? FUCK!
SOME OF YOU ARE ON, DAMN IT!
AND YOU?

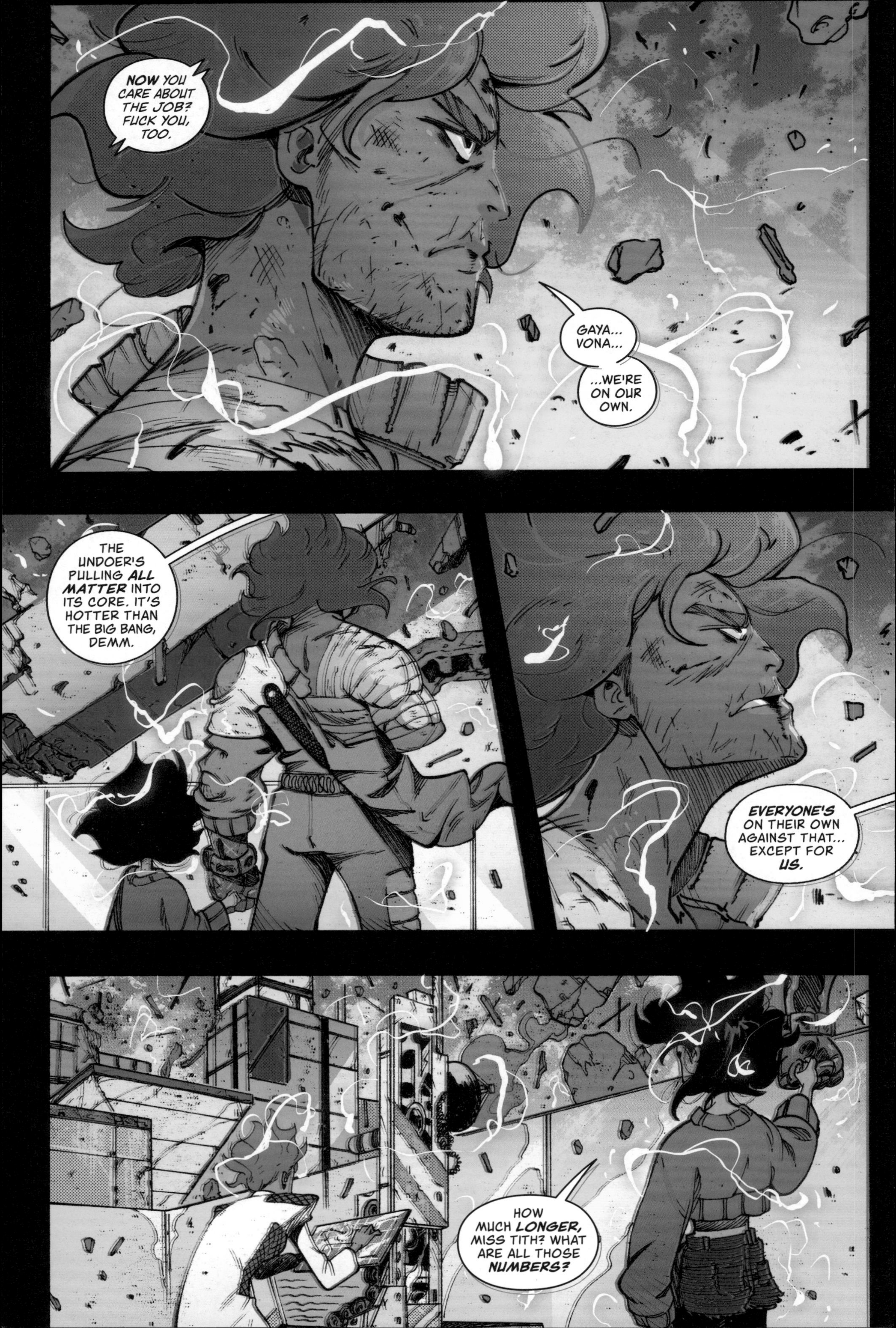
NOW YOU CARE ABOUT THE JOB? FUCK YOU, TOO.
GAYA... VONA...
...WE'RE ON OUR OWN.
THE UNDOER'S PULLING ALL MATTER INTO ITS CORE. IT'S HOTTER THAN THE BIG BANG, DEMM.
EVERYONE'S ON THEIR OWN AGAINST THAT... EXCEPT FOR US.
HOW MUCH LONGER, MISS TITH? WHAT ARE ALL THOSE NUMBERS?

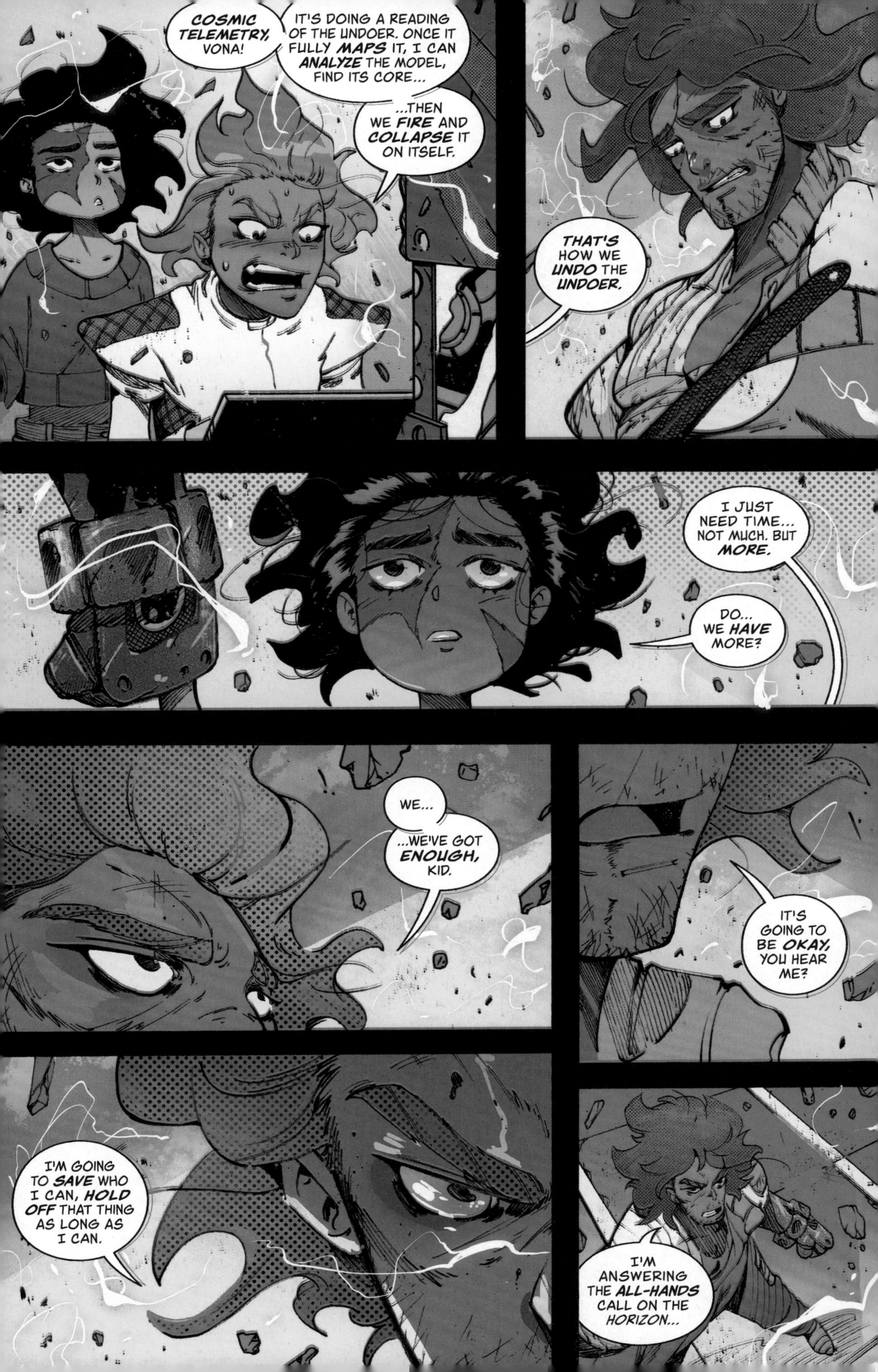
COSMIC TELEMETRY, VONA!
IT'S DOING A READING OF THE UNDOER. ONCE IT FULLY MAPS IT, I CAN ANALYZE THE MODEL, FIND ITS CORE...
...THEN WE FIRE AND COLLAPSE IT ON ITSELF.
THAT'S HOW WE UNDO THE UNDOER.
I JUST NEED TIME... NOT MUCH. BUT MORE.
DO... WE HAVE MORE?
WE...
...WE'VE GOT ENOUGH, KID.
IT'S GOING TO BE OKAY, YOU HEAR ME?
I'M GOING TO SAVE WHO I CAN, HOLD OFF THAT THING AS LONG AS I CAN.
I'M ANSWERING THE ALL-HANDS CALL ON THE HORIZON...

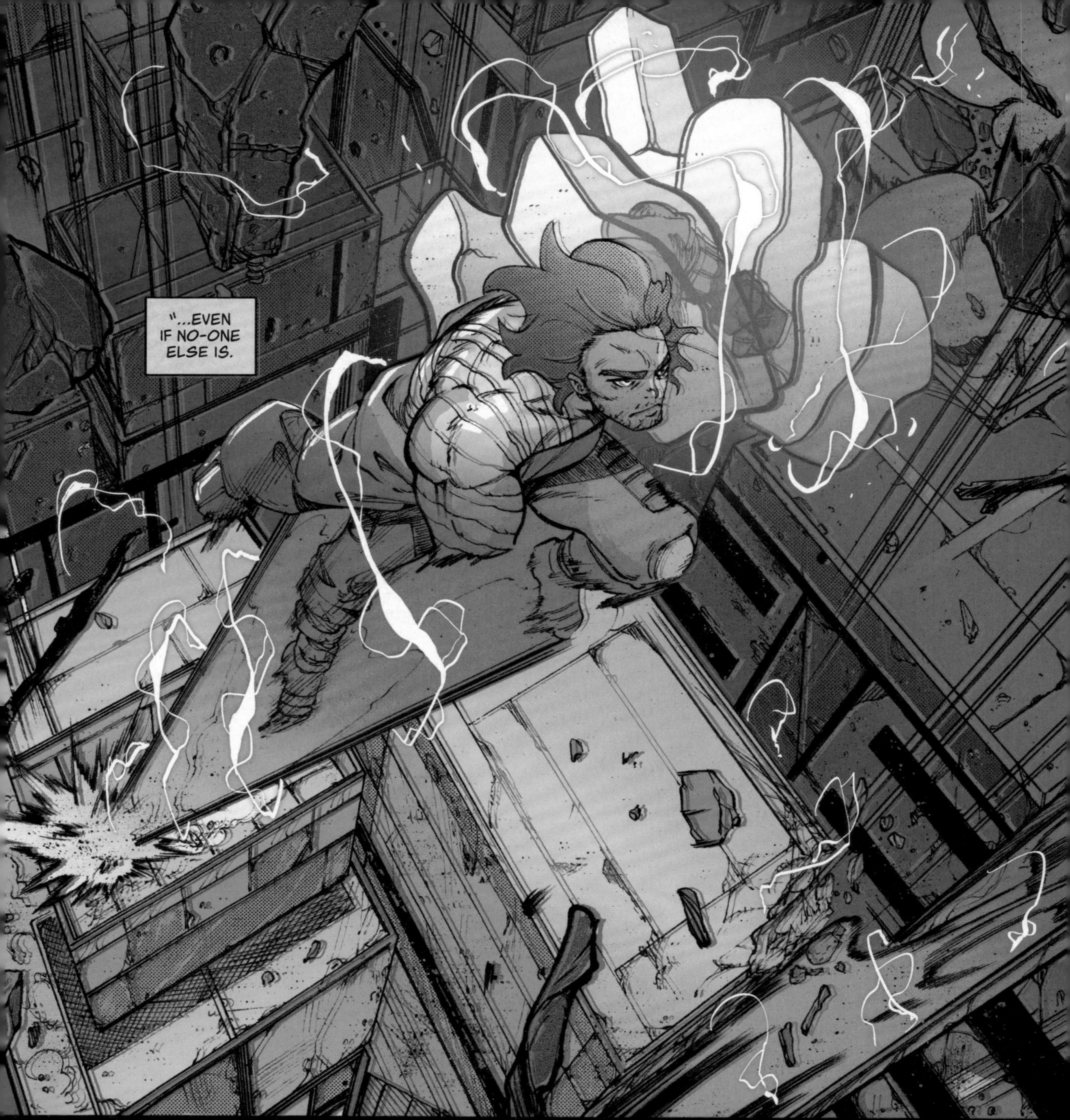
"...EVEN IF NO-ONE ELSE IS.
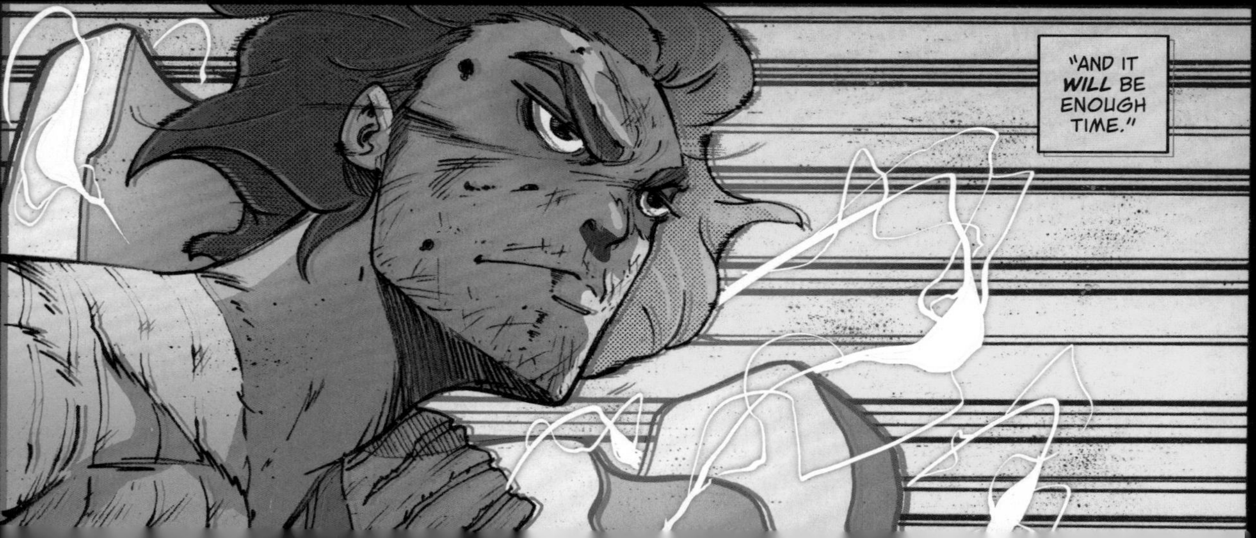
"AND IT WILL BE ENOUGH TIME."

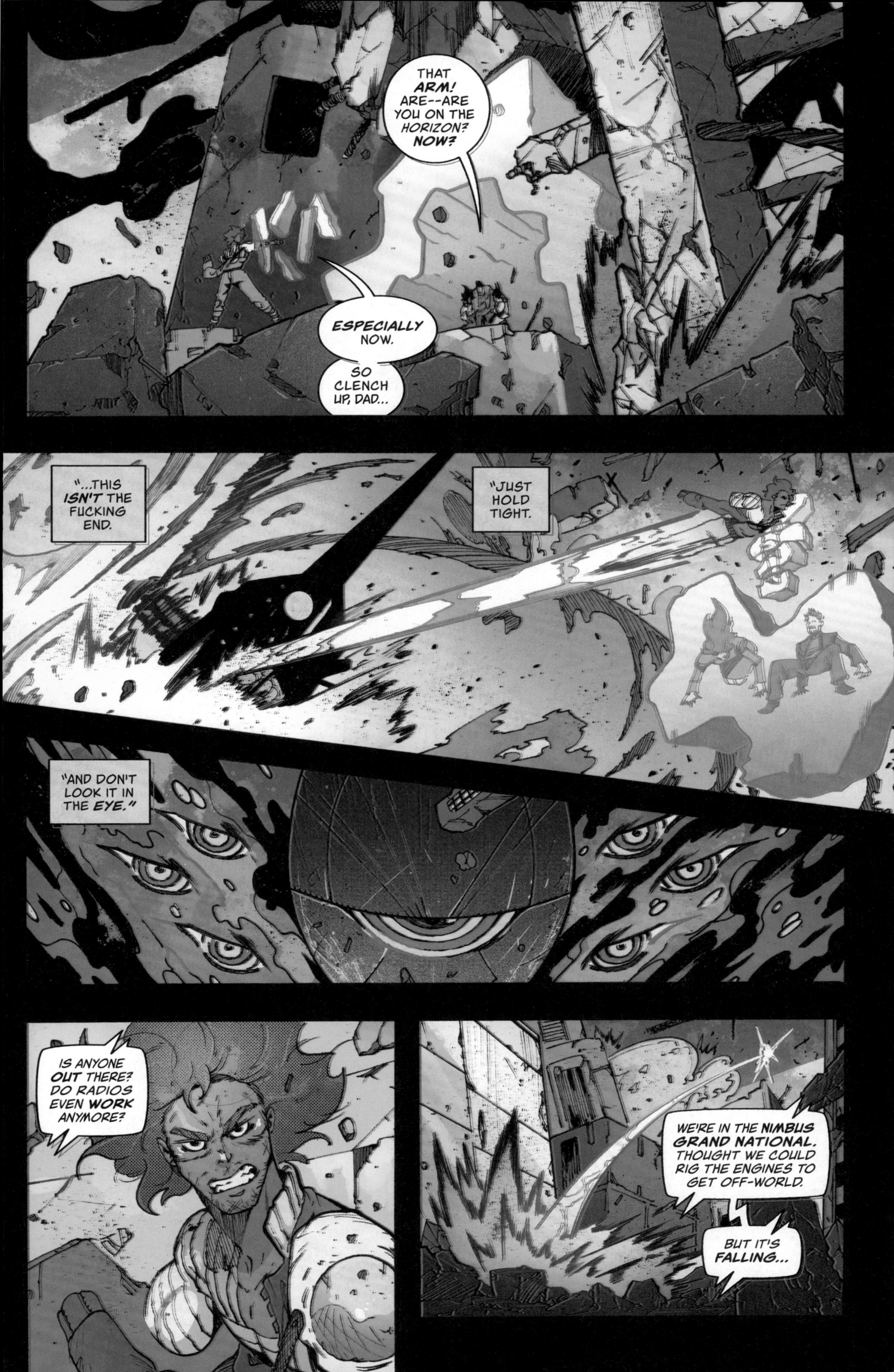

THAT *ARM!* ARE--ARE YOU ON THE *HORIZON?* *NOW?*
ESPECIALLY NOW.
SO CLENCH UP, DAD...
"...THIS *ISN'T* THE FUCKING END.
"JUST HOLD TIGHT.
"AND DON'T LOOK IT IN THE *EYE.*"
IS ANYONE *OUT* THERE? DO RADIOS EVEN *WORK* ANYMORE?
WE'RE IN THE *NIMBUS GRAND NATIONAL.* THOUGHT WE COULD RIG THE ENGINES TO GET OFF-WORLD.
BUT IT'S *FALLING...*

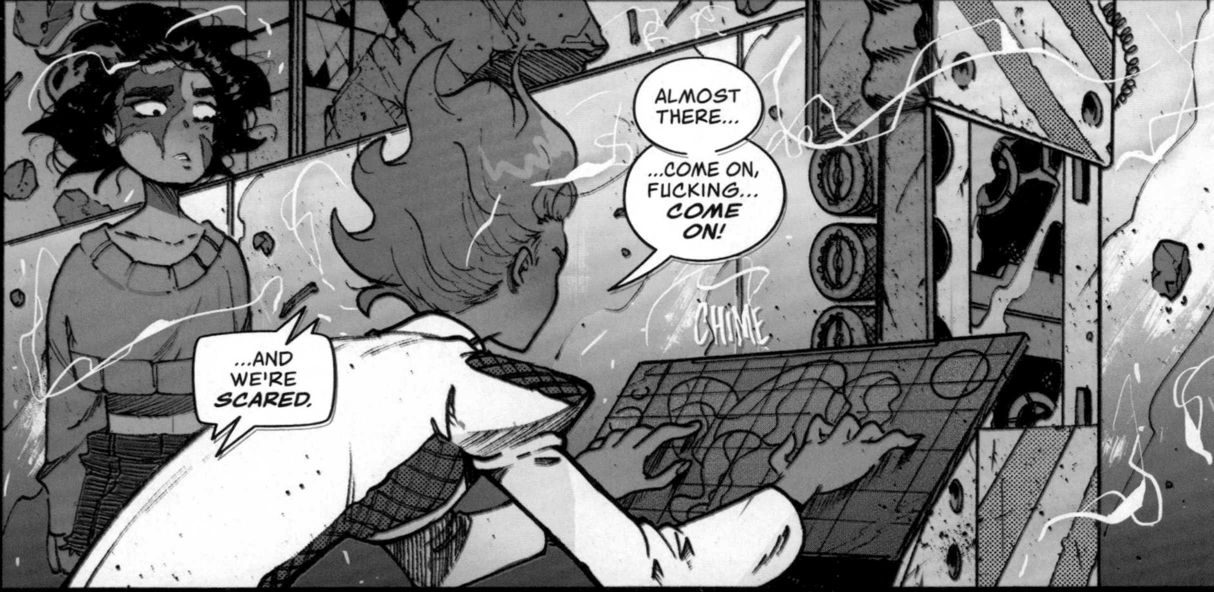
ALMOST THERE...
...COME ON, FUCKING... COME ON!
CHIME
...AND WE'RE SCARED.
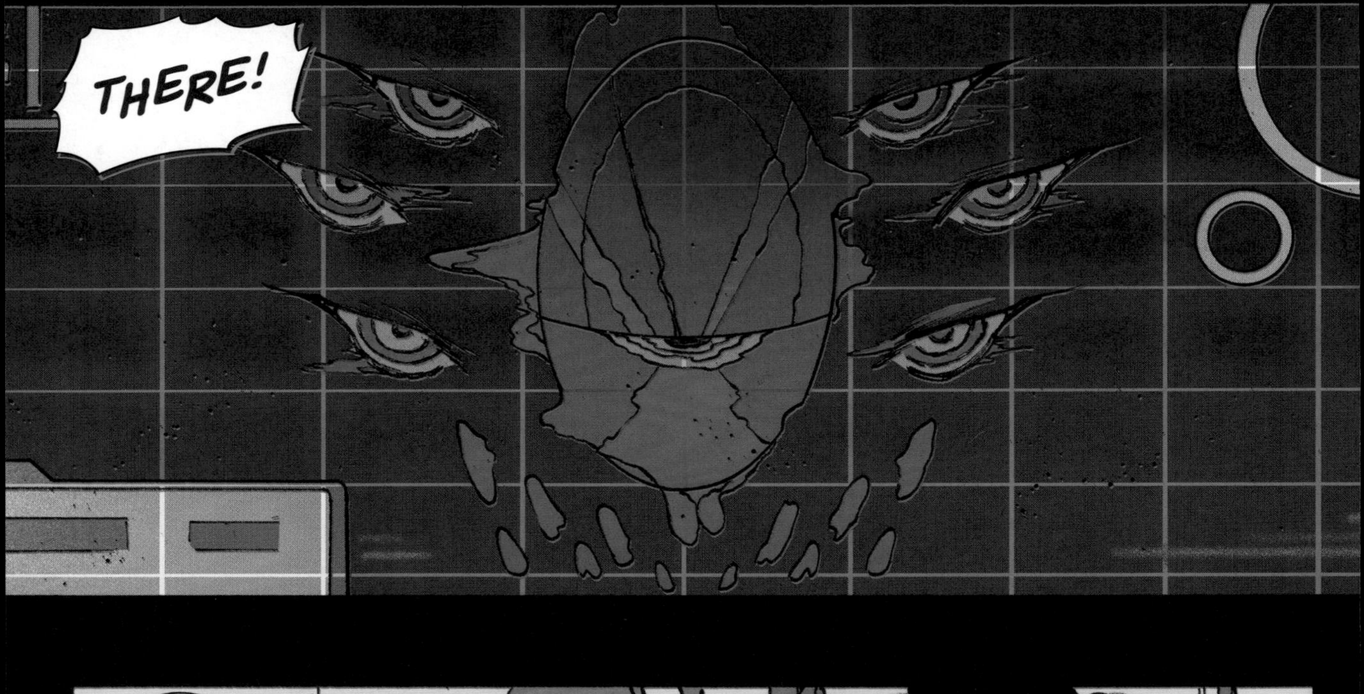
THERE!
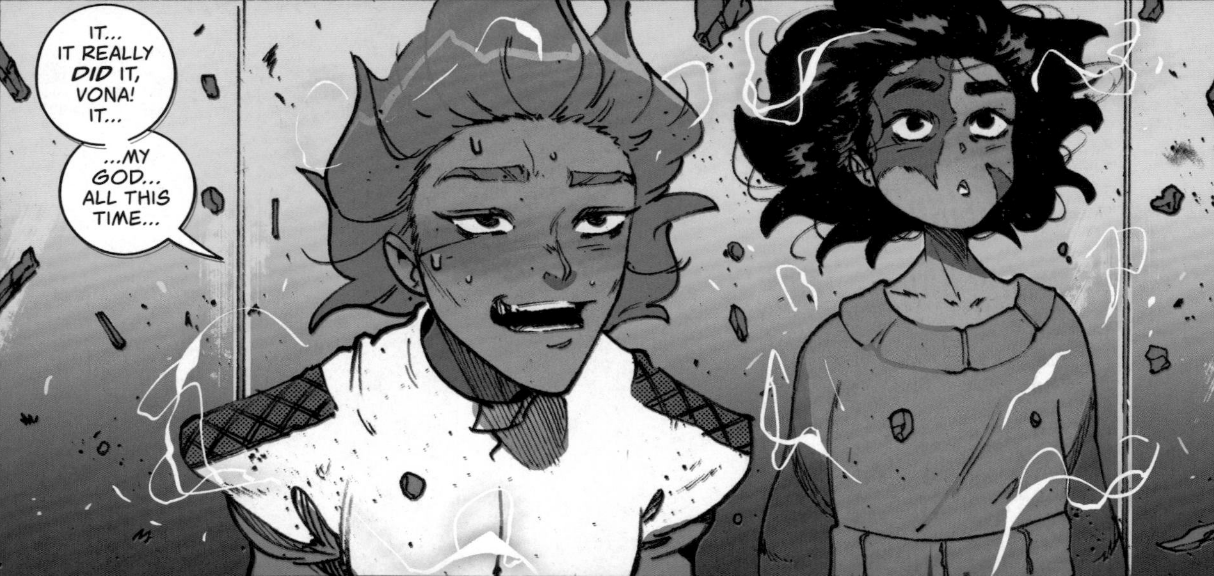
IT... IT REALLY DID IT, VONA! IT...
...MY GOD... ALL THIS TIME...

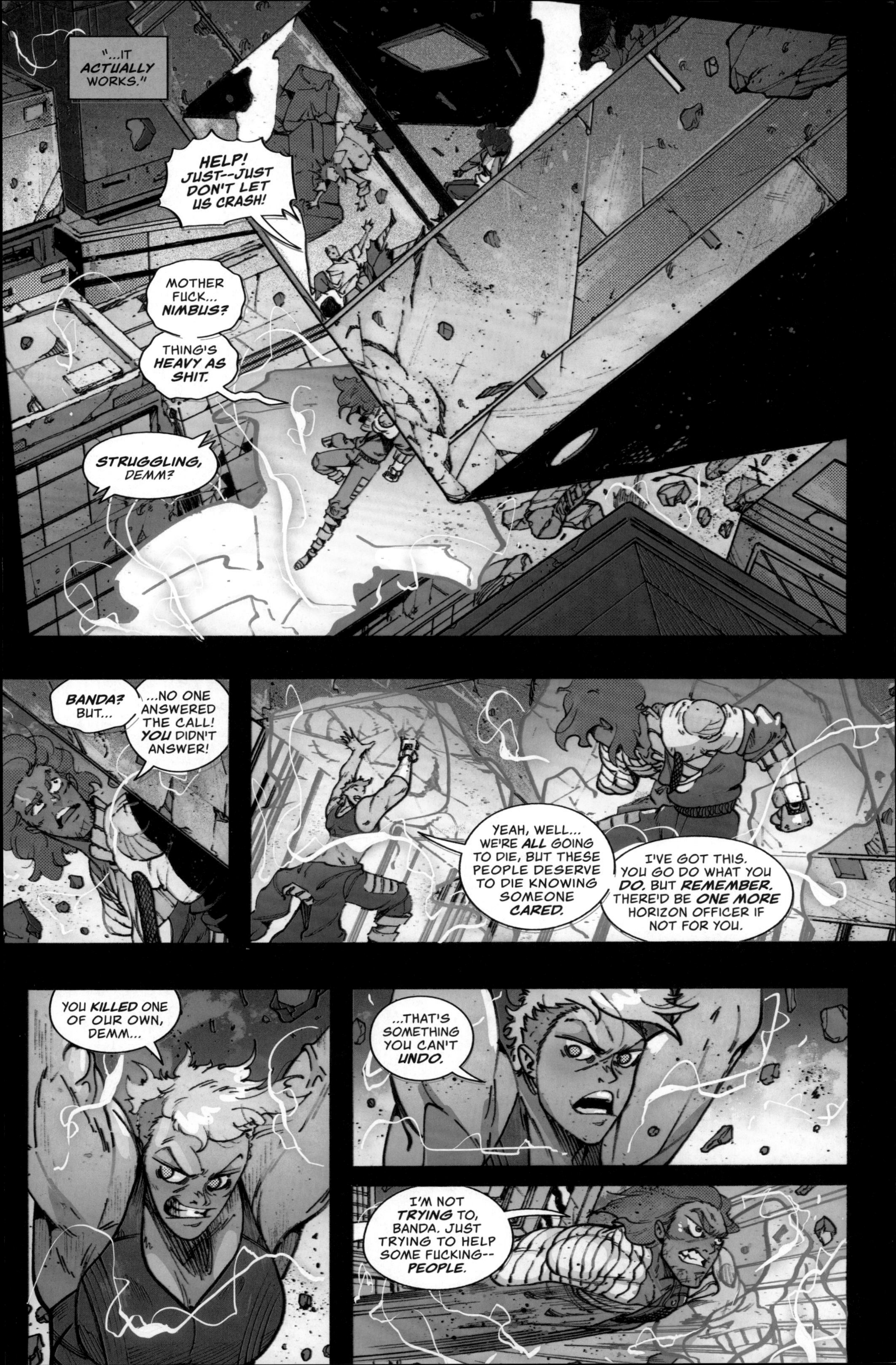
"...IT ACTUALLY WORKS."
HELP! JUST--JUST DON'T LET US CRASH!
MOTHER FUCK... NIMBUS?
THING'S HEAVY AS SHIT.
STRUGGLING, DEMM?
BANDA? BUT...
...NO ONE ANSWERED THE CALL! YOU DIDN'T ANSWER!
YEAH, WELL... WE'RE ALL GOING TO DIE, BUT THESE PEOPLE DESERVE TO DIE KNOWING SOMEONE CARED.
I'VE GOT THIS. YOU GO DO WHAT YOU DO. BUT REMEMBER. THERE'D BE ONE MORE HORIZON OFFICER IF NOT FOR YOU.
YOU KILLED ONE OF OUR OWN, DEMM...
...THAT'S SOMETHING YOU CAN'T UNDO.
I'M NOT TRYING TO, BANDA. JUST TRYING TO HELP SOME FUCKING-- PEOPLE.

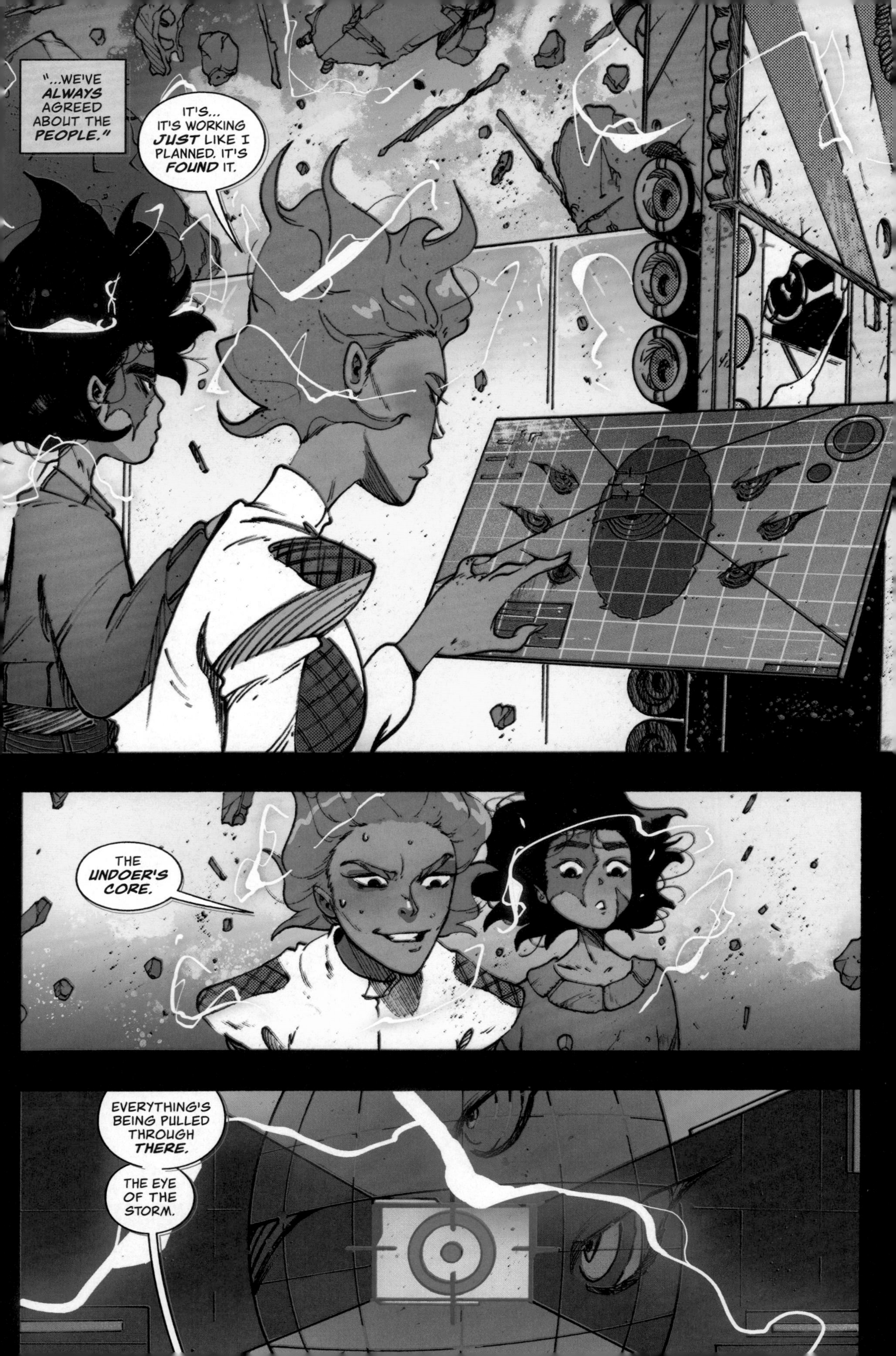
"...WE'VE ALWAYS AGREED ABOUT THE PEOPLE."
IT'S... IT'S WORKING JUST LIKE I PLANNED. IT'S FOUND IT.
THE UNDOER'S CORE.
EVERYTHING'S BEING PULLED THROUGH THERE.
THE EYE OF THE STORM.

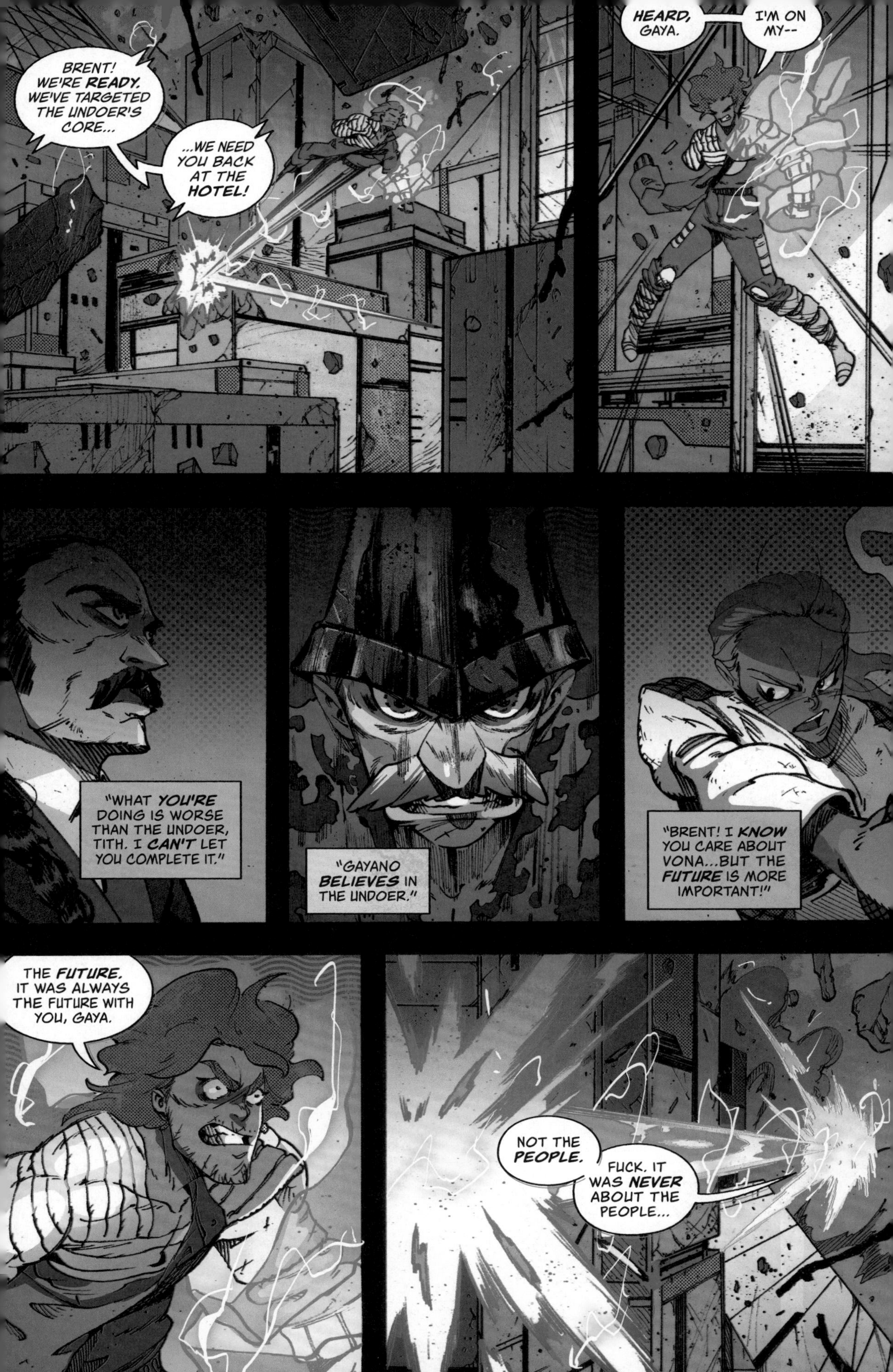
BRENT! WE'RE READY. WE'VE TARGETED THE UNDOER'S CORE...
...WE NEED YOU BACK AT THE HOTEL!
HEARD, GAYA.
I'M ON MY--
"WHAT YOU'RE DOING IS WORSE THAN THE UNDOER, TITH. I CAN'T LET YOU COMPLETE IT."
"GAYANO BELIEVES IN THE UNDOER."
"BRENT! I KNOW YOU CARE ABOUT VONA...BUT THE FUTURE IS MORE IMPORTANT!"
THE FUTURE. IT WAS ALWAYS THE FUTURE WITH YOU, GAYA.
NOT THE PEOPLE.
FUCK. IT WAS NEVER ABOUT THE PEOPLE...

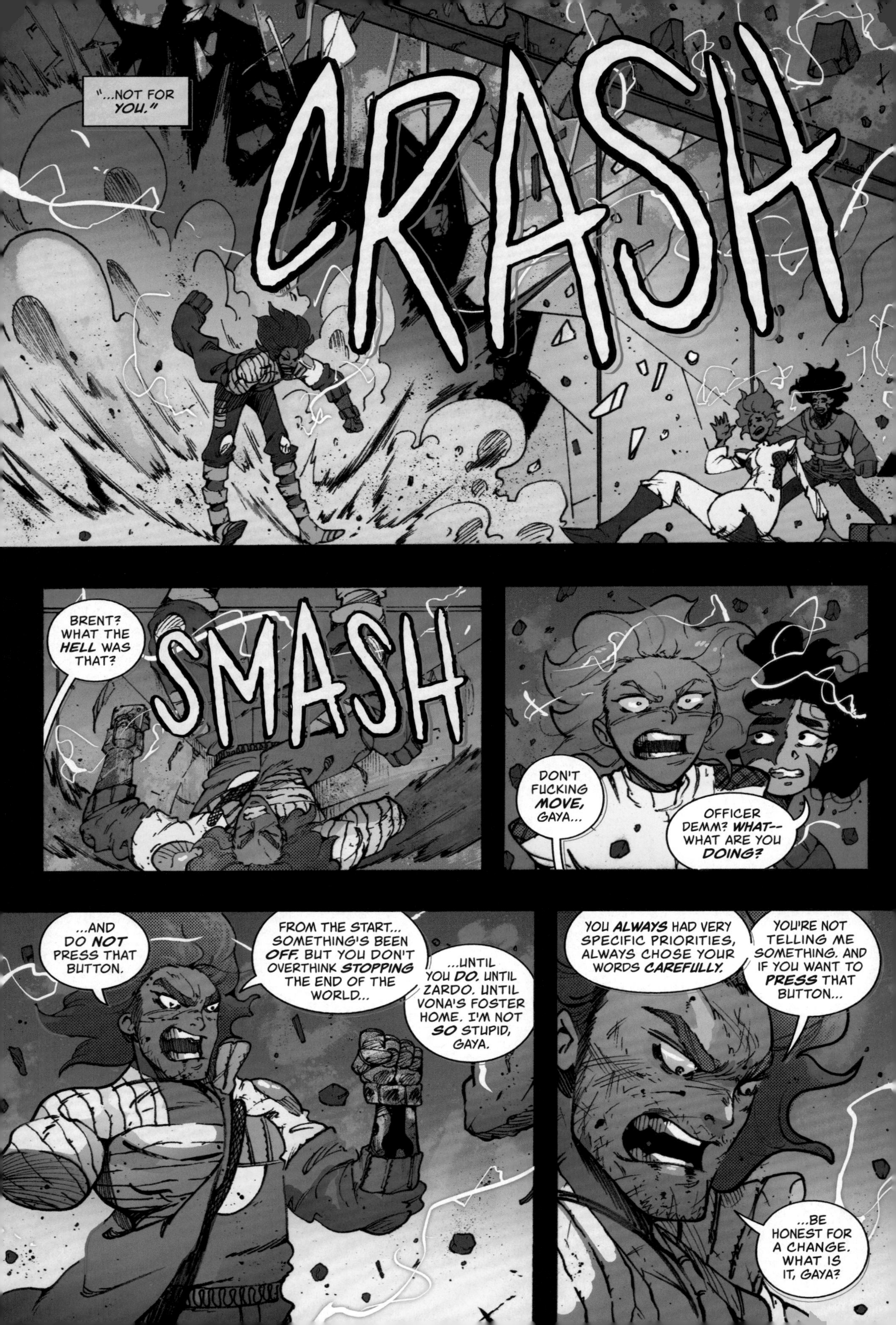

"...NOT FOR YOU."
CRASH
BRENT? WHAT THE HELL WAS THAT?
SMASH
DON'T FUCKING MOVE, GAYA...
OFFICER DEMM? WHAT-- WHAT ARE YOU DOING?
...AND DO NOT PRESS THAT BUTTON.
FROM THE START... SOMETHING'S BEEN OFF. BUT YOU DON'T OVERTHINK STOPPING THE END OF THE WORLD...
...UNTIL YOU DO. UNTIL ZARDO. UNTIL VONA'S FOSTER HOME. I'M NOT SO STUPID, GAYA.
YOU ALWAYS HAD VERY SPECIFIC PRIORITIES, ALWAYS CHOSE YOUR WORDS CAREFULLY.
YOU'RE NOT TELLING ME SOMETHING. AND IF YOU WANT TO PRESS THAT BUTTON...
...BE HONEST FOR A CHANGE. WHAT IS IT, GAYA?

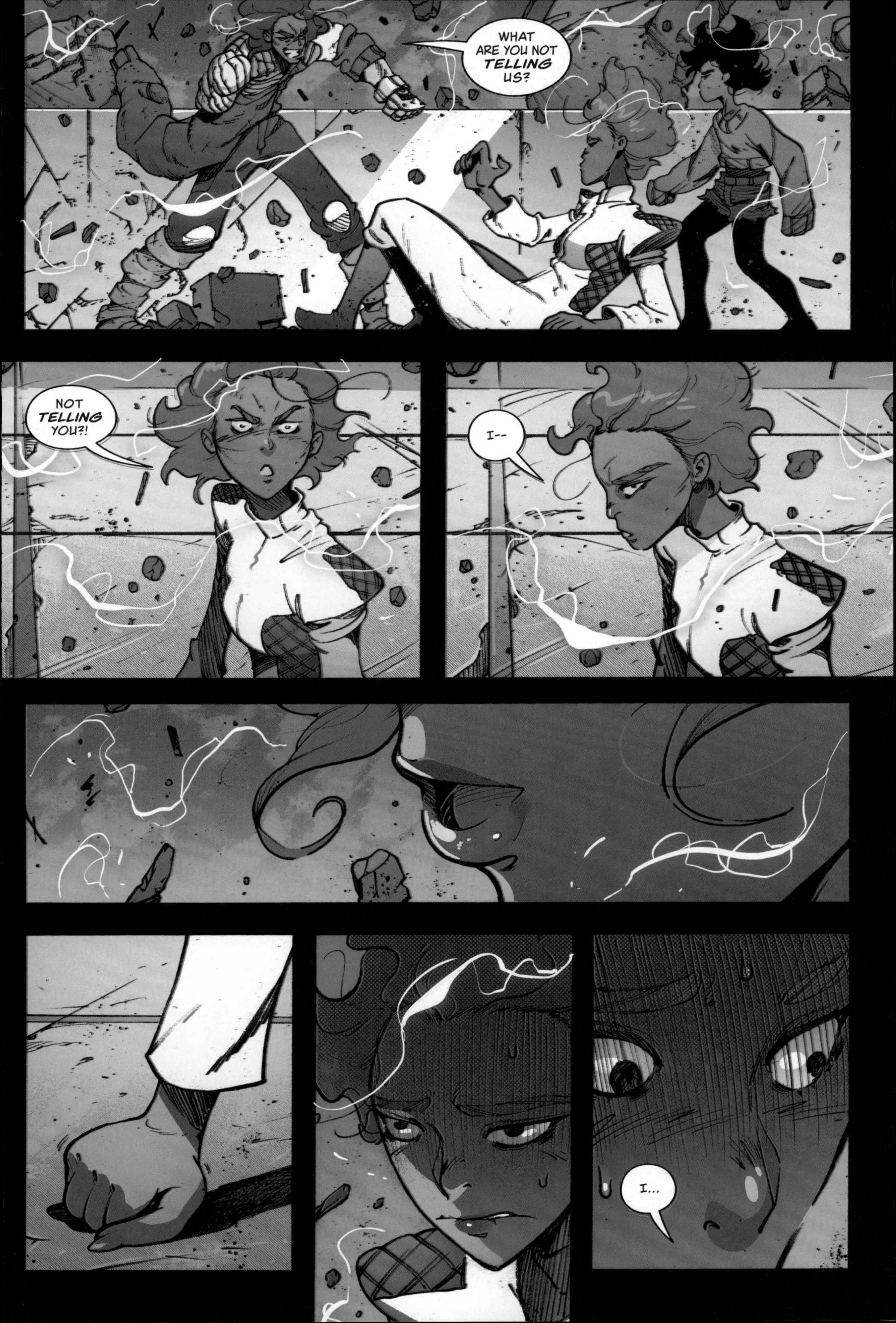
WHAT ARE YOU NOT TELLING US?
NOT TELLING YOU?!
I--
I...

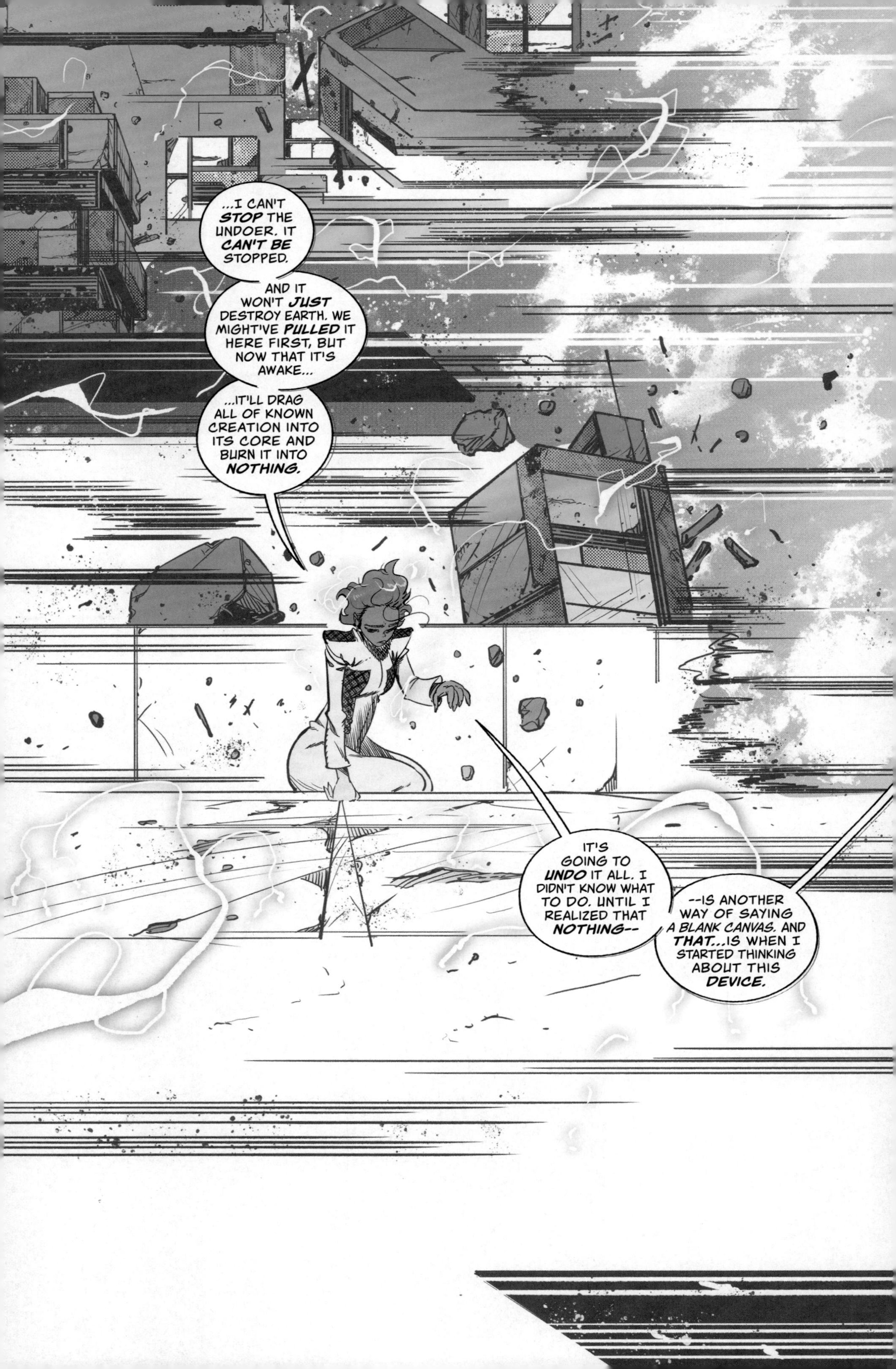
...I CAN'T STOP THE UNDOER. IT CAN'T BE STOPPED.
AND IT WON'T JUST DESTROY EARTH. WE MIGHT'VE PULLED IT HERE FIRST, BUT NOW THAT IT'S AWAKE...
...IT'LL DRAG ALL OF KNOWN CREATION INTO ITS CORE AND BURN IT INTO NOTHING.
IT'S GOING TO UNDO IT ALL. I DIDN'T KNOW WHAT TO DO. UNTIL I REALIZED THAT NOTHING--
--IS ANOTHER WAY OF SAYING A BLANK CANVAS. AND THAT...IS WHEN I STARTED THINKING ABOUT THIS DEVICE.

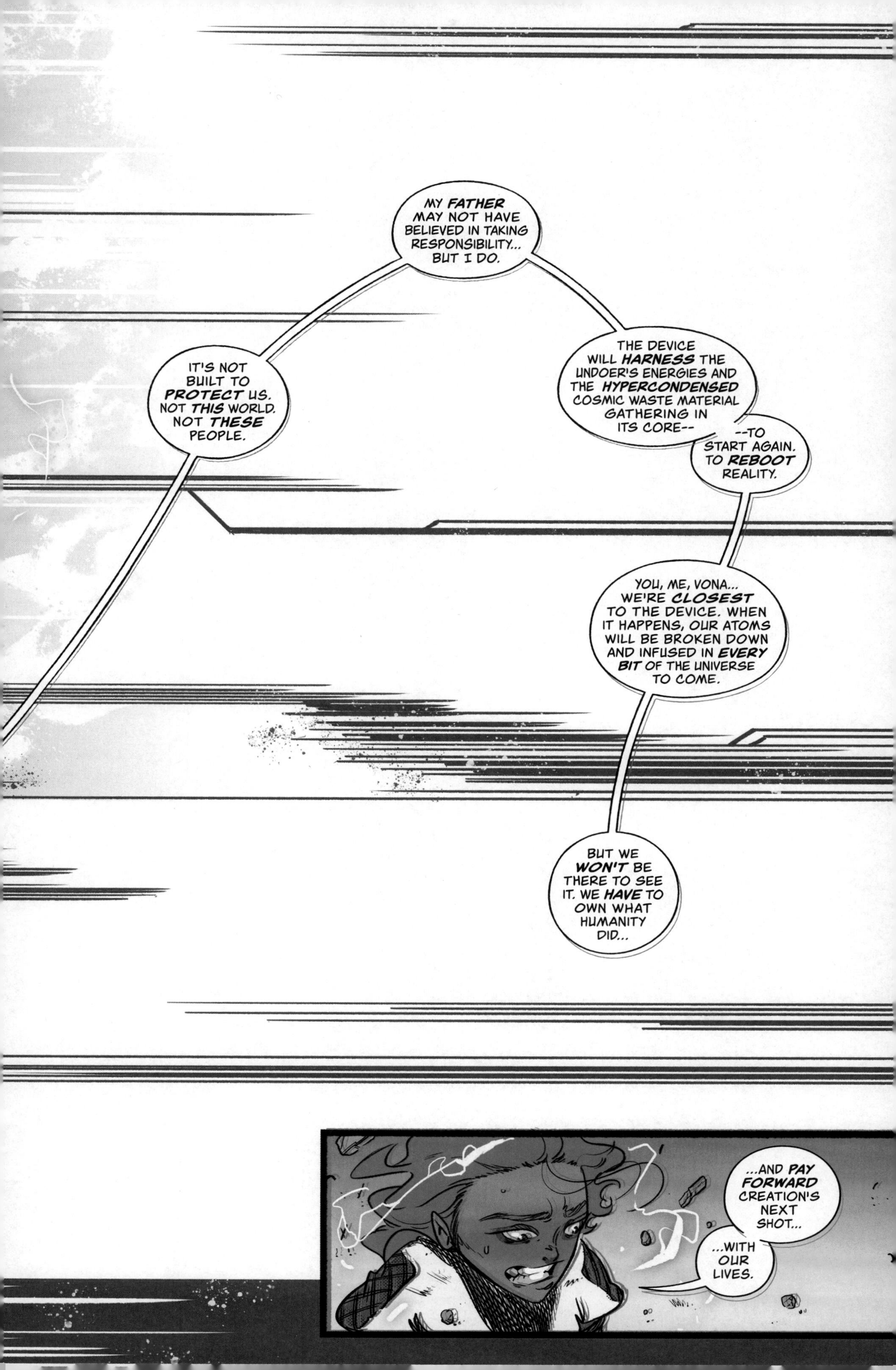
IT'S NOT BUILT TO PROTECT US. NOT THIS WORLD. NOT THESE PEOPLE.
MY FATHER MAY NOT HAVE BELIEVED IN TAKING RESPONSIBILITY... BUT I DO.
THE DEVICE WILL HARNESS THE UNDOER'S ENERGIES AND THE HYPERCONDENSED COSMIC WASTE MATERIAL GATHERING IN ITS CORE--
--TO START AGAIN. TO REBOOT REALITY.
YOU, ME, VONA... WE'RE CLOSEST TO THE DEVICE. WHEN IT HAPPENS, OUR ATOMS WILL BE BROKEN DOWN AND INFUSED IN EVERY BIT OF THE UNIVERSE TO COME.
BUT WE WON'T BE THERE TO SEE IT. WE HAVE TO OWN WHAT HUMANITY DID...
...AND PAY FORWARD CREATION'S NEXT SHOT...
...WITH OUR LIVES.

OUR...

...LIVES?!

OUR...

...OUR LIVES.

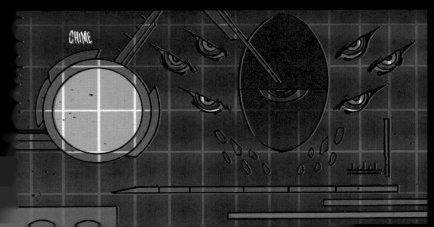

YOU...YOU SAID WE WERE *SAVING* THESE PEOPLE. *STOPPING* THE APOCALYPSE... BUT YOU WANT US TO *RIDE* IT INTO THE DARK?

I DIDN'T HAVE A CHOICE, BRENT...I NEEDED TO, I HAD TO DO SOMETHING.

CHIME

LISTEN.

LISTEN...

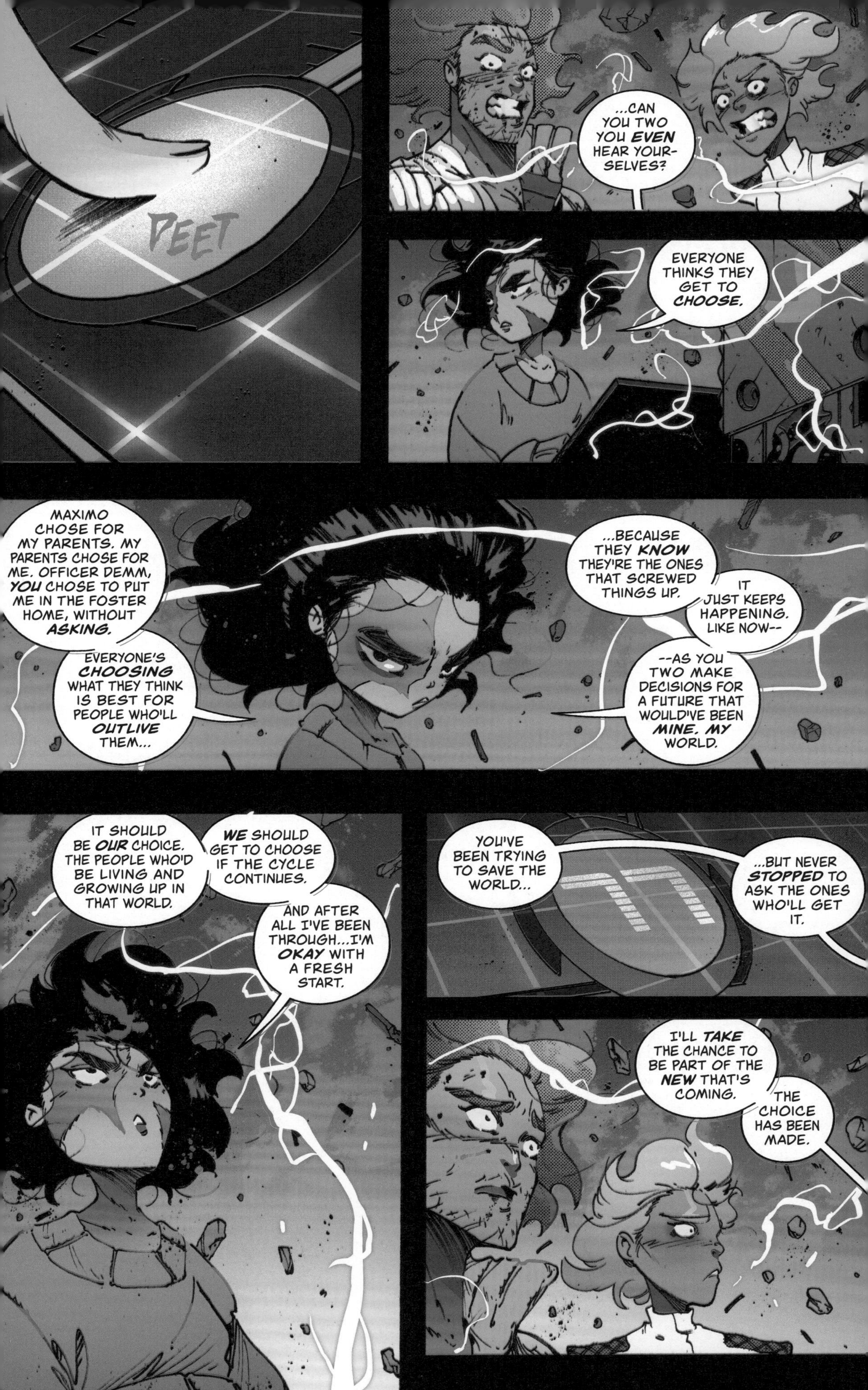
DEET
...CAN YOU TWO YOU EVEN HEAR YOUR-SELVES?
EVERYONE THINKS THEY GET TO CHOOSE.
MAXIMO CHOSE FOR MY PARENTS. MY PARENTS CHOSE FOR ME. OFFICER DEMM, YOU CHOSE TO PUT ME IN THE FOSTER HOME, WITHOUT ASKING.
EVERYONE'S CHOOSING WHAT THEY THINK IS BEST FOR PEOPLE WHO'LL OUTLIVE THEM...
...BECAUSE THEY KNOW THEY'RE THE ONES THAT SCREWED THINGS UP.
IT JUST KEEPS HAPPENING. LIKE NOW--
--AS YOU TWO MAKE DECISIONS FOR A FUTURE THAT WOULD'VE BEEN MINE. MY WORLD.
IT SHOULD BE OUR CHOICE. THE PEOPLE WHO'D BE LIVING AND GROWING UP IN THAT WORLD.
WE SHOULD GET TO CHOOSE IF THE CYCLE CONTINUES.
AND AFTER ALL I'VE BEEN THROUGH...I'M OKAY WITH A FRESH START.
YOU'VE BEEN TRYING TO SAVE THE WORLD...
...BUT NEVER STOPPED TO ASK THE ONES WHO'LL GET IT.
I'LL TAKE THE CHANCE TO BE PART OF THE NEW THAT'S COMING.
THE CHOICE HAS BEEN MADE.

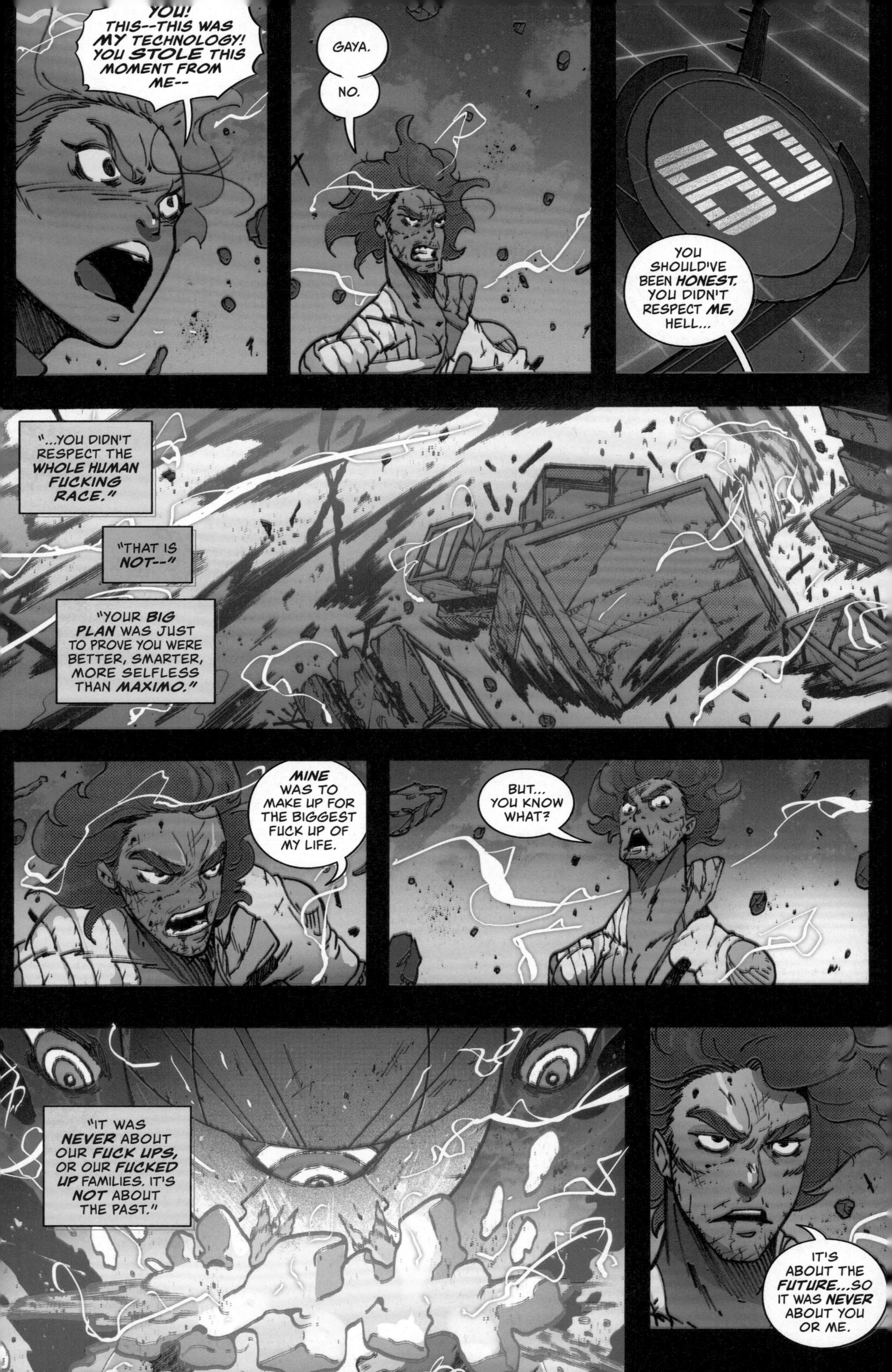
YOU! THIS--THIS WAS MY TECHNOLOGY! YOU STOLE THIS MOMENT FROM ME--
GAYA.
NO.
YOU SHOULD'VE BEEN HONEST. YOU DIDN'T RESPECT ME, HELL...
"...YOU DIDN'T RESPECT THE WHOLE HUMAN FUCKING RACE."
"THAT IS NOT--"
"YOUR BIG PLAN WAS JUST TO PROVE YOU WERE BETTER, SMARTER, MORE SELFLESS THAN MAXIMO."
MINE WAS TO MAKE UP FOR THE BIGGEST FUCK UP OF MY LIFE.
BUT... YOU KNOW WHAT?
"IT WAS NEVER ABOUT OUR FUCK UPS, OR OUR FUCKED UP FAMILIES. IT'S NOT ABOUT THE PAST."
IT'S ABOUT THE FUTURE...SO IT WAS NEVER ABOUT YOU OR ME.

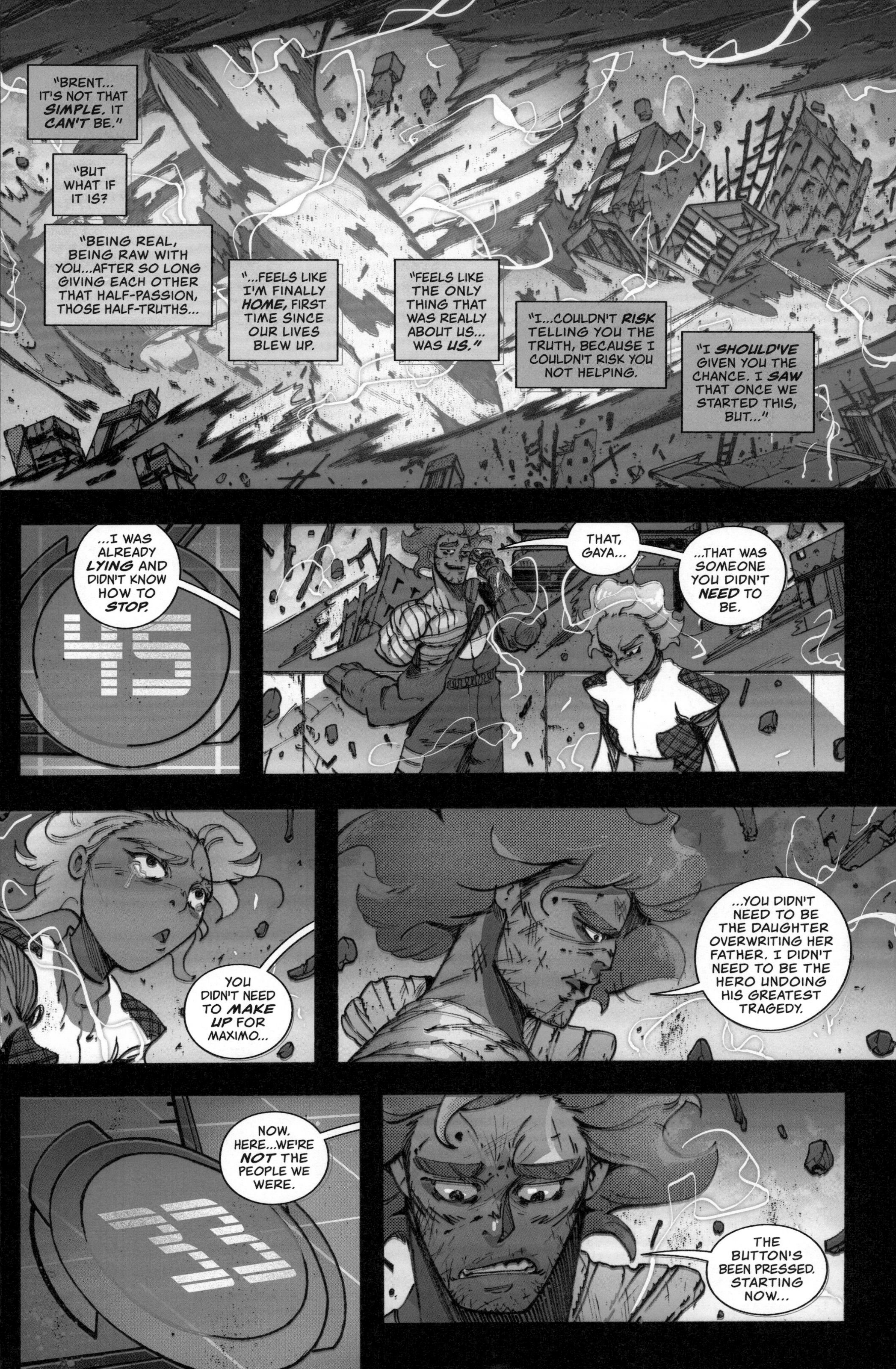

"BRENT... IT'S NOT THAT SIMPLE. IT CAN'T BE."
"BUT WHAT IF IT IS?
"BEING REAL, BEING RAW WITH YOU...AFTER SO LONG GIVING EACH OTHER THAT HALF-PASSION, THOSE HALF-TRUTHS...
"...FEELS LIKE I'M FINALLY HOME, FIRST TIME SINCE OUR LIVES BLEW UP.
"FEELS LIKE THE ONLY THING THAT WAS REALLY ABOUT US... WAS US."
"I...COULDN'T RISK TELLING YOU THE TRUTH, BECAUSE I COULDN'T RISK YOU NOT HELPING.
"I SHOULD'VE GIVEN YOU THE CHANCE. I SAW THAT ONCE WE STARTED THIS, BUT..."
...I WAS ALREADY LYING AND DIDN'T KNOW HOW TO STOP.
45
THAT, GAYA...
...THAT WAS SOMEONE YOU DIDN'T NEED TO BE.
YOU DIDN'T NEED TO MAKE UP FOR MAXIMO...
...YOU DIDN'T NEED TO BE THE DAUGHTER OVERWRITING HER FATHER. I DIDN'T NEED TO BE THE HERO UNDOING HIS GREATEST TRAGEDY.
NOW. HERE...WE'RE NOT THE PEOPLE WE WERE.
THE BUTTON'S BEEN PRESSED. STARTING NOW...

...WE'RE **BOTH** THIS *MOMENT*...

...AND NOTHING MORE.

TOOK YOU *LONG* ENOUGH.

FUCK, GAYA...

21

"...YOU'VE *ALWAYS* MADE ME *NEW.*"

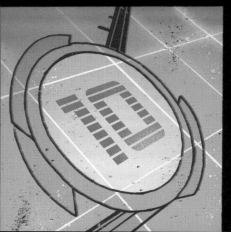

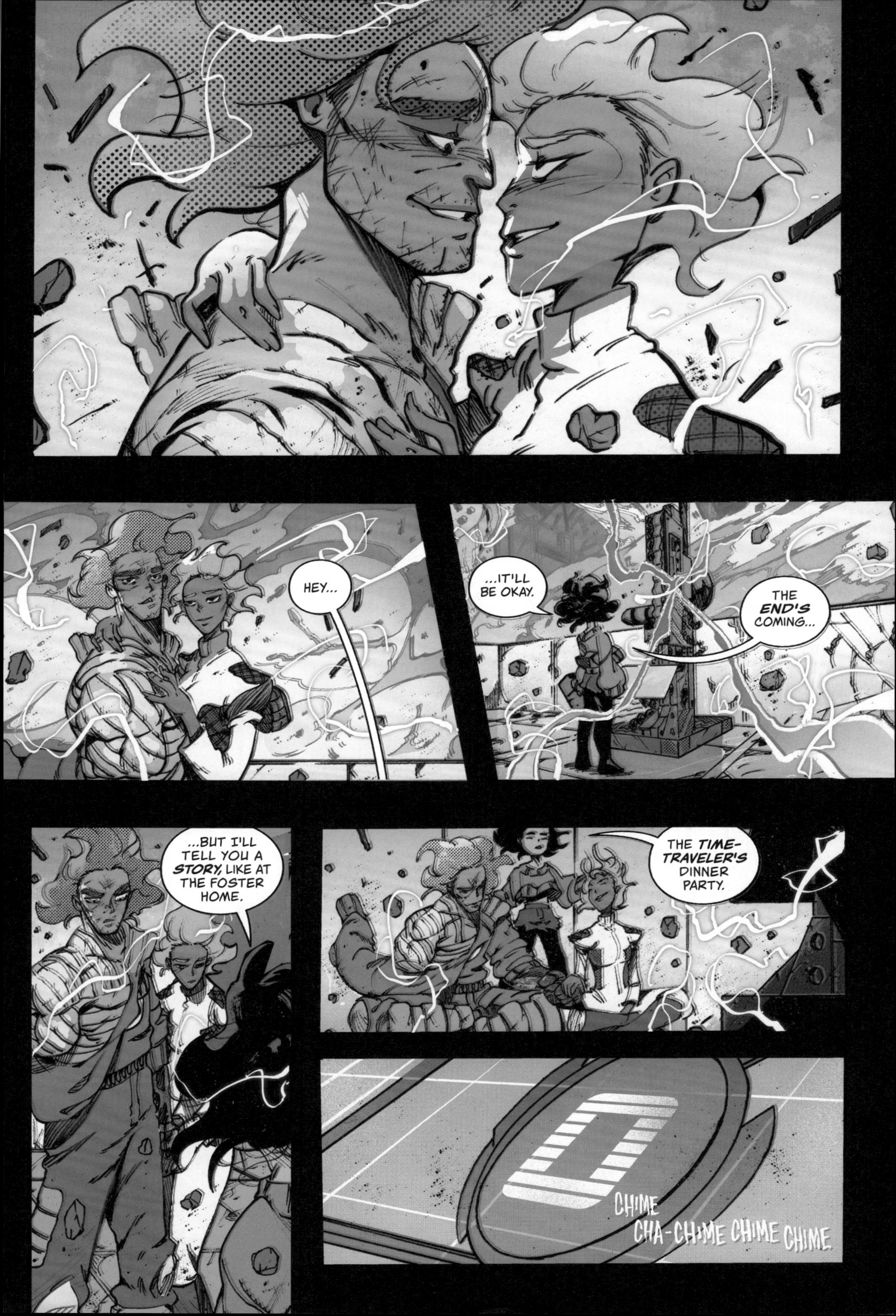
HEY...
...IT'LL BE OKAY.
THE END'S COMING...
...BUT I'LL TELL YOU A STORY, LIKE AT THE FOSTER HOME.
THE TIME-TRAVELER'S DINNER PARTY.
CHIME
CHA-CHIME CHIME CHIME

"THE TIME-TRAVELER WAS A GENIUS AND A DREAMER.

"THANKS TO THE LATTER, NO ONE KNEW HE WAS THE FORMER.

"HIS WHOLE LIFE WAS BUILT AROUND ONE IDEA.

"TIME TRAVEL, OF COURSE. WHAT DID YOU THINK?

"NOTHING ELSE MATTERED.

"HE COULD'VE SOLD A THOUSAND PATENTS, COWED TESLA AND EDISON.

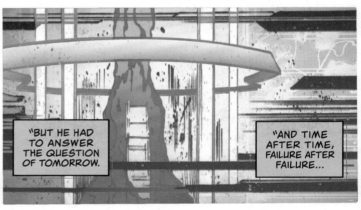

"BUT HE HAD TO ANSWER THE QUESTION OF TOMORROW.

"AND TIME AFTER TIME, FAILURE AFTER FAILURE...

"...HE GREW MORE AND MORE BITTER."

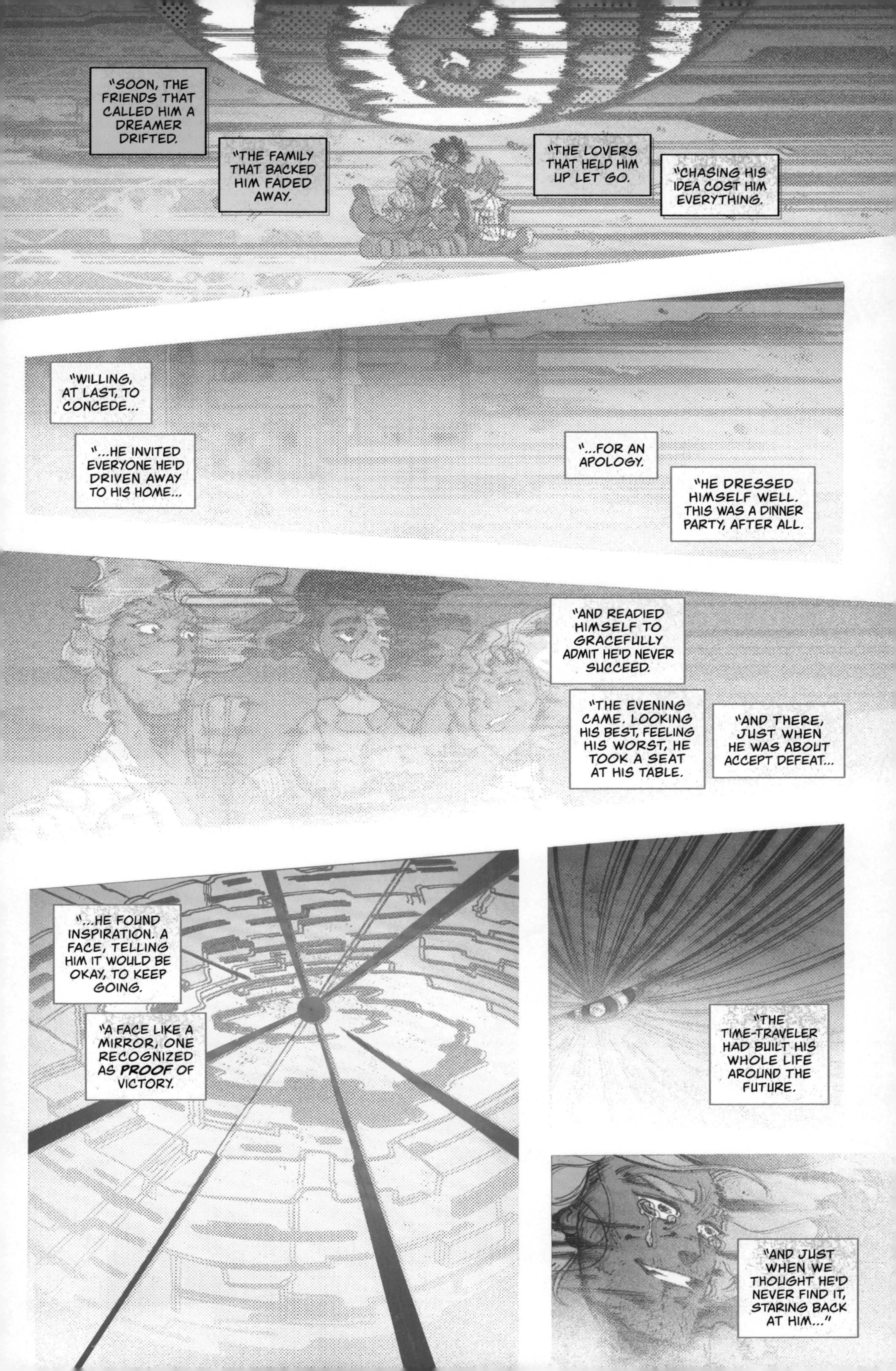
"SOON, THE FRIENDS THAT CALLED HIM A DREAMER DRIFTED.
"THE FAMILY THAT BACKED HIM FADED AWAY.
"THE LOVERS THAT HELD HIM UP LET GO.
"CHASING HIS IDEA COST HIM EVERYTHING.
"WILLING, AT LAST, TO CONCEDE...
"...HE INVITED EVERYONE HE'D DRIVEN AWAY TO HIS HOME...
"...FOR AN APOLOGY.
"HE DRESSED HIMSELF WELL. THIS WAS A DINNER PARTY, AFTER ALL.
"AND READIED HIMSELF TO GRACEFULLY ADMIT HE'D NEVER SUCCEED.
"THE EVENING CAME. LOOKING HIS BEST, FEELING HIS WORST, HE TOOK A SEAT AT HIS TABLE.
"AND THERE, JUST WHEN HE WAS ABOUT ACCEPT DEFEAT...
"...HE FOUND INSPIRATION. A FACE, TELLING HIM IT WOULD BE OKAY, TO KEEP GOING.
"A FACE LIKE A MIRROR, ONE RECOGNIZED AS ***PROOF*** OF VICTORY.
"THE TIME-TRAVELER HAD BUILT HIS WHOLE LIFE AROUND THE FUTURE.
"AND JUST WHEN WE THOUGHT HE'D NEVER FIND IT, STARING BACK AT HIM..."

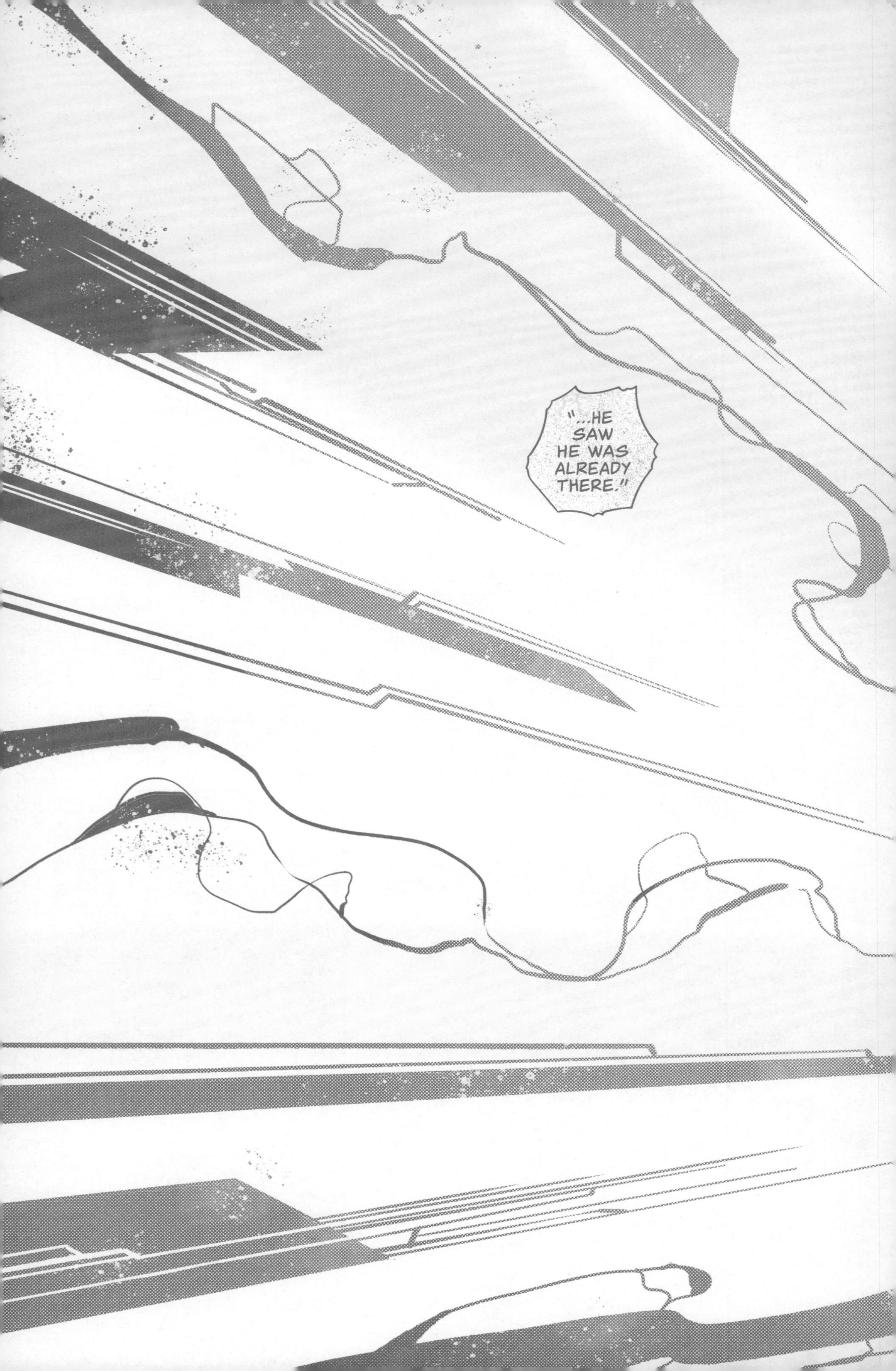
"...HE SAW HE WAS ALREADY THERE."

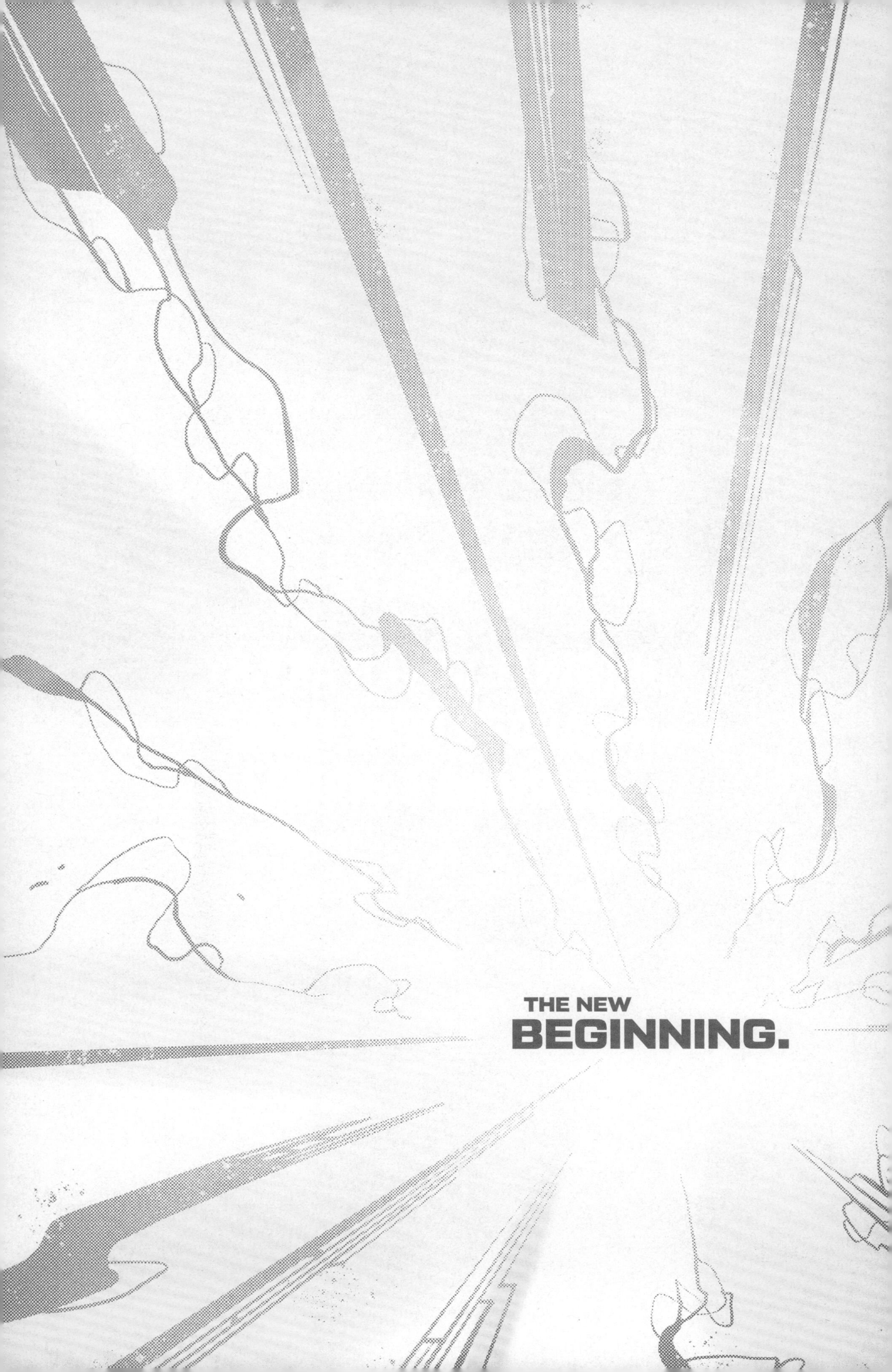
THE NEW
BEGINNING.

ORIGINAL COVER ART BY
RICARDO LÓPEZ ORTIZ
& TRIONA FARRELL

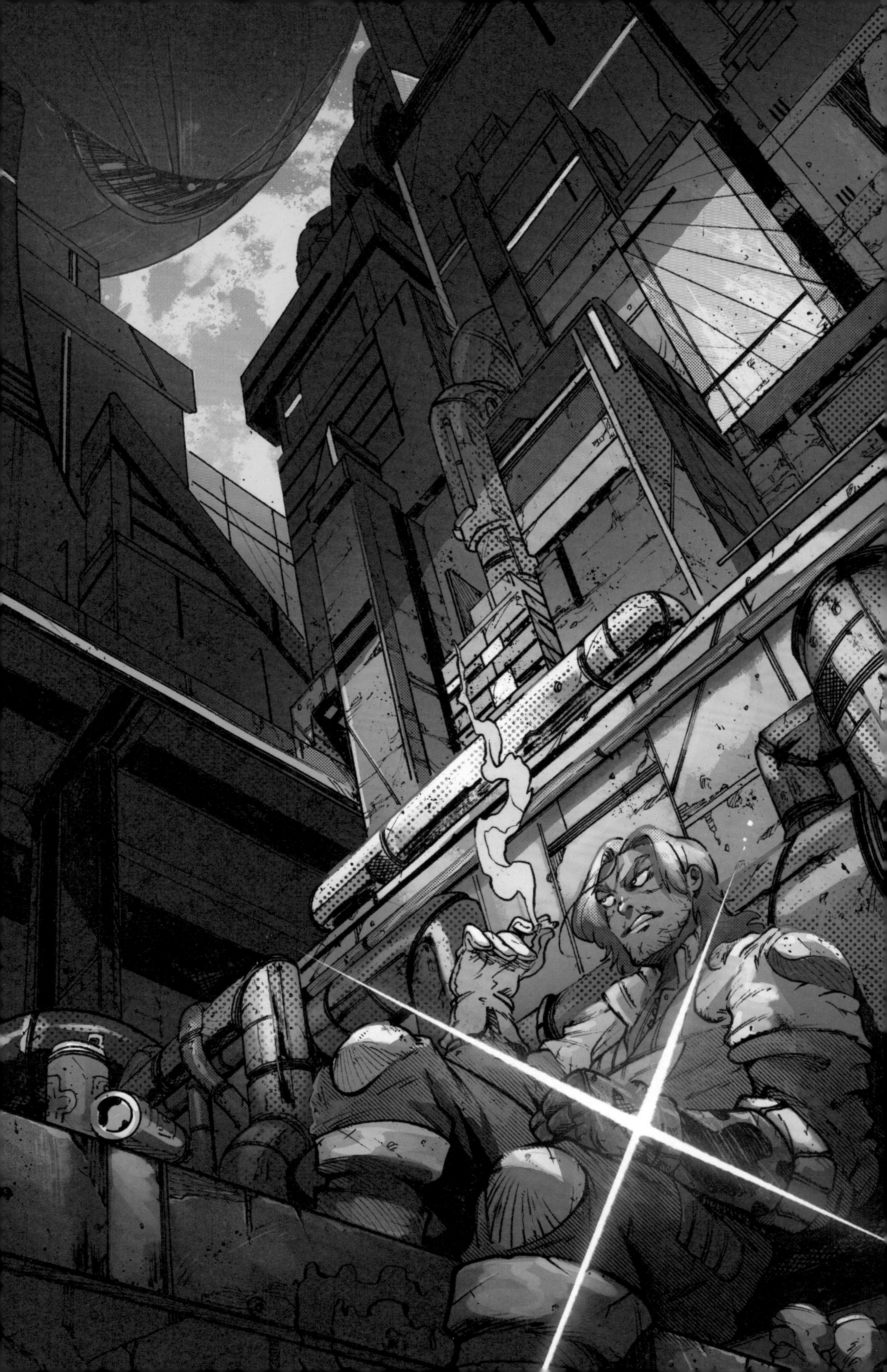

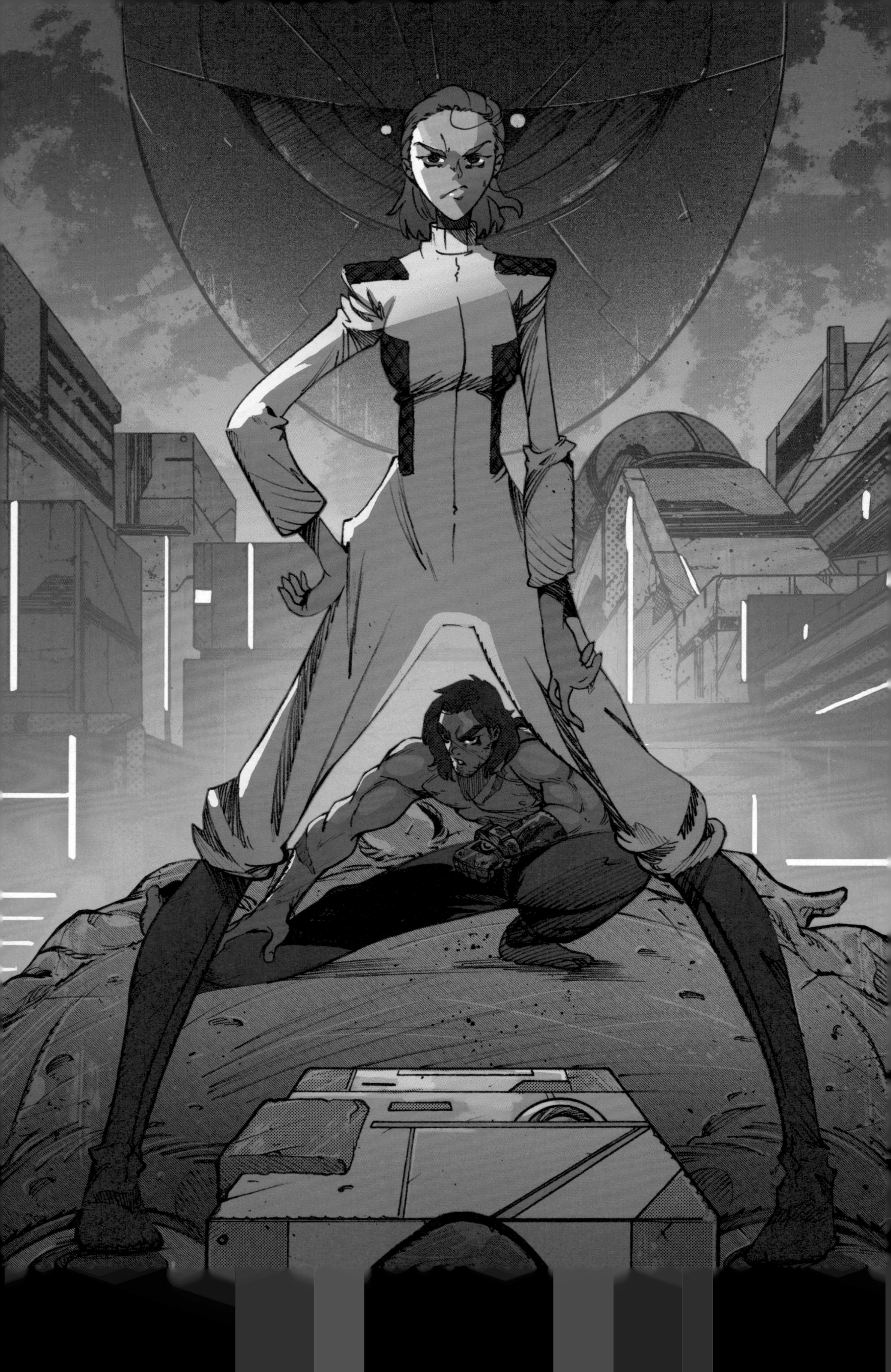

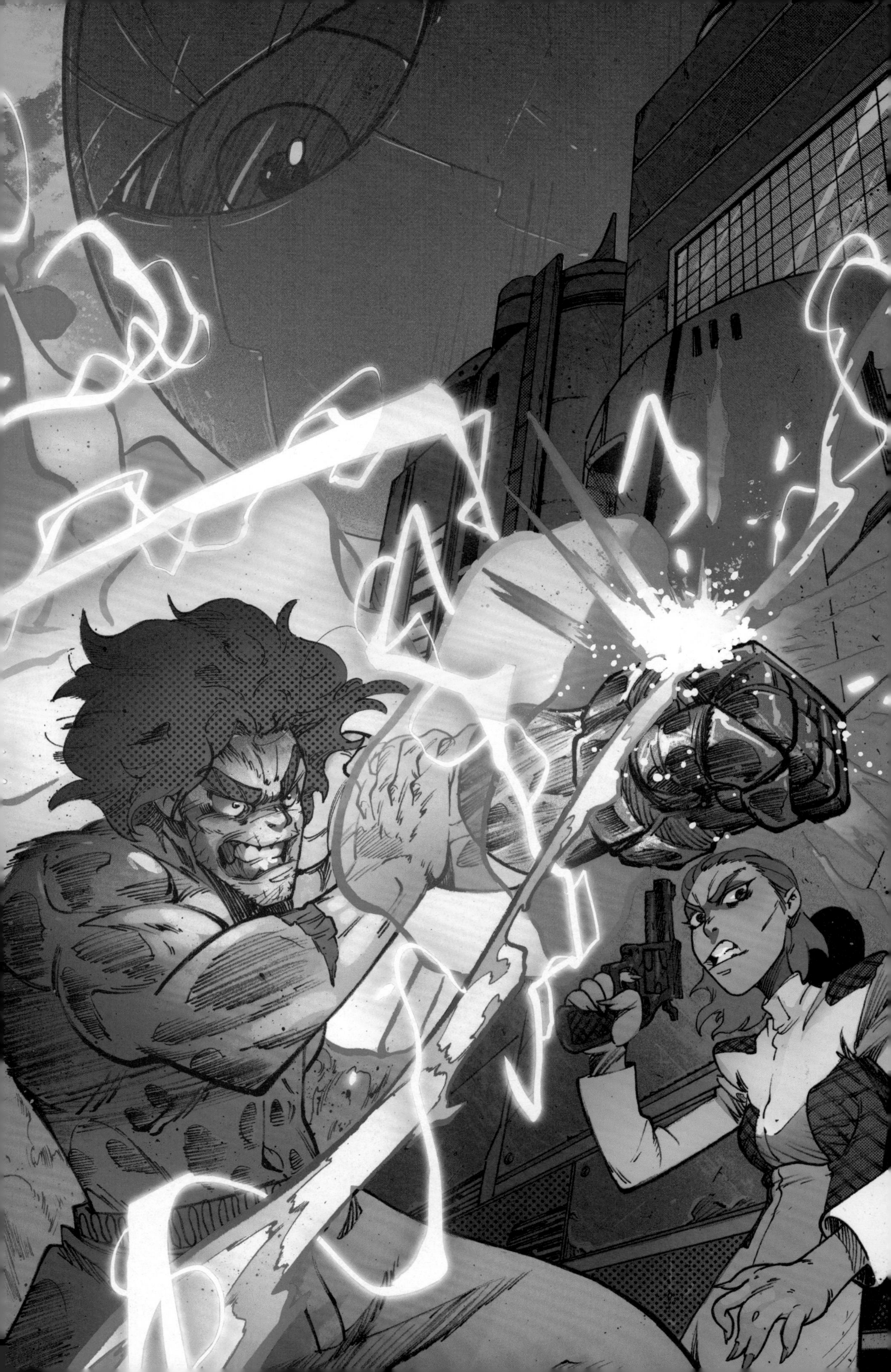

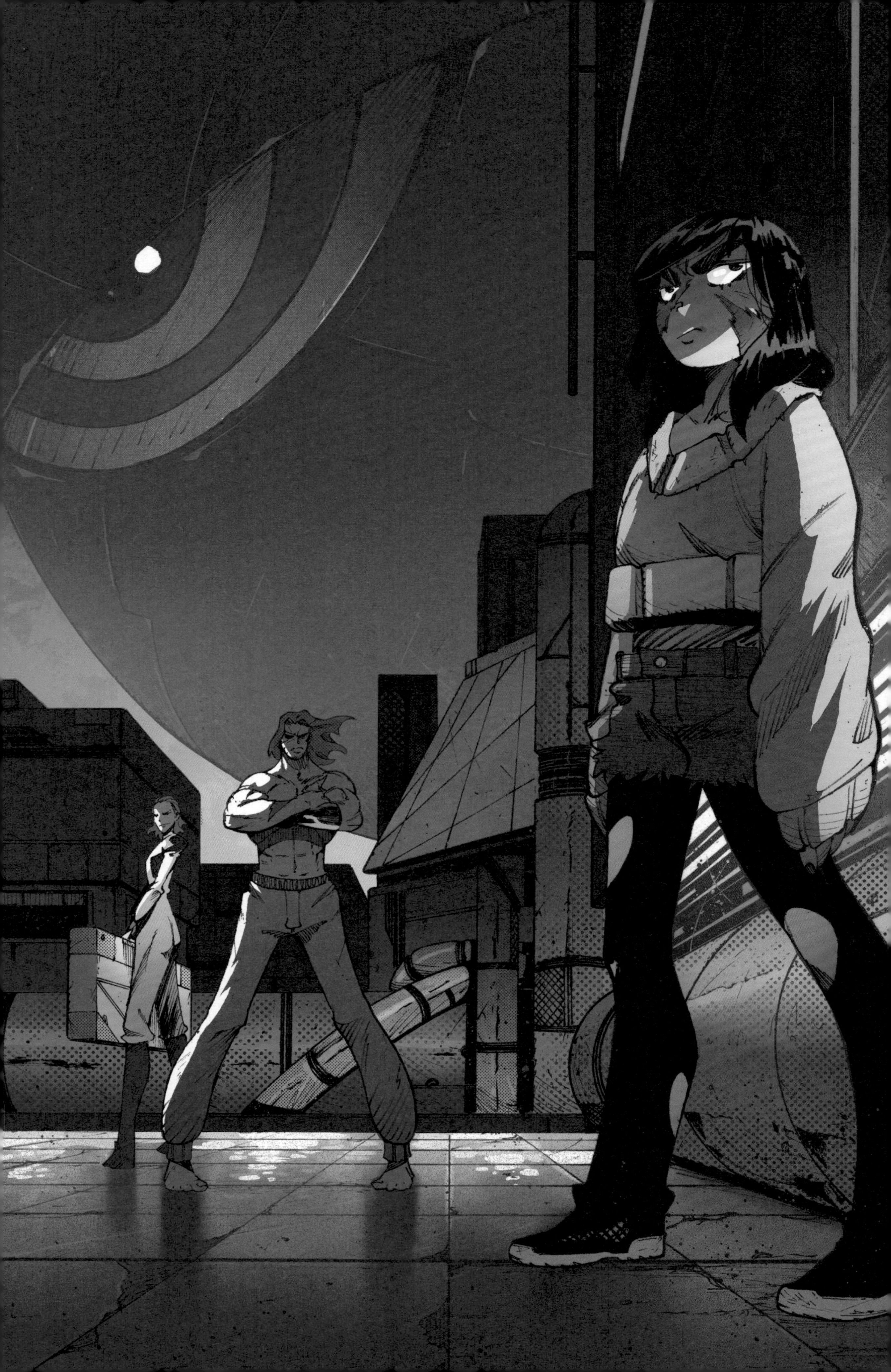

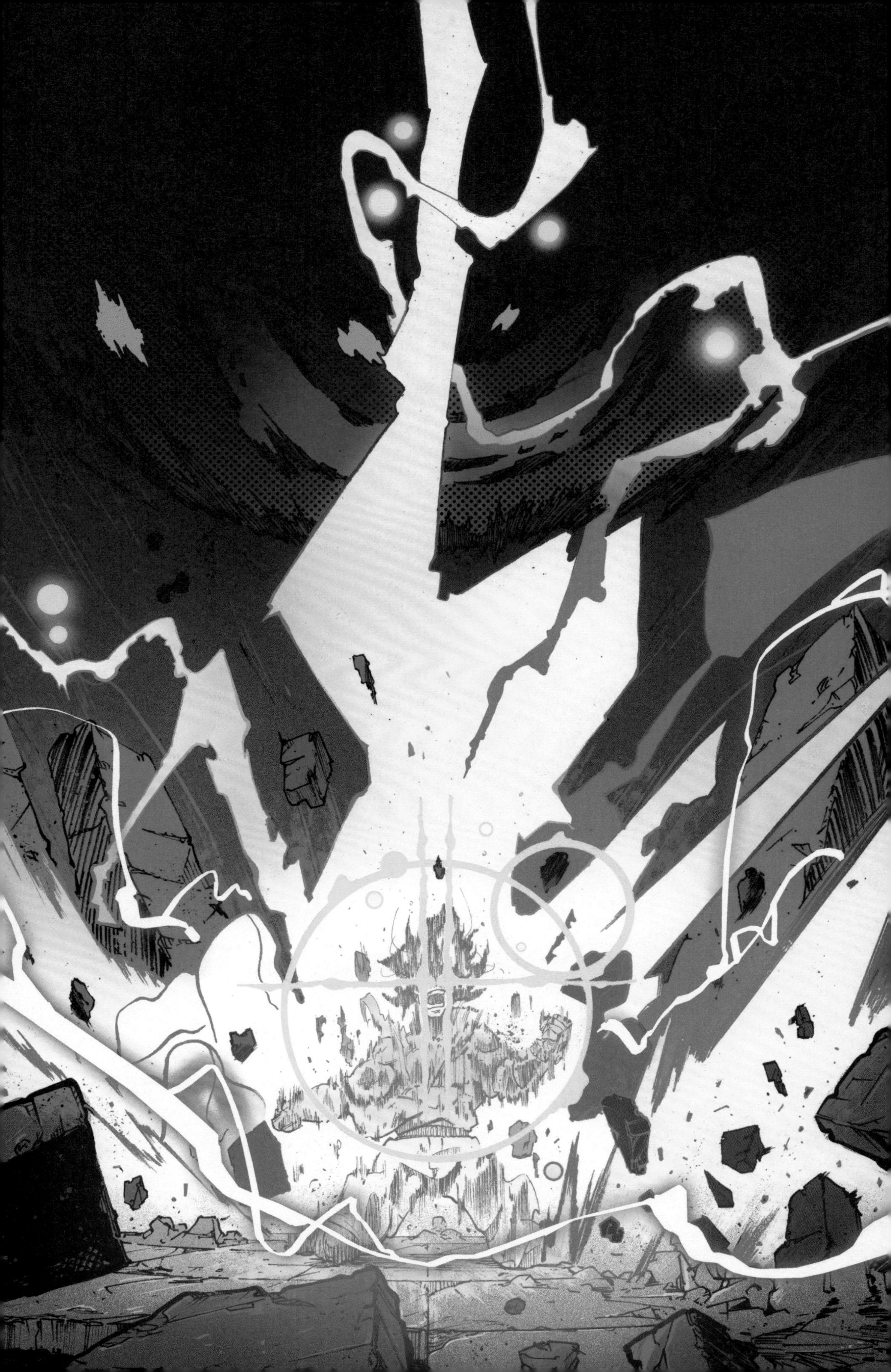

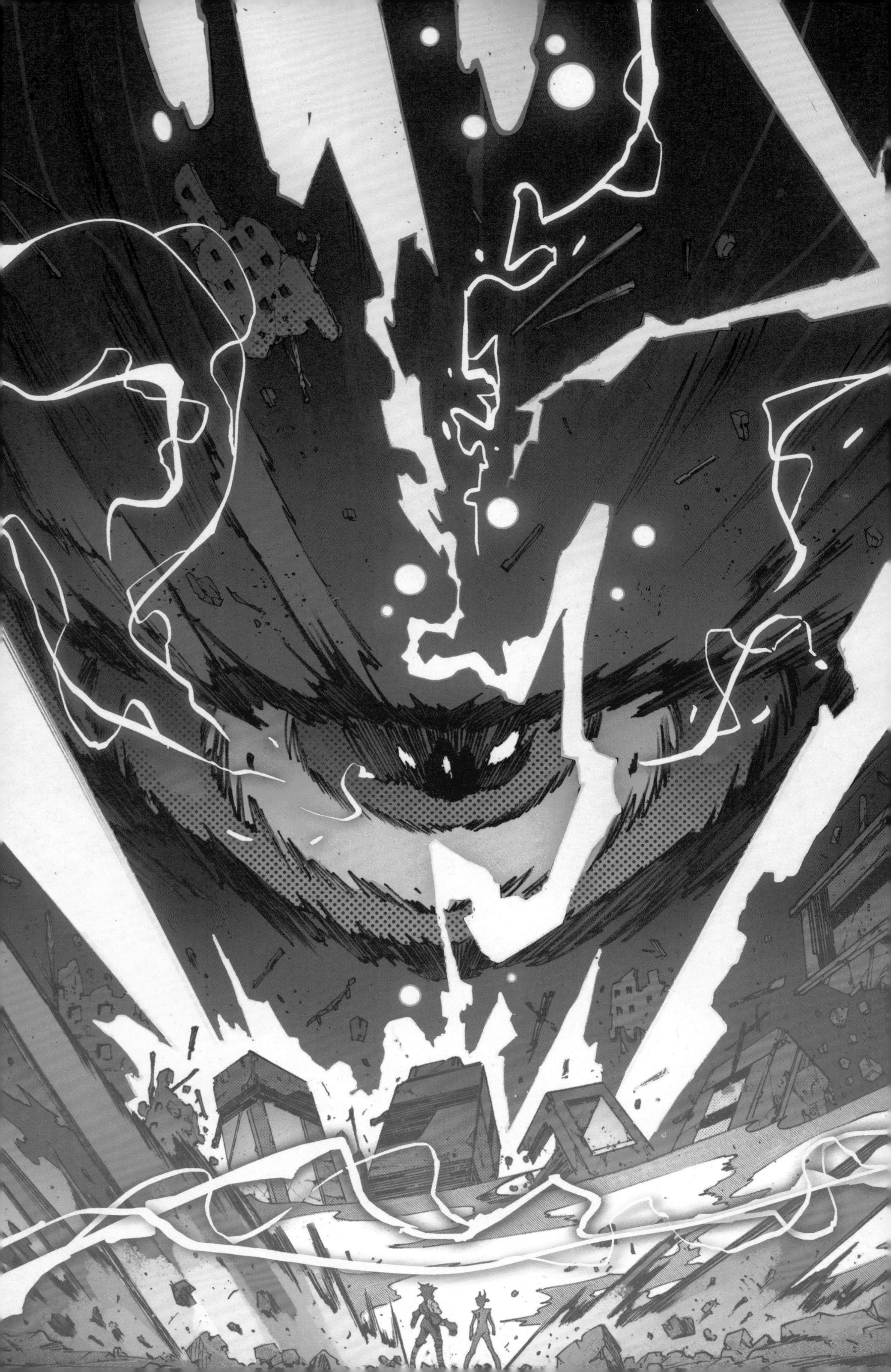

CREATORS

STEVE ORLANDO | WRITER

Steve Orlando writes and edits. His many works including VIRGIL, UNDERTOW, and stories in the Eisner Award Nominated OUTLAW TERRITORY at Image Comics. He has also written MIDNIGHTER and MIDNIGHTER AND APOLLO, both nominated for GLAAD awards, as well as JUSTICE LEAGUE OF AMERICA, BATMAN AND ROBIN ETERNAL, SUPERGIRL, and WONDER WOMAN for DC Entertainment.

RICARDO LÓPEZ ORTIZ | ARTIST

Ricardo López Ortiz is a Brooklyn, NY based comic book artist and illustrator hailing from Puerto Rico. He's known for his work on Marvel's WAR OF THE REALMS: WAR SCROLLS (2019), BLACK PANTHER VS. DEADPOOL, WEAPON X, TOTALLY AWESOME HULK MONSTERS UNLEASHED, and CIVIL WAR 2: KINGPIN, as well as HIT-GIRL: COLOMBI, WOLF, and ZERO for Image Comics.

TRIONA FARRELL | COLOR ART

Triona Farrell is a colorist from Dublin, Ireland. She has worked with numerous companies such as Dark Horse, Image, and Marvel on titles such as BLACKBIRD, BLACK WIDOW, and TERMINATOR. Numerous books of hers have been nominated for Eisner Awards, including CROWDED.

In her spare time she follows many nerd activities and reads comics.

THOMAS MAUER | LETTERER

Thomas Mauer has lent his lettering and design talent to numerous critically acclaimed and award-winning projects since the early 2000s. Among his recent works are Aftershock Comics' GODKILLERS and MILES TO GO, ComiXology Presents' IN THE FLOOD and THE DARK, Image Comics' HARDCORE and THE REALM, and A Wave Blue World's MEZO and THE 27 RUN.

He lives with his wife and children near Magdeburg, Germany. He enjoys woodworking, and is trying to teach himself 5-string banjo.

SEBASTIAN GIRNER | EDITOR

Sebastian Girner is a German-born, American-raised comic editor and writer. His editing includes such series as DEADLY CLASS, SOUTHERN BASTARDS and THE PUNISHER. He lives and works in Brooklyn with his wife.

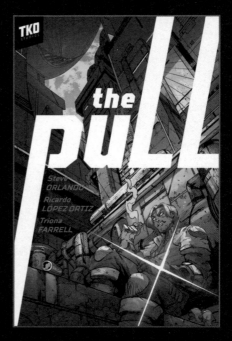
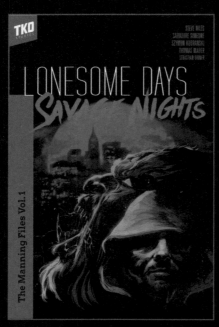
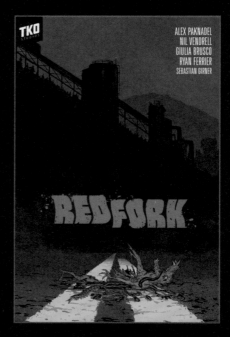